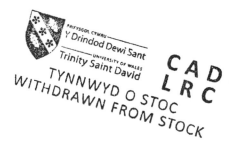

THE CHANGING VOICES
OF EUROPE

Glanville Price

THE CHANGING VOICES
OF EUROPE

Social and political changes
and their linguistic repercussions,
past, present and future

Papers in honour of Professor Glanville Price

edited by

M. M. PARRY,

W. V. DAVIES and R. A. M. TEMPLE

Published by the University of Wales Press
in conjunction with the
Modern Humanities Research Association
CARDIFF
1994

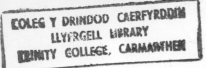
© the Contributors, 1994

British Library Cataloguing-in-Publication Data.
A catalogue record for this book is available from
the British Library

ISBN 0–7083–1259–4

401.
99
Bou.

*Typeset at Create Publishing Services Ltd., Bath
Printed in Great Britain by Cromwell Press, Melksham, Wiltshire*

Contents

Dedication

A colloquium on a theme which would encompass both Romance and Celtic linguistics seemed the most fitting way of marking the retirement of a scholar who has dedicated so much energy and enthusiasm to studying these two language families. Once the decision was taken to organize one at Gregynog, the University of Wales conference centre, there was no difficulty in obtaining from friends and colleagues a rich and varied programme of papers reflecting Professor Glanville Price's wide-ranging linguistic interests, nor in drawing together, in July 1992, a large group of scholars eager to show their appreciation of his work and friendship and to wish him well for the future. Revised versions of the papers given at Gregynog constitute the bulk of the present volume.

Glanville Price was born in Rhaeadr, Wales, in 1928 and attended Llandrindod Wells Grammar School. His French studies led him via the University College of North Wales, Bangor (1946–50), where he also studied German, to the Sorbonne (1950–53). Here he prepared his *doctorat de l'Université de Paris* with a thesis (presented in 1956) on word order in the chronicles of Froissart. In 1954 he married Christine Thurston, who was to support and encourage him throughout his career. Four years as French master, first at Wade Dean Grammar School, Widnes, and then at Llangollen Grammar School, were followed by lectureships in French at St Andrews (1958–64) and Leeds (1965–6). In 1967 he became Professor of French at Stirling and finally in 1972 he returned to Wales, to the Chair of French at the University College of Wales, Aberystwyth. Between 1975 and 1987 his title was Professor of Romance Languages, a more accurate description of his research and teaching interests (the latter including French and Spanish linguistics and Romanian).

Eloquent testimony to the former are the 9 books, 91 articles and chapters and 123 reviews he has produced to date. His perceptive and stimulating articles on historical linguistics have made an important contribution to the study of French syntax, particularly to the study of negation, word order, and personal and demonstrative pronouns (Price 1961, 1962, 1966a, 1968, 1969a, 1979, 1990, are among the most influential). Clarity of thought and presentation contributed to the widespread success also of his well-known textbooks, *The French Language, Present and Past* (1971, translated into German in 1988) and *An Introduction to French Pronunciation* (1991). Generations of students have benefited and will continue to benefit from them, as they will from his excellent revision of L. S. R. Byrne and E. L. Churchill's *A Comprehensive French Grammar* (1986 and 1993).

Within Romance, in addition to French and, to a lesser extent, Occitan, he has shown an abiding interest in Romanian and Romania. Lecture tours in Romania and broadcasts on the BBC Romanian Service, as well as radio and television programmes in Welsh, have helped to promote an awareness and an understanding of that country and its people. Matching his enthusiasm for Romanian has been Glanville Price's lifelong concern with minority languages and with the Celtic languages in particular. Although he was born in a long-anglicized part of Wales, he has acquired an excellent command of Welsh. His first book, *The Present Position of Minority Languages in Western Europe: A Selective Bibliography* (1969), made a valuable contribution to what has become a major area of research and was followed by numerous other publications reflecting his interest in minority languages, notably *The Languages of Britain* (1984) and his articles on Occitan and Gaelic (Price 1964, 1966b, 1976–8, 1978–80).

Glanville Price's bibliographical and editorial activities have contributed significantly to promoting research in modern languages and relate to all three of his main areas of study. In addition to the above-mentioned bibliography of minority languages, he published in 1977, with Kathryn F. Bach, *Romance Linguistics and the Romance Languages: A Bibliography of Bibliographies*. To *The Year's Work in Modern Language Studies*, which he edited from 1972 to 1991 (jointly from 1975), with a year's break during which he was Visiting Professor at the University of California, Berkeley, he has been an indefatigable contributor: at various times over the years he has contributed sections on Breton and Cornish, Occitan, Romansh, Romanian as well as French, and scholars have benefited greatly from the candour and clarity of his comments. His editorial acumen has been much appreciated by other members of the Committee of the Modern Humanities Research Association, whose Chairman he was from 1979 to 1990. He was also for many years a member of the Council of the Philological

Society. He is a member of the Advisory Board of the Princess Grace Library in Monaco, whose series of volumes on Irish and Celtic studies includes *The Celtic Connection* (1992), which he edited and to which he contributed several sections. He is currently General Editor of Blackwell's important series of comprehensive reference grammars of modern European languages, of which French, Russian and Welsh are already published (German, Italian, Portuguese and Spanish are in preparation), while his most recent editorial commitment is to an *Encyclopedia of European Languages.* This and his appointment as Research Professor at the University of Wales, Aberystwyth, may reassure us that retirement from teaching will not mean a cessation or even a reduction of scholarly activities. We trust that he will long continue to provide an energetic example and cheerful encouragement to the rest of us.

Dymunwn ymddeoliad ffrwythlon i Glanville a phob hapusrwydd yn y dyfodol iddo ef a'i wraig, Christine.

Mair Parry, Winifred Davies, Rosalind Temple
Aberystwyth, 1994

Glanville Price: selective bibliography

1961. 'Aspects de l'ordre des mots dans les *Chroniques de Froissart*', *Zeitschrift für romanische Philologie*, 77, 15–48.

1962. 'The negative particles *pas, mie, point* in French', *Archivum Linguisticum*, 14, 14–34.

1964. 'The problem of modern literary Occitan', *Archivum Linguisticum*, 16, 34–53.

1966a. 'Contribution à l'étude de la syntaxe des pronoms personnels sujets en ancien français', *Romania*, 87, 476–504.

1966b. 'The decline of Scottish Gaelic in the twentieth century', *Orbis*, 15, 365–87.

1968. 'Quel est le rôle de l'opposition *cist/cil* en ancien français?', *Romania*, 89, 240–53.

1969a. 'La transformation du système français des démonstratifs', *Zeitschrift für romanische Philologie*, 85, 489–505.

1969b. *The Present Position of Minority Languages in Western Europe: A Selective Bibliography*, Cardiff: University of Wales Press.

1971. *The French Language, Present and Past*, London: Edward Arnold [German translation, *Die französische Sprache*, 1988].

(ed.). 1975. *William, Count of Orange: Four Old French Epics*, London: Dent.

1977. [with Kathryn F. Bach] *Romance Linguistics and the Romance Languages: A Bibliography of Bibliographies*, London: Grant & Cutler.

1976–8. 'Gaelic in Scotland at the end of the eighteenth century. (The evidence of the *Statistical Account of Scotland* [1791–9])' (first part), *Bulletin of the Board of Celtic Studies*, 27, 561–8; (second part) ibid., 28 (1978–80), 234–47.

1979. '"*Point* nie bien plus fortement que *pas*" – Vaugelas que veut-il dire?', in *Festschrift Kurt Baldinger zum 60. Geburtstag* (ed. Höfler, M., Vernay, H. and Wolf, L.), Tübingen, Niemeyer, 245–54.

1982. 'Romance studies in Great Britain', in *Trends in Romance Linguistics and Philology* (ed. Posner, R. and Green, J. N.), Vol. 4, The Hague: Mouton, 127–70.

1984. *The Languages of Britain*. London: Edward Arnold.

1986. Revision of Byrne, L. S. R. and Churchill, E. L., *A Comprehensive French Grammar*, Oxford: Blackwell; 4th edn., completely revised and rewritten, 1993.

1987. *Ireland and the Celtic Connection*, Gerrards Cross: Colin Smythe, for The Princess Grace Irish Library, Monaco. (Also includes Owen, M. E., *A Celtic Bibliography*, edited by Glanville Price.)

1990. 'The origins and syntax of *ne ... goutte*', in *Variation and Change in French. Essays presented to Rebecca Posner* (ed. Green, J. N. and Ayres-Bennett, W.), London: Routledge, 201–9.

1991a. 'Romance numerals', in *Indo-European Numerals* (ed. Gvozdanović, J.), Berlin: Mouton de Gruyter, 447–96.

1991b. *An Introduction to French Pronunciation*, Oxford: Blackwell.

(ed.). 1992. *The Celtic Connection*, Gerrards Cross: Colin Smythe, for The Princess Grace Irish Library, Monaco.

1992–3. '*Eulalia*, v. 15, once again', *Romance Philology*, 46, 464–7.

1993. '*Pas (point)* without *ne* in interrogative clauses', *Journal of French Language Studies*, 3, 191–5.

(ed., with Coman Lupu). 1994. *Hommages offerts à Maria Manoliu-Manea*. Bucharest: Pluralia/Logos.

Tabula Gratulatoria

Professor D. E. Ager, Aston University

Professor Lloyd Austin, Cambridge

Gwenllian Awbery, University of Wales College of Cardiff

Wendy Ayres-Bennett, Queens' College, Cambridge

Stephen Barbour, Middlesex University

Professor P. J. Bayley, Gonville & Caius College, Cambridge

Helen E. Beale, University of Stirling

Geoffrey Bromiley, University of Durham

Dr Monique Burston, University of Melbourne

Aidan Coveney, University of the West of England, Bristol

Joe Cremona, Trinity Hall, Cambridge

Professor David Crystal, University of Wales, Bangor

Winifred V. Davies, Prifysgol Cymru, Aberystwyth

Professor Alan Deyermond, Queen Mary and Westfield College, London

Professor Jacques Durand, University of Salford

Emeritus Professor D. J. Fletcher, University of Durham

John N. Green, University of Bradford

R. Geraint Gruffydd, Aberystwyth

Ruth E. Harvey, Royal Holloway, University of London

Robert and Dorothea Havard, University of Wales, Aberystwyth

Marged Haycock, Prifysgol Cymru, Aberystwyth

Marie-Anne Hintze, University of York

Charlotte Hoffmann, University of Salford

Catrin Redknap, University of Wales, Cardiff

Glyn Tegai Hughes, Tregynon

Bob Morris Jones, University of Wales, Aberystwyth

Elin Haf Gruffydd Jones, Cynllun Mercator, Prifysgol Cymru, Aberystwyth

Emyr Tudwal Jones, Prifysgol Cymru, Aberystwyth

Mari C. Jones, Peterhouse, Cambridge

Kathryn Klingebiel, University of Hawaii at Manoa

A. L. Lepschy, University College London

Giulio Lepschy, University of Reading

John M. A. Lindon, University College London

Dr Ceridwen Lloyd-Morgan, Llyfrgell Genedlaethol Cymru

Professor Ian Lockerbie, University of Stirling

Professor and Mrs R. A. Lodge, Newcastle University

Martin Maiden, Faculty of Modern and Medieval Languages, University of Cambridge

Maria Manoliu, University of California, Davis

Roger and Mercedes Mills, University of Wales, Aberystwyth

Professor Valerie Minogue, University College of Swansea

Howard Moss, University College of Swansea

Brian Mott, University of Barcelona

Malcolm Offord, University of Nottingham

M. Mair Parry, Prifysgol Cymru, Aberystwyth

D. G. Pattison, Magdalen College, Oxford

Ralph Penny, Queen Mary and Westfield College, London

Rebecca Posner, University of Oxford

Christopher J. Pountain, Queens' College, Cambridge

Ian Press, University of London

Gwen Mary Rice, Department of Italian, University College of Swansea

Professor Peter Rickard, Emmanuel College, Cambridge

Felicity Roberts, Prifysgol Cymru, Aberystwyth

Cecilia Robustelli, University of Reading

W. Rothwell, Cheadle Hulme

Professor Dorothy Sherman Severin, University of Liverpool

Christopher Smith, University of East Anglia, Norwich

John Charles Smith, University of Manchester

R. Nigel Smith, Pembroke College, Oxford

Professor Emeritus A. J. Steele, Edinburgh

Dr Jill Taylor, University of Exeter

Rosalind A. M. Temple, Prifysgol Cymru, Aberystwyth

Derick S. Thomson, University of Glasgow

David Thorne, Coleg Prifysgol Dewi Sant, Llanbedr Pont Steffan

Professor James Trainer, University of Stirling

Margaret and John Trethewey, University of Wales, Aberystwyth

Professor D. A. Trotter, University of Wales, Aberystwyth

Professor J. R. Watson, University of Durham

Professor David A. Wells, Modern Humanities Research Association

Max W. Wheeler, University of Sussex

Yr Athro J. E. Caerwyn Williams, Canolfan Uwchefrydiau Cymreig a Cheltaidd, Aberystwyth

Roy and Erni Wisbey, King's College, London

Roger Wright, Dept of Hispanic Studies, University of Liverpool

Bristol University Library

Department of French, University of Leeds

Exeter University Library

The Library, Royal Holloway, University of London

The Library, University of Durham

The Library, University of Warwick

Modern Languages Faculty Library, University of Oxford

Mont Follick Library, Department of Linguistics, University of Manchester

School of Modern Languages, University of Wales, Lampeter

Trinity College, Oxford

The Ward Library, Peterhouse, Cambridge

University of Newcastle upon Tyne

University of St Andrews

Acknowledgements

It is not possible to name the many colleagues who have encouraged us as this volume has developed. The names of those who have contributed papers, and patiently complied with our occasional revisions of conventions, are of course to be found in the following pages; but we are equally grateful to the many others who have been generous with their advice and encouragement, particularly in the very early stages, and who have been prevented from contributing papers by time constraints, or by our need to keep to the theme chosen for the colloquium and book. We owe a particular debt of gratitude, however, to Margaret Parry, whose calm efficiency was invaluable during the organization of the colloquium, and to Dorothy Evans who stepped into the breach to see us through the final few days.

The project has benefited from financial assistance from various sources. We are very grateful to Professor D. A. Wells and the committee of the Modern Humanities Research Association for their generous financial support of the volume in recognition of Glanville Price's long-standing commitment to the Association, particularly through his energetic work on the committee and for the Association's publications. We should also like to thank the following for their generous support of the colloquium: Professor K. O. Morgan and the University of Wales, Aberystwyth; Roger Mills and the Department of European Languages, University of Wales, Aberystwyth; Barclays Bank Regional Office, Shrewsbury, and Barclays Bank, Aberystwyth Branch; Lloyds Bank, Aberystwyth Branch; Midland Bank, Aberystwyth Branch; National Westminster Bank, Aberystwyth Branch; Students' Bookshops Ltd, and especially the staff of the Penglais Bookshop, Aberystwyth.

And, finally, thanks to David, Rhys and Catrin for giving up their dining table for many an editorial meeting.

The contributors

Wendy Ayres-Bennett, University Lecturer in French and Fellow of Queens' College, Cambridge

Stephen Barbour, Reader in Modern Languages, Middlesex University

Joseph Cremona, formerly University Lecturer in Romance Philology and Fellow of Trinity Hall, Cambridge

Winifred V. Davies, Lecturer in German, University of Wales, Aberystwyth

John N. Green, Professor of Romance Linguistics, University of Bradford

Charlotte Hoffmann, Lecturer in German, University of Salford

Mari C. Jones, University Lecturer in French and Fellow of Peterhouse, Cambridge

Kathryn Klingebiel, Assistant Professor in the Department of French, University of Hawaii at Manoa

Bedwyr Lewis Jones, late Professor of Welsh, University College of North Wales, Bangor

Giulio Lepschy, Professor of Italian, University of Reading

R. Anthony Lodge, Professor of French, University of Newcastle upon Tyne

Maria M. Manoliu, Professor in the Department of French and Italian, University of California, Davis

Malcolm Offord, Reader in French, Nottingham University

M. Mair Parry, Senior Lecturer in Italian, University of Wales, Aberystwyth

Rebecca Posner, Professor of the Romance Languages, University of Oxford, and Professorial Fellow of St Hugh's College

Christopher J. Pountain, University Lecturer in Romance Philology and Fellow of Queens' College, Cambridge

J. Ian Press, Professor of Slavonic and Comparative Linguistics, Queen Mary and Westfield College, University of London

Rosalind A. M. Temple, Lecturer in French, University of Wales, Aberystwyth

Derick S. Thomson, Emeritus Professor of Celtic, University of Glasgow

David A. Thorne, Senior Lecturer in Welsh Language and Literature, St David's University College of Wales, Lampeter

Roger Wright, Senior Lecturer in Spanish, University of Liverpool

Introduction:

The Changing Voices of Europe

The development of greater economic and political integration within Europe, set in motion with the establishment of the European Community, and now carried a further step towards fulfilment with the abolition of border controls, has inevitably raised the question of linguistic integration, despite the EC's declared commitment to linguistic pluralism. The spread of dominant languages at the expense of weaker ones has always characterized the history of language, but as the world has grown smaller through industrialization, education and mass communication the process has accelerated, with even major world languages such as French becoming concerned about their fate. The unification of East and West Germany and the collapse of post-war political structures in Eastern Europe have also begun to have linguistic repercussions of various kinds. The effects of social and political events on a language's development can range from subtle influences on its phonetic and grammatical structure to far-reaching changes in usage and status within a broader speech context.

This volume brings together a series of papers, many of which were presented at the colloquium held in Gregynog, that seek not only to disentangle and comment on the complex linguistic issues that face Europe today and their implications for the future, but also to analyse the effect of political and social change on linguistic behaviour in past centuries. The papers focus particularly on those language groups to whose study Professor Price has made a significant contribution, namely Romance and Celtic. In addition, the importance of the German linguistic community within Europe is recognized by the inclusion of three papers on the current sociolinguistic situation in Germany. Barbour's contribution is a comparative study of the spread of German and English within Europe and their respective roles as

symbols of national identity. Complex questions of identity faced by
German immigrants from the former Soviet Union are discussed by
Hoffmann, while Davies examines linguistic identities in an urban
community in central Germany. Nevertheless, there are many groups
of languages that it has not been possible to include, such as Slavonic,
Baltic, languages not normally associated with a specific territory (for
example, Romani), and languages introduced to Europe by recent
waves of immigration from Africa and Asia. Many of these, however,
are mentioned briefly in the review of Europe's languages contained in
Lepschy's discussion of linguistic status and language policy.

The linguistic problems facing the European Community, which so
far has no co-ordinated language policy, emerge clearly from the essays
in Coulmas (1991). Possible options are reviewed by Posner, who
stresses the need for mutual tolerance and the importance of fostering
multilingualism among the general population of Europe, while introducing some rationalization at the level of official Community
languages. The growth in prestige and the spread of some languages
inevitably diminishes the use of others and, at a national level, the
standardization of one language variety may render particularly difficult the situation of other languages with fewer speakers. Lepschy
considers the extent to which Europe's rich linguistic heritage can or
should be maintained and the need for or acceptability of direct
intervention, questions which are taken up in many of the other
contributions: Green, Parry, Press and Thomson consider situations of
language shift in one or more 'minority' or 'lesser-used'[1] languages in
Spain, Italy, France and Scotland today, highlighting the importance
of positive attitudes towards a language on the part of its speakers, if it
is to survive. Speakers' attitudes are also seen as crucial to the maintenance of the local variety in Davies's study of the relationship between
language and dialect in Mannheim, and in Temple's analysis of linguistic aspirations for minority languages in France as European integration advances. There is, however, the danger, as seen particularly in
the Spanish developments described by Green, that political disaffec-
tion may encourage the proliferation of rather artificial 'languages'
lacking in historical and cultural justification.

Intricately linked with issues of language promotion and survival is
the complex process of standardization. With reference to the development of the highly normalized French language, Ayres-Bennett
examines the relationship between two essential components of standardization, namely elaboration and codification. One casualty of the
French standardization process was the vernacular of *ancien régime*
Paris discussed by Lodge. Others were the Occitan dialects of southern
France, and the effect of a prolonged diglossic relationship with French

on a particular area of their grammar is described by Klingebiel. On our own doorstep, the pervasive influence of English on the structure of Welsh cannot be denied and less obvious, but no less worrying, is the loss of poetic creativity that B. L. Jones fears will derive from the erosion of its oral base.

The Breton situation described by Temple and Press illustrates how the insensitive imposition of a standard language or variety can arouse passionate emotions and cause a crisis of identity in speakers of the less-favoured varieties. In the case of Romanian, Manoliu documents the emergence of two standard varieties as a result of political and social divergences in the Romanian communities on either side of the Atlantic. Speakers of languages whose very existence is under threat may find that attempts to select a norm can provoke conflict that may hinder the development or even the survival of the language, an issue raised in the contributions of Green, Press and Parry. Conflict, however, is not inevitable and can be avoided in different ways: Posner mentions the 'tolerant "polynomic" standardization of related varieties' aimed for in Corsica, whereas in the Welsh context M. C. Jones provides evidence of the gradual displacement of the geographical dialects by a non-regional composite variety and the spread of a new oral standard coinciding with a halt in the decline in Welsh speakers. The crucial role of the Welsh translation of the Bible in the development of the Welsh literary standard and the nature of subsequent updatings are examined by Thorne.

It might be assumed that social and political change is likely to have more far-reaching effects, be they positive or negative, on lesser-used languages. Such an assumption has been encouraged by the fact that, on the whole, supporters of lesser-used languages have been enthusiastic about Europe, since most of them have high expectations of a European Community where stateless nations and groups would be able to join forces in order to lobby for greater linguistic concessions (see Temple). However, even some of the major languages whose status has been taken for granted are perceived by their speakers as being in need of support if they are not to be adversely affected by developments in Europe and lose ground in the future. For example, in the context of the EC, the Danes are concerned that their language may lose its official status (*Guardian*, 19.6.92) and the Germans are said to be concerned that their language will never attain its deserved status as an official *and* working language on a par with French and English (*Der Spiegel*, 27.4.92); at the same time, Offord's contribution to this volume shows how worried the French are about the international standing and the structural integrity of their language. In contrast, Pountain's critical examination of syntactic anglicisms in Spanish illustrates how dire warnings about the threat posed to the essential structure of the indigenous language are often exaggerated.

Survival of linguistic varieties in the face of social and political change is perhaps the most obviously pressing issue to be raised by our contributors. Many focus on the contemporary situation, but it is clear from contributions such as Cremona's study of the fate of Arabic in Malta that significant insights may be gained and lessons drawn from the past. Conversely, the sociolinguistic study of present situations enables us to understand more clearly past phenomena, as evidenced in Wright's essay on orthographic conventions and literacy skills in tenth-century Spain. We would hope that a greater linguistic awareness of both present and past situations would help us to work towards a more responsible and tolerant, but equally rich, multilingual community of the future.

MMP, WVD, RAMT.

Note

[1] The traditional label, 'minority languages', is often nowadays replaced by others, such as 'lesser-used' or 'regional' languages, in an attempt to avoid any implication of minor significance or status. Problems of terminology and definition, involving the very concept of 'minority language' and the often contentious classification of a variety as a 'language' or a 'dialect', are discussed in detail by Lepschy and also by Green.

Reference

Coulmas, F. (ed.). 1991. *A Language Policy for the European Community. Prospects and Quandaries*, Berlin: Mouton de Gruyter.

1

How many languages does Europe need?

GIULIO LEPSCHY

1. The famous English physicist Freeman Dyson, in the chapter called 'Clades and Clones' of his autobiographical book *Disturbing the Universe*, recounts that in his youth he enjoyed mountaineering, and once, at the age of 17, in 1940, when he was climbing in Wales, he had an accident and was taken to the Llandudno hospital with a deep cut in his head. There he was kept for two days. I quote:

> I was put into a ward with nine other patients. I was washed and fed, my hair was cut and my scalp was sewn up. But my efforts to engage the nurses and patients in friendly conversation failed completely. Nobody, except for the doctor who sewed me up, uttered a single word of English in my presence. Everybody else, patients and nurses and visitors, spoke exclusively Welsh and pretended not to understand me when I spoke English. The Welsh language is beautiful and I enjoyed listening to the music in their voices. But their message was unmistakably clear. I was an alien, and the sooner I got onto the train back to England the better.
>
> This was a sobering experience for an English boy accustomed to consider the words 'English' and 'British' as synonymous. After six hundred years as a conquered people, and seventy years of compulsory education in the language of the conquerors, the Welsh of Llandudno were still Welsh. When one of the oppressors happened to fall into their hands, they tended his wounds and taught him a lesson he would never forget. (Dyson 1979, 218–19)

Dyson goes on to develop a parallel between biological and cultural evolution, and to suggest that linguistic diversity helped to keep small communities separate from each other, so that random genetic fluctuation could be significant. This is why clades, or different branches in the evolutionary tree, accompany leaps forward, whereas clones, or populations in which the individuals are genetically identical, are evolutionary dead-ends. Linguistic diversity, Dyson suggests, is similarly essential for cultural progress. The disappearance of a language, however little used, impoverishes our culture, as the disappearance of a species impoverishes the ecosphere.

The parallel between linguistic variety and biological variety, and in particular between languages and species, was of course familiar to nineteenth-century linguistics. In a more modern perspective many interesting articles on this topic were collected a few years ago, under the title *Biological Metaphor and Cladistic Classification* (Hoenigswald and Wiener, 1987).

The line taken by Dyson is somewhat surprising, as one might imagine natural scientists to be in favour of linguistic uniformity, which would allow quicker and more effective circulation of information; scholars working in the humanities are expected instead to be more sensitive to the unique richness represented by separate tongues and different linguistic and cultural traditions.

The situation is in fact more complicated than this crude distinction might suggest. We find for instance a famous linguist like Antoine Meillet being less than enthusiastic about the proliferation of language variety, and upholding instead the universality of civilization and scientific progress which seems to require and encourage the use of a common language. In a remarkable book on the languages of Europe, published in 1918 (and in a second edition, with a large statistical appendix by Lucien Tesnière, in 1928), Meillet has very trenchant observations to make about the absurdity of setting up dialects of peasants as languages of culture, while in the process isolating their speakers and depriving them of the opportunity to be educated through the medium of a great language of civilization with world-wide currency. His comments about Irish are so scathing that readers may find them shocking, especially as they come from one of the greatest scholars in the history of Indo-European studies.

2. The situation is also far from straightforward from the viewpoint of political and ideological assumptions.

On the one hand the democratic tradition, at least since the nineteenth century, has favoured self-determination and the right to national independence for individual communities, each being usually identified on the basis of its distinctive language. In our century this line has been upheld by the League of Nations and then by the United Nations, against the principle of *cuius regio, eius lingua* which allows the language of a ruling power to be imposed upon a subject nation. Unesco (1953) recommends education through the medium of the mother tongue, a principle not easy to interpret, let alone apply, for instance in a situation like that of Italy, where the mother tongue, for the majority of the population, until very recently, was different from literary Italian.

On the other hand the Enlightenment ideals seem to favour the use of a common language which allows different communities to understand each other. This tradition opposes the divisive, xenophobic attitudes which, by stressing the essential peculiarity of each separate linguistic tradition, end up with a denial of our common humanity, and for instance in the trend represented by the formula '*Muttersprache und Geistesbildung*' take on racist implications:

> The mother tongue paves the way on which a people *(Volk)* becomes conscious of itself, expands the community based on ties of blood and life-soil into a historically effective communion of thought and action, and crowns it, through the creation of permanent values benefiting all the living and future members of the *Volk*.

No, I am not making up this repulsive rubbish. Here is the original in all its splendour:

> Die Muttersprache bahnt den Weg, auf dem ein Volk sich seiner selbst bewusst wird, die in den Bindungen des Blutes und des Lebensbodens angelegte Gemeinsamkeit zur geschichtlich wirksamen Gemeinschaft des Denkens und Handelns ausbaut und durch das Schaffen bleibender, allen lebenden und künftigen Volksgliedern zu gute kommender Werte krönt. (Weisgerber 1943, 83)

The question is made more complicated by the fact that it does not just imply a two-way opposition between a local, native language, and another, different one, imposed from outside or from above. These linguistic problems are usually part of the history of the formation of national states, which often become independent breaking away from a larger, external power, and by the same token suppressing the internal differences between their separate constituent regions. It is a sort of tripartite model in which the national language establishes itself at the expense both of a larger, supranational medium, and of local varieties.

'How many languages does Europe need?' is of course a rhetorical question, not because the answer is already known, but because one is not expected. It would in fact be impossible to give a sensible answer. It is however a question which people ask, for instance when they see the incredible amount of time and resources devoted to translation by the bureaucracy of the European Community. The question could be reformulated into two problems. The first is: How many languages are actually used in Europe? And the second is: Should one encourage or discourage the present variety? The answer one gives naturally affects minority languages (or, to use a label now current, lesser used languages: LULs), however they are defined.

These two problems are in fact interrelated, because the answer to the first partly depends on the answer to the second. The attitude we have towards linguistic diversity, LULs, dialects, etc., inevitably contributes towards determining what goes into any linguistic map of Europe we may try to draw up. I propose to discuss the two questions below. The first is covered in sections 3–5, and the second in section 6.

3. According to the *Statistical Report on the Languages of the World as of 1985* (Décsy 1986–8) there are about 3,000 languages in the world (the figure is double in Grimes (1988), based on the consideration of the number of Bible translations needed to reach all communities in the world). Among the five continents, Europe is linguistically the poorest: Africa has over 1,000 languages, Oceania over 700, Asia just under 700, America over 500, and Europe 117.

The list I have prepared for the Einaudi *Storia d'Europa* (Lepschy 1993) includes 34 states (after German unification, and before the collapse of the Soviet Union and of Yugoslavia) and 138 languages. This higher figure is due to the fact that for the south-eastern boundary of Europe, I have followed the border that separates the former Soviet Union from Turkey and Iran, and I have therefore included the Caucasus, which adds about 20 languages to the list. Décsy gives instead the lower figure of 117 because he accepts the line that goes from the Caspian to the Black Sea along the Kuma-Manyč depression, north of the Caucasus.

Perhaps I can briefly say something about the linguistic situation of the former Soviet Union, and then abandon the topic for the purposes of this paper. In the linguistic policy of the Soviet Union we can distinguish different periods. The first (1917–30) was inspired by Lenin's theories. Against the Tsarist practice of imposing Russian throughout the empire, Lenin forcefully stated that all languages, however small or apparently insignificant and lacking a written tradition, were to be considered as absolutely equal, and that all citizens were entitled to education in their native tongues. The Soviet Union recognized 130 nationalities and over 100 different languages. In 1924 there existed school text-books in 25 languages; in the early thirties the figure had reached 104; in the seventies it had dropped to 45. The second, Stalinist, phase, without openly rejecting Lenin's stand, reverted to the imposition of Russian (which was anyway the mother tongue of about half the population of the Union), and advocated the use of Cyrillic also for languages which had been originally endowed with a Latin alphabet. In 1958–9 the principle of education in the mother tongue was officially abandoned (Kirkwood 1989, 39, 49).

For the purposes of this discussion I propose to disregard about half of these languages, which belong to the European part of the former Soviet Union but are not usually associated with the European linguistic tradition. These include Indo-European languages belonging to the Iranian family, like Tadzhik, Talysh, Tat; Semitic languages such as Assyrian; and a host of languages, listed below in Appendix B, belonging to three large families:

(a) Ugro-Finnic or Uralic, which also includes Hungarian, introduced into Central Europe in the ninth century, Finnish, brought to Europe in prehistoric times, Estonian, Livonian (replaced by Lettish), and Lapp;

(b) Altaic, which includes the Turkic family, with Turkish, used in the European part of Turkey, and the Mongolian family;

(c) Caucasian, which includes Georgian, with a literature going back to the tenth century.

We are left with a number of European languages (almost seventy) which is roughly double the number of states (thirty-four). But this ratio of 2:1 is far from suggesting the great complexity of the linguistic situation. In fact the terms of the problems have not been simplified by removing from our list about eighty 'exotic' languages used in the regions of the Urals and the Caucasus. The real difficulties are posed by situations which are quite familiar, like the Italian one.

Should Italy contribute one unit (that is, Italian) to our list of European languages, apart from a sprinkling of 'alloglottic' minorities, that is communities speaking French, German, Albanian, Greek, etc.? This is the solution adopted by Décsy (1986–8, III, 19) who states that Italian is spoken by 56,000,000 people, although 'with many distinct regional variations', whatever that may mean exactly, and only counts as one in his list of 117 languages for Europe.

Or should Italy add to the list its fifteen or so regional dialects, which are in effect separate Romance languages (Ligurian, Piedmontese, Lombard, Venetian and so on)? This is the line taken by Barbara Grimes (1988, 377–80), although her list of languages used in Italy is eccentric, and in some details downright bizarre.

In any case, there is a third possibility, considering not just fifteen or so, but hundreds or thousands of local dialects, on the ground that they are distinctly different from each other in phonology, grammar and vocabulary, although usually mutually intelligible within the same region. In this case Italy by itself would provide a number of languages larger than that traditionally attributed to the whole world.

Another problem is posed by the difficulty of establishing the number of speakers for different languages. I am basing my figures on Décsy 1986–8 (adding in brackets figures from Grimes 1988, preceded by a 'G', or from other sources, as indicated, if they are considerably different). I am not at all confident about the correctness of these figures, and in some cases I have serious doubts about the possibility of obtaining reliable data. Often these statistics are based not on observation of linguistic behaviour (which might raise its own problems anyway), but on self-evaluation, which is notoriously untrustworthy. Keeping in mind these reservations, I provide the data, grouped by state, in Appendix A.

We can think of the panorama emerging from Appendix A as formed by superimposing on a map of Europe two sets of interdependent historical data, resulting on the one hand from the formation of separate states, and on the other from the spread of languages. The linguistic history of Europe, looked at from the viewpoint of today, reveals three main language families – Romance, Germanic and Slav – which have shown considerable force of expansion throughout the world (particularly English in the Germanic family, and Spanish and Portuguese in the Romance). The Celtic family has been retreating, since the period between the fifth and the third centuries BC in which it stretched across Europe to Asia Minor, and is now besieged by English and French. The Baltic languages (Lettish and Lithuanian), Greek, Albanian, and, outside the Indo-European family, Basque, Hungarian, Finnish, Estonian, survive in an entrenched condition.

4. We can also look at the same map from the viewpoint of LULs (see Price 1969; Pogarell 1983). The definition of LULs is controversial. I do not intend to offer a definition and even suspect that a workable one may not be feasible. The notion seems to imply on the one hand numerical considerations, and on the other lack of recognition, cultural or bureaucratic. But both these criteria are difficult to apply unequivocally.

Numerically, one assumes that a LUL is used less within a relevant context, but defining the term 'relevant' is problematic. German is a LUL in Italy, but not in Europe; in South Tyrol, which is part of Italy, Italian is a LUL. 'Minority language' or 'LUL' are labels sometimes used to indicate a 'small' language, with reference to a unit which may be larger than the individual state: Slovenian is certainly a LUL in Italy, Austria and Hungary, and it was a LUL in the former Yugoslavia; even though it is the language of the majority in Slovenia (with about 2,000,000 speakers), some would still consider it a LUL in

Europe. On the other hand Ukrainian, with its 36,500,000 speakers in the Ukraine, although it was a LUL in the former Soviet Union, is not a 'small' language in Europe; it may however find its place in a discussion of LULs on account of its having lived in the shadow of two culturally more powerful neighbours, Polish and Russian. Similarly, situations like those of Belgium and Switzerland are often mentioned in this context, owing to the friction and unequal prestige of the languages involved. The French of Geneva, which is a LUL in Switzerland, enjoys a degree of prestige, relative to metropolitan French, greater than that of German Swiss (let alone Schwyzertütsch) compared with metropolitan German.

Rather than trying to introduce unsatisfactory definitions I shall just produce, in Appendix B, a list of all the languages which are used by a minority of the population in one or more European states. It is interesting to note that almost all European languages appear in this list, the only exceptions being Czech, Icelandic, Maltese, Norwegian, Portuguese and Spanish.

5. In the context of LULs we must also consider the questions related to recent immigration. The difficulty here is that figures may change considerably from year to year, and that it is not always easy to distinguish temporary residence (on the German *Gastarbeiter* model) from permanent immigration. To give an idea of the trend I shall quote data for different years. GERMANY, figures for 1989 (followed, in brackets, by those for 1975): 1,613,000 (543,000) Turks; 610,000 (416,000) Yugoslavs; 520,000 (292,000) Italians. FRANCE, figures for 1982 (1975): 795,000 (440,000) Algerians; 765,000 (475,000) Portuguese; 431,000 (130,000) Moroccans; 334,000 (230,000) Italians; 321,000 (265,000) Spaniards. UNITED KINGDOM, figures for 1986–8 (1975): 583,000 (452,000) Irish, presumably in a majority native speakers of English; 1,025,000 (over 1,000,000) of non-EC origin. (For the linguistic situation in Britain see Trudgill, ed., 1984; L. M. P. 1985.) ITALY, which used to be a source of emigrants has recently become a target for immigration: non-EC immigrants have risen from 35,000 in 1975 to 236,000 in 1989, to an estimated 650,000 in 1991.

6. The panorama is complicated not only for the number and variety of the languages involved, but also for the diversity of their resilience, status, and degree of institutional recognition. A detailed examination of the language policies of different states and of the various legal

provisions in place for the safeguard of LULs would require a separate study. In general there seem to be three main lines one can take towards language policy:

(a) The first consists in a deliberate striving towards linguistic uniformity, through the spread of a major language and the suppression of LULs by excluding them from the schools and the media and discouraging their public use.

(b) The second is a non-interventionist attitude, which promotes linguistic freedom and leaves all idioms to fend for themselves: let a hundred flowers bloom and coexist happily, and if some are stronger than others, let them prevail, and if some are weaker than others, let them succumb.

(c) The third is an interventionist attitude in favour of LULs: if we wish a LUL to survive, we must protect it, and give it the possibility of competing with more powerful rivals. It must be allowed, encouraged, and if necessary imposed, in schools from the kindergarten through to the university and the graduate research institute, in literary, scholarly and scientific writing, in the media (from newspapers to film to the all-powerful television), in administration, and in government.

It seems to me that the choice of one or another of these options can be argued for reasonably, but it is basically not a question of finding the correct solution to a problem, by examining the evidence available and using the model of rational, scientific explanation. The discussion is too closely associated with our attitudes and beliefs, and their ideological and political ramifications.

Perhaps the best I can do is to present my own personal experience in this field. I was born and grew up in Venice, and I consider myself a native speaker of two languages, Venetian (which is generally considered to be a 'dialect' in the sense current in the Italian tradition – it is in fact a separate Romance language), and standard Italian (in one of its northern varieties, which differ in some phonological details from, but are not less prestigious than, Tuscan). As a linguist I have also worked in the area of Italian dialectology. So I have both a professional interest in and a personal commitment to Italian dialects in general, and Venetian in particular with which much of my early intellectual and human experience is bound up. The Italian department where I work, at the University of Reading, was founded by Luigi Meneghello, another speaker of Venetian (in his case a variety of Vicentino) and one of the most notable contemporary Italian writers, who in his books has illustrated in a striking way the energy, vitality and subtlety of his native dialect, and the exciting richness provided by a background (traditional, in Italy, up to recent years) in which written language (and all the culture that goes with it) was an idiom (literary Italian) altogether different from that used in speech, which was endowed with its own separate culture, not less elaborate, and in some ways more alive and authentic than that associated with the written language.

On the basis of this experience, I cannot share the first position mentioned above, although it was quite widespread in the left-wing, democratic tradition in which most of my friends were nurtured in Italy after the war. I remember a conversation I had in my teens with an older friend, who was to become a brilliant Italianist. 'What do you think will happen to the dialects?', I asked. 'I hope they die out as quickly as possible', was the answer, not less poignant for having itself been given in dialect. This attitude was based on the Jacobin assumption that dialects symbolized backwardness, illiteracy and obscurantism, and that progress and emancipation could come only through the use of the national language. Unfortunately an analogous position was also upheld by reactionary ideologies, like those of purism on the one hand, and of fascist nationalism on the other.

As a linguist, I have greater sympathy for the second, *laissez-faire*, hands-off, position. I have to accept, however, that this implies a fairly rapid disappearance of the dialects.

The third, protectionist, hands-on, position may appear in some contexts the most civilized and desirable choice. But I must confess that, at least from my Italian viewpoint, it elicits some reservations. Here again I should like to quote a conversation I had some time ago with a friend and colleague who is an eminent Welsh Italianist, also interested in Italian LULs. 'If you want a language to survive,' he told me, 'you must treat it in all respects as a language of culture, and in particular as the medium for education. Otherwise the battle will inevitably be lost: the LUL will become a "vernacular", and in time it will be replaced, in all areas of usage, by the dominant standard.'

This I found troubling, because my commitment to Venetian is connected with the fact that it represented speech, and that it coexisted in a sort of symbiosis (and had done so for centuries) with literary Italian. Literary Italian was our 'other' language, the one of the written word, of books, of schooling. Venetian has of course a rich literary tradition, but the authors belonging to that tradition were part of a culture which used Latin and Italian as its main medium. It is not unjustified to say that Italian literature includes works written in Latin and in many dialects, as well as in Italian, and that therefore the Venetian plays by Goldoni, or the poems by Maffio Venier, belong to Italian literature. In fact sometimes we felt that we had invented literary Italian in Venice, when a speaker of Venetian, Pietro Bembo,

had written his *Prose della volgar lingua* at the beginning of the sixteenth century – but we were perhaps pushing local patriotism too far.
The idea, however, of having to study Venetian at school, of learning
history, chemistry and mathematics through the medium of Venetian,
or of reading the classics of English, Russian, and perhaps even Italian
literature in Venetian translation, I would have found (and I would still
find) engaging perhaps, but rather bizarre.

I think that part of my reluctance is based on the feeling that this
would have been a way of spoiling the dialect, of making it into another
parochial, little, restricted and restricting standard language of culture,
depriving us of our marvellous, lively and powerful idiom, which we
were able to contrast with the national written language.

Going back to my title: How many languages does Europe need?, my
inclination would be to answer: as many as there are, as spoken
languages. People should not be deprived of their speech. But, please,
as few as possible, as written standards, languages of culture to be used
for scholarly and scientific publications. The prospect would not please
me of having to read a technical linguistic monograph on barriers and
locality written in the dialect of Modena, or a great European novel
written in Milanese. In fact, part of the charm of Manzoni's *Promessi
sposi* would be lost if we did not have to interpret his Tuscan through
his native Milanese. You may think that I want to have my cake and eat
it too. Well, I am not sure that that is so deplorable.

Appendix A

Languages of Europe

These are given by state (see section 3 above) and exclude the former
Soviet Union. The figures come from Décsy (1986–8) unless otherwise
specified. As indicated above, the reliability of these data is problematic, Décsy's figures seem to be sometimes approximate, or extrapo-
lated for 1985. The first figure, immediately after the name of the state,
represents the total population. This may differ from the total of the
speakers for a number of possible reasons: (a) the statistical sources
may be different; (b) some groups are considered bilingual and are
therefore counted twice; (c) some sections of the population may be
unaccounted for in the language assessment; (d) immigrant workers or
guest workers (particularly from extra-European countries) are sometimes disregarded. I have refrained from intervening on individual
figures as this would have made it more difficult to compare them with
each other. I have however occasionally added figures given by Grimes

(1988), preceded by the letter 'G', if they were considerably different or gave information missing from Décsy.

ALBANIA 3,000,000: Albanian 2,900,000; Greek 100,000; Arumanian 50,000; Romany 30,000

ANDORRA 45,000: Spanish 30,000; Catalan 12,600; French 2,400.

AUSTRIA 7,579,000: German 7,359,000; Serbo-Croatian 80,000 (G 28,000); Slovenian 50,000; Hungarian 20,000.

BELGIUM 9,872,000: Flemish 5,800,000; French 3,200,000 (G 4,000,000); German 120,000 (G 150,000); Letzeburgisch 20,000.

BULGARIA 8,969,000: Bulgarian 8,000,000; Turkish 450,000 (G 846,000); Macedonian 200,000; Romany 170,000; Armenian 30,000; Gagauz 12,000; Tatar 10,000; Albanian: number unknown.

CYPRUS 662,000: Greek 480,000; Turkish 180,000 (G 120,000); Armenian 2,000 (G 23,000).

CZECHOSLOVAKIA 15,466,000: Czech 11,000,000; Slovak 3,400,000 (G 4,720,000); Hungarian 700,000; German 300,000 (G 200,000); (G Romany 220,000); Polish 100,000; Ukrainian 100,000.

DENMARK 5,112,000: Danish 5,000,000; Faeroese (in Faeroe Islands) 45,000; German 23,000; Greenlandic (Eskimo) 3,000; Romany 2,000; there is a small minority of Lapp speakers.

FINLAND 4,873,000: Finnish 4,470,000 (G 4,900,000); Swedish 311,000 (G 341,000); Karelian 40,000; Romany 6,000; Lapp 2,000.

FRANCE 54,872,000: French 45,000,000 (G 51,000,000); Occitanic (including Gascon) 8,000,000 (G 10,000,000); (Franco-Provençal less than 2,000,000 total, with minorities in Italy and Switzerland, according to *Encyclopaedia Britannica* 1983, vol. 4, 279); German 1,300,000; Dutch 1,200,000 (perhaps a mistake for 120,000; according to G 90,000); Breton 700,000; (G Catalan 260,000); (G Corsican 200,000); Italian 100,000; Basque 90,000; Romany 10,000.

GERMANY 78,105,000: German 77,600,000; Polish 200,000; Sorb of Lusatia 150,000; Romany 75,000; Ukrainian 70,000; Danish 50,000; Hungarian 40,000; Frisian 10,000; Adygey 500.

GREECE 9,884,000: Greek 9,000,000; Arumanian 200,000 (G 50,000); Macedonian 170,000; Turkish 150,000; (G Albanian 140,000); Romany 70,000; Bulgarian 30,000; (G Armenian 20,000); Meglenite 8,000; Judeo-Spanish 1,000.

HUNGARY 10,161,000: Hungarian 10,000,000; German 300,000; Romany 300,000; Slovak 100,000; Serbo-Croatian 40,000; Slovenian 25,000 (G 4,000); Romanian 10,000.

ICELAND 250,000: Icelandic 250,000; Danish 2,000.

IRELAND 3,575,000: English 3,500,000 (G 2,600,000); Irish 750,000 (120,000 in everyday usage).

ITALY 56,998,000: Italian 56,000,000; Sardinian: estimates vary from 1,200,000 to 159,000; Friulian 625,000; German 300,000, plus 13,000 in small linguistic enclaves; Albanian 260,000 (82,000 claiming everyday usage); Occitanic 200,000; Slovenian 80,000; French 70,000; (G Franco-Provençal 70,000); Ladin 50,000; (G Catalan 15,000); (G Romany 16,000); (G Greek 20,000); (G Serbo-Croatian 3,500).

LIECHTENSTEIN 27,000: German 27,000.

LUXEMBOURG 366,000: Letzeburgisch 355,000; German 350,000; French 350,000.

MALTA 360,000: Maltese 360,000 (G 300,000); English 200,000.

MONACO 28,000: French 25,000; Occitanic 5,000.

NETHERLANDS 14,437,000: Dutch 14,000,000; Frisian 350,000 (G 700,000); German 120,000.

NORWAY 4,145,000: Norwegian 4,000,000; Lapp 28,000; Finnish 20,000.

POLAND 36,887,000: Polish 35,000,000; Ukrainian 1,500,000; (G German 1,400,000); Belorussian 300,000; Kashubian 200,000; Romany 30,000; Yiddish 3,000; Slovak 2,000; Karaim 300.

PORTUGAL 10,045,000: Portuguese 10,000,000; Romany 20,000.

ROMANIA 22,683,000: Romanian 19,000,000; Hungarian 2,100,000; German 400,000; Serbo-Croatian 200,000; Romany 150,000; Turkish 30,000; Ukrainian 30,000; Tatar 25,000; Armenian 20,000; (G Bulgarian 10,000); Gagauz 10,000; Polish 10,000; Greek 10,000.

SAN MARINO 23,000: Italian 23,000.

SPAIN 38,435,000: Spanish 28,000,000; Catalan 8,500,000; Gallego or Galician 3,000,000; Basque 700,000; Romany 80,000; Mozarabic 5,000. There is also a small community of Gascon speakers in the Aran Valley.

SWEDEN 8,335,000: Swedish 9,000,000 (curiously the figure is higher than that given for the population); Finnish 500,000 (G 300,000); Lapp 10,000; Romany 10,000.

SWITZERLAND 6,500,000: German 4,200,000; French 1,200,000; Italian 800,000; Romansch 65,000.

TURKEY (EUROPEAN) 3,000,000: Turkish 3,000,000; Albanian 60,000; Bulgarian 60,000; Armenian 50,000; Serbo-Croatian 20,000; Greek 10,000; Judeo-Spanish 8,000.

UNITED KINGDOM 56,890,000: English 59,650,000 (curiously the figure is higher than that given for the population; G 55,000,000); Welsh 750,000 (G 575,000 including 32,700 monolinguals); Gaelic in Scotland 150,000 (G 89,000 including 477 monolinguals); French 140,000 (this is the total figure for the population of the Channel Islands, which are not part of the United Kingdom but dependencies of the British crown; only a minority speak Norman dialects; G 14,000); Romany 40,000;

Polish 20,000; Irish; data not available, perhaps 5,000; Manx 300, as a second language, in the Isle of Man (which is not part of the United Kingdom but a British crown possession); Cornish 50.

USSR (EUROPEAN) 194,476,000 (out of a total of 282,820,000 including the Asiatic part): see observations above.

VATICAN 1000: Italian 850; Swiss German 150.

YUGOSLAVIA 22,997,000: Serbo-Croatian 16,000,000 (Serbian 10,000,000; Croatian 6,000,000); Slovenian 2,000,000; Macedonian 2,000,000 (G 1,386,000); Albanian 1,400,000; Hungarian 600,000; Italian 300,000; Turkish 250,000; Romanian 150,000; Romany 100,000 (G 600,000); Slovak 50,000 (G 100,000); Ukrainian 23,000; (G German 23,000); Istro-Rumanian 1,000.

Appendix B

Minority languages

These are also described as lesser used languages (LULs) (see section 4), and they exclude the former Soviet Union. The figures come from Décsy (1986–8) unless otherwise specified; 'G' refers to figures given by Grimes (1988), quoted if they are considerably different or give information missing from Décsy.

ADYGEY (Caucasian): 500 in Germany.

ALBANIAN: 1,400,000 in Yugoslavia; 140,000 in Greece; 82,000 in Italy; 60,000 in European Turkey; an unknown number in Bulgaria.

ARMENIAN: 50,000 in European Turkey; 30,000 in Bulgaria; 20,000 in Greece; 20,000 in Romania; 2,000 (G 23,000) in Cyprus.

ARUMANIAN: 200,000 (G 50,000) in Greece; 50,000 in Albania.

BASQUE: 700,000 in Spain; 90,000 in France.

BELORUSSIAN: 300,000 in Poland

BRETON: 700,000 in France.

BULGARIAN: 60,000 in European Turkey; 30,000 in Greece; 10,000 in Romania.

CATALAN: 8,500,000 in Spain; 260,000 in France; 15,000 in Italy; 12,600 in Andorra.

CORNISH: extinct from the beginning of the nineteenth century; a few hundred people can read it, and a few dozens can use it in conversation.

CORSICAN: (G 200,000 in France (Corsica)); two dialects, one of Sardinian type, one of Tuscan type.

DANISH: 50,000 in Germany; 2,000 in Iceland.

ENGLISH: 200,000 in Malta.

FAEROESE: 45,000 in Denmark (Faeroe Islands).

FINNISH: 500,000 (G 300,000) in Sweden; they prefer Swedish to be used in schools and in public life; 20,000 in Norway.

FLEMISH/DUTCH: (G 90,000 in France); in Belgium the hostility between Flemish (5,800,000) and French (3,200,000, G 4,000,000) speakers goes back to the origins of the Belgian state in 1830. For the Flemish the standard is not a local variety, but Dutch, officially accepted since 1898, and sanctioned by law since 1973.

FRANCO-PROVENÇAL: less than 2,000,000, in France, Switzerland, Italy (G 70,000 in Italy).

FRENCH: 3,200,000 in Belgium; 1,200,000 in Switzerland (including an enclave in the German speaking Canton of Bern); 70,000 in Italy; 2,400 in Andorra. See also Norman French.

FRISIAN: 350,000 (G 700,000) in the Netherlands; 10,000 in Germany.

FRIULIAN: 625,000 in Italy (Friuli).

GAELIC: 150,000 (G 89,000) in Scotland, in 1971 (including, according to Grimes 1988, 477 monolinguals).

GAGAUZ (Turkic): 12,000 in Bulgaria; 10,000 in Romania.

GALLEGO or GALICIAN: 3,000,000 in Spain.

GASCON: a small community in the Aran Valley in Spain. In France Gascon is counted with the Occitanic varieties.

GERMAN: (G 1,400,000 in Poland); 1,300,000 in France (Alsace); 400,000 in Romania; 300,000 (G 200,000) in Czechoslovakia; 300,000 in Hungary; 300,000 (South Tyrol) plus 13,000 in small linguistic enclaves in Italy; 120,000 (G 150,000) in Belgium; 120,000 in the Netherlands; 23,000 in Denmark (Northern Schleswig, which became Danish in 1920); (G 23,000 in Yugoslavia); Swiss German: 150 in Vatican City.

GREEK: 100,000 in Albania; (G 20,000 in Italy); 10,000 in Romania; 10,000 in European Turkey.

GREENLANDIC: 3,000 Eskimo speakers in Denmark.

HUNGARIAN: 2,100,000 in Romania; 700,000 in Czechoslovakia; 600,000 in Yugoslavia; 40,000 in Germany; 20,000 in Austria.

IRISH: 120,000 in everyday usage in 1971 in Ireland, where it is the official language; data not available for United Kingdom (perhaps 5,000).

ISTRO-RUMANIAN: 1,000 in Yugoslavia.

ITALIAN: 800,000 in Switzerland; 300,000 in Yugoslavia.

JUDEO-SPANISH: 8,000 in European Turkey; 1,000 in Greece.

KARAIM (Turkic): 300 in Poland.

KARELIAN (Uralic): 40,000 in Finland.

KASHUBIAN: 200,000 in Poland.

LADIN: 50,000 in Italy (Dolomites).

LAPP (Uralic): 28,000 in Norway; 10,000 in Sweden; 2,000 in Finland; a small minority in Denmark, entitled to mother-tongue schooling since 1965.

LETZEBURGISCH: 20,000 in Belgium.

MACEDONIAN (Slavic): 2,000,000 in Yugoslavia; 200,000 in Bulgaria; 170,000 in Greece.

MANX: 300 people, who learnt it as adults, in the Isle of Man, a British crown possession; the last native speaker, Mr Ned Maddrell, died in 1974 (Price 1987, 6).

MEGLENITE (a variety of Romanian): 8,000 in Greece.

MOZARABIC (Semitic): 5,000 in Spain.

NORMAN FRENCH: Décsy 1986–8 gives 140,000, the total population of the Channel Islands (dependencies of the British crown); Grimes 1988 gives 14,000, but apparently 'It is impossible to estimate with any precision how many still speak the various dialects of Channel Island French' (Price 1984, 211).

OCCITANIC: estimated from 1,500,000 (C. E. C. 1986) to 10,000,000 in France; 200,000 in Italy; 5,000 in Monaco.

POLISH: 200,000 in Germany, including a community in the Ruhr region going back to the nineteenth century (C. E. C. 1986); 100,000 in Czechoslovakia; 20,000 in United Kingdom; 10,000 in Romania.

ROMANIAN: 150,000 in Yugoslavia; 10,000 in Hungary.

ROMANSCH: 65,000 in Switzerland.

ROMANY: 300,000 in Hungary; (G 220,000 in Czechoslovakia); 170,000 in Bulgaria; 150,000 in Romania; 100,000 (G 600,000) in Yugoslavia; 80,000 in Spain; 75,000 in Germany; 70,000 in Greece; 40,000 in United Kingdom; 30,000 in Albania; 30,000 in Poland; 20,000 in Portugal; (G 16,000 in Italy); 10,000 in France; 10,000 in Sweden; 6,000 in Finland; 2,000 in Denmark.

SARDINIAN: estimates vary from 159,000 to 1,200,000, in Italy (Sardinia).

SERBO-CROATIAN: 200,000 in Romania; 80,000 (G 28,000) in Austria; 40,000 in Hungary; 20,000 in European Turkey; (G 3,500 in Italy).

SLOVAK: 3,400,000 (G 4,720,000) in Czechoslovakia; 100,000 in Hungary; 50,000 (G 100,000) in Yugoslavia; 2,000 in Poland.

SLOVENIAN: 2,000,000 in Yugoslavia; 80,000 in Italy; 50,000 in Austria; 25,000 (G 4,000) in Hungary.

SORB OF LUSATIA: 150,000 in Germany; for this West-Slavic enclave see Stone 1972.

SWEDISH: 311,000 (G 341,000) in Finland.

TATAR (Turkic): 25,000 in Romania; 10,000 in Bulgaria.

TURKISH: 450,000 (G 846,000) in Bulgaria; 250,000 in Yugoslavia; 180,000 (G 120,000) in Cyprus; 150,000 in Greece; 30,000 in Romania.

UKRAINIAN: 1,500,000 in Poland; 100,000 in Czechoslovakia; 70,000 in Germany; 30,000 in Romania; 23,000 in Yugoslavia.
WELSH: 750,000 (G 575,000) in the United Kingdom (including, according to Grimes 1988, 32,700 monolinguals).
YIDDISH: 3,000 in Poland.

Appendix C

Other languages used in the European part of the former Soviet Union (see section 3 above).

(a) Ugro-Finnic or Uralic: Ingrian, Karelian, Komi-Permyak, Komi-Zyrian, Lud, Mari/Cheremis, Mordvin, Olonec, Samoyed, Vepsian, Votic, Votyak, Yurak.
(b) Altaic: Turkic family, with Azeri, Balkar, Bashkir, Chuvash, Gagauz, Karachay, Karaim, Karapapakh, Kazakh, Kirgiz, Kumyk, Nogay, Tatar, Turkmen, Uzbek; Mongolian family, with Kalmyk.
(c) Caucasian: Abaza, Abkhazian, Adygei/Circassian, Adzhar, Agul, Akhvakh, Andi, Archi, Avar/Tses, Bagvalal/Kvanadin, Bats/Tush, Botlikh, Budukh, Chamalal, Chechen, Dargva/Darghin, Godoberi, Hunsi/Nakhad, Ingush, Kapuchi/Bezhita, Kabardin, Karata, Khinalug, Khvarshi, Kryz/Dzhek, Lak/Kazikymyk, Lezghian, Rutul, Shapsug, Svan, Tabasaran, Tindi, Tsakhur, Tses/Dido, Udi, Zan/Chan/Laz/Mingrelian.

References

C. E. C. 1986. *Linguistic Minorities in Countries Belonging to the European Community. Summary Report Prepared by the Istituto della Enciclopedia Italiana*, Luxembourg: Office for the Official Publications of the European Community.
Dauzat, A. 1953. *L'Europe linguistique. Nouvelle édition, refondue et mise à jour*, Paris: Payot (first edition, 1940).
Décsy, G. 1986–8. *Statistical Report on the Languages of the World as of 1985*, 5 vols., Bloomington: Eurolingua.
Dyson, F. 1979. *Disturbing the Universe*, New York: Harper and Row.
Grimes, B. (ed.). 1988. *Ethnologue. Languages of the World*, eleventh edition, Dallas, Texas: Summer Institute of Linguistics (first edition, 1951).
Hoenigswald, H. M. and Wiener, L. F. (eds.). 1987. *Biological Metaphor and Cladistic Classification. An Interdisciplinary Perspective*, London: Pinter.

Kirkwood, M. (ed.). 1989. *Language Planning in the Soviet Union*, London: Macmillan.

Lepschy, G. 1993. 'Le lingue degli europei', in *Storia d'Europa*. Vol. 1, Turin: Einaudi, 867–910.

L. M. P. 1985. *The Other Languages of England, Linguistic Minorities Project*, London: Routledge and Kegan Paul.

Meillet, A. 1918. *Les Langues dans l'Europe nouvelle*, Paris: Payot (second edition, 1928).

Pogarell, R. 1983. *Minority Languages in Europe. A Classified Bibliography*, Berlin: Mouton.

Price, G. 1969. *The Present Position of Minority Languages in Western Europe. A Selective Bibliography*, Cardiff: University of Wales Press.

—— 1984. *The Languages of Britain*, London: Arnold.

—— 1987. *Ireland and the Celtic Connection. A Lecture Given at the Princess Grace Irish Library on Friday 27 September 1985*, Gerrards Cross: Colin Smythe.

Stephens, M. 1976. *Linguistic Minorities in Western Europe*, Llandysul: Gomer Press.

Stone, G. 1972. *The Smallest Slavonic Nation. The Sorbs of Lusatia*, London: Athlone Press.

Tesnière, L. 1928. 'Statistique des langues de l'Europe', in Meillet 1928, 291–484.

Trudgill, P. (ed.). 1984. *Language in the British Isles*, Cambridge: Cambridge University Press.

Unesco, 1953. *The Use of Vernacular Languages in Education*, Paris: Unesco.

Walter, H. 1991. *Les Langues dans l'Europe des douze. Communication au XVIIᵉ Colloque international de linguistique fonctionnelle*, Université de León 5–11 juillet 1990, in press.

Weisgerber, J. 1943. *Die volkhaften Kräfte der Muttersprache*, Frankfurt: Diesterweg (first edition, 1939).

2

Romania within a wider Europe: conflict or cohesion?

REBECCA POSNER

Let me start by making clear that Romania here is used in the sense of the 'community' of speakers of Romance languages and not for the name of the country, which for clarity's sake I shall call by its older English name of Rumania. My use of the designation Romania already implies that I am regarding the languages, if not their speakers, as a coherent group. The feeling of coherence, like most ethnic perceptions, is based on history. To some extent too, within Europe, there is geographical cohesion, as, leaving out Rumania, the Romance area is a continuous one. We cannot ignore the fact, however, that Romance languages are used outside of Europe, and that, indeed, there are more non-European than European speakers of Spanish and Portuguese, and even, perhaps, of French.

The historical basis of Romance identity needs no elucidation here: except in Rumania, there has been no definite break in tradition between the Roman era and the present day, even though the genetic make-up of the inhabitants of the area has changed. Christianity became part of that tradition, and even the schism in the Western Christian Church at the Reformation had comparatively little effect on Romance cohesion, except in marginal areas. True, Rumanian participation in the Romance tradition is, to say the least, doubtful, not least because Orthodox rather than Roman Christianity has for the most part shaped its traditions. Nineteenth-century linguists characterized the language as 'semi-Romance', and it is only after the establishment of an autonomous nation-state that the Romance nature of Rumanian was emphasized and accepted. Today we are witnessing a re-run of mid-nineteenth century national and linguistic conflicts in Rumania and Moldavia – probably fed by the underlying desire of the Romance speakers to be associated with the cultural and economic advantages of their Western confrères.

But the very ideological motives that led the Rumanians to seek identification with the Romance West prompted ruptures within the West. Assertion of nationhood, associated with the establishment of the modern state, was to split the perceived unity of the neo-Roman world. We recall that 'Roman' and 'Latin' were the usual names for written vernacular varieties until the thirteenth century, and that the more conservative form of Latin remained a vehicle for serious writing until the sixteenth century (and, of course, the language of the Roman Church until quite recently). But French shook off its Romance identity comparatively early; even in the nineteenth-century heyday of comparative philology French scholars were reluctant to consider their language in terms of a member of the Romance family, rather than as a *sui generis* creation (especially after 1870 when they tended to spurn Romance philology as a German invention). On the other hand, the cultural prestige associated with the French language did attract, particularly in the seventeenth and eighteenth centuries, the admiration of other Romance speakers, who adopted features of French language and style, with the effect that cohesion between the Romance languages was increased rather than diminished. The prestige long persisted, so that French was the normally taught second language in other Romance countries – a tradition finally broken in Italy, perhaps, only in 1992 when the requirement for competence in French was abandoned by the Diplomatic Service.

However, it can be objected that the prestige of first Latin, and then French, has not affected only the Romance-speaking countries (Posner 1992a). The Latino-Romance tradition invested the whole of Western Europe with a degree of cultural unity, certainly before the Reformation, and to some extent before industrialization and concomitant nationalism. It has even been suggested (Gellner 1983) that if industrialization had hit Western Europe in the High Middle Ages, then Latin would have remained the universal culture language, there might have been no standardization of vernaculars, and the translators and interpreters of the EEC would be out of a job. A proposal, advanced in 1974, that Latin should be the working language of the European Community (Coulmas 1991) was doomed to failure, however, as by that time Latin was no longer a universal élite language in Europe. Before the Reformation, however – Germanophone, as well as Romanophone – continental Europe used Latin as the language of serious writing (Henkel and Palmer (eds.) 1992), even translating German compositions into Latin, perhaps to give them wider currency. Norman England, of course, preferred the use of French for many purposes, and

French remained the fashionable language of cultured Germans and Russians, as well as the language of diplomacy, well into the nineteenth century.

The linguistic legacy of Rome, then, was not bequeathed exclusively to Romance speakers. Yet few doubt that they have always been conscious of the close relationship between their languages and Latin, to such a extent that someone like Montaigne could claim to make himself understood throughout Romanophone Europe by judicious choice of elements from French, Latin and Gascon. The influence of Latin on the standardized languages, especially in orthography and lexicon, is such that even today there can be a degree of mutual comprehension between their users.

Any feeling of cohesion among Romance speakers must have originated, however, in an impulse to differentiate themselves from 'the others' – in the first place the German 'others' who were encroaching on their territory, but who in some cases also became incorporated themselves into the Romance fellowship. Whereas the language of Rome was the legacy that all Europe inherited, 'Romance' was recognized as a distinct entity first in those peripheral areas where confrontation with German forced speakers to re-evaluate the status of their language. The Strasbourg Oaths of 842, sworn in both Roman and Teutonic tongues, may mark the first division into the two blocs (Posner 1993c). Within German-speaking Europe, from the twelfth century on, there were attempts to bolster Germanic patrimony, by disputing the French claim to Charlemagne as one of themselves: curiously, the controversy was conducted in Latin rather than in German (Schnell 1992). The confrontation between Germanic- and Romance-speaking Europeans came further into the open, and eventually into popular mythology, with Herder (1744–1803), whose claim that the mother tongue is the soul of the nation made manifest, is thought to be a German reaction to 'insultingly proud Romance neighbours to the west and ... hopelessly crude Slavic neighbours to the east' (Fishman 1972, 46). It was mainly against the French, rather than the other Romance peoples, that the German movement was directed, as the cultural hold of the French language in fashionable circles was resented by the upwardly mobile. Later in the nineteenth century Latin was also to be treated with hostility, in moves to deprive the classical gymnasium of its prestige and influence. In this conflict between German and Romance, the French themselves perhaps stood somewhat apart, as the myth persisted that their nobility was of Frankish, that is Germanic, extraction, partaking both of Germanic energy and Roman elegance (Poliakov 1974). The tone-setting élite could therefore claim to represent the best of both worlds, whereas the common people, who were to triumph in the Revolution, were purportedly of less privileged native Celtic stock (*nos ancêtres, les Gaulois*).

Today it is those Romance languages that are still in similar confrontations with representatives of other language families, that assert their 'Romanceness' by boasting the names 'Romance' or 'Latin' – Rumanian, the Swiss and Italian so-called Rhaeto-Romance varieties, the liturgical language of the Sephardic Jews. The original emergence of Romance as a separate bloc, I claim, was a consequence of conflict between European peoples, whereas the maintenance of Latin as a culture language preserved a degree of harmony within a linguistically divided Europe. Such cultural fellowship as persisted was, however, threatened with dissolution at the time of the Reformation, which split Western Europe roughly along the same lines as linguistic differences. It was the establishment of modern states that eventually rent asunder the European unity that we now seek to restore.

This picture of medieval and early modern Europe divided into two powerful linguistic blocs – Germanic and Romance – leaves on the margins 'older' European languages, Celtic, Albanian, Greek, Basque, Finnish, Lithuanian, and takes no account of the Slavonic languages, which some would claim have never wholly taken up residence in the 'European house'. We should obviously avoid the temptation to treat, like Smits (1989), Germanic and Romance as representative of 'Eurogrammar'; the European Science Foundation project 'Eurotyp' casts its nets much wider in an attempt to home in on typological features that can be said to characterize European languages, including those outside the Indo-European family. My aim is much more modest. It is to try and situate the modern Romance languages within the common European house and to suggest how linguistic conflict may be resolved and greater cohesion achieved within a changing Europe. I do not ask, with Professor Lepschy, how many languages the new Europe needs: the answer to that question must be, I agree, 'As many as possible'. Rather I ask how Europeans can maximize linguistic interchange without wasting resources on bread-and-butter translation and interpreting of routine communications.

As we enter the single market, four of the nine community languages are Romance (French, Italian, Portuguese and Spanish), to which we should add Catalan which since 1990 is also used for community publications. Taken as a unit, Romance mother-tongue speakers form a substantial group within the community. German, however, is the single language with most speakers, and if we count English as a Germanic language, this language family is numerically the strongest within Europe. English, with its extra-European connections, is the foreign language of choice throughout Europe, as elsewhere in the world, with French coming a poor second.

Linguistically, as a product of the fusion of the German and Romance linguistic traditions, English seems ideally suited to form the basis of a Eurospeak, as it already has for the language of science: the contributors to Coulmas (ed.) (1991) see as the only alternative to the adoption of English the promotion of polyglottism among a wider section of the population. Harald Weinrich (see Coulmas 1991, 28) has suggested that, to avoid English monopolizing the language market, it should be restricted to the status of second foreign language for European learners. Guy Jucquois (1991) advocates that, instead of promoting one European language (inevitably English), a whole range of second languages should be taught, in a fairly random fashion, so that within any reasonably sized group of Europeans there will be at least one individual who can cope with any language required.

Such limitation of individual educational choices, however, would seem to go against the spirit of the age. Resistance to English is understandable, as one of the cohesive qualities of the Community is the wish to hinder the encroachment of American values on the European heritage. I need hardly add that English-speaking linguists would view with dismay any move that may further decrease interest in foreign languages among our compatriots. But is there any alternative to English?

Would a Romance language, for instance, serve better as a lingua franca? We recall that the name 'lingua franca' itself derives from the Romance interlanguage used by Crusaders, and which then formed the base for a Mediterranean maritime *sabir*, which some believe then was spread by Portuguese slavers to the New World, to become eventually creole languages. The Romanophone nations retain, perhaps, enough cohesion to press for their own modern community lingua franca, or 'Romance Eurospeak'. But should it be based on one national language? And if so, which?

French is the Romance language with the most European speakers, although Spanish and Portuguese outstrip it world-wide. French is also the language most used in interchange within the Community bureaucracy, and in written Community documents, perhaps because of the location of offices within French-speaking territories. It has the great advantage of having established itself as the language of all Frenchmen, and of some others, and of being eminently teachable, because strictly codified. The corollary of this is, however, that its purist, intolerant stance has resulted in many speakers of French, both as a mother tongue and as a second language, suffering from severe linguistic insecurity. The Jacobinist doctrine of the national language has, in the past, led to conflict and domination of minority language communities. It has been, somewhat cynically, suggested that the present rather more flexible linguistic attitudes came into fashion in France only after it was recognized that French was losing its international status and so required a boost by the promotion of a new world-wide *Francophonie* – but even then old habits die hard. Besides, French is far from having prototypical Romance grammatical features: Coseriu (1988) sees it as outside '*le type roman*', which is better exemplified by the languages of 'Romania continua', running from Portugal through Spain, Catalonia, southern France and Italy.

French, especially in its spoken form, has undergone radical changes. Phonologically it presents difficulties for the non-native speaker (though not quite as great as the Lisbon-based European Portuguese variety). Morphologically it has reduced the inflectional elements that still persist especially in the verbal system of more centrally placed Romance languages, and it makes greater use of prefixed elements, and of word order, to signal grammatical function. Lexically, however, French remains Romance: even though the popular basic vocabulary is rather less central than that of other languages (Mańczak 1991), massive borrowing from Latin, especially from the fourteenth century onwards, 'relatinized' the language by introducing words in phonological, and orthographical, forms that appear much closer to more conservative Romance languages.

The most central Romance language, lexically and typologically, is standard Italian. By 'central' I do not mean 'neutral' or minimally idiosyncratic, which may apply better to Occitan or Catalan, as Raynouard (1816–21) dimly perceived when he identified '*la langue romane*' with the language of the troubadours. Italian, however, for all its idiosyncrasies, connects more directly and transparently with each of the other languages, sitting at the hub of the Romance web. This is partly because it is, in some senses, almost an invented language, codified on a conservative variety which harks back to Latin – a sort of surrogate proto-Romance. In the last century, when it still had relatively few mother-tongue speakers but enormous cultural prestige, it was adopted as the national language of unified Italy, purportedly bringing a degree of cohesion to the very diverse Romance languages spoken within the bounds of the Italian state. By 1987–8, according to a survey conducted by the Istituto Centrale di Statistica, 85 per cent of Italian citizens could express themselves in the national language, although 57 per cent still seemed to prefer dialect (Le Clézio 1991). Since the Second World War linguistic conflict has been almost absent within Italy, if we except those parts of the Alto Adige/South Tyrol where German speakers dominate. Autonomy of regions has allowed some flexibility of language policy, and there is a great deal of tolerance of regional differences within Italian.

In a way, the growth of the identification of the standard language with Italian national interests has made it less suitable for use as a European lingua franca, as favouring one nation-state over the others is bound to arouse hostility. Within Italy, however, as elsewhere in Europe, separatist movements have some support, and richer northerners seek to differentiate themselves from southern and Sardinian immigrants by promoting the use of their own regional varieties: the platform of the *Lega Lombarda*, for instance, includes the aim of reaffirming Lombard culture, history and language. If Italy were to go further along the road to regional autonomy, and to grant some sort of official status to the numerous Romance varieties used within its borders, the language of Dante and Petrarch could be viewed abroad as 'modern Latin', rather than as promoting the interests of Fiat or Olivetti.

It has many of the qualities required for an acceptable lingua franca: it is easily learnable, presents few pronunciation difficulties, and is tolerant of variation. It is already used by Romanophone (and even Greek) immigrant workers in Germanophone Switzerland, where the pressures of using two varieties of German seem to have led to the development of an underground lingua franca. It is readily accessible by Spanish, Galician, Portuguese, Catalan and Occitan speakers, though less so by the French, who also seem relatively impervious to appreciation of its beauties. Yet it forms part of the education programme of very few Europeans (in 1973–4, for instance, only 1.3 per cent of learners tackled Italian, compared with 83.8 per cent who chose English, cf. Ammon 1991). This is probably because it is still regarded as a 'fun' language – the language of holidays, art galleries and opera – rather than an economically viable asset. Even though the economic growth of Italy in recent times has been phenomenal, the lack of an extra-European dimension has been a hindrance to the expansion of its language as an international medium.

Spanish and Portuguese do have the non-European spread that Italian lacks: the majority of their speakers reside outside of Europe, and they rank just after English as world languages. Moreover, rather more cultural affinities are retained between European and American communities than is the case, for instance, for English. The existence of a Spanish-Italian interlanguage (*cocoliche* – see Meo Zilio 1993) in Argentina, spoken within a large community which still retains emotional, and some official, links with Italy, is evidence of the possibility of the development of a modern Romance lingua franca. However, within Spain, since the demise of Franco, who effectively suppressed dissident minorities, linguistic conflicts have become acute (see paper 10 by Professor Green in this volume), as indeed has always been the competition between Spanish and Portuguese (see Posner 1992 b, 1993 a, b). As things stand, the choice of any one of the Iberian tongues as a supranational language could spell only trouble.

It seems, then, that in present circumstances none of the Romance languages could replace English as the potential European language. Are we then to be left with the prospect of escalating budgets as more and more languages seek official status? The prospect for ourselves as professional linguists to expand language teaching is of course attractive, but we must beware of falling into the trap that ensnares many underdeveloped countries of spending more of our educational resources on the teaching of language skills than on education in science and humanities. Some limitation on the number of working languages used by the Community is surely desirable, even though we have no wish to see the decline of the diversity in European mother tongues.

The way in which Europe develops will determine our future choices. At present there still is some glimmer of hope (fast fading, alas) that Europe can become a federation of small nations rather than of large states. Each of these nations may indeed identify itself with a language, as part of its patrimony (assuming that cultural unity and geographical mobility within Europe will diminish manifestations of the other 'P-word' criteria for ethnicity, 'paternity' (or descent) and 'phenomenology' (or value systems) (Fishman 1977, 17)). However, espousal of the Swiss 'territorial principle' in promotion of a language may have its dangers: what of the languages without territory, like Yiddish or Romany, or those territories in which the language is not universally used, like Irish or Welsh? What seems certain is that in order to preserve cohesion within the small nations, some language policy will be necessary; a tolerant 'polynomic' standardization of related varieties (Thiers 1993) or promotion of multilingualism may be the least likely to spark off conflict.

A Europe of small nations would presumably preserve a host of small languages. The first task of educationalists would be then to foster in the school system a deep knowledge of the mother tongue and the patrimony it symbolizes, together with an appreciation of language in general, laying the foundation of regard for and ease of access to other languages, and promoting tolerant flexibility and clarity of expression in the use of the mother tongue in contact with non-native speakers. The next task would be to provide access to other Community languages, by widening the choice of foreign languages taught in the school system, but especially in increasing educational exchanges with other nations within the Community. I would, however, maintain that attempts to teach foreign languages to near-native standard at the lower levels are misguided, and that the alienation that besets some specialists in foreign languages, who are persuaded to relinquish their own national heritage in order to adopt 'foreign ways', should be shunned – unless voluntary expatriation is sought. So foreign languages for most Europeans would be counted as a tool, which can be used with more or less skill, but which should not be allowed to arouse feelings of insecurity and humiliation in less skilful users. Sneers about 'identikit' (Roche 1991) or 'pidginized' use should give way more to appreciation of attempts to communicate: the international community of scientists has already adopted simplified forms of English as an interlanguage, used frequently in groups of non-native speakers, in which, indeed, less tolerant mother-tongue speakers may feel out of place.

A better solution for Europe than the adoption of a 'Basic English' by all would, in my view, be the policy favouring passive multilingualism, with polyglot exchange, in which each speaker would use his own tongue, or an approximation thereto, but would strive to understand his interlocutors using their own languages. This is a strategy which has been advocated in Catalonia, where for the most part interlocutors speak nearly mutually comprehensible languages, but it was given a hostile reception when it was proposed for the European Community at the College of Europe in Bruges in 1978 (Coulmas 1991). As long as the Community remains broadly a Romance–Germanic coalition, knowledge of one variety from each of the language families may suffice for interactional purposes: I have suggested English and Italian as candidates for this role. As the Community widens, however, more language families may have to be catered for.

The Community may opt, post Maastricht, to continue as a loose confederation of nation-states, each with its own national language, which must be adopted as an official language of the Community. Such a confederation may conceivably survive as an economic entity, and may, indeed, save us from the wars that have up to now racked our continent; but linguistically and culturally it appears, to me at least, unviable and undesirable. In present conditions all we could envisage is that we shall be engulfed into the only great power that remains, one which resolutely imposes English on its multi-ethnic population. A Parisian Disneyland is a step in this direction, a disastrous one for those of us who feel, like President Mitterand, that *'ce n'est pas ma tasse de thé'*.

References

Ammon, U. 1991. 'The status of German and other languages in the European Community', in Coulmas (ed.), 1991, 241–53.

Coseriu, E. 1988. 'Der romanische Sprachtypus. Versuch einer neuen Typologisierung der romanischen Sprachen', in Albrecht, J., Lüdtke, J. and Thun, H. (eds.), *Energeia und Ergon. Sprachliche Variation – Sprachgeschichte – Sprachtypologie. Studia in honorem Eugenio Coseriu Band I. Schriften von Eugenio Coseriu (1965–1987)*, Tübingen: Narr, 207–24.

Coulmas, F. 1991. 'European integration and the idea of the national language. Ideological roots and economic consequences', in Coulmas (ed.), 1991, 1–37.

—— (ed.). 1991. *A Language Policy for the European Community: Prospects and Quandaries* (*Contributions to the Sociology of Language* 61), Berlin: de Gruyter.

Fishman, J. A. 1972. *Language and Nationalism. Two Integrative Essays*, Rowley, Mass.: Newbury House.

—— 1977. 'Language and ethnicity', in Giles, H. (ed.), *Language, Ethnicity and Intergroup Relations*, New York: Academic Press, 15–56.

Gellner, E. 1983. *Nations and Nationalism*, Oxford: Blackwell.

Henkel, N. and Palmer N. (eds.). 1992. *Latein und Volkssprache im deutschen Mittelalter 1100–1500. Regensburger Colloquium 1988*, Tübingen: Niemeyer.

Jucquois, G. 1991. 'La diversité linguistique européenne. Données politiques et économiques d'un aménagement linguistique', *La Linguistique*, 27, 29–58.

Le Clézio, Y. 1991. 'Dialectes et modernité: la situation linguistique en Italie en 1990', *La Linguistique*, 27, 59–74.

Mańczak, W. 1991. *La Classification des langues romanes*, Krakov: Universitas.

Meo Zilio, G. 1993. 'The acquisition of a second Romance language by immigrants in Latin America', in Posner, R. and Green, J. N. (eds.), 559–90.

Poliakov, L. 1974. *The Aryan Myth*, London: Chatto-Heinemann, for Sussex University Press.

Posner, R. 1992a. 'Language', in Jenkyns, R. (ed.), *The Legacy of Rome: A New Appraisal*, Oxford: Oxford University Press, 367–98.

—— 1992b. 'Linguistic conflict between Romance languages – and how to resolve it', *Journal of the Institute of Romance Studies* 1, 17–26.

—— 1993a. 'Language conflict or language symbiosis? Contact of other Romance varieties with Castilian', in Mackenzie D. and Michael, I. (eds.), *Hispanic Linguistic Studies in honour of F. W. Hodcroft*, Oxford: Dolphin Books, 89–106.

—— 1993b. 'Language conflict: decline, death and survival', in Posner, R. and J. N. Green (eds.), 1993, 41–76.

—— 1993c 'Latin to Romance (again!): Change or genesis?', in van Marle, J. (ed.), *Historical Linguistics 1991. Papers from the Tenth International Conference on Historical Linguistics,*, Amsterdam: Benjamins.

—— and Green, J. N. (eds.). 1993. *Trends in Romance Linguistics and Phil-*

ology 5: *Bilingualism and Linguistic Conflict in Romance*, Berlin: Mouton de Gruyter.

Raynouard, F.-J. 1816–21. *Choix des poésies originales des troubadours*, 6 vols., Paris: Firmin Didot.

Roche, N. 1991. 'Multilingualism in European Community meetings – a pragmatic approach', in Coulmas (ed.), 1991, 139–46.

Schnell, R. 1992. 'Lateinische und volksprachliche Vorstellungen. Zwei Fall-beispiele (Nationsbewusstsein; Königswahl)', in Henkel, W. and Palmer, N. (eds.), 123–41.

Smits, R. J. C. 1989. *Eurogrammar. The Relative and Cleft Constructions of the Germanic and the Romance Languages*, Dordrecht: Foris.

Thiers, G. 1993. 'Language contact and Corsican polynomy', in Posner, R. and Green, J. N. (eds.), 253–70.

3

Was there ever a Parisian Cockney?

R. ANTHONY LODGE

Introduction

The starting-point for this discussion is a subjective impression. A foreign visitor to London, possessing only a limited acquaintance with English, will, I believe, be quickly struck by the gulf which separates the pronunciation of standard English (Received Pronunciation, or RP) from the speech of indigenous lower-class Londoners. Non-standard lexis and syntax will no doubt compound the foreigner's difficulties, but here we will be concerned exclusively with questions of pronunciation or 'accent'. Pronunciation variables characteristic of London English, such as [ð]/[v], [θ]/[f], vocalization of preconsonantal [l], and glottalization of intervocalic [t], are used by large numbers of speakers in the capital. They are commonly grouped together under the label 'Cockney', and are readily parodied by other British speakers of English. In Labovian terms, they have achieved the status of socio-linguistic 'stereotypes' (Labov 1970, 188). Qualification is essential, of course, for we are dealing as ever with social, spatial and stylistic continua: Cockney pronunciation, like RP, exists nowhere in a pure state (not even within the sound of Bow Bells), and does not suddenly stop at the city boundary. Even so, in London English, divergences between the local vernacular and high-status speech norms are often very considerable.

Can as much be said of the pronunciation of Parisian French? It would be absurd to deny the existence of social and stylistic variation in Parisian speech, and the presence of important variables distinguishing the lower-class Parisian vernacular from other regional varieties of French. The 'Parigot' accent certainly exists and French speakers of French are very aware of it (Mettas 1979, 16–18). However, are Parigot pronunciation norms as divergent from those of the high-status standard as those of Cockney from RP? Are they as divergent from those of other northern French cities? More importantly perhaps, are there as many people whose speech approximates closely to them? Questions like these are exceptionally hard to answer in scientific terms, but my impression is that the sociolinguistic profiles of the two capitals are not identical, and that, arguably, the persistence of a strongly divergent local vernacular is nowadays more evident in London than it is in Paris. This prompted me to ask whether there ever was a Parisian equivalent of Cockney and to undertake a brief historical comparison of the standard–vernacular relationship in the two capitals. The results, I think, throw interesting light on the social history of French and invite us to devote further research into the development of vernacular speech in the French capital.

1. A framework for comparison

Traditional histories of French have two abiding characteristics. Firstly, they tend to be concerned with only one aspect of the language's development – the literary standard – to the exclusion of other varieties. Secondly, they tend to be overwhelmingly ethnocentric and to take little account of work on other languages. In this paper I shall be concerned with the spoken language rather than with the written standard, and, to allow us to look at the development of Parisian French in terms applicable to English as well as French, I shall base my exposé on the general model of language standardization proposed by Haugen (1966):

	Form	Function
Society	SELECTION	ACCEPTANCE
Language	CODIFICATION	ELABORATION

What does this table mean? On the level of *society*, before the process of language standardization can get under way, there needs to be a *selection* of a dialect which is ultimately to form the basis of the standard. The selected dialect will subsequently be diffused and ultimately *accepted* by the relevant population as the standard language. On the level of *language*, the oral vernacular which is moving towards the status of standard language needs to undergo an *elaboration of functions*, that is an expansion of its linguistic resources in order to allow it to perform additional functions in society, as a written language, as a language of administration, education, etc. At the same time, variation within it must be minimized through a process of *codification*, that is through the production of dictionaries and grammar books legitimizing certain linguistic items and rejecting others. Here the point needs to be made that, although the written language is readily amenable to codification, elimination of variation from speech is impossible to achieve. As literacy develops, writing exercises an increasing influence on speech (see Straka 1981, 222–45), but despite this, variability in speech can never be completely suppressed. In this paper we will compare London English and Parisian French with regard to the processes of selection, codification and acceptance. Elaboration of function is of lesser relevance.

2. Development of spoken norms in London English

2.1 Selection

What characterized the vernacular languages in the Middle Ages was not the absence of norms, but the proliferation of them: each town, each region had its own consensus speech norms (local norms, supralocal norms, regional norms, etc.). In England the process of selection of a single norm began later than it did in France, since the domination of French speakers meant that English was not the standard in the relevant period (Price 1984, 217–31). It was only in the fifteenth century that London English began to be regarded as a superior form of the language (Strang 1970, 161). But what do we mean by 'London English'? The speech of the capital cannot be said to have been homogeneous, for London speech naturally shadowed the different socio-economic relationships which the various sections of London society had with each other and with the outside world.

The lower socio-economic groups evidently had strong network ties within the city and with the rural communities of Kent and Essex which were the principal suppliers of food, so it comes as no surprise to learn that Cockney speech is closely related to the south-eastern dialects of English, particularly to Kentish (Leith 1983, 38). The higher social groups, on the other hand, had arguably less dense network ties within the city and more extended links with the wider world outside. However, they cannot be said to have constituted a monolithic social grouping. In sixteenth-century England a distinction has to be drawn between the merchant and financial classes on the one hand, and the landed aristocracy on the other. This distinction cannot be a rigid one since members of the merchant class persistently sought to buy themselves into the aristocracy. Even so, the interests of the two groups were at variance and tensions between them culminated in the English Civil

War and the triumph of the former over the latter. As a consequence, it is in the speech of the London merchant classes rather than that of the aristocracy that we have to look for the origins of RP. Historians of English seem unanimous in affirming that their speech bore a strong affinity with the dialect, not of London itself, but of the East Midlands, that is, of the triangle formed between Oxford, Cambridge and London (Leith 1983, 38; Samuels 1963).

2.2 Codification

The codification movement, which got under way in English in the seventeenth century, inevitably took as its model the dialect of the dominant group in London (that is the business class), and this led to the automatic stigmatization of forms considered to fall outside the norm, beginning, predictably, with the speech of the lower classes in the capital itself. Literary authors, particularly dramatists, joined in the movement and exploited for comic purposes the speech of the uncultivated Cockney and the Kentish peasant. The ridiculing of other dialects of English followed. As for the grammarians themselves, although there were various attempts in the eighteenth century to set up an Academy on the French model, these came to nothing in the face of the inveterate pragmatism of the English middle classes. Consequently, the codification of English took place entirely under the aegis of private individuals like Dr Johnson, rather than under that of an official body (see Leonard 1929; Baugh and Cable 1978, 258–94).

2.3 Acceptance of the standard

The *laissez-faire* attitude which characterized the codification of English also characterized the diffusion of the norms of the standard language into the provinces. If the royal administration and the national Church took the king's English into all the corners of the kingdom, this dialect nevertheless remained the preserve of the literate, and before the end of the nineteenth century few attempts were made to induce the population at large to adopt it. In the mean time, the Industrial Revolution brought the mushrooming of great conurbations such as Manchester, Birmingham and London, with the working classes developing their own urban varieties based on the pre-existing local dialect. Sociolinguistic norms are always most constraining at the top and at the bottom of the social hierarchy: while the norms of upper middle-class speech coalesced in the nineteenth-century public schools to reinforce the solidarity of the ruling élite, heavily stigmatized local vernaculars like Cockney reinforced their own norms to strengthen bonds between members of communities located at the bottom of society. This polarized sociolinguistic situation has been somewhat attenuated over the course of the twentieth century, but in many British cities, including the capital, low-status vernaculars remain extremely persistent (see Ryan 1979; Milroy 1992, 213). That said, recent surveys indicate that the London vernacular is currently spreading some way beyond the city itself, into parts of East Anglia for example (Trudgill 1986, 46–57).

After this cursory overview of what appears to have happened in London English, let us now compare, point for point, developments in Parisian French over the same period.

3. Development of spoken norms in Parisian French

3.1 Selection

Few people dispute that the origins of standard French are to be found in the 'parler de Paris' (Walter 1988, 82), but, as was the case in London, this does not take us far, given the size of late medieval Paris and the heterogeneity of its speech. Accurate estimates of the population of Paris in the sixteenth century are impossible to find (Descimon 1989, 69), but historical demographers agree that, until it was overtaken by London in the nineteenth century, Paris was one of the most populous cities, if not *the* most populous city, in western Europe. It was perceived by contemporaries as 'non urbs sed orbs' ('not a city but a world'). The number of its inhabitants in the sixteenth century has been pitched at between 200,000 and 300,000, this variation being attributable not simply to the sparseness of reliable data, but to an extent also to sizeable fluctuations in the population of the city. Paris was like an accordion, drawing people in from the surrounding countryside (and from the provinces) in great numbers in times of prosperity, and expelling them in equally large numbers in times of dearth. In view of all this, the speech of Paris over this period can only have been highly variable.

The extent of variability in Parisian speech has in the past been understated by linguistic historians, partly because of problems of data, but mainly, one suspects, because historians were really interested only in the development of the standard (and normally literary) form of the language. However, there are good reasons for rejecting this unidimensional approach to the language's history: since all language change has its origins in language variation, it is in fact impossible to make sense of, say, the sound changes which have taken place in French since the sixteenth century, without as full an appreciation of this variability as the data will allow.

Social stratification in the speech of Paris probably developed as early as the thirteenth century (Delbouille 1962), although the explanations offered for this stratification are not always convincing: traditional histories of the language imply that upper-class usage somehow represents the 'authentic' form of Parisian French, with the speech of the lower social groups constituting corrupt deviations from that high-status norm. In reality, it is just as likely that the process worked the other way round, with the lower groups retaining archaic vernacular features in their speech while the upper groups initiated their own distinctive language variety to set themselves off from the rest. The development of *argot* in early modern Paris implies a parallel strengthening of distinctive speech norms at the bottom of society as well as at the top.

As was the case in London, the speech of the lower social groups in sixteenth- and seventeenth-century Paris was a variable mixture of elements drawn from the dialects of the surrounding countryside, notably Picard, Norman and Champenois. Paris depended for its economic life upon trade up and down the Seine, and, like all medieval and early modern towns, lived in close relationship with the surrounding rural communities upon whom it depended for food and other primary agricultural products (leather, wood, flax). The linguistic consequences of this are visible in the speech of some of the peasants appearing in Molière's plays: the peasants in *Dom Juan*, for instance, apparently live in the country, but the features used to characterize their rustic speech are in fact all stigmatized by contemporary grammarians as belonging to the lower social groups resident in Paris itself (Lodge 1991, 494).

What can be said about the speech of the upper social groups, the merchant, financial and administrative classes and the aristocracy (the *ville*, the *palais* and the *cour*)? We have plenty of evidence to show that from an early date the upper groups sought to distinguish themselves linguistically from those located further down the pile. How did they contrive to do this? Was it by adopting the speech of a dialect located outside the capital as happened in London? This possibility is not to be totally discounted: it is conceivable that for much of the sixteenth century the speech of the higher nobility resident in Paris maintained reminiscences of the court's prolonged stays along the Loire and in Touraine (Walter 1976, 201; Joseph 1987), for the court did not establish itself on a long-term basis in Paris until the first third of the sixteenth century. Even then, the city offered a thoroughly uncongenial environment for the landed aristocracy: life there was precarious – plague, food shortages and riots were commonplace until the nineteenth century – and offered few opportunities for the country sports which mattered so much to them. In view of this, it is by no means surprising that the king and his court should have preferred to live much of their lives at a safe distance, in châteaux located outside the city.

Paris was above all the domain of the traders, financiers and legal men who controlled the business life of the city. As in London, it was the speech of the upper bourgeoisie which came ultimately (by the mid-eighteenth century) to provide the basis of the national norm, just as it was their financial power which came to dominate the national economy. However, unlike what happened in London, their speech cannot be linked to a dialect outside the city. Instead, upper middle-class norms seem to have developed out of elements present in sixteenth-century Parisian speech, selected in an apparently arbitrary fashion to distinguish, I would argue, the upper social groups from the lower. It is precisely the arbitrary and conventional nature of this selection which gave such social importance to grammarians in the seventeenth and eighteenth centuries.

3.2 Codification

The codification movement in seventeenth-century France reflected the strivings of the upper social groups to achieve identity and status and was throughout a highly political process, involving conflict between the upper and the lower social groups and between competing elements within the upper groups themselves. Hence the involvement of the state and the foundation of the Académie Française. Underlying the whole grammatical debate there lay the question of which part of the upper social group constituted the ultimate repository for the norm – the court or the city? The growth of the market economy in the eighteenth century eventually resolved the matter in favour of the latter, but what seems to have united both parties was their hostility to the speech of the lower social groups, not only in the provinces, but also in the capital.

Codification of the norms of upper-class speech led to the automatic stigmatization of forms situated outside the norm. Dramatists like Cyrano de Bergerac and Molière joined in the movement, poking fun in their plays at the uncultivated speech of the capital and surrounding countryside. Given the social motivations of this codification process, it is more than likely that the norms adopted by the high-prestige standard were conditioned to a significant degree by the low-status language variety from which it was being distinguished. In this perspective, a knowledge of low-status varieties of Parisian French in the seventeenth. and eighteenth centuries becomes indispensable for an

overall understanding of language change over this period. On the
general principles involved here see Milroy (1992, 123 ff.).

What do we know about uncultivated speech in Paris under the
ancien régime? A large body of evidence dating from the sixteenth
century onwards attests the existence of a lower-class vernacular which
diverged markedly from upper-class norms in lexis, syntax and pronunciation. This evidence is a good deal more plentiful than that
worked on by Wyld (1920) for English, but the French sources have not
in my view been explored with the thoroughness they require. Valuable
groundwork has been carried out by Stimm (1980) and Lathuillère
(1984). The source material consists, firstly, of a large number of
comments on pronunciation judged to be incorrect by grammarians
between the sixteenth and nineteenth centuries. These judgements were
brought together and published over a century ago (Thurot 1881), and
have been thoroughly analysed. Secondly, there exists an unknown
quantity of letters and journals written by lesser educated people which
betray the influence of their everyday speech. These have not been
systematically worked on (Brunot 1966, t. 10, pp. 438–43). Thirdly, we
have a sizeable corpus of burlesques, comedies and political tracts
replicating with varying degrees of conventionality the speech of the
common man of the seventeenth and eighteenth centuries. Some of
these texts were in fact written in non-standard spelling purporting to
represent the pronunciation of vernacular speech and it is these that I
wish to concentrate on here. Although a number of them were analysed
many decades ago by Nisard (1872), Rosset (1911) and Sainéan (1920),
it seems to me that the time has now come to look at them afresh in the
light of variationist principles.

The most important of these texts are listed in Appendix A, but it has
to be added that a substantial quantity of other texts relevant to the
study of uncultivated Parisian speech remains largely unexplored and
unedited in libraries and archives (see Nisard 1872, 319–436; Rosset
1911, 36–46). Moreover, our list deliberately excludes a very large
number of literary texts written in the second half of the eighteenth
century which purported to evoke lower-class speech and which have
come to be known as the *genre poissard* (see Moore 1935). The word
poissard (first attestation 1531) designated traders in the Paris markets
along with their uncouth speech, and was associated particularly
strongly with foul-mouthed female fish-sellers. However, in the middle
years of the eighteenth century it was adopted by poets and playwrights
like Caylus, Vadé and Lécluse, to denote the style they had created
embodying certain features drawn from vernacular speech. These
authors evoked lower-class speech in such a sentimental and stylized
way, through the use of a tiny set of oft-repeated Parisian features, that

it led Brunot (1966, t. 6.2, p. 1215 and t. 10.1, p. 269) to see them merely as an 'artifice littéraire' and to dismiss their documentary value out of hand. Brunot's *parti pris* has undoubtedly contributed to the general neglect of written texts evoking lower-class Parisian speech.

If the linguistic value of many of the literary *poissard* texts is limited, does the same go for the other texts listed in Appendix A? Are we dealing here with nothing more than a highly durable convention of the Parisian stage? It is entirely to be expected that the representations of lower-class speech found in these texts will owe a great deal to convention and stereotyping, and this makes the difference between them and the literary *poissard* texts one of degree, not of kind. The authors were all writing within the constraints of a tradition (be it literary or not) and had to use linguistic forms whose social meaning the audience (presumably a literate one) would recognize. It is clear that in many cases the speech forms represented were selected by authors not primarily for reasons of realism, but on account of the particular social meaning of the variables involved. However, such insights into the social meaning of linguistic variables in times past should not be discarded lightly. They are in fact of considerable importance to linguistic historians, for 'what is relevant to change is not the linguistic function of a structural unit, but the social meaning carried by its various realisations' (Bynon 1977, 213). Sociolinguistic stereotyping is not the prerogative of literary authors; rather it is a normal and integral part of everyone's linguistic behaviour (Lyons 1981, 275). The fact that we are dealing with stereotypes does not automatically mean that the forms occurring have no relationship with actual usage.

In Appendix B we quote extracts from three texts drawn respectively from the sixteenth, seventeenth and eighteenth centuries. The phonological variables which feature most prominently in them are the following:

(i)	[ɛr] – [ar]	*tarre* (*terre*, 'earth')
(ii)	distribution of [ɛ], [wɛ], [wa]	*drai* (*droit*, 'right')
(iii)	[o] – [jo]	*biau* (*beau*, 'beautiful')
(iv)	[jɛ̃] – [jã]	*bian* (*bien*, 'well')
(v)	[ĩ] – [ɛ̃]	*Robain* (*Robin*)
(vi)	distribution of [o], [u]	*estoumaque* (*estomac*, 'stomach')
(vii)	[ɥi] – [i]	*depis* (*depuis*, 'since')
(viii)	[ɔ] – [œ] in initial syllables	*quemence* (*commence*, 'begins')
(ix)	elision of post-vocalic [r]	*jou* (*jour*, 'day')
(x)	elision of aspirate [h]	*l'haut* (*le haut*, 'the top')

(xi)   [tj] – [kj]; [dj] – [gj]   *piquié; Guieu* (*pitié,* 'pity';
                                                        Dieu, 'God')

(xii)   [nj] + vowel – [ɲ]   *ignia pas* (*il n'y a pas,* 'there is
                                                        not')

(xiii) [lj] + vowel – [ʎ]   *il y glia* (*il y a,* 'there is')
(xiv)   elision of post-consonantal   *pus* (*plus,* 'more')
        [l]
(xv)   elision of post-consonantal   *raisonnabe* (*raisonnable,*
        [l]/[r] before final schwa   'reasonable')

The phonological variants listed here are all in fact attested in modern dialect surveys of the Ile-de-France (see Wüest 1985). Furthermore, they were all thoroughly stigmatized by generations of grammarians writing throughout the period: it is unlikely that grammarians would have hurled their thunderbolts at purely literary artifices. What is caricatural in the texts and what confers on them their air of artificiality is not the linguistic forms in themselves, but the larger-than-life accumulation of stigmatized items in short stretches of discourse. The texts can, in my view, be used to shed light upon Parisian spoken language under the *ancien régime*, provided some sociolinguistic expertise is used in interpreting what they signify.

A significant feature of them is that they are not linguistically homogeneous: they vary from author to author and they vary over time. A quantified analysis of linguistic variables in these texts could well throw important light on the progress of linguistic change. At the very least it would give us an indication of what items speakers believed to be outside the norm at a particular time, and how salient they perceived them to be. It may be possible, in some cases, to make direct correlations between changes in the prominence of particular non-standard forms in our texts with changes in their vitality in vernacular speech, reflecting the spread of new forms and the decline of old ones. In all such cases, however, we are likely to be confronted with a time lag since stereotyped attitudes are more deep-rooted in society and evolve more slowly than independent, individual assessments. In other cases changes in the stereotype found in our texts may actually correlate inversely with the vitality of particular forms in real-life usage: a vernacular variant may lose prominence not because it has disappeared, but, on the contrary, because it has lost stigmatization through being absorbed into the standard language. This is clearly what happened with regard to developments in the distribution of [ɛ], [wɛ] and [wa] in words such as *roi, droit* and *soir*. In the seventeenth century comic and satirical writers very heavily exploited social variation in the use of this feature. When, in the second half of the eighteenth century, an author such as Vadé ceased to use this feature as a marker of lower-class style, we can be sure that the question of the acceptability of [wa] in upper-middle-class speech had been more or less decided.

When we put together the evidence provided by texts like this with that available in other sources, notably grammars and dictionaries, it seems quite clear that there existed in *ancien régime* Paris a distinctive low-status vernacular, comparable in many respects to London's Cockney. We must assume, of course, that this vernacular, like all vernaculars, was highly variable and never existed in a pure form: we are dealing, as always in spoken language, with quantitative differences in the distribution of key linguistic variables. There was a socio-linguistic continuum between the Louvre at the top and the Place Maubert at the bottom of the social strata. We are dealing also with a stylistic continuum, for it is more than likely that upper-class Parisians, whose speech in formal situations approximated closely to high-status norms, used features in their spontaneous style which they themselves commonly attributed to members of less prestigious social groups.

What this vernacular lacks is a name. While London had its Cockney, it is difficult to find a name for lower-class speech in *ancien régime* Paris. In the eighteenth century it looked for a while as though the term which was emerging for the purpose was *poissard*, but the literary associations of the term appear to have rendered it too ambiguous. The term *parigot* is a recent creation first attested in 1886. Following Sainéan and Nisard, Wüest (1985) writes limply of the *patois de Paris*.

3.3 Acceptance of the standard

If we accept (*pace* Brunot) that an urban vernacular corresponding in some degree to the image provided in these texts did have a real existence in the seventeenth and eighteenth centuries, we are compelled to ask: what has happened to it since? Nisard (1872, 123) asserts that, by the time he wrote his study of popular speech, the old Parisian dialect had disappeared. Given the long persistence of low-status varieties in British cities over this period (in London as elsewhere), this is surprising. What made sociolinguistic developments in Paris so different? By what stages did the old vernacular disappear as the standard dialect was diffused downwards? Did it in fact disappear completely and are there not relic forms still to be found in Parisian pronunciation? Questions such as these call for a good deal of research. As an opening shot, it could be suggested that the crucial period for the reduction in the ancient gap between upper and lower-class speech in Paris was the middle decades of the nineteenth century (see Mettas 1979, 30).

The linguistic policy of the *ancien régime* had been more or less the same as that followed by the state in Britain – one of *laissez-faire*. Things changed in 1793 when the monarchy was abolished and a new ideology of the nation became predominant. The Jacobins and their successors in the nineteenth century adopted a *dirigiste* policy of linguistic assimilation, persecuting non-standard varieties not only in the non-French-speaking periphery and in the *patois*-speaking countryside, but also in the capital itself. That said, the importance of official language-planning policies in the development of French can easily be overstated. Education policy in the first half of the nineteenth century undoubtedly affected working-class speech in Paris, but compulsory primary education only became general in the latter part of the century, and it is unlikely to have had much impact unless it was part of a more fundamental economic and demographic process.

The fate of the old Paris vernacular in the nineteenth century is more fully understood if we relate it to transformations of the traditional working-class communities of Paris whose identity it expressed. Industrialization, large-scale immigration from the provinces and a steep demographic rise evidently affected these communities profoundly in the first half of the nineteenth century. However, similar developments occurred on an even larger scale in London. What was different in Paris? Whereas in London the upper groups seem to have sought simply to distance themselves as far as possible from the lower and to turn their back on them, in Paris they sought more actively to break up working-class identity, just as they strove to destroy regional identities in the provinces. Education policy, particularly under the Third Republic, played an important part, but interventionism went much further: as everyone knows, the social life of Paris for much of the nineteenth century was marked by serious conflict. Middle-class fear of the lower social groups was very real, for it was the Paris 'mob' who had, after all, sparked off the revolutions of 1789, 1830 and 1848. The removal of the threat posed by the working-class communities of central Paris became a matter of great middle-class concern: their break-up and removal to the *faubourgs* were clearly major components of Haussmann's programme of *assainissement* in the 1850s and 1860s, and the suppression of the Paris Commune in 1871 took this process to its ultimate conclusion. It is easy to see how the destruction of these communities with their tight social networks had devastating sociolinguistic consequences for the old urban vernacular.

However, it would be quite incorrect to assert that all traces of the old Parisian dialect have now disappeared. They survive in the syntax of colloquial French and in *argot* and other non-standard vocabulary which so mark off colloquial varieties of French from the formal variety (see Hunnius 1975, Hausmann 1979). More importantly for the main thrust of this paper, many of the pronunciation features we discussed earlier (see above pp. 43–4) were still widely occurring in Parisian speech in the earlier part of the twentieth century (see Bauche 1920; Straka 1981), and relic forms undoubtedly persist in uncultivated Parisian speech even today, forming the basis of the 'Parigot' accent. Moreover, the fact that lower-class Parisian *appears* nowadays to be less divergent from other northern vernaculars, when compared with Cockney within British English, may be attributable to the greater dominance of Paris within France, and to an earlier spreading of low-status as well as high-status Parisian features to the surrounding regions, ironing out differences.

Conclusion

This comparison of the sociolinguistic history of Paris with that of London has revealed close similarities between them, and also import-ant differences. Both cities saw the triumph by the mid-eighteenth century of the capitalist financial and merchant classes at the expense of traditional land-based aristocracies, leading to the adoption of their sociolect as the dominant linguistic norm. Both cities show evidence for the existence in the early modern period of a distinctive lower-class vernacular related (at the beginning at least) to the rural dialects in the surrounding countryside. We looked at some of the data related to the Parisian vernacular in the seventeenth and eighteenth centuries: there did seem to exist at this time a Parisian equivalent of Cockney.

What came subsequently to distinguish the sociolinguistic histories of the two capitals were the different relationships holding between the upper and lower social groups located within them. Language diversity reflects social and geographical barriers, the level of integration of any given group into the wider society being inversely related to the extent to which it maintains a distinctive vernacular. Whereas in nineteenth-century London, as in other British cities, relationships between the upper and lower social groups were segregational and allowed a longer persistence of working-class communities with their tight social net-works, in Paris they were overtly conflictual, leading to the breaking up of traditional working-class groups and their greater assimilation into French society at large. This may go some of the way to explaining the stronger persistence of Cockney in London compared with its equiv-alent in Paris.

Appendix A

1544(?) *Epistre du biau fys de Pazy par autre que Marot*, ed. A. Grenier, *Oeuvres complètes de C. Marot*, Paris: Garnier, 1951, t. 1, 275–80.

1644 *Nouveaux Compliments de la Place Maubert, des Halles ...* ed. E. Fournier, *Variétés historiques et littéraires*, Paris: Jannet, 1859, t. 9, 229–39.

1648 *Discours d'une harengère sur le retour de Mon^r de Brousselle*, partial ed. in Moore 1935, 43–5.

1649 *La Gazette de Halles touchant les affaires du temps*, partial ed. in Moore 1935, 45–7.

1649 *La Gazette de la Place Maubert ou Suitte de la Gazette des Halles, touchant les affaires du temps*, partial ed. in Moore 1935, 47–8.

1649 *Les Menaces de harengères faites aux boulangers, à faute de pain*, partial ed. in Moore 1935, 51–2.

1649 *Le Caquet des marchandes poissonnières et harengères des Halles, sur la maladie du Duc de Beaufort*, partial ed. in Moore 1935, 55–60.

1649–52 *Agréables Conférences de deux paysans de Saint-Ouen et de Montmorency sur les affaires du temps*, ed. F. Deloffre, Paris: Les Belles Lettres, 1961.

1652 Le sieur Berthaud, *La Ville de Paris en vers burlesques*, ed. P.-L. Jacob, *Paris ridicule et burlesque au XVIIe s.*, Paris: Delahaye, 1859, esp. 107, 152–3, 163.

1654 Cyrano de Bergerac, *Le Pédant joué*, ed. J. Prévot, in: *Cyrano de Bergerac: Oeuvres complètes*. Paris: Belin, 1977, esp. Act II, scenes 2 and 3; Act V, scenes 8–10.

1665 Molière, *Dom Juan*, ed. W. D. Howarth, Oxford: Blackwell, 1958, esp. Act II, scene 1.

1666 Molière, *Le Médecin malgré lui*, ed. R. Jouanny, Paris: Garnier, 1962, esp. Act I, scenes 4 and 5.

1678 Letter supposedly from an inhabitant of Ville d'Avray, published in *Le Mercure galant*, janvier. See Moore 1935, 17.

1731–48 N. Jouin, *Harangues des habitants de Sarcelles à Mgr l'archevêque de Paris*, ed. in *Le Vrai Recueil des Sarcelles*, Amsterdam: au dépens de la Compagnie, 1764.

1739 A.-C.-P. de Caylus, *Le Porteur d'iau ou Les Amours de la ravaudeuse*, Troyes: Oudot.

1743 J.-J. Vadé, *La Pipe cassée*, ed. in *Oeuvres de M. Vadé*. The Hague: P. Gosse, t. I, 1759.

1750 Coustelier, A.-U., *Lettres de Montmartre*, London.

1754   Boudin, P. *Madame Engueule ou Les Accords poissards*, Paris.

1755   Anon., *Les Spiritueux Rébus de Margot la mal peignée*, Troyes: Oudot.

1756   J.-J. Vadé, *Les Raccoleurs*, Paris: Duchesne.

1756   *Poissardiana ou Les Amours de Royal Vilain et de Mlle. Javotte*, Paris: Grenouillère.

1759   A.-C. Cailleau, *Le Goûter des porcherons*, Paris: Cailleau.

1764   Ami du feu Vadé, *Amusement à la grecque ou les Soirées de la Halle*, Paris: Cuissart.

1773   Anon. *Les Porcherons* (poème en sept chants), Paris: Meurant.

1780 (?)   A.-C. Cailleau, *Le Waux-hall populaire ou Les Fêtes de la Guinguette*, Paris: Cailleau.

1789–93   Political pamphlets listed by Moore 1935, 340–2.

Appendix B

(1) Extract from *Responce de la Dame au jeune fils de Paris* (c. 1544):

> De ma par, je vouray montré
> Si vouravé bonne memoise,
> Notre jeu de bille d'ivoise
> Et ma zobbe d'un fin dra noir.
> Vous varriez, si voulé veoir,
> Tou mes manchesons de velour,
> Mes soulié qui ne son pas lour.
> Pour enjamber notre ruissiau,
> Et ma cotte de dra de Siau
> Bien teinte, que me la donna
> Le sise Jean, quan ordonna
> Et voulut par son testamen
> Que je l'eusse soudainemen.
>   Ha! si j'estien tou deu ensemble
> Je vous contesoy, ce me semble,
> Cen mille bon peti propo.
>   (ed. Grenier, t. 2, 278–9)

(2) Extract from Cyrano de Bergerac's *Le Pédant joué* (1654):

Gareau

O! par le sangué va-t'en charcher tes poursuiveux. Aga qu'il est raisonnabe aujourd'huy, il a mangé de la soupe à neuf heures. Et si je ne veux pas dire comme ça moy? Tanquia qu'à la parfin je nous en revinsmes. Il apportit de ce païs-là tant de Guiamans rouges, des Hemoroïdes vartes, et une grande espée qui atteindret d'icy a demain. C'est à tout ces farremens que ces mangeux de petis enfans se batont en deüil. Il apportit itou de petis engingorniaux remplis de naissance, à celle fin de conserver, ce feset-il, l'humeur ridicule, à celle fin, se feset-il, de vivre aussi longtems que Maquieu salé. Tenez n'avous point veu Nique-doüille, qui ne sçauret rire sans montrer les dants?

(ed. Prévot, 184)

(3) Extract from Jouin's *Harangues des habitans de Sarcelles* (1748):

A nossigneurs les mitriers
ramassés à Paris cheux les Grands
Augustins
Au moüas de Mai 1748

Gn'a pas mal de tems, Nossigneurs, que j'ons aïeu l'honneur de vous faire present d'une magnière de petit Sarmon que j'avions affuté pour Monsigneur l'Archeveque á la Coque. L'an nous a dit du depis que vous l'aviais quasiment loüangé. Je n'en ons pas battu nos femmes pour ça, comme vous pensez. Parguié pis donc que vlà qu'est comme ça, j'ons rumainé à par nous & j'ons pensé que falloit core vous bailler sti-là que je venons de bredouiller a Monsigneur de Biaumont du Repaire, notre nouviau Minitrier.

(*Le Vrai Recueil des Sarcelles*, t. 2, 5–6)

References

Bauche, H. 1920. *Le Langage populaire*, Paris: Payot.
Baugh, A. C. and Cable, T. 1978. *A History of the English Language* (3rd edn.), Englewood Cliffs: Prentice-Hall.
Brunot, F. 1966. *Histoire de la langue française* (nouvelle édition), Paris: A. Colin.
Bynon, T. 1977. *Historical Linguistics*, Cambridge: Cambridge University Press.
Delbouille, M. 1962. 'La notion de "bon usage" en ancien français', *Cahiers de l'Association Internationale des Études Françaises*, 14, 10–24.
Descimon, R. 1989. 'Paris on the eve of Saint Bartholemew', in Benedict, P. (ed.), *Cities and Social Change in Early Modern France*, London: Unwin Hyman, 67–104.
Haugen, E. 1966. 'Dialect, language, nation', repr. in Pride, J. B. and Holmes, J., *Sociolinguistics*, Harmondsworth: Penguin, 97–111.
Hausmann, J. L. 1979. 'Wie alt ist das gesprochene Französisch?', *Romanische Forschungen* 91, 431–44.
Hunnius, K. 1975. 'Archaïsche Züge des langage populaire', *Zeitschrift für französische Sprache und Literatur*, 85, 145–61.
Joseph, J. E. 1987. *Eloquence and Power*, London: F. Pinter.
Labov, W. 1970. 'The study of language in its social context', repr. in Pride, J. B. and Holmes, J., *Sociolinguistics*, Harmondsworth: Penguin, 180–202.
Lathuillère, R. 1984. 'Pour une étude de la langue populaire à l'époque classique,' in *Mélanges de langue et littérature médiévales offerts à Alice Planche*, Nice: Centre d'Etudes Médiévales, and Paris: Les Belles Lettres, 278–86.

Leith, D. 1983. *A Social History of English*, London: Routledge and Kegan Paul.

Leonard, S. A. 1929. *The Doctrine of Correctness in English Usage 1700–1800*, Madison: University of Wisconsin.

Lodge, R. A. 1991. 'Molière's peasants and the norms of spoken French', *Neuphilologische Mitteilungen*, 92, 485–99.

Lyons, J. 1981. *Language and Linguistics*, Cambridge: Cambridge University Press.

Mettas, O. 1979. *La Prononciation parisienne*, Paris: Selaf.

Milroy, J. 1992. *Linguistic Variation and Change*, Oxford: Blackwell.

Moore, A. P. 1935. *The genre poissard and the French Stage of the Eighteenth Century*, New York: Columbia U.P.

Nisard, C. 1872. *Etude sur le langage populaire ou patois de Paris et de sa banlieue*, Paris: Franck.

Price, G. 1984. *The Languages of Britain*, London: Arnold.

Robert, P. 1965. *Dictionnaire de la langue française*, Paris: Société du Nouveau Littré.

Rosset, T. 1911. *Les Origines de la prononciation moderne*, Paris: A. Colin.

Ryan, E. B. 1979. 'Why do low-prestige varieties persist?', in Giles, H. and Sinclair, R. (eds.), *Language and Social Psychology*, Oxford: Blackwell, 145–57.

Sainéan, L. 1920. *L'Argot ancien*, Paris: Champion.

Samuels, M. L. 1963. 'Some applications of Middle English dialectology', *English Studies*, 44, 81–94.

Stimm, H. (ed.). 1980. *Zur Geschichte des gesprochenen Französisch. Zeitschrift für französische Sprache und Literatur*, Beiheft 6. Wiesbaden: Franz Steiner.

Straka, G. 1981. 'Sur la formation de la prononciation française d'aujourd'hui.' *Travaux de Linguistique et de Littérature de Strasbourg*, 19, 161–248.

Strang, B. 1970. *A History of English*, London: Methuen.

Thurot, C. 1881. *De la prononciation française depuis le commencement du XVIe siècle, d'après les témoignages des grammairiens*, Paris: Imprimerie nationale.

Trudgill, P. 1986. *Dialects in Contact*, Oxford: Blackwell.

Walter, H. 1976. *Le Dynamique des phonèmes dans le lexique français contemporain*, Geneva: Droz.

Walter, H. 1988. *Le Français dans tous les sens*, Paris: Laffont.

Wüest, J. 1985. 'Le "patois de Paris" et l'histoire du français', *Vox Romanica*, 44, 234–58.

Wyld, H. C. 1920. *A History of Modern Colloquial English*, Oxford: Oxford University Press.

4

Elaboration and codification: standardization and attitudes towards the French language in the sixteenth and seventeenth centuries

WENDY AYRES-BENNETT

1. Introduction

The image of the sixteenth century as the age of richness, expansion and creativity countered by the restrictive codification and control of the seventeenth century has been a commonplace of the history of French at least since Brunot. It is a view which is broadly espoused, for instance, by Lodge (1991) in a recent 'overview article' which examines the standardization of French in the light of wider sociolinguistic thinking, and notably the theories of Haugen (1972) and the Milroys (1985).[1] In Haugen's terms, the sixteenth century is thus the period of elaboration and the seventeenth century the age of codification.

However, a number of scholars have challenged this picture, notably as regards the sixteenth century, arguing that although it perhaps has pedagogic value, it masks the reality which is, perhaps inevitably, more complex. For example, John Joseph's monograph entitled *Eloquence and Power* includes a detailed case study of sixteenth-century French, highlighting not only the elaborative elements, but also the signs of control (Joseph 1987, 132–59). Trudeau's study of what she terms 'the inventors of good usage' is at pains to stress the importance of normative activity in the sixteenth century (Trudeau 1992, 142), as is Kibbee's article (1990) on attitudes to linguistic variation during that century. Somewhat less attention has been paid, however, to the equally important question of whether there are elaborative elements in the seventeenth century, although as early as 1974 Marzys suggested that perhaps in many respects the seventeenth century was less 'classical' than the sixteenth 'si le classicisme implique rationalité et durée' ('if classicism implies rationality and permanence') (Marzys 1974, 327).

It is my aim here to contribute to the debate as to whether the traditional view of the sixteenth century as the period of elaboration and the seventeenth century as the age of control is correct by focusing especially on the seventeenth century. This will raise broader issues as to whether Haugen's theoretical model of standardization in terms of selection, codification, elaboration and acceptance (see below) can indeed be translated into some sort of temporal sequence, with these 'stages' having real time correlates. I shall also consider whether there is a tendency for the processes of elaboration and control to have most effect on one or more levels of linguistic structure. For instance, it is generally agreed that elaboration is primarily lexical, since the need for greater variety of function necessarily involves the elaboration of vocabulary (Milroy and Milroy 1985, 31). Joseph, however, seems less clear on this point. On the one hand, he asserts that the 'modernization' of the lexicon is generally the prime focus for elaboration (1987, 101) and that phonology, as a 'closed system' is most rarely affected by it (ibid., 97). Moreover his definition of elaboration as 'the addition of *structural or lexical* [my emphasis] elements to the synecdochic dialect, resulting from and necessary for its functioning in the domain appropriate to standard languages' (ibid., 93) seems to exclude the phonological. On the other hand his case study of the sixteenth century, which I shall discuss later, does include some examples of phonological elaboration.

2. Haugen's model of standardization[2]

One of the most influential models of standardization that has been proposed is that of Haugen, which I shall use here in my discussion of the standardization of French. It may be schematized in the following way:

Table 1: Haugen's model of standardization (Haugen 1972, 110)

	Form	Function
Society	SELECTION	ACCEPTANCE
Language	CODIFICATION	ELABORATION

For Haugen, codification concerns the form of the language, or its linguistic structure including phonology, grammar and lexicon. Its target is to achieve 'minimal variation in form' (Haugen 1972, 107) for efficient communication. In its purest – and hypothetical – form this implies a one-to-one relation between form and function so that each word ideally has one spelling and one pronunciation, each word one meaning (and vice versa) and all utterances utilize the same grammatical framework.[3] Elaboration, on the other hand, is related to the functions of language and strives for maximal variation in function, the enabling of a language to fulfil all necessary communicative functions (ibid., 107–8). Of necessity a balance has to be maintained between these two processes, since elaboration of function may lead to complexity of form, and unity of forms entails rigidity of function. Haugen adds that neither of these two processes can proceed very far until a model is selected as the basis of the norm.[4] For this norm to become the basis of the standard language is must be accepted by the community, albeit by only a small but influential group of speakers.

As I have suggested, an important question is whether this theoretical model or schema has real time correlates or temporal ordering. Haugen himself is not explicit on this point, although his comment on selection implies that this must occur early on in the standardization process. He also describes the four aspects as crucial 'steps' in the development from a 'dialect' to a language, and lists them in the following order in his summary (ibid., 110): (a) selection of the norm; (b) codification of form; (c) elaboration of function; (d) acceptance by the community. Joseph and Lodge, on the other hand, suggest that elaboration precedes control. To quote Joseph (1987, 109): 'the histories of standard languages reveal the same pattern over and over: elaboration triggers control'.[5] Thus in the case of French he speaks of a taste for the magnificent and monumental being replaced by a desire for subtlety and simple elegance which is connected with the onset of the control process (ibid., 144). Nevertheless, in his case study of the sixteenth century he identifies elements of control as well as elaboration (see below), and I shall likewise argue that, whereas the seventeenth century is primarily dominated by the control imperative, it too contains elaborative elements. Indeed the processes of elaboration and control appear to be on-going, even if only at what Joseph (ibid., 108) terms 'maintenance level', since new technology and new needs lead to elaboration which in turn may stimulate control, as evidenced, for instance, in the well-known twentieth-century attempts to control neologisms and especially Anglo-American borrowings in the French lexicon.[6] It is perhaps for this reason that the Milroys assert (1985, 27) that the processes of selection, acceptance, diffusion and maintenance are only hypothetical stages and do not necessarily follow in temporal succession; for instance, in their view maintenance starts quite early in the process.

Evidence from the history of French suggests that it is mistaken to see the processes as occurring in strict succession. Explicit discussion of the norm for standard French is found from the earliest grammar of French onwards (Palsgrave 1530), and continues until the middle of the seventeenth century when the question is settled to some extent in the work of Vaugelas (1647). However, whilst the élitist quality of Vaugelas's norm remains, there are subsequent shifts in the eighteenth century to a norm firmly based on past written usage, and subsequent events and changes in the sociocultural situation of French – including above all the French Revolution – necessitate the rethinking of a norm based on Court usage.[7]

I want now to consider to what extent features of elaboration and control are represented in the sixteenth and seventeenth centuries and to examine which levels of linguistic structure are most affected by these processes.

3. The sixteenth century

3.1 Elaboration in the sixteenth century

Elaboration involves two interrelated processes: the spread of what Joseph terms the 'synecdochic dialect' to new domains of usage which are ones appropriate for a standard language, and the resulting and essential addition of elements to that 'language' to enable it to carry out those new functions (see Joseph 1987, 93).[8] According to Joseph, there are two stages in the process. During an initial period when translation activities are of prime importance, there is direct borrowing from the superposed 'high' system (henceforth H), which in the case of French means primarily Latin, but also to a lesser extent Italian and Greek. This is a period of 'transference' when the language is simply peppered with borrowed words which lack equivalents in French, the 'low' system (L) undergoing the standardization. Regularly such borrowing engenders resentment, typified in the sixteenth century by Henri Estienne's polemic (1578, 1579) against Italianisms at Court. In a second period of 'nativization', the transferred elements become assimilated either minimally by adapting them to the phonological and morpho-syntactic constraints of the borrowing language or maximally by *calquing* (Joseph 1987, 93–5). In the case of French, however, there are at least two other major sources of enrichment. Notably in the sixteenth century French equally borrows from the dialects or, for example, from technical registers. Moreover, it creates words using material from within its own system either by derivation or composition, or indeed by semantic change.

Although the sixteenth century undoubtedly witnessed the peak of elaborative efforts in France, the spread of French to fresh domains and the concomitant adoption of terms to express the new còncepts involved began much earlier. For instance, while popular sermons and pious texts were attested early in French, towards the end of the Middle Ages French was also used in religious, moral and philosophical texts.[9]

The external factors – whether political, cultural, religious or social – favouring elaboration in the sixteenth century are well documented (cf. Joseph 1987, 132–4; Trudeau 1992, 13). These include the advent of printing from about 1470 which meant much wider diffusion for the written vernacular; Humanist attempts to bring Latin closer to its classical purity rendering the classical language less able to express all that was necessary for modern life and focusing attention instead on how the vernacular could be 'improved'; the Renaissance engendering an enhanced desire to translate the great classical works into French and adding a new language – Italian – to the superposition; and the Reformation with its demands for the laity to have direct access to the Bible in the vernacular which were met, for example, by Olivetan's complete translation of the Bible for Protestants published in 1535.[10] The *Ordonnances de Villers-Cotterêts* have traditionally been considered to be symbolic of changing attitudes to the vernacular. Following a series of royal edicts aiming to remove Latin from legal proceedings, these also excluded other vernaculars from court proceedings, deeds and judgments by asserting that they should be written down 'en langage maternel françois et non aultrement' ('only in the French mother tongue'). Recent research has, however, questioned whether this phrase was always interpreted as referring exclusively to French (Trudeau 1992, 40); evidence suggests that it was also interpreted by certain lawyers and historians as including any vernacular spoken in France, since of course French was not in fact the 'mother tongue' for the majority of speakers in France, but rather their local dialect or patois.

French steadily consolidated and strengthened its position as it was increasingly used in new domains (Rickard 1968; Picoche and Marchello-Nizia 1989, 27). For instance, the need to educate barbers, surgeons and apothecaries led to medical works being composed in French, such as Ambroise Paré's *Methode pour traicter les playes faictes par hacquebutes* (1545). Works on mathematics by Peletier du Mans and Forcadel appeared in French and there were equally works in French on the subjects of astrology, the natural and physical sciences, and important texts on geography such as André Thévet's *Cosmographie de Levant* (1554). Even dialectics (Ramus, Fouquelin) and of course grammar (Meigret) opened their doors to the vernacular (Rickard 1968, 5–6).

With the spread of French to new domains came an awareness of the language's inadequacy and calls to improve and enrich it, such as Tory's *Champ fleury* (1529) or Du Bellay's *Deffence et illustration de la langue françoyse* (1549). Associated above all with the elaborative activity is the doctrine of *richesse* ('richness') of the Pléiade poets, typified in Ronsard's assertion 'plus nous aurons de mots en nostre langue, plus elle sera parfaitte' ('the more words our language has, the more perfect it will be') (Brunot 1906, 168). Much of the debate focuses on the lexical resources of French, just as much of the remedial elaboration is lexical. As Kibbee notes (1990, 61), Ronsard and contemporary grammarians and lexicographers were generally more tolerant of lexical borrowings – especially if they filled a conceptual gap – than of dialectal pronunciations or morphology.

Although some aspects of variation were viewed in a negative light by certain commentators (see below), for many variation was a positive factor since it enriched the language. For instance, Henri Estienne is largely concerned with expanding the expressive power of French by a wide range of means provided these fit in with the 'naïve puissance'('natural strength') of French. Thus archaisms and neologisms are deemed acceptable if they fulfil an expressive need and dialectal forms are considered a source of ornamentation. Even Italian borrowings, the butt of his satire, are permitted if they fill an expressive gap, as he argues is true of *charlatan* and *bouffon*. For Estienne, 'eloquence', the ability to say more with fewer words, is of prime concern so that he approves, for instance, of *pieça* ('long ago, long since') despite its lower-class origins and archaic flavour not least since it allows the translation of a passage of the Aeneid in fewer words (Kibbee 1990, 54–5). Throughout the period under discussion, the writing of grammars and the production of translations were viewed as complementary activities, and translators created neologisms through necessity. Thus Meigret, in theory not always enthusiastic about neologisms, in practice, as a translator himself, realized the need to accept them provided they were assimilated to French phonotactics (ibid., 56).

The focus of elaborative activity in the sixteenth century is thus undoubtedly lexical. This includes the addition of 'learned' words and borrowings from other languages, dialects, or registers and the admission of archaisms and neologisms, as well as the borrowing of meanings and notably the restoration of etymological meanings to French forms. However, there are also examples of conscious elaboration of the syntax of French in the sixteenth century. For instance, Joseph (1987, 142–4) cites imitation of the object infinitive construction or the Ciceronian period[11] as instances of elaboration, to which we may add other conscious imitations of Latin constructions such as the use of the subjunctive with *comme*, unattached participial clauses mirroring the

Latin ablative absolute construction, the *relatif de liaison* (beginning a sentence with a relative pronoun or adjective), or the use of *que si* parallel to Latin *quod si* with the meaning 'but if' or 'and if'. Here the influence of Latin is of prime importance. The influence of an H system, whether Latin or Italian, is also central to Joseph's morphological examples (ibid., 138–9). In the main these involve the addition of new derivational suffixes to French, some of which have found a permanent home in the language (for example, *-esque* from Italian), some of which have played a more marginal or temporary role (such as the Latin-based ending *-ieur* for the comparative). The other two morphological examples of elaboration cited by Joseph appear to be of a rather different nature. The origin of the first of these, the use of 'je' with a first person plural verb as in 'je serons bien', which was frequently heard at Court according to Palsgrave, is the subject of debate.[12] The other, the use of *estre* rather than *avoir* as the auxiliary verb in compound tenses of *estre*, may have been given new vigour because of the parallel use of the auxiliary 'to be' in Italian, but is equally a form which is not uncommon during the Old French period.

Clearly then elaboration may be morphological or syntactic as well as lexical or semantic. In addition, Joseph cites four examples of phonological elaboration: the pronunciation of [ɛr] for [ar] by courtiers as hypercoristic reaction to the popular tendency to open [ɛr] to [ar]; the substitution of [u] for [o] (for example, *chouse* for *chose*) before or after *s*, *l*, *r*, *m*, *n*, [ŋ], perhaps through the influence of a prestigious southern dialect, probably Lyonnais; the change [wɛ] to [ɛ] as the aristocratic norm in direct competition to the change [wɛ] to [wa] in the non-aristocratic norm, thereby giving [ɛ] as the court pronunciation, [wa] as that of Paris and the surrounding regions, and [wɛ] as that of the provinces and conservative urban usage; and spelling pronunciations based on etymological orthography. These are, however, different from the other examples in important respects. As Joseph himself recognizes (1987, 143–5), virtually all examples of elaboration beyond the phonological level require deliberate and authoritative introduction into the written language and are supported by a superposed H language (the exceptions of *je* with a first person plural verb and the use of the imperfect subjunctive in place of the conditional are examples about which I have already expressed reservations). This is, however, not obviously true for all his phonological examples. While it may be possible to see the influence of Latin in the case of spelling pronunciations and perhaps, although much less convincingly, the support of Italian in promoting the change [wɛ] to [ɛ], it is more difficult to see the influence of an independent H language in the case of the other two phonological examples. Moreover, rather than involving the addition of extra variants enriching the language and offering it new expressive resources, the phonological examples are often replacements adopted by one sector of society. Thus, while these are examples of variation, they are not so clearly examples of elaboration as we have defined it. Whereas variation may be introduced into the written language for stylistic or cosmetic reasons, this is not so obviously true in the case of pronunciation.

3.2 Codification in the sixteenth century

Codification or, in Joseph's usage (1987, 109), control is concerned with limiting the introduction of new elements and evaluating and hierarchizing the elements already present in a language. It often entails elimination of some of the variants, and goes with the claim that such elimination of the 'worse' form(s) guarantees perfection. As the Milroys point out (1985, 66), the prescriptive preference for one form over another implies that the alternatives are exactly equivalent. The necessity of assuming equivalence may explain the success of attempts to codify spelling, where there can be little argument over equivalence, but it proves much more problematic when we discuss syntax. For instance, if we say that 'to whom am I speaking?' is the only correct form, we ignore the fact that the choice of this in conversation rather than the more usual 'who am I speaking to?' will have cold connotations and mark social distance (ibid., 68). In other words the expressions may not in fact be equivalent in all respects and so the language through hierarchization may lose a source of either semantic or stylistic richness. Questions of codification are of course related to the selection of the norm in that controversies are usually settled by reference to some 'authority', whether this is a norm based on geographic, social, demographic or literary considerations, or whether it makes appeal to logic or more subjective criteria such as economy, euphony, clarity or purity (cf. Joseph 1987, 125).

In an authoritative article on the control of variation in the sixteenth century, Kibbee (1990, 49–50) notes that there had been complaints over variation in French well before Tory's famous appeal for French to be codified, and he quotes the anonymous fourteenth-century author of the Metz Psalter who laments the inconstancy of the Romance idiom. Whilst the sixteenth century was undoubtedly preoccupied with the expansion and promotion of the *richesse* of French, especially as regards the lexicon, Renaissance grammarians were also concerned with rules and stability and the removal, at least to some extent, of variation. Indeed, the mere fact of producing a description of '*the* French language' whether for foreigners or native speakers implies selection and codification of one of a large range of possible systems.

A constant theme of sixteenth-century commentators on the French language is the awareness that the language is changing rapidly, and the belief that this is a hindrance to its use in certain functions. We may cite, for instance, Guillaume Des Autels's description of changes in French pronunciation and orthography as 'cette peste, laquelle infecte les plus saines parties de nostre parole' ('this plague which infects the healthiest parts of our speech'), or Montaigne's assertion that he wrote his *Essais* in French because he was not writing for posterity, but that if he had been, he would have had to use 'un langage plus ferme' ('a more stable language'), that is, Latin (Brunot 1906: 128–9). Whereas early on in the century there was doubt expressed, for instance by Charles de Bovelles (1533), as to whether it was possible to reduce the vernacular to rules (cf. Trudeau 1992, 35–6), by the middle of the century Du Bellay (1549) asserts that rules are not only possible, but desirable, and Meigret in his grammar of 1550 equally favours rules provided they are not imposed but reflect usage. Clearly by the mid-sixteenth century early codification was beginning to reduce variation and control elaboration.

Of course, the calls for fixity in the sixteenth and seventeenth century are not necessarily identical, since the different socio-historical contexts of each age engender different attitudes to fixity. For early sixteenth-century grammarians the fixing of French entailed giving it the fixity of Latin and often forcing it into Latin models (see especially Dubois 1531). Fixity was considered as contributing to the prestige of a codified language, just as richness did. In the seventeenth century, however, fixity often, although not invariably, equates with restriction.

It would be, moreover, foolhardy to try and characterize individual grammarians as representatives of either elaboration or control. For instance, at the same time as Tory calls for French to be elaborated, he also demands control and seeks fixity for the language. Again, Henri Estienne promotes ideas of correctness and desires the removal of 'les corruptions et depravations que luy fait le menu peuple' ('the corrupt and depraved elements created by the common people'), but equally appreciates the vitality of certain popular expressions (Marzys 1974, 324).

In other words, it is often in practice difficult to separate off clearly elaboration and control, since the two processes frequently go hand-in-hand in the sixteenth century.[13] Whilst we have hitherto seen the advent of printing as a factor favouring elaboration, we could equally note its influence as an agent of control, since with the arrival of printing came an enhanced need for standardized norms and control of orthography to allow intercommunication.[14] The sixteenth century is thus a period of intense debate about French orthography – whether it should be learnèd, etymological, and give priority to meaning through for example the differentiation of homonyms, or whether, as Meigret and others argued, it should be phonological and reflect the reality of the spoken word (see Brunot 1906, 93–123). The failure of Meigret's attempted reforms put the norm for orthography firmly in the traditional camp, and Robert Estienne's dictionary, in turn influencing Nicot and seventeenth-century norms, established the basis for standard spelling today.

In short, to use Haugen's terms (see table 1), the sixteenth century is concerned not only with function, but also with form. However, the attitude adopted towards the form differs according to the level of language under discussion. On the whole there is a rather relaxed attitude towards the lexicon (although not exclusively so, the paradigmatic example being Henri Estienne's polemic against the excessive use of Italianisms at Court), but there is more control of spelling and morphology and to some extent pronunciation. In general, however, sixteenth-century grammarians have relatively little to say about syntax and word order.

Kibbee (1990) illustrates how the Renaissance quest for glory for the vernacular was reflected in attacks on variation of different kinds. Meigret (1550), for instance, sows the seeds of dislike of diachronic variation through evaluating forms on the basis of usage rather than their proximity to Greek and Latin forms. Likewise, synchronic geographic variation is censured in his criticism of Parisian pronunciations or 'corruptions' (for example, Meigret 1550, 7), or Palsgrave's attacks on dialectal forms found in authors.[15] There is equally criticism of synchronic sociolinguistic variation such as Meigret's castigation of the pronunciation of certain courtiers whom he brands as 'efféminés mignons' ('effeminate little dears') (1550, 7). In short, even in the sixteenth century we witness a desire for greater or lesser variation within the standard through the ranking of variants and the implied elimination of less acceptable usages. Thus the two currents, elaboration and codification, are coexistent: whilst some authors favoured expansion, others strove to find rules to limit variation which, as Kibbee notes (1990, 59–60), has both political and religious implications.

Joseph's case study of the sixteenth century (1987, 145–58) shows how there was already reaction to the elaborative activity we have discussed. For instance, the changes [ar] > [ɛr], [o] > [u], and [wɛ] > [ɛ] were all the subject of comment and control, the two new superlative endings were criticized (indeed -*issime* never achieved normality), and there was a general decrease in the influence of Latin as the century progressed.[16]

4. The seventeenth century

4.1 Codification in the seventeenth century

It is pointless to rehearse the well-known stages towards the codification of French in the seventeenth century which include the arrival at court of Malherbe and his annotations of Desportes's poetry, the foundation of the French Academy in 1635, and the publication of Vaugelas's *Remarques* in 1647. Since Vaugelas is generally considered the key representative of the new seventeenth-century ethic of control, I shall focus my discussion on his work. For Vaugelas codification serves various ends: it creates a linguistic and social élite (*la distinction*);[17] it guarantees intercommunication; it ensures others will find one's linguistic usage agreeable since hearers like to hear ideas expressed in the language they themselves would have chosen; and it contributes to the fixing of the language in its present state of perfection (Vaugelas 1647, Preface X, 2).

Although, as we shall see below, we should not overlook elaborative elements in the *Remarques*, equally we should not underestimate the degree of control. Berrendonner (1982, 34) notes how in the 'discours normatif' ('normative discourse') there are two types of procedure for masking the normative or prescriptive character of the discussion – those which hide the prescriptive approach itself, and those which aim to shift the responsibility from the grammarian. Both these tactics are found in Vaugelas. First, as Joseph points out (1987, 18), in practice there is not a great deal of difference between saying 'the best speakers say x (not y)' as we often find in Vaugelas, and 'say x not y', especially in the light of Vaugelas's assertion (1647, 355) that perfection must always be sought. Secondly, despite Vaugelas's claim that he is nothing but a 'simple tesmoin' ('simple witness') of good usage, his inclusion of the phrase 'la plus saine partie de' ('the soundest part of') in his definition of good usage as 'la façon de parler de la plus saine partie de · la Cour, conformément à la façon d'escrire de la plus saine partie des Autheurs du temps' (ibid., Preface II, 3)[18] is sufficiently vague and flexible to allow him to introduce his own personal preferences, as is evident for instance in his discussion of *pluriel* (ibid., 468–70).

Haugen asserts that the interaction of elaboration and codification is the domain of style: a complete language has its different styles, regional accents, sociolects, and so on which do not threaten its unity provided they are clearly differentiated in function and are relatively close together (Haugen 1972, 108–9). In Vaugelas's *Remarques* there appear to be two contrasting models for the French language – one, which we might term broadly sociolinguistic and we will discuss below, that recognizes variation in language and acknowledges that certain forms and expressions will be permissible in certain styles and registers (such as burlesque) but not in others. Many *Remarques* falling within this model could therefore be classed as stylistic rather than specifically grammatical. However, in the second mode, the 'codification model', the usage appropriate for one style or register is deemed the appropriate form for all French usage, and thus control dominates over elaboration.[19]

In this second model there is a simple division made between *le bon Usage* ('good usage') and *le mauvais Usage* ('bad usage'), the latter being represented by burlesque, comedy and satire (Vaugelas 1647, Preface VII, 3). One thus finds examples of low-register usages, such as *boutez-vous là* for *mettez-vous là*, being condemned in very strong terms. Furthermore, *le bon Usage* is equated with *le bel Usage* ('fine usage') and this is said to exclude anything which is deemed 'bas' or 'de la lie du peuple':

> Au reste quand je parle du *bon Usage*, j'entens parler außi du *bel Usage*, ne mettant point de difference en cecy entre le bon & le beau; car ces Remarques ne sont pas comme un Dictionnaire qui reçoit toutes sortes de mots, pourveu qu'ils soient François, encore qu'ils ne soient pas du bel Usage, & qu'au contraire ils soient bas & de la lie du peuple (ibid., Preface VII, 1).[20]

This gives us the following model:

Table 2:   The Codification Model

le bon Usage = *le bel Usage*
le mauvais Usage = *bas, de la lie du peuple*; associated with comedy, burlesque, satire

In this model, therefore, very high demands are made on all linguistic behaviour. As we shall see, this attitude contrasts sharply with the opinion expressed in the other model of usage found in the *Remarques*.

4.2 Elaboration in the seventeenth century

Whilst undoubtedly the peak of the expansion of French to new domains had been passed by the last two decades of the sixteenth century, elaborative activity did not cease in the seventeenth century. New territories continued to be added to France in the course of the century: part of Artois and Roussillon in 1659; Franche-Comté, the rest of Artois, Cambrai, Valenciennes and Maubeuge in 1678; Strasbourg in 1697. Moreover, the seventeenth century marks the first period of French colonial expansion with the settlement of Canada,

Martinique and Guadeloupe and the establishment of trading posts in Senegal and Madagascar. In the same way, French continued to expand its functions. For instance, Brockliss (1987, 278–9) notes how, from 1679 onwards, the law faculty began to include in its teaching the study of French law, and that within a few years professors of law were employed who broke with tradition by lecturing in the vernacular.

As well as the spread of French to new domains, the seventeenth century witnessed elaborative efforts of the type traditionally associated with the previous century. Since, as I have already indicated, Vaugelas is generally viewed as the very personification of the new ethic of control of the French language, it seems appropriate to concentrate our discussion on whether there are any elaborative features in the *Remarques*. Other writers on the French language could however be cited. It is not difficult, for instance, to identify elaborative efforts in the century in the shape of opponents to Vaugelas and the 'purists' – notably Scipion Dupleix and De la Mothe le Vayer (see Streicher 1936) who questioned the restrictive control of the purists. Perhaps more significantly, even those held to be paradigmatic organs or figures of control also allow some freedom. For instance, article 24 of the Academy's statutes establishes it as an organ of control in its assertion that the role of the Academy is to:

> travailler avec tout le soin et toute la diligence possible à donner des règles certaines à notre langue et à la rendre pure, éloquente et capable de traiter les arts et les sciences (Pellisson and d'Olivet 1858, I, 493).[21]

However, it has been pointed out (see Popelár 1968; Wolf 1983) that the Academy dictionary is not always as purist as one might imagine and contains, for instance, such expressions as *chier de peur* ('to shit with fear') or *il se noyerait dans son crachat* (literally 'he would drown in his own spit'; 'makes a mountain out of a molehill') (Wolf 1983, 116).

If we now turn to consideration of Vaugelas, we find that there are indeed elaborative elements in his *Remarques*. In a recent paper Bonhomme (1990) divided critics of Vaugelas into two camps: those who see Vaugelas as a 'simple witness' who, favouring a contemporary norm, is a 'modernist' and even a precursor of the structuralists, and those who highlight the prescriptive content of the *Remarques* and characterize Vaugelas as one of the fathers of normative grammar. As I have already suggested, it is probably more correct not to attribute these views to two types of critics of Vaugelas, but rather to consider them as two different positions adopted by Vaugelas himself (cf. Berrendonner 1990, 70). We have seen how the *Remarques* in many respects personify the control ethic, but there are equally observations in which a normative stance is not adopted.

In this other 'sociolinguistic' model Vaugelas asserts the relativity of good usage and presents a much more complicated network of values with words being considered more or less acceptable according to their style and situation. Here we encounter the importance of what Vaugelas himself terms 'la proprieté des mots et des phrases' ('appropriateness of word or phrase'), defined by Chiflet (1659, 148) as the ability to use the words or phrases appropriate to the subject being treated. Vaugelas recommends the choice of the right word according to the genre, register, context and style of the work. Thus in discussing *comme ainsi soit* he asserts, 'J'avoüe que dans une lettre il seroit exorbitant: mais qui ne sçait qu'il y a des paroles & des termes pour toutes sortes de stiles?' (1647, *470).[22] Alongside the simple characterization of usage as either 'good' or 'bad' we thus find the statement that there are rather three levels *within* good usage, *le bas* ('low'), *le mediocre* ('mediocre') and *le sublime* ('sublime'). This allows the possibility of having terms labelled *bas* or *familier* nevertheless constituting good usage:

> mais il y a bien de la difference entre un langage soustenu, & un langage composé de mots & de phrases du bon Usage, qui comme nous avons dit, peut estre bas & familier, & du bon Usage tout ensemble (ibid., Preface VII, 3).[23]

Furthermore, in this model, *le bon Usage* and *le bel Usage* are differentiated, as is suggested in Vaugelas's comment on the expression *pour l'heure*:

> Cette façon de parler pour dire *pour lors*, est bonne, mais basse, & ne doit pas estre employé dans le beau stile, où il faut dire *pour lors* (ibid., 192).[24]

According to Vaugelas the important thing is to avoid the mixing of levels, if one wishes to avoid appearing ridiculous. He adds that there are words and expressions appropriate for each of the three 'styles' and that the French language has wrongly been criticized for its poverty by poor speakers and writers. This is unjust since French 'a des magazins remplis de mots & des phrases de tout pris, mais ils ne sont pas ouverts à tout le monde, où (*sic*) s'ils le sont, peu de gens sçavent choisir dans cette grande quantité ce qui leur est propre' (ibid., 510–11).[25]

Table 3:   The Sociolinguistic Model

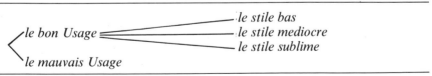

Consequently Vaugelas at times sanctions two or more variants, asserting the value of variety and leaving the speaker or writer with a choice of acceptable expressions. For instance, in discussing *sur les*

armes and *sous les armes* (ibid., 396–7) he argues that they are both acceptable and that it is misguided to use only one of them; rather since they are both good usage:

> il faut user tantost de l'un et tantost de l'autre, afin qu'il ne semble pas que l'on condamne celuy dont on ne se sert jamais, en quoy l'on auroit tort, & pour conserver d'ailleurs tout ce qui contribuë à la richesse de nostre langue; comme est de pouvoir dire une mesme chose de deux façons, plustost que d'une seule.[26]

This more interesting model, with its sociolinguistic emphasis, has tended to be overlooked in Vaugelas, since it is largely the codification model which is adopted by such successors as Bouhours. Within this more tolerant model elaboration is permissible. Although Vaugelas asserts that no one has the right to create new words, and especially not new phrases, in practice he at times adopts a more flexible attitude, especially as regards derivatives which fit into an established pattern. For example, discussing *devouloir* (ibid., 490–2), he mitigates his apparent absolute rejection of new words by asserting that 'cette sorte de composition de verbes semble avoir ce privilege, qu'on en peut former & inventer de nouveaux aubesoin, pourveu qu'on le face avec jugement & discretion, & que ce ne soit que tres-rarement'.[27] Even the calque from Latin, *transfuge*, is welcomed into French because it is deemed to fill a conceptual gap (ibid., 448–9).

Therefore, although the seventeenth century is clearly a period of very tight control, Vaugelas apparently realizes that elaboration is essential and inevitable and in consequence must be accepted. For instance, the use of *recouvert* for *recouvré* has been introduced 'contre la reigle, & contre la raison' ('against rule and reason'), but has nevertheless become established; Vaugelas therefore recommends that in a long work, where there is the opportunity, both alternatives should be exploited. He even admits that the usage of *la* for *le* by women, as when they reply to the statement 'quand je suis malade, j'ayme à voir compagnie' ('when I am ill I like to see people') with the words '& moy quand je *la* suis...' ('and when I am (ill)...') which he brands a fault, may eventually become established (ibid., 27).

If we turn our attention briefly to Vaugelas's preoccupations and attitudes towards different levels of linguistic structure, a noticeable feature is the increase in space devoted to syntactic questions compared with the previous century. Over one third of the *Remarques* are broadly concerned with questions of construction and word order and the promotion of *netteté* ('clarity') against structural ambiguity. In this area Vaugelas's judgements tend to be highly prescriptive, even to the point of placing unreasonable demands on the language. On more 'local' questions of agreement and government, however, he allows some flexibility as in his toleration of both *survivre à* and *survivre* with a direct object (ibid., 534).

As regards morphology, Vaugelas stresses that many mistakes are made, especially in the conjugation of verbs, and details numerous examples of errors made in speech (ibid., 572–3) such as the use of *j'alla* for *j'allay*, *il allit* for *il alla*, or *nous alliβions* for *nous allaβions*. However, even in this area, which is often thought to tolerate least variation, Vaugelas allows a little flexibility over verb morphology (for example, *Vesquit, vescut*, ibid., 108–9) and greater latitude over nominal gender, perhaps at times to a degree surprising to the modern reader. For instance, having asserted that the gender of *ouvrage* is masculine, Vaugelas concedes that women use the word in the feminine and that they should be allowed to do so (ibid., 445).

Even in the observation in which he denies that French tolerates new phrases, Vaugelas employs the vocabulary of elaboration and admits that this is an ongoing process:

> Ce n'est pas non plus, que comme nostre langue s'embellit & se perfectionne tous les jours, on ne puisse employer quelques nouveaux ornemens, qui jusqu'icy estoient inconnus à nos meilleurs Escrivains, mais le corps des phrases & la diction doit estre tousjours conservé, & l'essence & la beauté des langues ne consiste qu'en cela (ibid., 510).[28]

Moreover, in the Preface, Vaugelas mentions the ground he has not been able to cover, which includes discussion of the history of the language and of the success of the elaborative efforts which have resulted in the richness and perfection of French as witnessed for instance in translations of classical texts.[29] Thus not only is there a continuation of elaboration in the seventeenth century, albeit on a much reduced scale, there is also pride expressed in the richness and wealth of the French language.

5. Conclusion

We may conclude by noting that a neat categorization of the sixteenth century as the age of elaboration and the seventeenth as the age of control is not possible. Whilst this picture may represent the dominant features of each period, it fails to reflect the complex interaction of the processes throughout the centuries which have led to the emergence of 'standard French'. Rather than seeing elaboration and codification as temporally based 'stages', it thus seems more realistic to view them as constructs in a model which is useful to the understanding of the standardization process. Evidence suggests that both elaboration and codification are ongoing processes, and that their continuance is indeed essential to the health of a language.

Notes

1 Extensive use of these works had been made previously, for instance, by Joseph (1987). For discussion of Haugen's theory, see below section 2, and Lodge and Jones (this volume).

2 Note that there is considerable variation in the use of terminology between theorists. For instance, whilst for Joseph 'standardization' includes a number of stages, starting with the initial firing of patriotism when the virtues of the vernacular are extolled, through a period of translation and using the vernacular in standard language functions to a period of complaint about the vernacular's ineloquence and so on, the Milroys (1985, 8) employ a narrower definition of it as 'the suppression of optional variability in language'. It is the broader definition which will be employed here, and the terms 'codification' or 'control' used for the narrower sense. The Milroys further comment that it is very difficult to separate such concepts as linguistic prescription, normalization and standardization (ibid., 2). I shall consider the selection of a norm and prescription of correct usages as facets of the process of standardization.

3 Lodge (1991, 98) argues that since uniformity is deemed the ideal state, the written language, which tolerates less variation, is considered of greater worth. One may contrast this with Vaugelas's assertion of the primacy of the spoken word (for example, Vaugelas 1647, 470).

4 There is an extensive body of literature concerned with the selection of a norm for French; see, for example, Berrendonner 1982, Budagow 1961, Caput 1972, Glatigny 1989, Klinkenberg 1982, Marzys 1974, Padley 1983, Settekorn 1988, Trudeau 1992, Winkelmann 1990 and Wolf 1983.

5 See Lodge (1991, 97): 'After an oral vernacular has been "selected" and "elaborated" it will still contain within it fluidity of usage. The process of standardization requires that this variation be suppressed.'

6 See, for example, Muller 1985, 40–6, and Offord (this volume).

7 On this, see, for example, Settekorn 1988, 83–134.

8 In this respect, therefore, elaboration is not merely concerned with function as in Haugen's model, but also involves form.

9 For the spread of French to new domains in the fifteenth century, see Rickard 1976.

10 Note too how Calvin chose to translate his own work, the *Christianae religionis institutio*, into French in 1541.

11 I am unhappy about Joseph's example (E13) of the use of the imperfect subjunctive in place of a conditional as an instance of elaboration. Rather than being the conscious imitation of a Latin construction, it is an alternative which had been in the language from the earliest times (indeed the use of the imperfect subjunctive in conditional clauses was the more usual Old French construction) and still survived as a variant.

12 Joseph (1987, 139) tentatively suggests a Norman origin for it.

13 Joseph (1987, 145) comments that in the climate of elaboration of the sixteenth century certain control decisions, such as the establishment of rules for the agreement of the past participle with *avoir*, were actually elaborative in nature.

14 Note that Tory (1529) views his work on typography as a first step in a vast programme for fixing all of French usage (cf. Trudeau 1992, 25).

15 Kibbee (1990, 56) notes how Palsgrave criticizes phonetic ([r] > [z]) and morphological (*j'ay conclud*) as well as lexical regional variation.

16 Of course, not all cases of elaboration were the subject of control. There was no control, for instance, of spelling pronunciations or of the use of *-esque*. Two of the other instances of control cited by Joseph, the prohibition in the name of logic of such double comparatives as *plus hauçor* and the ridicule of *pieça* because of its low-class origins, were, however, defended by Henri Estienne (Joseph 1987, 157). Inconsistency is a constant feature of the application of control. For instance, Joseph (ibid., 158) rightly asks why, if *pieça* ('long since, long ago') is to be criticized, *naguère* ('not long since, a short time ago') should not equally be censured, since a case could be made against it on similar grounds.

17 See especially Settekorn (1988) which discusses the standardization of French in the light of Bourdieu's theory of a linguistic market.

18 Note that throughout the use of 'i'/'j' and 'u'/'v' has been modernized. The quotation reads: 'The way of speaking of the soundest part of the Court in conformity with the way the soundest part of contemporary authors write.'

19 Cf. Bonhomme (1990) who distinguishes three 'norms' in Vaugelas: 'la norme organisatrice' ('organizing norm'), 'la norme préservatrice' ('preserving norm') and 'la norme prescriptive' ('prescriptive norm'). This last category is similar to my 'codification or control model' in which the usage of one sector of society, *le bon Usage*, is made to equate with French usage *tout court*. Significant in this model is Vaugelas's usage of the term 'français' (see Ayres-Bennett forthcoming).

20 'Moreover, when I speak of *good usage*, I also include *fine usage*, since I make no difference in this between what is good and what is fine; for these remarks are not like a dictionary which includes all kinds of words provided they are French, although they are not in fine usage, but are on the contrary low-register, common, and of the dregs of the people.'

21 'To work with all possible care and diligence to give fixed rules to our language, and to make it pure, eloquent and capable of treating both the arts and the sciences.'

22 The asterisk indicates the second set of a duplicate set of pagination in the text of the *Remarques*. The quotation reads, 'I admit that in a letter it would be excessive, but who does not know that there are words and terms for all sorts of styles?'

23 'But there is a great difference between an elevated use of language and a language composed of words and expressions of good usage which, as we have said, may be low-register and familiar and at the same time constitute good usage.'

24 'This expression for *pour lors* is good (usage) but low-register and should not be used in fine style in which *pour lors* should be used.'

25 '... has stores full of words and phrases of all values; but they are not all open to everyone, or, if they are, few people are able to choose from this great quantity what is appropriate to them.'

26 'One should use now one, now the other, so that it does not appear that the one which is never used is condemned, which would be wrong, and so that one keeps, moreover, all that contributes to the richness of our language; for example, being able to say the same thing in two ways rather than one.'

27 'This type of verb formation has this advantage that one can form and invent new ones as required, provided this is done with judgement and discretion, and only very rarely.'

28 'It is not the case either, since our language is improving [literally 'becoming more embellished'] and becoming more perfect every day, that one cannot use a few new embellishments, which were unknown to our best writers until now, but the body of phrases and style must always be preserved, and the essence and beauty of languages consist entirely in that.'

29 Vaugelas (1647, 560–70) is, however, highly critical of the neologisms of Ronsard, Du Vair and other 'great men' who thought they were enriching the language with them, but in his view were mistaken.

References

Ayres-Bennett, W. 1987. *Vaugelas and the Development of the French Language*, London: Modern Humanities Research Association.

——forthcoming. '"tres-estrange & tres-François": l'usage du terme "français" au XVIIe siècle et la tradition de la latinitas'. To appear in the Conference Proceedings of the XIX Congreso Internacional de lingüística e filoloxía románicas (Santiago,1989).

Bédard, É. and Maurais, J. (eds.). 1983. *La Norme linguistique*, Quebec: Publications du Gouvernement du Québec; Paris: Le Robert.

Berrendonner, A. 1982. *L'Eternel grammairien. Etude du discours normatif*, Berne: Peter Lang.

Bonhomme, M. 1990. 'Les rapports norme-structure dans les *Remarques* de Vaugelas', in Liver, R., Werlen, I. and Wunderli, P. (eds.), *Sprachtheorie und Theorie der Sprachwissenschaft. Festschrift für Rudolf Engler zum 60. Geburtstag*, Tübingen: Narr, 69–82.

Bovelles, Ch. de, 1533. *Liber de differentia vulgarium linguarum, & Gallici sermonis varietate*. Paris: R. Estienne.

Brockliss, L. W. B. 1987. *French Higher Education in the Seventeenth and Eighteenth Centuries. A Cultural History*, Oxford: Clarendon Press.

Brunot, F. 1905–53. *Histoire de la langue française des origines à nos jours*, Paris: A. Colin (especially vol. 2 (1906), vol. 3 (1909) and vol. 4 (1913–24)).

Budagow, R. A. 1961. 'La normalisation de la langue littéraire en France aux XVIe et XVIIe siècles', *Beiträge zur Romanischen Philologie*, 1, 143–58.

Caput, J.-P. 1972. 'Naissance et évolution de la notion de norme en français', *Langue française*, 16, 63–73.

Chiflet, L. 1659. *Essay d'une parfaite grammaire de la langue françoise*, Antwerp: Jacques van Meurs.

Du Bellay, J. 1549. *La Deffense et illustration de la langue francoyse*, Paris: A. l'Angelier.

Dubois, J. (or Sylvius). 1531. *Jacobi Sylvii Ambiani in Linguam Gallicam Isagωge*, Paris: R. Estienne.

Estienne, H. 1578. *Deux dialogues du nouveau langage françois italianizé et autrement desguizé, principalement entre les courtisans de ce temps*, Geneva: R. Estienne.

—— 1579. *Project du livre intitulé De la precellence du langage françois*, Paris: Mamert Patisson.

Glatigny, M. 1989. 'Norme et usage dans le français du XVIe siècle', in Swiggers and Van Hoecke 1989, 7–31.

Haugen, E. 1972. 'Dialect, language, nation', in Pride, J. B. and Holmes, J. (eds.), *Sociolinguistics. Selected Readings*, Harmondsworth: Penguin, 97–111. (First published 1966 in *American Anthropologist*, 68, 922–35.)

Joseph, J. E. 1987. *Eloquence and Power. The Rise of Language Standards and Standard Languages*, London: Frances Pinter.

Kibbee, D. A. 1990. 'Language variation and linguistic description in sixteenth-century France', *Historiographia Linguistica*, 17, 49–65.

Klinkenberg, J.-M. 1982. 'Les niveaux de langue et le filtre du "bon usage" du discours normatif au discours sociolinguistique', *Le français moderne*, 50, 52–61.

Lodge, R. A. 1991. 'Authority, prescriptivism and the French standard language', *Journal of French Language Studies*, 1, 93–111.

Marzys, Z. 1974. 'La formation de la norme du français cultivé', *Kwartalnik neofilologiczny*, 21, 315–32.

Meigret, L. 1550. *Le Tretté de la grammere françoeze*, Paris: C. Wechel.

Milroy, J., and Milroy, L. 1985. *Authority in Language. Investigating Language Prescription and Standardisation*, London: Routledge and Kegan Paul.

Muller, B. 1985. *Le Français d'aujourd'hui*, revised edition translated from the German by A. Elsass, Paris: Klincksieck.

Padley, G. A. 1983. 'La norme dans la tradition des grammairiens', in Bédard and Maurais 1983, 69–104.

Palsgrave, J. 1530. *Lesclarcissement de la langue francoyse*, London: J. Hawkyns.

Pellisson, P. and d'Olivet, P.-J. T. 1858. *Histoire de l'Académie française par Pellisson et d'Olivet*, ed. by Livet, Ch.-L., 2 vols., Paris: Didier.

Picoche, J. and Marchello-Nizia, C. 1989. *Histoire de la langue française*, Paris: Nathan.

Popelár, I. 1968. 'Das Akademiewörterbuch von 1694 – Das Wörterbuch des "Honnête Homme"?', *Beiträge zur Romanischen Philologie*, 7, 303–10.

Rickard, P. 1968. *La Langue française au seizième siècle. Etude suivie de textes.* Cambridge: Cambridge University Press.

——. 1976. *Chrestomathie de la langue française au quinzième siècle*, Cambridge: Cambridge University Press.

Settekorn, W. 1988. *Sprachnorm und Sprachnormierung in Frankreich. Einführung in die begrifflichen, historischen und materiellen Grundlagen*, Tübingen: Niemeyer.

Streicher, J. 1936. *Commentaires sur les Remarques de Vaugelas*, 2 vols., Paris: Droz.

Swiggers, P. and Van Hoecke, W. 1989. *La Langue française au XVIe siècle: Usage, enseignement et approches descriptives*, Louvain: Leuven University Press; Peeters.

Tory, G. 1529. *Champ fleury*, Paris: Gourmont.

Trudeau, D. 1992. *Les Inventeurs du bon usage (1529–1647)*, Paris: Minuit.

Vaugelas, C. F. de, 1647. *Remarques sur la langue françoise utiles à ceux qui veulent bien parler et bien escrire*, Paris: J. Camusat and P. Le Petit.

Winkelmann, O. 1990. 'Französisch: Sprachnormierung und Standard-sprache', in Holtus, G., Metzeltin, M., and Schmitt, C. (eds.), *Lexikon der Romanistischen Linguistik*, Tübingen, vol. 5. 1, 334–53.

Wolf, L. 1983. 'La normalisation du langage en France. De Malherbe à Grevisse', in Bédard and Maurais 1983, 105–37.

5

Protecting the French language

MALCOLM OFFORD

The defence and illustration of the French language has come a long way since 1539 and article 111 of the Ordonnance of Villers-Cotterêts, which prescribed that all judicial documents should be expressed in 'langage maternel françois' and not Latin; it has also come a long way since 1549 and Joachim du Bellay's *Deffence et illustration de la langue francoyse*, or since 1629 and the meetings in the home of Valentin Conrart, which were the precursors of the *Académie française*. The *Académie* officially came into being in January 1635, although it did not receive full parliamentary approval until 16 July 1637 (see especially Cooper 1989, 3–11). From the time of the Revolution language became an ever more important political issue, particularly in the area of education, culminating in the education laws of Jules Ferry of 1881–4. However, debate about the French language was rarely in the public domain before the twentieth century.

1. Concern in the twentieth century for the French language

The second half and particularly the last quarter of the twentieth century have witnessed a remarkable upsurge of concern about the language. This has taken three distinct forms: the opinions of individuals, government action and pressure from private organizations.

1.1. The opinions of individuals

These have tended to be extremely critical of current trends in the language and have at times been expressed through violent outbursts, often in books with highly emotive titles, the best known of which is, of course, *Parlez-vous franglais?* of 1964 by René Etiemble.[1]

Some attitudes seem rather difficult to substantiate; for example, one cannot help being struck by the rather eccentric claims made for the therapeutic benefits of French by Michel Popov of the *Féderation européenne des sciences sociales* in a paper issued before the Seoul Olympics:

> Quant au rayonnement de la langue française sur les cinq continents, il peut, vu son caractère olympique en tant que langue de rencontre et de compréhension des Peuples et de rapports interpersonnels directs, jouer un rôle de dynamisme équilibrant pour l'autostructuration neuromotrice des Athlètes. Sa clarté physiologique, sa mesure, sa concision, dans une période postindustrielle, peuvent lui assurer des articulations délimitées de gestes d'ensembles et de langages ensembliers pour Adultes en activité.[2]

A less vocal, less chauvinistic view also exists but for obvious reasons does not grab the headlines like the previous group of writers: Jacques Cellard (ex-language correspondent of *Le Monde*)[3] and Claude Hagège, especially (1987), are the major exponents of this view, which advocates minimum interference with the language. The middle course, that of 'gentle dirigisme', was especially advocated by Aurélien Sauvageot (1973).

1.2. Government action

Since the middle 1960s successive governments have set up a number of organizations with ever-increasing briefs. The role of these organizations has been, amongst other things, to supervise the quality of French used in official documents and the media, to make provision for new terminology and to safeguard the position of French on the international scene. Government action and legislation in linguistic matters has been well documented in recent years.[4] To summarize the situation as far as government bodies are concerned: the *Haut Comité pour la défense et l'expansion de la langue française* was established in 1966; in 1972 the first *Commissions de terminologie pour l'enrichissement du vocabulaire français* were charged with recommending new technical vocabulary; *Franterm*, the terminological powerhouse, was created in 1980; in 1984 the *Haut Comité* was revamped and divided into three complementary bodies, the *Commissariat général de la langue française*, the *Comité consultatif de la langue française,* and the *Haut Conseil pour la langue française*. The latter was given the major task of preparing the summit meetings of Francophone heads of state (four to date, Paris twice (the latest November 1991), Quebec and

Dakar; the next is to be held in Mauritius in 1993). Its official function is to 'préciser le rôle de la francophonie et de la langue française dans le monde moderne; rassembler les données et confronter les expériences, notamment dans les domaines de l'enseignement, de la communication, de la science et des techniques nouvelles; distinguer les enjeux et les urgences et proposer des perspectives d'action' ('to define the roles to be played by Francophonia and the French language in the modern world; to collect data and compare experiences, especially in the following domains – teaching, communication, science and recent technological advances; to identify issues and matters of urgency and to propose appropriate courses of action') (Répertoire 1992, 23).

The importance attached to maintaining Francophonia as a significant international force is reflected in the creation in 1986 of a *secrétaire d'Etat chargé de la francophonie*, promoted to *ministre délégué à la francophonie* in 1988, who 'propose toutes mesures, anime et oriente l'action des administrations intéressées et est en charge de la coopération avec les organismes internationaux à vocation francophone' ('proposes measures, prompts and directs the actions of the appropriate administration and is in charge of co-operation with international Francophone bodies') (Répertoire 1992, 24). The first minister, Alain Decaux, was replaced by Catherine Tasca in the cabinet reshuffle of May 1991. The latest reorganization of these government bodies and clear proof of the continuing commitment of the previous government to linguistic matters occurred in June 1989 with the establishing of the *Délégation générale à la langue française* and the *Conseil supérieur de la langue française*. The former 'met en œuvre . . . toutes actions visant à la diffusion et la défense de la langue française. Elle coordonne les travaux effectués en matière de terminologie, les actions visant à l'enseignement et la diffusion du français par les moyens autres que scolaires, et les actions menées au plan international pour le développement de l'usage du français' ('puts into effect . . . decisions aimed at spreading and defending the French language. It co-ordinates efforts made in the area of terminology, plans for teaching and spreading French other than via schools, and plans carried out on the international plane for promoting the use of French'); the latter 'a pour mission d'étudier . . . les questions relatives à l'usage, à l'aménagement, à l'enrichissement, à la promotion et à la diffusion de la langue française en France et hors de France' ('the latter's mission is to study . . . matters relating to the use, management, enriching, promotion and extension of the French language both within and outside France') (Répertoire 1992, 22). After the elections of March 1993, bringing about a change of government, Jacques Toubon was appointed *ministre de la culture et de la francophonie*. It is unfortunately too soon to discern what attitude the new government may adopt in relation to the organizations inherited from the previous administration.

The different tones of government concern are well illustrated by the following series of remarks made by the heads and other leading figures of various official agencies.

1.2.1. To begin with, a pessimistic tone from Bernard Billaud, the last of the *commissaires généraux de la langue française*, who said in a document published before the 1989 Dakar summit of Francophone heads of state (Dakar 1989, 25):

> Je sais qu'il est mal venu aujourd'hui de parler de défense de la langue, car la notion de 'défense' est suspecte: elle suppose une tournure d'esprit jugée frileuse et étriquée et elle se heurte au courant dominant qui veut faire de l'anglais la langue de communication universelle, à l'exclusion de toute autre. Au risque de susciter plus de quolibets que d'encouragements je vais répéter que notre langue est menacée et que cette menace retentit sur l'avenir de notre peuple.[5]

1.2.2. Next, a resigned tone, as illustrated by the following comment in the *Lettre de la Francophonie*, published by the *Délégation générale à la langue française* (numéro spécial, November 1990, p.iv):

> Il serait vain, en effet, d'ignorer l'attrait qu'exerce, à tort ou à raison, la langue anglaise dont le ministre français chargé de la Francophonie, Alain Decaux, n'hésite pas à estimer que les francophones doivent accepter de la subir 'comme on subit les orages ou les étés torrides'.[6]

Pierre Maillard, French ambassador, reporting on a meeting between members of the *Association pour la défense du français et du patrimoine linguistique européen* with members of the *Groupe d'étude pour le développement et l'usage de la langue française* (a group of Euro-MPs)[7] said:

> Diverses solutions [to the problem of the diversity of languages in the EC] ont été évoquées, langue unique, bilinguisme, réduction à trois ou quatre des langues officielles, les autres restant langues d'usage, mais sans statut officiel. L'examen de cette importante question sera activement poursuivi avec, en ce qui nous concerne, la ferme volonté d'éviter tout système qui, à défaut de donner au français une place exclusive – ce qui serait évidemment à nos yeux la solution idéale – risquerait à terme d'affecter la position privilégiée qui selon nous doit être la sienne dans les institutions européennes.[8]

1.2.3. Next, an alarmist tone, in the words of Philippe Rossillon, ex-*rapporteur général du Haut Comité de la langue française*:[9]

> Tous les indicateurs ... sont au rouge: disparition de la recherche et des colloques scientifiques en français, cours dispensés directement en anglais

dans un nombre croissant d'écoles ou d'instituts supérieurs, multiplication des établissements bilingues, tentative de l'introduction de l'anglais dans le cycle primaire par l'Education nationale, courrier adressé en anglais aux administrations françaises, anglicisation rampante de Bruxelles, usage de l'anglais dans la communication interne de nombreuses entreprises privées au capital partiellement anglais ou américain, usage de plus en plus fréquent de l'anglais dans la publicité, dépôt de plus en plus majoritaire des marques de fabrique et raisons sociales en anglais ou faux anglais.[10]

1.2.4. Next, a much more aggressive tone: Philippe Rossillon again, who is quoted as saying:[11]

On observe un effort à la fois colossal et insidieux de la part de l'Angleterre, et surtout des Etats-Unis, pour faire de l'anglais la langue universelle ... L'impérialisme culturel américain tend à imposer l'anglais comme langue universelle. L'impérialisme culturel français, infiniment plus faible, cherche à empêcher l'anglais de devenir une langue universelle, en consolidant l'usage du français auprès de 3% de la population mondiale, en essayant de conserver ou d'arracher une petite place pour le français.[12]

In similar vein, but also with what appears as a slightly devious intention, a document reporting the setting up of the *Conseil supérieur de la langue française* makes the following statement:

Pour enrayer la baisse sensible de la demande en langue française, ses [du *Conseil*] recommandations suggéreront des démarches plus réalistes et plus offensives que par le passé. Il s'agit moins en effet d'empêcher la connaissance d'autres langues en France que de faire en sorte que le français pénètre davantage dans les pays non-francophones, et en premier lieu dans les pays les plus industrialisés.[13]

The jingoistic triumphalism of earlier years is happily absent from recent declarations.

1.2.5. And lastly, perhaps the most realistic attitude, well and frequently expressed by Léopold Senghor, one of the founder members of the current conception of Francophonia and indefatigable promoter of the French language, who wrote in the Dakar document (1989, 13):

Une de mes convictions est qu'il ne s'agit pas de remplacer l'anglais comme première langue de communication internationale. La superpuissance américaine n'est pas près de s'affaisser. Il est question de se placer au second rang, mais surtout de faire adopter le français comme langue de culture.[14]

The 1990 report on the situation of French in the world states very soberly (Rapport 1990, 14):

Globalement, l'évolution du nombre de francophones, ces dernières années, apparaît relativement limitée, de l'ordre de 4% de 1985 à 1989.

Cet accroissement est très sensiblement inférieur aux prévisions qui avaient pu être faites au début des années 1980 et s'explique notamment par la régression des taux de scolarisation dans nombre de pays et par la dégradation des conditions et de la qualité de l'enseignement[15]

and (1990, 16): 'L'aventure francophone, qui apparaît exaltante à bien des égards, demeure fragile' ('The francophone adventure, which in many respects seems elating, is in fact fragile').

1.3. Private organizations

It is not only individuals and the government who are concerned about the status and quality of the French language. During the second half of the twentieth century many organizations have sprung up in France and throughout the French-speaking world which express sometimes very moderate, but sometimes very strong views, about the threats to the French language posed by English in particular and about its future role in the world.

The important role played by these organizations has been noted on a number of occasions. Stélio Farandjis, secretary-general of the *Haut Conseil de la francophonie*, has declared:[16] 'Tous les pays défendent leur langue. Mais la France est effectivement la seule à posséder des organismes structurés' ('Every country defends its language. But France is in actual fact the only one to have a system of developed organizations'), and Philippe de Saint-Robert, first *commissaire général de la langue française*, has congratulated them,[17] since they 'servent de relais dans le public à l'action des pouvoirs publics, et dont la mission d'information et de mobilisation est ... plus importante que jamais' ('serve as staging posts between the public and the action of official bodies; their mission to inform and mobilize is ... more important than ever'). However, Rapport, 1990, 399–402 mentions only a very small number of the organizations and makes no reference to their contribution to maintaining French.[18] Xavier Deniau, a prime mover in the francophone world (but without official status), paid a glowing tribute to them in the pre-Dakar-summit document already referred to. He said (1989, 56, 57):

La contribution des associations à la francophonie, je ne dirais pas qu'elle est essentielle parce qu'elle est plus que ça encore. Ce sont les associations qui ont créé la francophonie. Les gouvernements et les administrations ne sont venus que bien longtemps après. Vous en aviez déjà depuis longtemps, mais surtout depuis 1960 où il y a eu une véritable explosion du système associatif en France qui quadrillait le monde francophone ... Les associations ont été très antérieures à l'activité des Etats. Elles continuent à jouer un rôle très important.[19]

He claims that they have a difficult task:

> C'était ... leur reconnaissance par les Etats, ou par les gouvernements, qui était relativement difficile ... En France c'est parce qu'il y a une volonté de monopole de la part des administrations et de l'Etat dès qu'il s'agit d'une affaire publique. Et du moment que la francophonie est devenue affaire nationale, il y a une véritable jalousie (et le terme n'est pas trop fort) de la part des administrations à l'égard des associations qui, souvent, connaissent beaucoup mieux le milieu, les hommes, que ne les connaissent les administrations elles-mêmes ... Je crois que les associations resteront un élément essentiel, et que, faire de la francophonie sans les associations, c'est-à-dire, sans les liens naturels qui réunissent des hommes (*sic*) par la voie de la profession ou des centres d'intérêts communs, me paraît une absurdité.[20]

2. Organizations concerned with safeguarding the French language

2.1. Lists of organizations

In 1977 the *Association francophone d'accueil et de liaison* published an *Annuaire de la Francophonie* containing information about organizations based in France; in 1980 this was expanded to include organizations from other parts of the world dedicated to the cause of defending the French language and the concept of Francophonia. The *Commissariat général de la langue française* combined forces with AFAL in 1984 to produce the first edition of the *Répertoire des organisations et associations francophones*. Further editions appeared in 1987 and 1989, the most recent in 1992. These *Répertoires* are an invaluable resource for anyone investigating the protection of the French language and culture.

Although we have said above that there has been a dramatic growth in the number of organizations committed to protecting the French language in the second half of the twentieth century, there were of course similar organizations in operation much earlier. See Appendix 1.

2.2. Chronological appearance of France-based organizations

There were in fact many more organizations in existence at this time, although they did not have necessarily an exclusively linguistic brief like those mentioned in Appendix 1. The list presented in Appendix 2 details the chronological appearance of France-based organizations which still exist and are recorded in the 1989 and 1992 *Répertoires*. Presumably other organizations have been created and then disbanded before they could appear in the *Répertoires* (like the *Office de la langue française* mentioned in Appendix 1). It should also be noted that not all the organizations which appear in the *Répertoires* are accompanied by the date of their creation.

The differences between the two sets of statistics for the pre-1990 period may be explained by reference to the criterion for inclusion in the *Répertoires* mentioned in the next section.

Apart from that, the statistics scarcely require any comment. Taking the 1992 *Répertoire* as a basis for discussion, of the 241 organizations for which the *Répertoire* provides a date, 15 came into existence before the First World War and only 7 between the wars. Really dramatic development occurs after the 1960s, the 1970s registering more than a 50 per cent increase over the previous decade, and the 1980s, breaking the hundred threshold, more than doubling that tally. The 1990s have got off to an impressive start and promise to exceed the record set by the 1980s.

2.3. The number of organizations

The production of the 1992 *Répertoire* was undertaken by the *Centre de documentation et d'information* of the *Délégation générale à la langue française* (directed by Josseline Bruchet, who had also overseen the production of the previous editions). It is in this *Répertoire* that for the first time the main criterion for including organizations and the methods used for recording their names are explained (*Répertoire* 1992, 5):

> Le principal critère de sélection des organismes cités est l'emploi et la diffusion de la langue française dans le monde culturel, scientifique et technique francophone. Les associations qui figurent dans ce répertoire ont été relevées dans le *Journal officiel de la République française* intitulé 'Associations' puis contactées. Les associations étrangères nous ont été indiquées par les organismes officiels des pays concernés. Certaines d'entre elles ne se trouvant pas dans ce répertoire, soit n'ont pas répondu après deux rappels, soit n'ont pas souhaité, pour cette année, s'y voir présenter.[21]

From the last sentence it is clear that the *Répertoires* cannot avoid gaps in their service, because of organizations not replying to requests (after being written to a number of times) or simply not wishing to be included (although it is difficult to understand why that should be). The ebb and flow of the organizations and the aleatory nature of their inclusion is underlined by a comparison of the last three editions of the *Répertoire*.[22] The 1987 *Répertoire* records the names of 246 organizations devoted to the francophone cause; the 1989 edition 318, an increase of 72 over the previous edition. However, 87 organizations figure in the 1989 *Répertoire* which were not recorded in the 1987 version. Reference to the dates of entry of the organizations reveals on the other hand that only 20 organizations came into existence between the appearance of the 1987 *Répertoire* and that of 1989. A similar pattern emerges if the 1992 *Répertoire* is compared with the 1989 edition: 115 organizations are recorded for the first time in 1992, but of these 55 were established before 1989 (another 19 are entered without a date); 22 organizations are recorded for 1989, 13 for 1990 and 6 for 1991.

The *Répertoires* contain names of organizations which are based not only in France but throughout the Francophone world and beyond. The figures given in Appendix 3 show the extent to which the present and future of Francophonia is a concern of countries other than France.

One or two organizations are included more than once in these figures, since they are represented in more than one country (for example, the *Association des universités partiellement ou entièrement de langue française* has offices in France, Haiti, Madagascar, Morocco and Senegal). That said, a total of 220 organizations based in France itself in 1989 and 271 in 1992 remains. (This number includes two organizations based in New Caledonia, both concerned with the Pacific Ocean area, the *Association pour la diffusion des thèses sur le Pacifique francophone* and the *Centre de rencontres et d'échanges internationaux du Pacifique* and one in Guadeloupe, the *Association pour la connaissance des littératures antillaises*; because of the DOM–TOM status of Guadeloupe and New Caledonia, it seems appropriate to consider these three organizations as forming part of the France-based contingent.)

In the 1989 *Répertoire* official organizations account for 19 of the total number of organizations – 6 international, 3 based in France, 2 in Senegal and 1 in Burkina Faso, and 13 national, 9 in France, 2 in Belgium and 2 in Canada. Deducting the France-based ones from the total of 220 leaves 208 non-governmental organizations based in France. For the 1992 edition the figures are as follows: 14 international organizations (7 based in France, 3 each in Canada and Senegal and 1 in Burkina Faso), and 19 national ones (15 in France, 2 each in Belgium and Canada); consequently there are 238 private France-based organizations.

2.4. The names of the organizations

The names chosen by the organizations have their own interest and certainly provide ample proof of what has been called the 'riche vie associative' in France. See Appendix 4.

Excluded from the 1989 list are such evocative titles as *Le Clair-mirouère du temps, INTERMEDIA, Les Nuits francophones Rhône-Alpes, Les Taxis de la Marne*, all of which fail to appear in the 1992 list. The names included in the 1992 *Répertoire* seem much more prosaic, *Les Dossiers d'Aquitaine et d'ailleurs* being the most imaginative.

3. The meaning of Francophonia

In a speech delivered to the members of the *Haut Conseil de la franco-phonie*, ambassadors, the press, top civil servants and 'associations' in March 1985, one year after the creation of the *Conseil*, President Mitterrand said: 'En France plus de 300 associations reçoivent des aides de l'Etat au titre de la francophonie. Elle s'en servent bien en général, mais cette multiplicité entraîne une certaine dispersion' ('In France there are more than 300 organizations which receive aid from the State in the name of Francophonia. In most cases they use it well, but this multiplicity produces a certain dispersion of impact'). According to a more recent brochure published by the *Haut Conseil de la francophonie* and describing its work,

> De nombreuses associations se consacrent à la francophonie, dans les domaines les plus divers, de l'enseignement à la recherche scientifique en passant par la littérature ou la presse. Elles constituent un riche tissu et leur liste remplit un répertoire entier.[23]

But what is meant by 'la francophonie'?

The term Francophonia has developed a number of values. Deniau 1992, 14–26 mentions a linguistic, a geographical, a spiritual and mystical, and an institutional meaning. To justify the last, he says (1992, 26):

> en effet, l'appartenance linguistique et géographique à un même ensemble provoque chez les individus un sentiment de participation qui se traduit dans la réalité par la naissance d'associations et d'organisations publiques et privées.[24]

This definition, which might have been thought to apply neatly to the organizations under review, does little to remove the ambiguity which seems to be inherent in the names of many of these organizations. A common alternative to 'francophone' in the titles is 'de langue française', which unfortunately does not reduce the problem. Both these expressions may, at their weakest, refer to the French-speaking world in a very general way, without especially evoking the French language, but rather relating to any matter of common concern to the countries sharing the French language. At the other extreme, at their strongest, they refer specifically to the French language, and the main thrust of the organization in question will be a preoccupation with the quality of French used by the members of the organization or by those people over whom the organization has some influence or even by any speaker of French, whatever her or his origin. In addition, in some cases 'francophone' is contrasted with 'français', where the focus is upon French and non-French nationality.[25]

4. The aims of the organizations

The 1984 *Répertoire* is the only edition to have attempted a thematic categorization of the organizations. Its 'liste thématique' extends over 50 pages, covering approximately one thousand organizations 'ayant une activité éditoriale'. This list was prepared by the *Comité de liaison national des associations culturelles*, and in fact has very little to do with Francophonia, let alone the French language – strangely (or perhaps significantly) it does not have a section on defending the French language, although four linguistics societies are recorded. Amongst the categories mentioned are agriculture 13, astrology 3, astronomy 4, literature 97, history 188, medicine 10, mycology 8, natural sciences 40.

The *Répertoires* assemble organizations with a highly variable range of involvement in and commitment to the French language. Indeed, some of the organizations included in the *Répertoires*, a small minority, it is true, have nothing at all to say about the language. This is the case, for example, with *Lions international de France*, whose objects are 'de perfectionner [la] francophonie et de préparer ... un monde meilleur' ('to enhance Francophonia and prepare ... a better world'), but who are absent from the 1992 edition. Also to be included here is the body with perhaps the widest remit of any of the organizations, the *Académie des sciences, des arts et des lettres*, which groups together members of various national academies and representatives of government to discuss cultural and scientific problems affecting Europe and which obviously does not concern itself with national matters, such as the fate of the French language, as also (not surprisingly) the *Association France–Algérie* and the *Association francophone internationale des directeurs d'établissements scolaires*.

Some of the remaining organizations devote themselves exclusively to defending and promoting the language. Others combine a concern for the language with another, often professional, interest; for example, organizations proposing terminologies, organizations promoting the teaching of French, organizations encouraging links between France and other francophone countries, organizations promoting French and francophone culture. For yet others, the language is a side-issue, but is mentioned regularly in their literature. Time and space do not permit adequate discussion of such organizations here (see Offord 1993).

5. *Conclusion*

The boast that three hundred or so organizations are committed to the cause of protecting Francophonia (see above) needs to be examined in the light of the foregoing analysis. The difficulty resides in the interpretation to be put upon the term 'Francophonie': the ambiguity inherent in the term has been highlighted above, where it has been shown that it may at one level be applied to the language exclusively but at others can refer to any aspect of human endeavour undertaken by French speakers. However, as hinted earlier, and as will be demonstrated in a paper following this one (see Offord 1993), concern with the language is a leitmotiv running through the constitutions of many of the organizations, even of those whose major concern is with a matter far removed from the language. The statement made by President Mitterrand in 1985 (quoted above) seems to provide only lukewarm approval of the work of the organizations, and that is certainly the impression gained by Xavier Deniau (see above). However, the energy and commitment of the leaders of these organizations cannot be questioned, and although one may at times be distressed by the chauvinism of certain statements issuing from them, it is clear that they provide an important service to the French-speaking world. The most strident in its attitude is the recently created *Association francophone avenir*, which lists amongst its aims (*Répertoire* 1992, 55): 'dénoncer l'emprise de la langue anglaise en France; s'élever contre le bilinguisme français-anglais en France'('to denounce the ascendancy of the English language in France; to rise up against French-English bilingualism in France'). The organizations referred to in this paper make available much valuable information about the position and condition of French in France and the rest of the world, they publicize meetings and *stages*, they provide meeting-places for those sharing their convictions and keep the state of the French language in the forefront of the minds of as many leaders of francophone countries as possible. As will be demonstrated elsewhere, what is surprising, considering the large number of organizations listed in the *Répertoires*, is the small degree of overlap of interest between them. Specialization seems to be the name of the game. The somewhat haphazard way in which organizations are recorded in the *Répertoires* was mentioned earlier. What is clear, however, is that not only are numbers increasing as time progresses, but that there is also enthusiasm on the part of the leaders of the organizations to have them registered in the *Répertoires*. In fact certain names occur frequently as president of several organizations.[26] It is also quite evident that much of the impetus for an individual organization derives from the personality and commitment of its founder, and as that person disappears from the scene, so the impact of the organization declines. This would go some way to explaining why certain organizations are prepared to correspond regularly and provide generous documentation about themselves, whereas others seem extremely reluctant to enter into correspondence or discussion, despite friendly gestures on the part of interested parties. This is all the more sad in the case of certain organizations which used to co-operate in this respect but have now ceased doing so.

6. *A personal note*

I have always been a great admirer of the endurance of Edmond Edmont in criss-crossing France on his bicycle on behalf of Jules Gilliéron and the *Atlas linguistique de la France*. I have also read with great interest in the various linguistic atlases appearing under the auspices of the *CNRS* of the exploits and ingenuity of field workers when eliciting evidence of the rapidly disappearing dialects of France. So much so that, because not all the organizations I had written to had deigned to reply, and new ones had appeared in the 1992 *Répertoire* which I did not discover until the end of March 1992, I thought I would conduct my own small piece of field work. Consequently I allowed myself five days in Paris to track down and interview a certain number of organizations. My diary reads as follows:

Day 1: planned route.
Day 2: raining but excited; first foray; a number of organizations cluster around same address; should be able to kill many birds with one stone; on arrival discover office opens only between 10 and 1 on my last day; disillusioned.
Day 3: raining; located first address but could find no evidence of organization; imprisoned in courtyard for quarter of an hour unable to find way out; second address turned out to be a pet shop; third open between 9 and 12; I arrived at 14.50; fourth address: business on right sent me left, business on left sent me right; found a plaque bearing name of organization but no sign of an office; fifth address turned out to be a private apartment, but no one at home. Abandoned field work for the day.
Day 4: raining; disagreement between *arrondissement* number given in the *Répertoire* and map; decided to follow map; discovered large forbidding

black door with no evidence of any organization; returned to address 3 of Day 3 – open, but scarcely came up to expectations: the name, the *Association pour la promotion de la langue française dans le monde du travail* led me to believe that its object was to protect the French language in the workplace; as I joined a queue of African and Oriental faces and consulted the receptionist, it became clear that I was in a literacy centre; scoured every nook and cranny of next location; again no sign of life; fed up.

Day 5: last chance; returned to address located on Day 2; welcomed with open arms, laden with brochures and publicity – only trouble was I was already familiar with this organization; the others at the same address had moved; a bitter-sweet experience. Edmond Edmont, eat your heart out! Returned to security of my office in England.

A strange discrepancy emerged between the grandiose entries appearing in the *Répertoires* and reality on the ground. The organizations seem more like Scarlet Pimpernels leaping to the aid of a much-loved language, and proving extremely elusive to anyone wanting to pin them down. However, when an encounter actually occurs, it can be both warm and fruitful.

Appendix 1

Bengtsson (1968) mentions the following organizations:

the *Haut Comité pour la défense et l'expansion de la langue française*, founded in 1966 (a government body)

the *Office de la langue française*, founded 1937, discontinued 1942

the *Cercle de Presse Richelieu*, 1953, becoming *Défense de la langue française* in 1958, and continuing to function

the *Office du vocabulaire français*, 1957 (does not feature in the 1980 *Annuaire*)

the *Fédération du français universel*, 1963 (disappears from the 1987 *Répertoire*)

the *Association pour le bon usage du français dans l'administration*, 1967 (does not figure in the 1984 *Répertoire*).

Appendix 2

The chronological appearance of France-based organizations:

Recorded in both the 1989 and 1992 *Répertoires*:

1838	*Société des gens de lettres de France*
1859	*Société d'éthnographie de Paris*
1860	*Alliance israélite universelle*
1873	*Office de promotion de l'édition*
	Société de législation comparée

1883	*Alliance française*
1892	*Syndicat national de l'édition*
1893	*Comité du rayonnement français*
1902	*Association des professeurs de langue vivante de l'enseignement public*
	Mission laïque française
	Société des poètes français
1911	*Association des professeurs de lettres*
1916	*Renaissance française*
1919	*Fédération française des Sociétés de sciences naturelles*

Recorded in the 1992 *Répertoire* only:

| 1856 | *Association de l'Œuvre d'Orient* |
| 1915 | *Comité catholique des amitiés françaises dans le monde* |

	1989	*1992*
1920–9	4	4
1930–9	4	2
1940–9	6	9
1950–9	16	13
1960–9	30	30
1970–9	42	49
1980–9	91	101
1990		12
1991		5
Total	207	241

Appendix 3

The number of organizations in Francophonia and elsewhere:

	1989	*1992*
in Europe:		
Belgium	26	30
Switzerland	7	9
Italy	2	3
Austria	1	1
Denmark	1	1
Finland	1	1
Germany	1	1
Luxembourg	1	0
Netherlands	0	1
Spain	0	1

in North America:

Canada	41	40
USA	4	6
Haiti	0	1

in South America:

Brazil	4	2
Chile	3	2
Argentina	1	0

in Africa:

Senegal	2	6
Burkina Faso	1	1
Ghana	1	0
Madagascar	0	1
Morocco	0	1
Togo	0	1
Tunisia	0	1
Zaïre	1	0

in Asia:

India	1	1
Total	99	111

Appendix 4

The names of the organizations:

	1989	1992
Académie	3	3
Agence	1	2
Alliance	3	3
Amicale/Amis/Amitié	4	1
Assemblée	0	1
Association	76	98
Atelier	2	1
Bureau	0	1
Centre	12	13
Cercle	4	3
Club	1	1
Comité	9	10
Communauté	1	2
Conférence	2	2

Conseil	1	2
Fédération	7	8
Festival	0	3
Fondation	3	5
Groupe	2	2
Groupement	2	2
Institut	6	8
Ligue	2	1
Mission	2	1
Office	7	3
Rencontre	2	3
Société	14	15
Union	8	9

Notes

[1] Others include Grandjouan 1971, Thévenot 1976, Le Cornec 1981, Duneton 1984, de Broglie 1986, Laurent 1988.

[2] 'As far as the expansion of the French language throughout the five continents is concerned, it is possible for it, given its Olympic character as well as its use as a linguistic meeting-place and a language enabling comprehension among Peoples and of direct interpersonal relations, to play an equilibrating dynamic role in the neuromotor autostructuring of Athletes. Its physiological clarity, its moderation, its conciseness, in a postindustrial period, will guarantee it delimited articulations of collective gestures and languages for active Adults' (*sic*).

[3] See especially the collections of his newspaper articles, 1985 and 1986.

[4] See especially Guenier 1985, de Broglie 1986, Ager 1987 and 1990, Ball 1988, Rickard 1989, Offord 1990 and 1993, Judge 1993.

[5] 'I realize it is barely acceptable these days to speak of defending the language, because the idea of "defence" is suspect: it suggests a narrow-minded, hypersensitive attitude and it runs counter to the dominant trend which sees in English the universal language for communication, to the exclusion of all others. At the risk of incurring more jeers than encouragements, I persist in repeating that our language is threatened and that this threat has repercussions on the future of our nation.'

[6] 'It would, in fact, be ridiculous to ignore, rightly or wrongly, the attraction exercised by the English language, an attraction which according to the *ministre chargé de la Francophonie*, Alain Decaux, in no uncertain terms, French-speakers must be prepared to suffer "in the same way as we suffer storms and scorching summers".'

[7] Reported in the *Bulletin de liaison*, 4 (November 1985), p. 5 of the *Association*.

[8] 'Many solutions have been proposed [to the problem of the diversity of languages in the EC] – a single language, bilingualism, reducing the official languages to three or four, the others remaining as working languages but without any official status. Consideration of this important question will be actively pursued with, as far as we are concerned, the firm desire to avoid any arrangement which, by failing to give French an exclusive position – in our view

obviously the ideal solution – would in the long run endanger the privileged position which should in our opinion be its by right within the European institutions.'

9   Reported in Rapport 1990, 55.

10 'All the indicators ... stand at red: the disappearance of research and scientific conferences in French, lessons given directly in English in an increasing number of schools or institutions of higher education, an increase in bilingual institutions, the attempt to introduce English into primary schools by the *Education nationale*, mail addressed in English to French administrative bodies, rampant anglicization in Brussels, the use of English in internal communication within many private companies whose capital is partially English or American, the increasingly frequent use of English in advertising, the registering of a majority of trademarks and company names in English or pseudo-English.'

11 At the Angers *Assemblée générale* of the *Association internationale des villes francophones de congrès* (see *Dialogues* (December 1983), p. 4, 'Evocation de la francophonie').

12 'It is possible to observe an effort which is at one and the same time colossal and insidious on the part of England, and especially the United States, to make English the sole world language ... American cultural imperialism tends to impose English as the sole world language. French cultural imperialism, which is infinitely weaker, seeks to prevent English from becoming a world language by consolidating the use of French among 3 per cent of the world population, by attempting to preserve or claw back a small space for French.'

13 'To counter the obvious reduction in demand for the French language, [the *Conseil*] is to make recommendations suggesting that more realistic and more offensive steps be taken than in the past. It is in fact less a question of preventing a knowledge of other languages in France than of facilitating a fuller penetration of French into non-French-speaking countries, and especially into the most industrialized ones.'

14 'It is one of my convictions that what is at stake is not a matter of replacing English as the first language of international communication. The American superpower is not on the verge of collapse. What is at stake is for French to assume a secondary position, but especially to get French adopted as a language of culture.'

15 'Globally speaking, in recent years, growth in the number of French-speakers appears relatively limited, of the order of 4% from 1985 to 1989. This increase is very noticeably lower than the forecasts which had been made at the beginning of the 1980s and may be explained particularly by the decline in the numbers of children receiving education in many countries and the deterioration in the conditions and quality of teaching.'

16 Reported in *Dialogues*, December 1983.

17 Reported in the *Bulletin de liaison* of the *Association pour la défense du français et du patrimoine linguistique européen*, 4, November 1985, p. 3.

18 This attitude accords with comments made from the government perspective by de Broglie 1986, 225 and from the perspective of the organizations themselves by Xavier Deniau, mentioned in what follows.

19 'I would not say that the contribution of the organizations to Francophonia is essential, because it is much more than that. It is the organizations which have created Francophonia. Governments with their administrations arrived on the scene long afterwards. They [the organizations] have been around for a long time already, but especially since 1960, when there was a veritable explosion in

the network of associations in France, which went on to embrace the whole of the French-speaking world ... The organizations predate the State's involvement. They continue to play a very important role.'

[20] 'It was ... being recognized by the States, or the governments, that was relatively difficult for them. In France this is because there is a desire on the part of the government and the State to impose a monopoly as soon as an affair in the public domain is concerned. And from the moment that Francophonia became a national matter, there was a veritable jealousy (and the term is not too strong) on the part of the administration with regard to the organizations, which often had a fuller knowledge of the circumstances and personalities involved than the administration itself ... I believe that the organizations will remain an essential element, and that to create Francophonia without the organizations, that is without the natural bonds linking men [*sic*] by means of their professions or common interests, is an absurdity.'

[21] 'The main criterion for selecting the organizations quoted is the use and expansion of the French language in the French-speaking cultural, scientific and technical world. The organizations which appear in this inventory have been taken from the *Journal officiel de la République française* entitled "Associations" and then contacted. Foreign organizations have been referred to us by the official bodies of the countries concerned. Some which do not appear in this inventory either did not reply after two reminders or did not wish to be recorded this year.'

[22] The first international edition, of 1980, contained details of 254 organizations; that of 1984 a slight decrease, to 245.

[23] 'A number of organizations are dedicated to Francophonia, in the most diverse domains, from teaching to scientific research via literature or the press. They constitute a rich canvas and fill a complete inventory.'

[24] 'In fact, belonging linguistically and geographically to one and the same collectivity arouses a sense of participation among the individuals concerned; this sense of participation is manifested in reality by the development of both public and private organizations.'

[25] Compare the description of the objectives of the *Association des écrivains de langue française* in the *Répertoires*: 'Faire connaître les œuvres et les écrivains français et francophones' ('To make known French and French-speaking works and writers'). Rapport 1990, 36 also refers to the additional difficulty of distinguishing 'francophones occasionnels' ('occasional French-speakers') and 'francophones réels' ('genuine French-speakers').

[26] This point is examined in more detail in Offord 1993, 181, 182; suffice it to mention here that Xavier Deniau is associated with at least five organizations and 5 rue de la Boule Rouge is the home of four.

References

Ager, D. 1987. 'La politique linguistique de la France contemporaine', *ACTIF*, 31–40.

—— 1990. *Sociolinguistics and Contemporary French*, Cambridge: Cambridge University Press.

Ball, R. 1988. 'Language insecurity and state language policy: the case of France', *Quinquereme* (11), 95–105.

Bengtsson, S. 1968. *La Défense organisée de la langue française: étude sur l'activité de quelques organismes qui depuis 1937 ont pris pour tâche de veiller à la correction et à la pureté de la langue française*, Uppsala.

Cellard, J. 1985 and 1986. *Histoire des mots*, 2 vols., Paris: La Découverte (*Le Monde*).

Cooper, R. L. 1989. *Language Planning and Social Change*, Cambridge: Cambridge University Press.

Dakar 1989. *Troisième sommet de la francophonie*, Paris: Commissariat général de la langue française/Mermon.

de Broglie, G. 1986. *Le Français pour qu'il vive*, Paris: Gallimard.

Deniau, X. 1992. *La Francophonie*, Paris: PUF, 2e éd.

du Bellay, 1549. *La Deffence et illustration de la langue francoyse*, ed. Chamard, H., Paris: Didier, 1945.

Duneton, C. 1984. *A hurler le soir au fond des collèges*, Paris: Seuil.

Etiemble, R. 1964. *Parlez-vous franglais?* Paris: Gallimard.

Grandjouan, O. 1971. *Les Linguicides*, Brussels: Duculot.

Guenier, N. 1985. 'La crise du français en France' in *La Crise des langues*, Paris: Le Robert, 5–38.

Hagège, C. 1987. *Le Français et les siècles*, Paris: Odile Jacob.

Judge, A. 1993. 'French: a planned language?' in Saunders, C. (ed.), *French Today; Language in its Social Context*, Cambridge: Cambridge University Press, 7–26.

Laurent, J. 1988. *Le Français en cage*, Paris: Grasset.

Le Cornec, J. 1981. *Quand le français perd son latin*, Paris: Belles-Lettres.

Offord, M. 1990. *Varieties of Contemporary French*, London: Macmillan.

—— 1993 'Protecting the French language – the role of private organizations', *French Cultural Studies* (4), 167–84.

Rapport 1990. *Etat de la francophonie dans le monde, Rapport 1990*, Paris: Haut Conseil de la Francophonie (la Documentation française).

Répertoire 1992. *Organisations et associations francophones*, Paris: Délégation générale à la langue française (la Documentation française).

Rickard, P. 1989. *A History of the French Language*, 2nd edn., London: Unwin Hyman.

Sauvageot, A. 1973. *Français d'hier ou français de demain?* Paris: Nathan.

Thévenot, J. 1976. *Hé! La France, ton français fout le camp*, Brussels: Duculot.

6

Language standardization and political rejection: the Romanian case

MARIA M. MANOLIU

As has been often pointed out, the choice of a particular dialect or register as a standard is usually based on considerations of socio-political and/or cultural 'prestige' (see for example, Price 1976). The phenomenon dealt with in this paper originates in a very different psycho-political attitude, since what is involved is not the prestige of a given register but the rejection for political reasons of a certain type of speech. More specifically, we consider how such rejection has differently affected an Eastern European language, Romanian, in its homeland in the communist and post-communist era and in the freer ambience of the Western world.

For some forty-five years after the Second World War, Romanian underwent two major splits:

(i) in Romania itself, between the 'official language', which came to be referred to as *limbă de lemn* ('wooden language') or, in French, *langue de bois*, see Thom (1987) and Manoliu (1988, 1989), and the language of intellectuals as reflected mainly in literary periodicals; and

(ii) between these two registers on the one hand and the language of the newspapers and other publications of Romanian emigrants, especially in America, on the other hand. This latter phenomenon, i.e. the rejection by emigrant communities, for political reasons, of features of Romanian as written in Romania is still in evidence, appearing at various levels but particularly in the choice of innovative lexical procedures.

The first part of the paper will analyse the innovative procedures in the literary periodicals published in Romania, which were aimed at opposing – at least by their high intellectual level and their linguistic register –

the clichés of daily papers that were invaded by the characteristics of a 'wooden language'.

The second part will present the ways and means of innovating in the language of the Romanian papers published in the United States by those strata of immigrants who aimed to eliminate any trace of changes that had occurred in the Romanian language as it had developed in their native land, voicing, in this way, their opposition to the regime in power.

1. The Romanian of intellectuals in Romania itself

Although Romania formed part of the Soviet bloc, Romanian periodicals, especially those of a literary character, contained throughout the communist period a high proportion of words and expressions drawn from Western European languages, foremost among them, in line with a long cultural tradition, French. This represented an act of covert political protest.

1.1. Borrowings

As in the past, the basis of Romanian adaptations from French is usually the written form rather than the oral sequence of phonemes. Many such borrowings have a corresponding term in standard Romanian (SR), for example:

(1) *sujet* 'subject' (Fr. *sujet*) – SR *subiect*; *policier* 'policeman' (Fr. *policier*) – SR *polițist*; *mefient* 'mistrustful' (Fr. *méfiant*) – SR *neîncrezător* 'mistrustful';

while others do not, for example:

(2) *truculență* 'vividness' (Fr. *truculence*), *propensiune* 'propensity' (Fr. *propension*), *coliziune* 'collision' (Fr. *collision*).

Anglicisms occasionally occur, for example:

(3) *flash-back* (the title of a column in the weekly periodical *România literară*), *ocurență*, *topică*, with the meaning of English 'occurrence', 'topic' respectively,

as do Latinisms, for example:

(4) *duct* 'approach', *summum* 'peak', *varii* 'various', and so on.

1.2. Derivation

Most innovations fall into this category, the suffix being morphologically integrated into Romanian patterns while the stems are sometimes not. There seems to be a particular liking for abstract nouns derived from adjectives by means of such general Romance suffixes as *-(it)ate* (cf. *amabilitate* 'amiability', *bunătate* 'goodness'), for example:

(5) *limpiditate* 'clearness' (cf. SR *limpezime* corresponding to the adjective *limpede*), *idealitate* 'idealness' (SR *ideal* 'ideal'), *poeticitate* 'poeticaliness' (from SR *poetic* 'poetical').

There are also cases in which there is no corresponding SR adjective, for example:

(6) *amenitate* 'amenity', *alteritate* 'otherness' (from Fr. *aménité*, *altérité*).

Other abstract nouns are formed by means of other, well-integrated, suffixes such as *-eţe*, *-oare*, for example:

(7) *imediateţe*, from *imediat* 'immediate'(cf. such old standard forms as *frumuseţe* 'beauty', from *frumos* 'beautiful'), *lentoare* 'slowness' from *lent* 'slow' (SR *încetineală* from *încet* 'slow') (cf. *amploare* 'ampleness').

Certain adjectives have a pseudo-derivative structure even when the corresponding nominal or verbal stem does not exist in Romanian, for example from a single issue (15.9) of *România literară* (hereafter *RL*):

(8) *grabă auctorială* 'authorial haste' – the noun stem **auctor* (cf. Latin *auctor*) does not exist in Romanian;

(9) *o proză expresionistă tensionată* 'a tense expressionist prose', which implies a non-existent verb **a tensiona* (cf. SR *tensiune* 'tension');

(10) *un lirism vaticinar* 'a prophetic lyricism', implying non-existent **a vaticina* 'to prophesy' (cf. Fr. *vaticiner*, but SR *a profeţi, profetic* – adjective);

(11) (*comunicare*) *terifiantă* 'terrifying communication', implying non-existent **a terifia* (cf. Fr. *terrifier*, Eng. *to terrify*, but SR *a înspăimânta*).

The adjectival participial form *-ant* (corresponding to the Romanian present participial ending *-ând*, for example *cântând* 'singing' from *a cânta* 'to sing'), which represents a reduction of relative clauses with an active verb, is also a recent borrowing from French, for example:

(12) *motive structurante ale imaginaţiei* (*RL*, 15.13) 'motifs which structure the imagination', *copiant* (ibid.) 'copying'.

The causative suffix *-iza* is very productive in verbal derivation, for example:

(13) *a minoriza* (ibid.) 'to transform into something minor' from *minor*; *a (se) ambiguiza* (ibid.) 'to transform (oneself) into something ambiguous' from *ambiguu* 'ambiguous', and so on.

1.3. Compounds

Compound forms range from unsurprising parasynthetic structures like *cosubstanţialitate* 'cosubstantiality' (*RL*, 15.9) to strange combinations of brand-new prefixes with more common stems, such as *cosmocomicărie* (ibid.) from *cosmo-* (as in *cosmopolit* 'cosmopolitan') + *comicărie* 'prank, buffoonery'.

1.4. Semantic transfer

Several items have undergone a semantic transfer. For example, in an utterance such as:

(14) *planimetria verticalei şi spaţialitatea spiralei* (*RL*, 15.13) 'the two-dimensionality of the vertical and the three-dimensionality of the spiral', *planimetria*, which in *Dicţionarul limbii romîne moderne* ('Dictionary of the Modern Romanian Language' 1958, hereafter *DLRM*) and *Mic dicţionar enciclopedic* ('Little Encyclopaedic Dictionary', 1978, hereafter *MDE*), is defined as either a part of topography or a part of geometry, is contrasted with *spaţialitatea* and so assumes the meaning of 'two-dimensionality', in accordance with the meaning of *plan* 'plane' as contrasted with *spaţiu* 'space'.

Ocurenţă, defined in *DLRM* and *MDE* as the form in which a mineral is found, has the meaning of English 'occurrence' in:

(15) *obiecte care au avut iniţial ocurenţa în durata reveriei* (*RL*, 15.13) 'objects which initially occurred in the course of the reverie'.

1.5. Neologisms as a window to the West

For our present purposes, a neologism is taken to be a form that occurs in neither *DLRM* nor *MDE* or, in some instances, in only one of them. In just two issues of *România literară*, from the period when the personality cult around Nicolae and Elena Ceauşescu was already fully developed, namely 15 (1982), nos 9 and 13, there are forty-two such neologisms. This illustrates an important characteristic of the literary style in question which renders it inaccessible both to less educated people in Romania itself and to various strata of emigrants who left Romania in the 1940s and 1950s. Examples (some of them given in context and commented on above) are:

(16) (forms given in neither dictionary): *alteritate* 'otherness', *auctorial* 'authorial', *a insolita* 'to render unusual' (the adjective *insolit* 'unusual' is itself given as a Gallicism in *DLRM* while *MDE* proposes a dual – that is, French and Latin – etymology), *lentoare* 'slowness', *limpiditate* 'clearness' (*DLRM* gives the synonyms *limpezime, limpeziciune,* and *MDE* gives *limpezime, limpezeală*), *mefient* 'mistrustful' (Fr. *méfiant*), *tensionat* 'tense', *truculenţă* 'vividness', *vaticinar* 'prophetic';

(17) (not in *DLRM*) *cizelură* 'chiselling' (from Fr. *ciselure* (*MDE*)), *summum* 'peak';

(18) (not in *MDE*) *amenitate* 'amenity', *propensiune* 'propensity', *superbie* 'haughtiness' ('rare' according to *DLRM*), *variu* 'varied' (a Latinism according to *DLRM*).

A few of these neologisms seem to have been rapidly integrated into the standard literary vocabulary. For example, whereas in 1958 *DLRM* lists *terifiant* and *insolit* as French words, twenty years later *MDE* accepts them with the qualification 'livresc' (i.e. found in books) and 'neologism' respectively.

The unlisted terms represent 52 per cent of the total (22 out of 42).[1] Thirteen (or 31 per cent) cannot be accounted for in terms of established derivational processes, for example *duct, terifiant, vaticinar,* and so on, a fact which could render them less easy to integrate and hence reduce their chances of survival.

Furthermore, judged according to the sociolinguistic criterion of necessity, other innovations that correspond to widespread standard forms are unlikely to survive; for example, in the following contexts, from *RL,* 15.9 (see examples (19), (20), (22), and (23)) and 15.13 (see (21)), *a proclama* could be substituted for *a clama* 'to claim' (see (19)), *a ajunge* or *a avea acces* for *a accede* 'to reach' (see (20)), *încetineală* or *zăbavă* for *lentoare* 'slowness' (see (21)), *neîncrezător* for *mefient* 'mistrustful' (see (22)), etc.:

(19) *lumina numai mie mi-a fost hărăzită, clamează acesta* 'the light has been granted only to me, this one [i.e. the author] claims'
(20) *autorul accede [...] într-o zonă de pure esenţe şi dimensiuni absolute* 'the author reaches [...] an area of absolute essences and dimensions'
(21) *să se mişte într-un spaţiu al lentorii* 'that one move [i.e. subjunctive] within a space of slowness'
(22) *în spiritul noii generaţii de prozatori, mefientă faţă de marile construcţii epice* 'in the spirit of the new generation of prose-writers, mistrustful of large epic constructions'.

Other unlisted forms, however, are not synonymous with standard forms. To take two further examples from *RL*, 15.13, *a minoriza* 'to render minor' could not be replaced by *a micşora* 'to make smaller' in (23), or *a se ambiguiza* 'to become ambiguous' by *a se dedubla* 'to take two forms' in (24):

> (23) *minorizări ale situaţiilor documentare* 'rendering minor the documentary situations'.
> (24) *era nevoit să se ambiguizeze în mărturisirea crezului politic şi moral* 'he was obliged to become ambiguous in the confession of his political and moral creed'.

2. Playing with semantic interpretations

2.1. Substandard Romanian in the 'official' communist press

As I have shown elsewhere (Manoliu 1988), the 'official' language of Romanian daily newspapers has been profoundly influenced by substandard registers elevated to the level of political discourse by ill-educated party officials, who were ignorant of or deliberately rejected more cultured registers. This 'new' political language was elaborated as a means of manipulation for political ends, aimed primarily at interposing a politically construed world between reality, thought, and language, and at severing the normal links between them. To achieve this purpose, political discourse made play with semantic features, with connotations, and with contextual meanings.

To decode most of the political clichés of the communist period in Romania, one had, so to speak, to play a game of antonyms, reversing the 'polarity' of lexemes and phrases and reinterpreting what would be positive connotations at the semantic level of invariants as negative meanings at the contextual level. So, widely used clichés such as:

> (25) *cel mai iubit fiu al poporului* 'the most beloved son of the people' (i.e. Ceauşescu);
> (26) *20 de ani lumină* 'twenty shining years' (with reference to the Ceauşescu period);
> (27) *epoca Ceauşescu – epoca de aur a istoriei României* 'the Ceauşescu era – the Golden Age of Romanian history';
> (28) *fericirea şi bunăstarea întregului popor* 'the happiness and the welfare of the whole people'

were decoded as, respectively, 'the hated tyrant who in no way represents the Romanian people'; 'twenty years of darkness'; 'the Ceauşescu period – the period of Romania's greatest suffering and greatest economic decline'; and 'the misery of the whole people'.

Sometimes, however, the fear that such a negative decoding might be too easy to access led to the quest for more sophisticated ways of concealing interpretations that would meet normal truth conditions. For example, the expression *muncă voluntară*, literally 'voluntary work', a key phrase in the 1950s and 1960s, easily decodable as 'involuntary, compulsory labour', was later replaced by *muncă patriotică* 'patriotic work'. A simple switch to the antonymous meaning 'anti- or unpatriotic work' would not be an appropriate representation of the situation. To arrive at the truth one must analyse those inherent features of the adjective which are reversible in the context. In this specific case, 'the usefulness of the activity for the nation' – a core feature of 'patriotic' – had to be inverted to 'useless, of no benefit either to the nation or to individuals', since, in most cases, the activity in question constituted compulsory manual labour on the part of intellectuals, who were totally lacking in the skills necessary for work in the fields or on building sites, with consequent damaging effects both on the individuals concerned and on the economy.

A further example is the avoidance of such terms as *inflaţie* 'inflation' and *scumpirea produselor* 'increase in the price of produce' by means of ambiguous expressions such as *reaşezarea preţurilor* 'the resetting of prices' (prices being governmentally controlled).[2]

2.2. 'Transitional' reinterpretations

The contemporary (that is, post-1989) language is not free of political clichés and substandard expressions of the same type as those imposed on it during the communist period. The same polarization and opposition between, on the one hand, the users of substandard Romanian as the vehicle of a communist regime and, on the other hand, educated people (most of them intellectuals, scholars and artists) who now have the opportunity to express openly their opposition to the ideology of the regime, is evident in a new type of rejection.

2.2.1.
When, for the first time for over twelve years, I returned to Romania in 1990, I discovered that various words and expressions that had still had their normal connotations when I left Romania in 1977 had meanwhile become virtually unusable. This is, for example, the case with:

(29) *comitetul executiv*, which I proposed to use (and had regularly used in America) as the Romanian title of the Executive Committee of the American-Romanian Academy, but for which I was obliged, in Romania, to substitute *consiliul director* (= more or less

'board of management') as the former term had come to be too specifically associated with the Communist Party.

2.2.2. Words or expressions used more recently by representatives of the mass media supporting the post-1989 regime (which are therefore not a carry-over from the Ceauşescu period) are also liable to be rejected, when considered tainted with neo-communist connotations. For example, on a return visit to Romania in 1991 I was advised to avoid, when addressing press conferences, the expression (30) *oameni de bine*, corresponding to French *hommes de bien*.[3] The explanation I was given links this rejection to the fact that, at the beginning of 1990, a TV commentator advanced the idea that moral features such as those implied by *oameni de bine* should be used as criteria for judging people and criticized the position of some opposition members who started to talk about judgements on the basis of the degree of involvement in the policies of the former regime.

2.2.3. Certain everyday colloquialisms used by President Iliescu in the course of political remarks have attracted attention precisely because of the fact that they belong to a linguistic register (with pornographic connotations) that is highly inappropriate for the context in which they were uttered. Consequently, many intellectuals now find it impossible to use these expressions without ironic intent. For example, an expression such as:

(31) *să fiarbă în suc propriu*, literally 'let them stew in their own juice', but having the idea of 'give them time to let their anger subside'

is likely to be interpreted ironically because of the fact that the President used it when urged to clear the streets of anti-government demonstrators (many of them intellectuals and students) who occupied University Square in Bucharest and the adjoining boulevard for some weeks in the spring of 1990.

Another example from the same source that has acquired similar overtones is provided by the expression:

(32) *nu-mi puneţi sula în coaste*, literally 'don't stick an awl in my ribs', that is 'don't hold a knife to my throat',

used by the President in response to opposition calls for decisive action at a particular moment of sociopolitical crisis.

2.2.4. A reverse phenomenon, the change from a negative to a positive connotation, is illustrated by the semantic evolution of the word *golan*. Before the events in University Square in April–May 1990 (see the comment on (31) above), the term had the derogatory meaning 'ruffian, vagabond, hooligan, good-for-nothing'. But in May 1990, it was used by the President with reference to the people protesting against 'neo-communism'. A slogan and a song dating from those days glorify the word *golan* by contrasting it with *activist* 'apparatchik, communist party functionary' with the result that *golan* acquired the meaning of 'a protestor against communism and conservative forces'. The refrain of the song runs:

(33)   *Mai bine haimana decît trădător*
          Mai bine huligan decît dictator
          Mai bine golan decît activist...
          Mai bine mort decît comunist.[4]

'Better a tramp than a traitor, better a hooligan than a dictator, better a *golan* than an apparatchik, better dead than communist.'

2.2.5. Those linked to conservative groups call into question words and expressions referring to Western democratic institutions. Even the term *democrație* 'democracy' has become a prime target of conserva-tive newspapers, which try to reverse its positive meaning by associ-ating it with derogatory expressions, as in:

(34) *În concluzie și cu mult înainte de a pomeni măcar a zecea parte din probe: s-o lăsăm mai ușurel cu democrația [...]. E la fel de utopică și de mincinoasă democrația ca și ideea comunistă! (Totuși iubirea* (1992) 72.3, p. 2). 'In conclusion and long before mentioning even a tenth of the evidence, let's forget about democracy [...]. It [= democracy] is just as Utopian and false as the communist idea!'

2.2.6. The most interesting phenomenon in this transitional period is, in fact, the absence of any prestige register, outside or inside the borders of Romania. In a euphoric interpretation of freedom of expression, writers and journalists use low colloquial registers, even pornographic expressions, as a kind of linguistic shock-therapy. In brief, they accept the previously rejected registers and reject not only former political clichés but also widely accepted registers (see for example the language of the extremist newspaper *România mare*).

3. American Romanian – a new standard?

Since Romanian has no official status in the United States, Romanian-language newspapers published there or in Canada can play a major role in the process of language standardization. Although newcomers from Romania have regularly brought in innovations that had appeared in Romania itself, these have frequently been rejected by many of those who belong to earlier strata of immigrants because of their 'communist' associations. On the other hand, the fact that terms absent from the contemporary standard in Romania itself occur widely in newspapers published in North America may confer on them the status of standard forms for Romanian-speaking communities served by these newspapers. The papers in question provide a substantial corpus of data illustrating the split between the two varieties of the language (indigenous and American) in respect of their ways and means of standardization.

The standardization of American Romanian has, as we shall see, been much influenced by American linguistic and socio-cultural patterns and by a sustained effort to preserve the cultural values of a tradition free of what one may term communist influence.

3.1. Romanian versus Romanian

3.1.1. The socio-cultural patterns of successive waves of Romanian immigrants to North America have been very different,[5] with the result that, in the process of standardization, American Romanian may have chosen variants that in Romania would be considered dialectal, e.g. *jiu* instead of *apă* 'water', *lichid* 'liquid', or *sos* 'sauce, gravy', as in:

> (35) *cartofii se servesc garnitură lângă carnea prăjită, peste jiul for-*
> *mat (Micromagazin* [a weekly published in New York], no. 114,
> p. 140) 'potatoes are served as a garnish with fried meat, on which
> the gravy is poured'.

or archaic, as in *ospătare* for *masă* 'meal', or substandard, for example *mișcați-vă!* (literally 'move yourself!') for *acționați!* 'act now!' or 'get a move on!'.

3.1.2. Differences (especially of a political nature) among Romanian immigrants may become a disintegrating factor at the linguistic level. A classic example, and one that is more than a mere matter of orthography, is that of the spelling of the phoneme /ɨ/ (a high central unrounded vowel). In many words, this may be represented either by *â* (see *a cânta* 'to sing') or by *î* (see *în* 'in') (depending on their Latin etymology), in accordance with the norms laid down by the Romanian Academy in 1932, or only by *î*, as prescribed by the Academy in 1953, for example *a cânta* or *a cînta* 'to sing', *cât* or *cît* 'how much', *pâine* or *pîine* 'bread'. Other examples are provided by 1932 *sunt*, 1953 *sînt* '(I) am, (they) are', and by the substitution of a hyphen in 1953 for the earlier use of an apostrophe to indicate the elision of a vowel, for example 1932 *m'a văzut, n'au venit*, 1953 *m-a văzut, n-au venit* 'he saw me', 'they have not come' (the full forms being *mă* 'me', *nu* 'not'). In spite of recent protests by Romanian linguists, the 1953 orthography is widely regarded as a symbol of oppression, imposed under Soviet influence, for the purpose of playing down the Latin origins of the Romanian language and its links with other Romance languages; cf. the alternative spellings given above with Latin *cantare* 'to sing', *quantum* 'how much', *panis* 'bread', and the use of an apostrophe in other Romance languages to indicate elision, for example French *il m'a vu* 'he saw me' [*me* + *a*], Italian *l'ombra* 'the shade' [*la* + *ombra*], Catalan *l'he vista* 'I have seen her' [*la* + *he*]. The 1953 orthography is therefore rejected in favour of the 1932 orthography by many Romanian Americans.

3.2. *English influence*

In spite of their different socio-cultural patterns and the fact that they arrived at different periods, the various strata of Romanian immigrants to North America have faced more or less the same new world, new institutions, new legal and social structures, for which they have had to find appropriate linguistic expression. This has been achieved by various means, ranging from unintegrated borrowings from English to semantic interference. We shall say no more about borrowings but shall concentrate on other widespread types of change affecting the lexical structure of American Romanian.

3.2.1. Romanian words have undergone semantic change under the influence of a cognate English word, for example:

   (36) *să lipsească de pe piață comoditățile cele mai elementare* (*Curierul* [California], Jan.–March, 1981) 'that the most elementary commodities are not to be found in the market'

– SR *comoditate* means 'comfortableness' or 'indolence'.

   (37) *oricine poate succede in America* (*Cuvântul Românesc* [Hamilton, Ontario], 1981, no 6) 'anybody can succeed in America'.

– SR *a succede* means 'to succeed' only in the sense of 'to follow'.

3.2.2. A Romanian word may change both its meaning and its categorial status under the influence of an English counterpart, for example:

(38) *oficialii români* (*Dreptatea* [New York], 1981, no. 10) 'the Romanian officials'.

– SR *oficialitățile* (SR *oficial* is only an adjective).

3.2.3. A Romanian word may change its form owing to its phonetic similarity to a semantically corresponding English word, for example:

(39) *o politică de amicabilă conviețuire* (*Cuvântul Românesc*, 1980, no. 3) 'a policy of amicable coexistence'

– *amicabil*, influenced by English *amicable*, corresponds to SR *amical* or *amiabil*.

3.2.4. A new Romanian word may be created by changing the meaning and to some extent the form of an English word under the influence of another Romanian word, for example *sofisticărie* 'complicated game, duplicity', as in:

(40) *acești ziariști nu pricep nici sofisticăria sovietică* (*Cuvântul Românesc*, 1980, no. 3) 'these journalists do not even understand Soviet duplicity.'

The word *sofisticărie* seems to be a cross between English *sophistication* and Romanian *șmecherie* 'cunning, duplicity'.[6]

3.2.5. American Romanian uses both suffixes and prefixes to form derivatives that do not exist in SR, as in:

(41) *vă așteptăm cu dragoste și frățietate adevărată* (*America* [Cleveland, Ohio], 75, 1981) 'we are waiting for you with love and true brotherliness'

– *frățietate*, corresponding to SR *frăție* 'brotherliness', has a redundant suffix *-tate* (see 'Neologisms as a window to the West' above, and examples (5) and (6) above); and

(42) *de a reînvia coexistențialismul* (*Cuvântul Românesc*, 1980, no. 3) 'to revive the principle of coexistence'

– *coexistențialism* corresponds to SR *principiul coexistenței (pașnice)* 'the principle of (peaceful) coexistence'. The American Romanian form looks at first sight like a compound of the prefix *co-* and the noun *existențialism* 'existentialism', but, since it clearly has nothing to do with philosophical existentialism, it can be only analysed as a derivative of the noun *coexistență* 'coexistence' and the suffixes *-al*, which derives adjectives from nouns (for example *structural* 'structural' from *structură* 'structure'), and *-ism*, which derives abstract nouns from adjectives (for example *structuralism* from *structural*).

3.2.6. According to a well-known linguistic universal, influences and borrowings first affect the category of the noun (see Moravcsik 1978). The fact that innovative lexical processes in American Romanian also affect verbs and adjectives is an indication that it has attained a certain degree of autonomy with respect to the standard language of Romania itself.

4. Conclusions

Despite the differences that now exist between the standard language in Romania and the language of the North American Romanian press, two underlying common features can be identified:

(i) on the one hand, both varieties are characterized by the rejection of words and expressions (and even morphological features) that are considered as being associated with the communist era – even when the referent has nothing to do with the political sphere;

(ii) on the other hand, either by way of conscious selection or as the result of language interference, both varieties draw on Western languages (including Latin) as a source for lexical innovations, thereby forging and strengthening ties with the Western world.

But the most interesting phenomenon in the changing patterns of present-day Romania consists in the rejection of any prestige register, of any linguistic constraints imposed by previous standard patterns, and of both the cultivated register of intellectuals and the political clichés of apparatchiks, in a euphoric search for freedom of expression.

Notes

[1] Of the twenty-two words in question, only three (*a culpabiliza* 'to induce feelings of guilt', *lentoare*, and *a tensiona*) figure in Florica Dimitrescu, *Dicţionar de cuvinte recente* ('Dictionary of Recent Words'), Bucharest, Albatros, 1982.

[2] The ways in which combinations of expressions and sentences are used in order to violate basic conversational maxims are discussed in Manoliu (1988).

[3] The meaning of *homme de bien* is nowadays expressed by the formula *om bine* (= Fr. *homme bien*).

[4] 'Imnul golanilor' ('The hymn of the *golani*'), from the record *Din cîntecele golanilor*. 1, Cristian Paţurcă, Laura Botolan and Dr. Barbi, Producer and Exporter: IRMAG SRL, August, 1991.

[5] It is beyond the scope of this paper to elaborate on the historical background, i.e. on the successive waves of Romanian immigrants to North America – for details, see Manoliu, 1985.

⁶ In any case, the suffix *-ărie* is not very productive in contemporary SR (cf. *apărie* 'a lot of water', an old Romanian formation from *apă* 'water').

References

Dicţionarul limbii romîne moderne, 1958. Bucharest: Academia R. P. Romîne.

Manoliu-Manea, M. 1985. 'A divergent standardization. American Romanian versus Standard Romanian', *Journal of the American Romanian Academy*, 6–7, 104–15.

—— 1988. 'Grice's conversational maxims and the Romanian political discourse', *Journal of the American Romanian Academy*, 11, 83–94.

—— 1989. 'Metamorphoses of time in Romanian political discourse', *Journal of the American Romanian Academy*, 12, 63–75.

Mic dicţionar enciclopedic, 2nd edn. 1978. Bucharest: Editura enciclopedică română.

Moravcsik, E. A. 1978. 'Universals of language contact', in Greenberg, J. H. (ed.), *Universals of Human Language*, Stanford: Stanford University Press, I, 93–120.

Price, G. 1976. 'Language standardization in the Romance field', *Semasia*, 3, 7–32.

Thom, F. 1987. *La langue de bois*. Paris: Juillard.

7

Syntactic anglicisms in Spanish: exploitation or innovation?[1]

CHRISTOPHER J. POUNTAIN

1. In this paper I wish to examine the hypothesis that foreign linguistic influence can bring about innovatory changes in a language's syntactic structure. The testing-ground for this hypothesis will be the influence of English on the syntax of present-day Spanish. The reality of English influence on the lexical, and possibly other, levels of Spanish is of course beyond dispute. But existing studies of anglicisms have not given the detailed attention to syntax that they might have done[2] and yet have tended, either explicitly[3] or implicitly,[4] to accept that innovatory change in Spanish syntax is being caused by English influence. The uncritical acceptance of this hypothesis is even more surprising since the weight of general linguistic opinion from Whitney onwards (see Haugen 1950, 224) goes against it by considering syntax as the level most resistant to foreign influence. It is surely time, then, that the matter received more detailed and considered investigation.

I intend to consider only data which are clearly established in modern Spanish. Many anglicisms prove to be either essentially ephemeral phenomena which blow hot and cold with fashion and establish no long-term footing in the language, or else they are transitional phenomena which remain recognizably 'foreign' until they are modified to suit the host system or vice versa. (See the distinction made between 'crude' and 'assimilated' anglicisms in Smith (1975); also the various criteria proposed in England and Caramés (1978, 80ff.).)

2. Syntactic anglicisms

2.1 The selectivity of foreign influence

I begin by posing a question which to my knowledge has never been posed, and on which I will insist repeatedly: why should English influence operate in some areas of Spanish syntax and not others? In other words, what is the basis for the selectivity of foreign influence? In the area of lexis, the answer to such a question is easily given: certain semantic fields associated with a characteristic area of anglophone culture (for example sport, technology, business) effectively lend not only words but indeed the concepts those words represent. But why, for instance, should the English passive be apparently so readily adopted in Spanish (see 2.2.1 'The English and Spanish passives' below) whereas, say, there is no reduction in the use of the personal *a* or the subjunctive, or any inclination to use the gerund as a nominal form (see 2.2.2 'Gerund structures' below)? One possible answer is that, as in the area of lexis, English lends syntactic constructions which increase rather than decrease the expressive possibilities of Spanish. Another answer, and the one I will principally argue for here, is that Spanish only borrows what it is in a sense disposed to borrow, patterns which are an extension or further exploitation of those which already exist in the language. These two answers are of course not mutually exclusive.

2.2 Some specific examples

2.2.1 The English and Spanish passives
Increase in the use of the *ser*-passive in Spanish has often been blanketly ascribed to the influence of English (Lorenzo 1971, 92; Pratt 1980, 209). *MEU* is, however, more discriminating, and regards as the true anglicism the passive sentence with (passive) subject first, for example:

(1a) X[5] Un crédito ha sido votado por el Congreso para los damnificados

'A credit has been voted by the Congress for the victims'

the 'acceptable' version being given as

(1b) Ha sido votado un crédito por el Congreso para los damnificados.

It is undeniable that (1b) is strongly preferred by many speakers. But it is far from obvious that the subject-first passive is inherently 'foreign' to Spanish. Examples are to be found regularly in formal register, the most famous being the *GRAE*'s assertion (255) that 'la construcción pasiva es poco usada en castellano'. The *ser*-passive is of course a notoriously 'difficult' area of modern Spanish: it is undoubtedly favoured in some registers rather than others (Green 1975), and the constraints on it are multiplex (Pountain 1992–3). It is no surprise that native speakers feel unease with a sentence like (1a) without being able to say exactly why: one informant accepted without demur such versions as

(1c) Este crédito ha sido votado por el Congreso para los damnificados

'This credit . . .'

(1d) Este crédito para los damnificados ha sido votado por el Congreso

commenting that the problem with (1a) lay not in the word order as such, but rather in the indefinite subject NP. Perhaps another ground for preferring (1d) to (1a) is that (1d) unites the noun and prepositional phrase constituents of the subject NP which are split in (1a).

A number of the syntactic areas supposedly susceptible to innovation through English influence are extremely volatile in the sense that historically they have been subject to long-term processes of restructuring. The passive is such an area. It may be that what we are witnessing today is a slight tendency in certain registers to restore a situation which has become eroded by the rise in frequency of alternative constructions, notably the reflexive passive,[6] and certainly it seems that the *ser*-passive was relatively more frequent in earlier stages of Spanish.[7] If so, then the growing acceptability of subject-first *ser*-passives can be seen within the context of this ongoing process of restructuring.

But to return to (1a). The existence of this sentence may be seen as due to the convergence of a number of semantic and pragmatic requirements: (a) the topicalizing of *un crédito*, which leads to its initial position; (b) the indefinite nature of *un crédito*; and (c) the expression of a *por* agentive phrase. None of the so-called 'alternatives' to the *ser*-passive can cope with these three requirements simultaneously: for example, the reflexive is incompatible with the expression of an agentive phrase:

(1e) ??Un crédito se ha votado por el Congreso . . .

'A credit itself has voted by the Congress'

and a preposed direct object with an active verb construction, while allowing the topicalizing order to be retained, is incompatible with the indefinite nature of the new object NP:

(1f) ??Un crédito lo ha votado el Congreso . . .

'A credit it-OBJECT has voted the Congress'.

On the other hand, the other 'passives' of Spanish (the reflexive and *estar*-passive) freely admit subject-first order, and while in Spanish sentence-types overall there is a well-known propensity to verb-first order (Green 1976), subject-first order is rarely impossible. In short, syntactic analogical pressure and semantic/pragmatic need seem to conspire to favour sentences like (1a), even without the supposed helping hand of English.

We should note also that the parallel with the English passive does not extend so far as to allow passivization on indirect and prepositional objects, and that, as I have argued elsewhere (Pountain 1992-3), the *ser*-passive is aspectually marked, in a way that its formal English counterparts are not, in the present and the imperfect tenses. The possible influence of English is thus at the very least highly selective in this area.

2.2.2 Gerund structures

The English and Spanish gerunds (*-ing/-ndo* forms) are very different in their syntactic properties. The gerund in Spanish almost never acts as an attributive adjective pure and simple: *hirviendo* 'boiling' and *ardiendo* 'burning' are the only candidates, but there is never any adjective-like agreement of gerund and noun (*agua hirviendo* 'boiling water', *casas ardiendo* 'burning houses'). Moliner (1982, 1394) also points out the restriction on the contrastive use of these two gerunds:

(2) *El agua hirviendo es la del puchero pequeño
     'The water boiling is that of-the pot small'
     ('The *boiling* water is in the small pot')
     (but *El agua caliente es la del puchero pequeño* 'The *hot*
        water ...')

     *La hoguera ardiendo está más lejos que la apagada
     'The bonfire burning is more distant than the one-which-has-
        been-extinguished'
     ('The *burning* bonfire is further away than the one which has
        gone out')
     (but *La hoguera encendida está más lejos que la apagada* 'The
        lighted bonfire ...')

The gerund never acts as a predicative adjective following a copula (although *estar* + gerund forms the present continuous aspectual form of the verb). The possible impact of English on Spanish in this area has made no inroads into these limitations, and this should be borne in mind in what follows.

2.2.2.1 *The gerund introducing an adjectival clause.*
This usage is only infrequently cited as an anglicism in the literature
(for example Lapesa 1963, 199), although it is regularly castigated by
purists, and the parallel with English is patent:

(3) X[5] Se han celebrado dos congresos tratando de la misma
        cuestión (*MEU* 51)
     'Themselves have held two conferences dealing with the same
        question'
     ('Two conferences dealing with the same question have been
        held')

(4) X Una señora halló al niño deambulando por el parque (ibid.)
     'A lady found OBJECT + the child walking around the park'.

The strict normative rule in Spanish is that the gerund must have an
adverbial value and that the implied subject of the gerund must be the
subject of the next higher clause: thus

(5) Me canso subiendo escaleras (*MEU*, 48)
     'Myself (I)-tire climbing stairs'
     ('I get tired climbing stairs')

Subiendo here has a causal adverbial value; (5) implies *Subir escaleras
me cansa* 'Going up stairs tires me'/*Me canso si, cuando subo escaleras* 'I
get tired if, when I go up stairs'. The implied subject of *subiendo* is *yo*,
which is also the subject of the higher clause verb *me canso*.
     But there are some precedents in Spanish for the gerund introducing
an adjectival clause: the usage referred to by *MEU*, 50, as the 'gerundio
del Boletín Oficial' is a well-known feature of this publication's rarefied
and idiosyncratic register:

(6) Mañana se publicará un decreto regulando la exportación de
        vinos (*MEU*, 50)
     'Tomorrow itself (it)-will-publish a decree regulating the
        exporting of wines'.

The usage is indeed recognized as anomalous within Spanish.[8] Yet
there are other structures in Spanish which create similar surface
patterns. In a sentence such as

(7) El presidente, comprobando que no había quórum, levantó la
        sesión ('acceptable' according to *MEU*, 48)
     'The president, establishing that not there-was (a) quorum,
        caused-to-rise the session'

the clause introduced by the gerund is strictly adverbial in nature
(*comprobando que no había quórum = ya que comprobó que no había
quórum* 'since he established that there was no quorum'). Yet the

boundary between adverbial and adjectival function in such clauses is surely hazy: it might equally be construed as a non-restrictive adjectival clause (*que comprobó que no había quórum* 'who established . . .').[9] The gerund is also used in the complements of an increasing number of verbs in modern Spanish. Of long standing is its use in the complements of verbs of perception such as *ver* 'see' and *oír* 'hear':

(8a) De madrugada oíamos manifestantes gritando eslóganes
      (*MEU*, 49)
      'In (the) early-morning (we)-heard demonstrators shouting
      slogans'.

MEU also mentions verbs of graphic representation such as *pintar* 'paint', *retratar* 'portray', *fotografiar* 'photograph', *dibujar* 'draw', and so on, as belonging to this category, for example:

(9a) Docenas de fotógrafos retrataban a los cardenales entrando
      en el cónclave
      'Dozens of photographers were-taking-pictures-of OBJECT
      the cardinals entering-GERUND into the conclave'.

In fact, native speaker judgments seem to suggest that the matter can be put rather more strongly. The basic difference in meaning between the infinitive complement and the gerund complement for such verbs is that the gerund indicates progressive aspect (Fente 1971, 103): where progressive aspect is obligatory, the infinitive is actually unacceptable:

(9b) *Docenas de fotógrafos retrataban entrar en el cónclave a
      los cardenales[10]
      '. . . entering-INFINITIVE . . .'

In such complement structures, significantly, the implied subject of the gerund is not the subject of the higher sentence: the subject of *gritando* in (8a) is the object of the higher sentence (*manifestantes*), and similarly the subject of *entrando* in (9a) is *cardenales*. It is no doubt this complement use of the gerund which has led to the 'photo caption' usage, which is admitted by *MEU*, 51, and by Seco (1989, 207), who glosses (10) and (11) by an elliptical structure involving a verb of perception:

(10) Las ranas pidiendo rey (Seco, 207) (Seco: *Las ranas están, en
      este relato, pidiendo rey* 'the frogs are, in this story, asking
      for a king')
      'The frogs asking-for (a) king'

(11) Napoleón pasando los Alpes (Seco, 207) (Seco: *Napoleón
      está, en este cuadro, pasando los Alpes* 'Napoleon is, in this
      picture, crossing the Alps')
      'Napoleon crossing the Alps.'

The complement use of the gerund accordingly brings it very close to introducing an adjectival clause,[11] and interestingly many Romance languages are able to commute such complement constructions with (preferentially, though not exclusively) non-restrictive relative clauses:

(8b) Oímos a los manifestantes(,) que gritaban/estaban gritando
'(We)-heard OBJECT the demonstrators(,) who were-shouting-IMPERFECT/were-IMPERFECT shouting-GERUND'

(9c) Docenas de fotógrafos retrataban a los cardenales(,) que entraban en el cónclave
'Dozens of photographers were-taking-pictures-of IMPERFECT OBJECT the cardinals(,) who were-entering-IMPERFECT into the conclave'

and compare French

(12a) Je l'ai vu qui parlait à la voisine
'I him-have seen who was-talking-IMPERFECT to the neighbour'
('I saw him talking to the neighbour')

which similarly foregrounds progressive aspect by contrast with

(12b) Je l'ai vu parler à la voisine (Fente 1971, 103)
'I him-have seen talk-INFINITIVE to the neighbour'
('I saw him talk to the neighbour').

Crucially, all the constructions examined above ((7), (8a), (9a), (10) and (11)) present a surface pattern N + gerund in which there are strong reasons for considering the clause introduced by the gerund to have, at least, partially, an adjectival value. The puristically castigated structures (3), (4) and (6) can be seen as a further exploitation of this pattern. Furthermore, we have seen how the exploiting of the opposition between gerund and infinitive in sentences like (8a) allows an aspectual discrimination within the non-finite verb which parallels that within the finite verb-system.

We must note too that this gerund usage is certainly not a recent innovation in Spanish, but has antecedents of long standing, as the following example from *Don Quijote* shows:

(13) En un instante se coronaron todos los corredores del patio de criados y criadas de aquellos señores diciendo a grandes voces: Bien sea venida la flor y la nata de los caballeros andantes (cit. Moliner 1983, I, 1393).

'In an instant all the corridors of the patio were crowned with manservants and maidservants of those lords (and ladies) saying (say-GERUND) aloud: Welcome to the flower of knight-errantry.'

2.2.2.2 *estar + siendo*

The paraphrase *estar + siendo* ('be-(ESTAR) + be-(SER)-GERUND) is very often (*MEU*, 50; Lorenzo 1971, 124; Kany 1945, 237–8; Gómez Torrego 1991, 22–3; Lorenzo 1990, 78; Pratt 1980, 210) considered an anglicism, and is apparently deliberately avoided by many writers, with the interesting possible consequence (Pountain 1992–3) that the imperfect tense of the *ser*-passive may be making good the 'gap' in the aspectual system, at least by comparison with English.

However, the form finds a natural place within the Spanish verb-system. There are restrictions on its use, as indeed in English: the progressive is not available with many adjective complements of *ser* because of the restriction that stative expressions are inconsistent with the progressive, as in

(14a) *John is being tall
(14b) *Juan está siendo alto
   'Juan is-(ESTAR) be-(SER)-GERUND tall'.

Spanish also appears to be more resistant than English to non-stative progressive *ser* + adj or noun expressions:

(15a) He's being naughty
(15b) Está siendo travieso
   '(HE)-is-(ESTAR) be-(SER)-GERUND naughty'

but

(16a) He's being creative
(16b) *Está siendo creativo
   '(He)-is-(ESTAR) be-(SER)-GERUND creative'.

However, this restriction may not be due to any restriction on *estar + siendo* as such. In what Quirk *et al.* (1972, 48) call the 'transitory condition of behaviour' use of the English progressive, the implication is often that the adjective is not an inherent property of the subject: therefore the corresponding Spanish structure *ser* + adjective, which precisely does imply that the adjective is an inherent property of the subject, is impossible. For example, the English sentence

(17a) I'm being very optimistic about the future

(even though normally I'm a pessimist) cannot be appropriately translated by the Spanish

(17b) Soy muy optimista con respecto al futuro
'(I)-am-(SER) very optimistic with respect to-the future'

since this would imply that I am by nature an optimist, which is quite the reverse of what is implied by the English sentence. On the other hand,

(17c) Estoy muy optimista con respecto al futuro
'I-am-(ESTAR) very optimistic with respect to-the future'

with its implication *aunque normalmente soy pesimista* ('although normally I am a pessimist'), is indeed appropriate. However, *estar* itself does not admit the progressive paraphrase:

(17d) *Estoy estando muy optimista...
'(I)-am-(ESTAR) be-(ESTAR)-GERUND very optimistic'.

Similarly, the English sentence

(18a) He's being very good at the moment

cannot be appropriately rendered in Spanish as

(18b) *De momento es/está siendo muy bueno
'At the moment (he)-is-(SER)/(he)-is-(ESTAR) be-(SER)-GERUND very good'

but would typically be expressed periphrastically, such as

(18c) De momento se comporta de manera buena
'At (the) moment himself (he)-behaves in (a) way good'.

Note once again that the supposed influence of the English progressive has been very selective in Spanish. Amongst the English uses of the progressive which are not available in Spanish are (following the terminology and examples of Quirk *et al.* 1972, 88ff.) politeness (*When will you be putting on another performance?*), limited duration (*The professor is typing his own letters (these days)*) and characteristic activity (*John's always coming late*), as well as the very well-known absence of any future time-referring use of the progressive in Spanish, by contrast with English; see also Fente (1971, 99ff.). Furthermore, as already noted, the model of English *to be being* + adjective has not been sufficient to encourage the introduction of *estar estando* + adjective to Spanish. The restriction on *estar estando* may be a 'stylistic' avoidance of the same verb as both auxiliary and main (though English *be being* is exactly cognate morphologically speaking), though it seems also to be consistent with the restriction on the progressive with stative expressions (for example English *I am being sad*/Spanish *Estoy estando triste*).

Looking now to the existing structure of Spanish, we should note two features which I believe are significant. First, many passivizable transitive verbs are non-stative and hence not subject to the restriction on the progressive, for example:

(19a) Los leñadores estaban cercenando los árboles
        'The woodcutters were-(ESTAR)-IMPERFECT felling-
        GERUND the trees'

which quite naturally demands a passive

(19b) Los árboles estaban siendo cercenados por los leñadores
        'The trees were-(ESTAR)-IMPERFECT be-(SER)-
        GERUND felled by the woodcutters'

if its aspectual value is to be maintained under passivization. Secondly, there is no general ban on *siendo* being the complement of an (ad-mittedly small) number of 'semi-auxiliary'[12] verbs in Spanish such as *seguir, continuar*. These two facts mean, respectively, that there is a slot which is naturally filled by the progressive passive, and that the surface model of V + *siendo*, as in

(20)   Sigue siendo interesante
        '(It)-continues be-(SER)-GERUND interesting'
        ('It continues to be interesting')

already exists.

Estar + *siendo* + pp therefore not only conforms to an existing syntactic model but is actually needed to fill what would otherwise be an anoma-lous structural gap in Spanish.[13]

2.2.3 Noun + noun (N + N) combinations
Occasional instances of N + N combinations are recorded in older usage (for example *patrón oro* 'gold standard' (Smith 1992, 826; Pratt 1980, 203)). Lapesa (1963, 203) cites *pájaro mosca* 'humming-bird' and *coche cama* 'sleeping car' as well-established examples, and also points out that proper name usage without *de* dates from the beginning of the present century (*Teatro Apolo, Cinema España, Instituto Rubio*). But it is clear that the significant increase in frequency of N + N constructions is of recent date, as is also the growth in the range of their functions (Pratt 1980, 203–6). Pratt suggests that the innovation attributable to English is the use of the N + N construction to render a function previously expressed by a preposition, whereas the 'traditional' N + N groups were more truly appositional, being essentially co-ordinate in nature. There has also been extension from simple N + N combinations to N + NP combinations: *trenes largo recorrido* 'long-distance trains',

premio fin de grado 'end of year prize', etc. (examples from Gómez Torrego 1991, 17).

However, even here it can be shown that the development is not inconsistent with the existing structure of Spanish. There are already some nouns in Spanish which regularly act as invariable adjectives: *macho* 'male' and *hembra* 'female' (for example *ardillas macho* 'male squirrels'), the points of the compass *norte* 'north', *sur* 'south', etc., and several colours: *lila* 'lilac', *malva* 'mauve', *rosa* 'pink', *violeta* 'violet' (for example *gafas rosa* 'pink glasses'). The latter also provide the model for complex colour adjectival expressions: *uniformes verde oliva* 'olive green uniforms', *cortinas verde oscuro* 'dark green curtains' (Smith 1992, 826). Cardinal numerals behave similarly: *el día uno* 'the first (day of the month)', *la página tres* 'page three', a formula which in fact is obligatory with higher numbers (*el ejemplo 43* 'example 43'). Like these formations, new combinations of N + N in Spanish essentially use the second noun as a defining adjective, and there is no possibility of changing the order of the two nouns: *macho ardilla and *verde oscuro cortinas are as impossible as *límite fecha. Thus in typical $N_1 + N_2$ combinations, N_1 is an extremely common noun with a wide field of reference and N_2 marks a very particular property or relation.

There are many more Spanish adjectives, such as *optimista* 'optimist(ic)', *hablador* 'talker/talkative', which are also used as nouns and are invariable in the singular. We should also note that in Spanish, unlike English, the boundary between nouns and adjectives is by no means always morphologically or syntactically marked: thus *francés* 'French (adj) and Frenchman', *bueno* 'good' and *(el)bueno* '(the) good one'. The use of an adjective as a noun is far from unusual in Spanish: what the influence of English seems to be doing is causing Spanish to exploit the reverse possibility – the use of a noun as an adjective – more fully than hitherto.

There is also evidence of ongoing internal productivity in this area. *Hombre* is indubitably used as the first item in a number of anglicisms which render the equivalent of English *-man*: as in *hombre-rana* 'frogman'. But *hombre-* has continued to participate in other combinations which do not have an obvious English base: *hombre masa* 'average man', *hombre-anuncio* 'sandwich man'. Smith (1992, 826) makes the same point about *fantasma*: although *buque fantasma* 'ghost ship' is a patent anglicism, *empresa fantasma* 'dummy company' is not so easy to attribute directly to English influence. Another group mentioned by Smith is N + *punta*: *hora punta* 'rush hour', *tecnología punta* 'leading edge technology', *tránsito punta* 'rush-hour traffic' (by association with *hora punta* 'rush hour'), *industrias punta* 'sunrise industries'.[14]

We should notice the 'economic' value of N + N combinations to Spanish. Many of these combinations are not gratuitous neologisms in the sense that they replace existing words, but economically label new concepts for which Spanish originally had no ready expression. It might also be said that Spanish is gaining something of the morphological transparency which is so characteristic of the Germanic languages in this area: the kind of transparency which allows, for example, the immediate perception of a semantic relationship between English *eye*, *eye+lash*, *eye+brow*, *eye+lid* that is not perceptible between Spanish *ojo*, *pestaña*, *ceja*, *párpado*. In short, Spanish N + N combinations are simultaneously fulfilling a semantic need and filling morphological gaps.

The proper name usage identified by Lapesa (1963, 203) (see above) must be a powerful potential force for analogy in the language. Although it is theoretically possible to create constructions with *de* for this purpose, it would be unnecessarily cumbersome and uneconomical: perhaps the motivating factor in change we are looking at here is the need for catching quick attention in the commercial world. *Bar 'Los Mirlos'*, *Automóviles Sánchez, SA*, *Tiendas Cortty* and such-like have now established a firm and invariable pattern within the language.

It is interesting to notice that Lapesa gives an alternative explanation of this phenomenon, one which to my knowledge has not been taken up by subsequent commentators. He attributes the elision of *de* in such expressions as *la calle Goya* to phonetic erosion of the initial segment of *de*, a well-known feature of colloquial Spanish.

Lastly, turning to the reverse side of the coin, I once again ask what Spanish has *not* borrowed from English in this area. As we have seen, the Spanish noun-adjective order is for the most part preserved, for example *coches patrulla* not **patrulla coches* 'patrol cars'. There are exceptions, but they are a tiny minority: *cine club* 'film club', *ciencia ficción* 'science fiction', which could in any case be construed in the 'Spanish' way as 'science which is fiction', etc. There is accordingly no major syntactic upset caused by these combinations.

Spanish combinations are limited to those in which the semantic link between the two nouns is fairly obvious and requires for semantic interpretation the supplying of largely predictable prepositional and verbal information. The more idiomatic and figurative combinations of English (for example *book worm*, *rainbow*) have not generally been adopted.

3. Conclusion

My conclusion is brief. In none of the syntactic areas of Spanish I have examined have I found any movements which cannot be understood as natural extensions of the existing structure of the language, consistent with expected types and directions of linguistic change, and in some cases recalling earlier stages of Spanish. They are all very volatile areas of constant change in the history of the language. The patterns which have sometimes been presented as being peculiar to English in fact, without exception, exist already in Spanish, and what is tending to happen is that Spanish is extending minority structures or 'capitalizing', to use a term I have introduced elsewhere (Pountain 1991), on its own resources. Furthermore, it has often been possible to show that such changes have important expressive advantages for Spanish. The sensationalist terms in which purist utterances are often couched are therefore without foundation: syntactic anglicisms do not lead to significant innovation in Spanish, but rather encourage the fuller and more effective use of existing possibilities.

Notes

[1] I am grateful to Wendy Ayres-Bennett and Rebecca Posner for their helpful comments on this paper at Gregynog.

[2] Lorenzo (1971) devotes approximately one page (91–2) of a 23-page article; Pratt (1980) devotes 10 pages (202–12) of a book of 273 pages.

[3] See Lorenzo's contention (1971, 91) that 'los más dañinos y peligrosos efectos del anglicismo operan en la sintaxis' ('the most harmful and dangerous effects of English are on syntax').

[4] For example, when purist commentators stridently disapprove of what they tend to call the 'perversion' of their language, perversion by definition implying something new and unfamiliar within the native system. Even Lorenzo (1971) indulges in such subjective modes of expression, speaking of certain English calques as 'verdaderas monstruosidades que revelan la ignorancia de los traductores' ('real monstrosities which betray the ignorance of the translators') (89) and referring to the acceptance of subject-first passives by university students as evidence that 'el mal ... está consumado' ('the damage has been done') (92). Estrany (1970, 199) speaks of 'la gran conmoción lingüística producida por el torrente de anglicismos que están invadiendo nuestro idioma' ('the great linguistic upheaval brought about by the torrent of anglicisms that are invading our language') and 'calcos sintácticos, traducciones calcadas de estructuras inglesas, que por negligencia o ignorancia nos llegan sin la depuración necesaria y pueden con el tiempo tergiversar las estructuras españolas' ('syntactic calques, word-for-word translations of English structures that, through negligence or ignorance, reach us without the necessary purification and can, in time, distort the Spanish structures'). Madariaga's famous, or rather infamous, article on spelling conventions (1966), couched in extremist vocabulary ('humillante', 'absurdo', 'lamentable'), begins with the statement that Spanish 'hoy es una colonia del inglés' ('has been colonized by the English language') (a position thankfully refuted by Lapesa (1966) and more recently by Smith (1991)).

[5] X is used here to denote an example judged unacceptable by purist commentators though clearly acceptable to many speakers.

6 See Cárdenas (1967–8, 160): '... la perífrasis de pasiva en castellano se ha visto superada por otras perífrasis verbales, en gran número y riqueza y con nuevas posibilidades expresivas: perífrasis con SE, *estar* + participio, *quedarse, volverse, hacerse, resultar*, etc. + participio (adjetivado), de algunos de cuyos matices carece el inglés' ('The periphrastic passive in Castilian has been superseded by a great many other periphrastic forms, offering new possibilities of expression: periphrasis with SE, *estar* + participle, *quedarse, volverse, hacerse, resultar*, etc. + adjectival participle, some of whose nuances are lacking in English').

7 Thus Moliner (1982, II, 655), who comments: 'Antiguamente, ... era más corriente que ahora en lenguaje coloquial la voz pasiva' ('In the past the passive voice was more common in colloquial language than it is now').

Such an assertion is extremely difficult to substantiate, however, even for written register (see De Kock and Gómez Molina 1985, 125, note 21). The most conveniently available illustrative statistics are those of Keniston (1937a and b). I reproduce these below, given in his original form x-y, where x represents the 'range' or number of texts in which the phenomenon was found, and y represents the 'frequency' or number of actual or projected occurrences. The figure in square brackets is my own calculation of y/x, and it will be seen that in nearly all cases the twentieth-century figures are lower than the sixteenth-century figures, the only exceptions being the Perfect and Pluperfect tenses.

Verb-form	16th Cent		20th Cent	
Pres	27–180	[6.67]	32–61	[1.91]
PresSubj			5–6	[1.20]
Imp	22–49	[2.27]	13.24	[1.85]
Pret	27–154	[5.60]	27–72	[2.67]
Fut	19–61	[3.21]	9–18	[2.00]
Cond	7–16	[2.29]		
Perf	9–12	[1.33]	15–35	[2.33]
Plup	4–4	[1.00]	11–15	[1.36]
Inf	27–117	[4.33]	30–72	[2.40]
PerfInf			4–4	[1.00]
PresPart	13–31	[2.38]	3–3	[1.00]
PerfPart	1–1	[1.00]		

8 Gili Gaya (1948, 172) says 'es contrario a la naturaleza del gerundio español su uso como atributo' ('It is contrary to the nature of the Spanish gerund to be used as an attribute').

9 Compare the 'adverbial' uses of relative clauses in Latin (Woodcock 1959, 108–9).

10 Note that the syntax of infinitive and gerund complements is different (though this is not, I think, strictly relevant to the matter in hand). The infinitive complement allows subject-verb inversion in the complement structure:
  Oímos a los manifestantes gritar eslóganes
  Oímos gritar eslóganes a los manifestantes
  ('We heard the demonstrators shout slogans')
whereas the gerund complement does not:
  Retrataban a los cardenales entrando en el cónclave
  *Retrataban entrando en el cónclave a los cardenales
  ('They photographed the cardinals entering the conclave')

The infinitive may also have a 'passive' function which is not available to the gerund:

Oí cantar una canción

*Oí cantando una canción

('I heard a song being sung')

[11] Moliner 1982, I, 1393 lists such usage under the heading of 'gerundio adjetival' ('adjectival gerund').

[12] This category is discussed in Green 1982.

[13] See Gómez Torrego (1991, 23): 'Su éxito en castellano se debe a que viene a llenar la casilla vacía correspondiente a la perífrasis activa "estar + gerundio"' ('Its success in Castilian is due to the fact that it fills the empty slot corresponding to the active periphrasis "estar + gerund"'): "El proyecto *está siendo discutido* estos días en la comisión" (por "se está discutiendo"); "El plan *está siendo elaborado* por los profesores del Centro" (por "Los profesores ... están elaborando...").'

[14] See, in similar vein, Spence (1989) on anglicisms in French.

References

Cárdenas, S. 1967–8. 'Voz pasiva en inglés y español', *Filología Moderna*, 29–30, 159–66.

De Kock, J. and Gómez Molina, C. 1985. 'La frecuencia de la pasiva en español y otras lenguas', *Revista Española de Lingüística*, 15, 117–31.

England, J. and Caramés Lage, J. L. 1978. 'El uso y abuso de anglicismos en la prensa española de hoy', *Arbor*, 390, 77–89.

Estrany, M. 1970. 'Calcos sintácticos del inglés', *Filología Moderna*, 38, 199–203.

Fente Gómez, R. 1971. *Estilística del verbo en inglés y en español*, Madrid: SGEL.

Gili Gaya, S. 1948. *Curso superior de sintaxis española*, 2nd edn., Barcelona: Spes.

Gómez Torrego, L. 1991. 'La lengua española hoy', in Ramos Gascón, A. (ed.), *España hoy: Cultura*, Madrid: Cátedra, 9–37.

GRAE = Real Academia Española, 1931. *Gramática de la lengua española*, Madrid: Espasa-Calpe.

Green, J. N. 1975. 'On the frequency of passive constructions in Modern Spanish', *Bulletin of Hispanic Studies*, 52, 345–62.

—— 1976. 'How free is word order in Spanish?', in Harris, M. (ed.), *Romance Syntax: Synchronic and Diachronic Perspectives*, University of Salford, 7–32.

—— 1982. 'The status of the Romance auxiliaries of voice', in Vincent, N. and Harris, M. (eds.), *Studies in the Romance Verb*, London: Croom Helm, 97–138.

Haugen, E. 1950. 'The analysis of linguistic borrowing', *Language*, 26, 210–31.

Kany, C. E. 1945. *American-Spanish Syntax*, Chicago: Chicago University Press.

Keniston, H. 1937a. *The Syntax of Castilian Prose*, Chicago: Chicago University Press.

—— 1937b. *Spanish Syntax List*, Chicago: Chicago University Press.

Lapesa, R. 1963. 'La lengua desde hace 40 años', *Revista de Occidente*, 3, 193–208.

—— 1966. '"Kahlahtahyood". Madariaga ha puesto su dedo en la llaga', *Revista de Occidente*, 12, 373–80.

Lorenzo, E. 1971. *El español de hoy, lengua en ebullición*, 2nd edn., Madrid: Gredos.

—— 1990. 'Anglicismos en el español de América', in García Domínguez, P. and Gómez Font, A. (eds.), *El idioma español en las agencias de prensa*, Madrid: Fundación Germán Sánchez Ruipérez, 65–82.

Madariaga, S. de, 1966, '¿Vamos a Kahlahtahyood?', *Revista de Occidente*, 12, 193–208.

MEU = Agencia Efe, 1986. *Manual de español urgente*, 3rd edn., Madrid: Efe.

Moliner, M. 1982. *Diccionario de uso del español*, Madrid: Gredos.

Pountain, C. J. 1991. 'Syntactic change and *génie de la langue*: on making the most of linguistic opportunity', paper read to the annual meeting of the Association of Hispanists of Great Britain and Ireland, Belfast.

—— 1992–3. 'Aspect and voice: questions about passivization in Spanish', *Journal of Hispanic Research*, 1, 167–81.

Pratt, C. 1980. *El anglicismo en el español peninsular contemporáneo*, Madrid: Gredos.

Quirk, R., Greenbaum, S., Leech, G., Svartvik, J. 1972. *A Grammar of Contemporary English*, London: Longman.

Seco, M. 1989. *Diccionario de dudas y dificultades de la lengua española*, 9th edn., Madrid: Espasa-Calpe.

Smith, C. 1975. 'Anglicism or not?', *Vida Hispánica*, 23, 9–13.

—— 1991. 'The anglicism: no longer a problem for Spanish?', in *Actas del XIII Congreso Nacional de AEDEAN*, Tarragona, 119–36.

—— 1992. *The Collins Spanish Dictionary*, 3rd edn., Glasgow: Collins.

Spence, N. C. W., 1989. 'Qu'est-ce qu'un anglicisme?', *Revue de linguistique romane*, 53, 323–34.

Woodcock, E. C., 1959. *A New Latin Syntax*, London: Methuen.

8

Logographic script and assumptions of literacy in tenth-century Spain

ROGER WRIGHT

Much has been discovered in recent years about the linguistic differences between literate and non-literate societies, and historical linguists have been able to relate these discoveries to our two types of evidence about linguistic situations of the past, that is, texts and reconstructions. But some societies fall into neither category, in that they have only a small proportion of literate people but none the less preserve some general assumptions from a more literate past. Tenth-century Spain is such a case. Furthermore, when we try and use their surviving texts as evidence for the nature of their speech, it is probable that our analysis is hampered by the fact that their originally phonographic orthography was probably taught and learnt in an essentially logographic manner (as in modern Britain): that is, one word at a time, rather than one letter at a time.

The way that we should analyse the social assumptions that lie behind the existence of texts written in the distant past is not at all self-evident (cf. Wright 1993a). At times writers wish to transcribe speech with some directness. For example, the earliest texts intentionally written in a Romance language, in the central Middle Ages, were prepared with morphology, syntax, vocabulary and spelling that were intended to be more or less isomorphic with at least some style of the regional vernacular. But before the invention of such specifically Romance writing methods, such language planning as there was, if any, was not based on this ideal of isomorphism with speech, and writers' intentions were nearly always in principle to attain the written features that had been deemed as correct centuries before by the late Roman grammarians. I intend to refer here, as examples of our difficulty, to texts of tenth-century north-western Spain. These were written towards the end of the period that predates the language-planning reforms in that area, which would later lead to the existence of written Galician, Leonese and Castilian. Thus they were prepared according to an orthographical system that corresponded to a long-distant stage of the language. For nobody can doubt that the vernacular of the area had developed considerably from that of a millennium earlier. In order to work out any details of the spoken language used by those who composed this documentary evidence, therefore, we need first to consider in general terms what happens to writing systems that survive into periods when both (a) the speech with which they were originally intended to correspond has developed markedly, and also (b) the proportion of people in society who are able to write has decreased appreciably, such that the skill may have been the province only of professionals. This has hardly been studied, in fact; the acquisition of literacy into a society has been investigated by several scholars, but the social and linguistic consequences of such disparity and simultaneous professionalization remain to be assessed. And yet in some respects, this is what has happened to Modern French and Modern English (although their spelling was never entirely phonemic). The related problems have ramifications for the historical study of all levels of language, although the orthography–phonology interface is the one to be considered in this chapter. Since writing is an artificial technique, whose acquisition depends on explicit instruction within an *ad hoc* kind of micro language planning, it is also of great importance to try to reconstruct the way in which writing and spelling were actually taught, at various places and times in the past. In the case of tenth-century north-western Spain the near total absence of explicit evidence from any contemporary commentator means that our best available method is to deduce details of that teaching process from comparing genuinely attested ('unemended') written forms with reconstructible pronunciations. Some printed versions are useless for this purpose, having been distorted ('emended') by modern editors; others are more reliable. The texts I have in mind are those such as in Mínguez Fernández (1976), Ubieto Arteta (1976), García Leal (forthcoming). One of Mínguez's is reproduced here as an Appendix.

Tenth-century Christian Spain was a society which functioned on a basis of written texts (documents of sale such as the one reproduced here, charters, sermons, letters, saints' lives, laws, liturgy, and so on) which were intended to be read aloud. Compared with the proportions for modern societies, it seems that not many people could write; but we have to bear in mind that the chance survival of several pieces of slate from the Salamanca area on which shepherds of (probably) the seventh century noted practical details in respectable written form, onto an untypically non-biodegradable surface, suggests that the ability to write in Visigothic society was more widespread than is often now assumed. The relative proportion in society of those who could write may well have declined by the tenth century, even if we include the Mozarabic immigrants often thought to have boosted their numbers. Even then, many more people could read without being able to write; and even those who could not read were not thereby cut off from the literate world, for historical research has come to suggest that most texts, however old-fashioned, seem to have been expected to be generally comprehensible when read aloud sympathetically (see for example McKitterick 1990, Wright 1993a), as they often are to children and illiterates today. Thus the social role of the reader-aloud (*lector*) in a community was an important one. It is hardly surprising, therefore, that Isidore of Seville had recently devoted careful consideration to the habits of a good *lector*, largely on that assumption of intelligibility if the *lector* did his job well (Banniard 1976). *Lectores* could also work as scribes (see Ganz and Goffart 1990, 917), so it seems reasonable to deduce that at least some of those who wrote had the needs of the reader-aloud much in mind. For example, in order to be binding, legal documents usually had to be first recorded in writing and then also read aloud by the actual scribe for confirmation by the interested parties. Several documents (such as the one in the Appendix) have near the end a first-person clause in which the first-person deixis refers to the depositor (rather than to the notary) including the words *relegente audivi* ('I heard it read aloud'): in this case, *Ego Ermildi in ac karta bendiccionis que relegente audibi manu mea* (signo) *fecit ante testibus mul[tis] tera[di]dit roboranda.* Presumably the witnesses could largely follow the oral version as well.

Tenth-century Christian Spain (and late early medieval pre-Reform Europe in general) is perhaps unusual in being a society of comparatively restricted literacy, in the sense that fewer people wrote than before, which had nevertheless maintained several social assumptions from an earlier time of much wider literacy. Yet it is probably more misleading than has been previously realized to analyse the nature of that restriction in the same perspective, and using the same terms, as those with which other societies are usually characterized, in which the proportion of literate people in society is numerically similar to that of the Late Early Romance world, but has in contrast developed from total illiteracy in the relatively recent past. For example, Stock (1983), Armistead (1986) and also myself (1990–1), have made what may be an unwarranted assumption that the work of anthropologists such as Goody, on the change from pre-literacy to literacy, will necessarily be relevant to societies such as those of tenth-century Spain. In this latter case, the continuing administrative and educational infrastructure, based on an inherited assumption of textual intelligibility, which continued to be valid, could well be more relevant to our assessment of the relationship between textual evidence and speech than are the actual numbers of writers. That is, the illiterate were not cut off from literacy then in the way that they are often seen to be in societies where the literate are pioneers in a new universe. The general population of tenth-century Europe need not be patronizingly dismissed as illiterate on merely comparative numerical grounds, if by that characterization we mean that it was untouched by literate culture (cf. McKitterick's comments, 1990, 2, on Stock 1983). Their society, essentially post-literate rather than pre-literate, could thus in some respects be said to be more like that of Modern English than that of the modern developing world; there is much to be said for the 'idea that written language has irreversibly changed the human mind' (Frith 1983, 603), and that irreversible change was not reversed by the decline in educational standards in either modern Britain or tenth-century León.

Historical linguists need therefore to investigate, if we can, the nature and role of literacy in a society before we can reconstruct speech from texts with any certainty. This applies to all societies of the past, in fact, for writing never reflects speech exactly. In the first place, no hitherto devised writing system is in practice a complete biunique representation of phonetic output. Even the narrowest transcription of tape-recorded natural vernacular is unlikely to represent exactly in its detached written units every detail of the speed, pitch, intonation, rhythm, resonation, and frequencies in a section of continuous speech. An orthography has a different function from an acoustic spectrogram, for orthographic texts are intended to communicate meaning, but a connected text in spectrogram form would communicate nothing at all. Such a direct textual representation of the sound alone is no help in practice, because what readers want are not such phonetic details but immediate indications of what the morphemes and the words are. For in reading, everything else is secondary; the immediate practical function of reading is to recognize the words rather than the sounds. As the modern specialists in teaching reading and writing stress, we 'read by eye' even if in part we 'write by ear' (Sampson 1985, 208; Frith 1980; Savin 1972). This is a linguistic universal, albeit of a vague kind; yet it is not the sort of universal that diachronic linguists are used to operating with, even if we subscribe to merely the weaker varieties of uniformitarian principles, because in fact although orthography and phonetics never match exactly, the closeness of the fit between speech and writing can vary widely at different places and times. This wide variation is largely the consequence of disparate manifestations of human inventiveness, sometimes institutionalized as socially purposive language planning. Apprentice writers are not usually taught phonetic script. That is always advanced study. Instead, apprentice writers are taught 'correct' written forms of words and morphemes. Thus in order for modern historical linguists to use those written texts as evidence for the phonetic or morphosyntactic nature of contemporary speech, we need to work out, if we can, how far each writer wrote his text according to set conscious principles of what he thought he 'ought' to write, and how far, if at all, he was directly trying to reproduce what he would say himself. As regards Late Early Romance, Pei and Muller and others have already been criticized extensively for expressing the latter view (sixty years ago). There is no need to dance on their graves any more, merely to point out that, in the light of subsequently-accrued sociolinguistic expertise, we now know that the writers could hardly have been able to express their own vernacular directly.

This remark presupposes that the results of sociolinguistic research into the present have direct relevance for societies of the past. In other words, it implies the 'uniformitarian' hypothesis. This is not, in fact, an invention of sociolinguists; it was used first by geologists, and then by philosophers of history (see for example Dray 1989). These latter have been discussing at length whether we are likely to understand events in the past better by analogy with similar and already well-understood phenomena of the present, or by detailed study of the original context. Clearly, we need to do both if we can, but at the very least those of us who are considering the sociolinguistic state of Early Romance communities should not postulate phenomena that directly contradict what we know about similar societies in the twentieth century (cf. Wright 1988). On the other hand, linguistic universals can only strictly apply to events outside the conscious control of the language user; and philosophers of history would mostly agree now (if not in their behaviourist phase) that to understand historical events that are even to some extent in the conscious control of the participants we need to try and get into their conscious minds. This is often, of course, impossible, in any strict sense, which is why historiography is always going to remain in large part a sequence of ifs and buts. Even so, despite the uniformitarian validity of some general principles, we need for present purposes to put to one side the search for universals, and look at the specific society that our texts come from to see what the authors thought they were doing. Different societies, different writers and different orthographical systems need to be assessed differently by the investigator.

Sometimes writers have consciously tried to reproduce speech. This has probably always been the initial intention of those who first invented (or adapted from elsewhere) writing systems for their own language. Speech, however, is a vague term. As is generally known, orthographical systems fall into two main categories. These are:

(a) the logographic systems, such as the one devised to transcribe Chinese, whose original intention was to signal morphemes as phonetically unanalysed wholes; and

(b) the phonographic systems, such as the Roman alphabet, whose original intention was to signal units of sound.

The theoretical distinction between the two is clear. But the picture tends to become confused, because, over time, most systems become a mixture of the two.

Research suggests that texts prepared with the logographic systems tend to be easier to read (by those who have learnt how), but that on the other hand the phonographic systems are easier to learn to write. It is not the case that either should be regarded as intrinsically more advanced or desirable than the other (Sampson 1985; Coulmas 1989). It seems plausible to propose that readers and writers in tenth-century Spain, like those in the modern English-speaking world, living in a society where speech sounds and the orthographic units of the traditionally 'correct' written forms often fail to correlate closely, operate a system that, although it was originally phonographic (using sounds as the basic unit), has come to work, at least partly, in a logographic manner (seeing words as the basic unit). This is not meant to be seen as in any sense a process of decay or corruption. Our present system works, and the important practical matter is to operate a system that works, whether or not it has a phonographic basis. It is conceivable, for example, that future generations will laugh at our own clumsy naïvety in operating with a writing system for Modern English that makes no attempt to reproduce on paper the nature of acoustic formants. It is already the case that Korean script could be seen as more advanced than ours, in a phonographic sense, in that it includes direct representation of distinctive features. An acoustic-formant-based writing system seems as odd a concept to us as written vocalic representation would have seemed to a Sumerian, because we are all used to operating with what we have been taught. But we can infer from the work of Schmandt-Besserat (for example, 1991) that the Sumerians' system was a sufficient and practical one for their perceived needs. So is ours now. So was that of tenth-century Spain. Chomsky and Halle (1968, 49) made the sensible comment that 'orthography is a system designed for readers who know the language' (and cf. Klima 1972). Orthographies are not designed to assist philologists of a millennium later. Let us assume that the strange appearance of documents such as many of those from tenth-century Spain corresponds neither to a desire to mystify, nor to endemic total stupidity and incompetence, nor to improbably precocious expertise in phonetic script (Wright 1991b, 1993a), but to a practical purpose.

At a slightly later period than the one I am centrally concerned with here, several approximations to spoken usage can be seen to be intentionally made in some eleventh- and twelfth-century documents in the Iberian Peninsula, at a time when the ancient systems were still in theory the only ones in use; these came to be used as the basis for the consciously isomorphic thirteenth-century standardizations of written Castilian, Catalan and Portuguese (Wright 1982, ch. 5). We cannot assume, of course, as Penny has shown (1991), that the correspondences they operated with were those of modern phonetic alphabets, but this was at least a period of phonographically-inspired spelling reform.

Most texts, however, are not prepared during or just after reforms of the writing system. Indeed, even if they are, reforms are sometimes specifically directed towards *not* representing speech; as with the late eighth-century reforms at the Frankish court which eventually led to the separate concept of Medieval Latin (Wright 1991c), aiming to revive 'correct' written forms that in fact reflected the speech of a whole millennium earlier: or several of the orthographical decisions taken in the eighteenth century by the newly established Royal Academy of the Spanish Language.

The nature of a spelling system can change unintentionally as well as being consciously invented and reformed. As a result, many writing systems work in practice on both semantic and phonetic levels. In the first place, logographic systems, over time, tend to acquire phonetic components. This has, in fact, happened to Chinese script (DeFrancis 1984; Coulmas 1989, 109), which nowadays aids the reader with both phonetic and semantic indicators. Conversely, on the other hand, phonographic systems, over time, become naturally more logographic as the inevitable consequence of phonetic change. This has happened to words written with the Roman alphabet in many languages, including Modern English and French, and also tenth-century Spanish Romance (see the studies by Emiliano and Varvaro in Wright, ed., 1991). In Sampson's words (1985, 203): 'the fact that the Roman letters originally stood for segmental sounds would not in principle be any bar to constructing a purely logographic script with them.' Thus in both kinds of system there is often a simultaneous appeal to recognition of both words and sounds. This fact has practical consequences for teachers. One method used in teaching reading in British schools, for example, involves the use of what are known as flashcards; the teacher says, for example, 'this word is [najt]', holding up a card with the written word *night,* and with this technique the pupil is encouraged to learn the word's written form as a whole. Pupils still need to be able to recognize the individual letters, of course (Besner *et al.* 1984), but there is no intermediate stage of mentally allotting particular sounds to each individual letter. This is just as well, because such a˙process would be positively unhelpful in words such as *night*. As a consequence of this method of teaching, when reading aloud words we know, at least, the word (and its lexical entry) is always the basic unit that inspires our pronunciation, rather than the individual letter. It may even perhaps be a universal truth, concerning the consumers of ostensibly phonographic scripts, that the letter-sound correspondences are utilized in reading individually, that is, sounded out as separate entities, only when we encounter a word we do not immediately recognize as a whole. Spelling-pronunciations, therefore, are due to poor readers, those who cannot read well enough to recognize the word concerned immediately ('by eye'), and thus have to have clumsy resort to piecemeal phonographic correlation. This simple and indeed obvious deduction is, even so, diametrically opposed to that which is standardly taught in university classes on Romance philology, in which spelling-pronunciations ('mots savants', 'cultismos' – such as the [-u] in *spiritum* that gave rise to Spanish *espíritu* 'spirit') are usually diagnosed as being the result of specifically erudite influence rather than of the reading incompetence that they actually attest (Wright 1993b).

Accordingly, it is worth considering the hypothesis that when people in tenth-century Christian Spain were taught to read (for they must have been taught somehow), they were indeed taught to recognize the letters, but as an aid to reading logographically; that is, the aim was to enable the apprentice reader to recognize whole, without clumsy piecemeal phonographical analysis, the written forms of at least those words that occurred commonly in their ordinary speech. That is, the orthographic forms would have been taught as single phonetically-unanalysed units. There is no immediately obvious way of knowing for certain if that was indeed the case, but the modern evidence suggests that it would at least have been a sensible method to use. The teacher in tenth-century Castile, as it were, might have held up a card or slate or plank or piece of bark or stone or leaf or parchment bearing the written letters I P S A and said 'this is [ésa]'; held up a card inscribed S U P E R (or even perhaps its abbreviation *sup*) and said 'this is [sóβre]'; held up a card with the letters P E T R U S and said 'This is [péðro]'. These are three words commonly found in documents, although only *ipsa* is in the one in the Appendix here. The fact that the written letter P in these three words actually corresponded in tenth-century Spain to an unvoiced bilabial plosive in P E T R U S, a voiced bilabial fricative in S U P E R, and to nothing at all in I P S A, might never have occurred to the pupils, and possibly not to the teacher either, who was not a theoretician of linguistics. In tenth-century Spain, we can reconstruct plausibly many such phonetic forms whose phonetic transcription would not have been exactly the same as their traditional 'correct' orthography. Words that a scribe was likely to read and write often, such as the word reconstructably pronounced [komplógo] in 933 – with possible variations – and written *conplacuit* in the text reproduced here (and also in that of 908 in Wright 1982, 166–7), would have been much simpler to teach and learn as whole units, particularly for those who were only learning to read rather than also to write – which was always the case, for it seems that it was normal practice to learn to read first and to write later if at all. More general principles of individual sound-letter correspondence would only be broached for recognizing words that were less common and less easy to recognize whole. For those who are learning only to read, in any language, such correspondences are only secondary; reading has to be based on a logographic recognition of the words and morphemes when (as in Modern English) the fit between the traditionally correct orthography and the speech sound is so often awkward and indirect. Since reading in tenth-century Spain seems to have been very often reading aloud, and intended to be immediately intelligible, it was essential to have a direct procedural link from the recognition of the written shape of the lexical item, to its oral production with its normal vernacular phonetics. In practice the oral rendering of both Modern English and these tenth-century texts would be greatly confused and indeed stultified by any attempt to read traditional spellings one letter at a time as if they were phonetic script. This is only common sense, and yet many Romance philologists have assumed that the reading of these texts can only have been phonographic, allotting one sound to each letter. Research evidence suggests that we do not after all read in that way, and that normal logographic reading could render the words, at least, intelligible to an unlettered audience, although the word-order might occasionally have been a problem (but see Blake 1991; and even if it was, see the transposition techniques proposed by Stengaard 1991, Korhammer 1980).

Since writing was usually taught only to people who had already learnt to read, as Riché established, writing would have been taught most practically on the basis of the already learnt reading techniques. Having already learnt to read, for example, the word written I P S A as [ésa], the apprentice scribe would probably have found it a comparatively simple operation subsequently to reverse the direction of inference and learn to write the word [ésa] as I P S A, still as a largely unanalysed whole. For the apprentice, morphology, of course, produced additional complications, since logographic script based on whole words is inherently insufficient for languages with non-syllabic morphemes such as the plural-marking final [-s] of Old Spanish. We can hypothesize that the root was taught as one logographic unit, and the suffix, however brief, as another. There is some evidence for this: orthographical treatises of that age devote a great deal of energy precisely to the operation of these combinatorial techniques. For example, for a scribe to know when to add in writing a final silent letter -M to nouns and adjectives needed extensive explicit teaching. So he received it, in, for example, Cassiodorus's *De Orthographia*, aimed at his protégés in Vivarium, Italy. In addition, the fact that many words were commonly written in the same widely accepted abbreviated form can only imply that these abbreviations were also taught as wholes (Bischoff 1990, 150–68; for Spain, Millares Carlo 1929, ch. 5); it is no great extension of the argument to propose the same for many words in unabbreviated form also.

An internal analysis of some written forms in tenth-century Galicia (Wright 1991b, partly based on Veiga Arias 1983 and the study of León in Pensado 1991) led me to the conclusion that the written form of a number of words was indeed taught in this way without phonetic analysis, during the teaching of writing as well as that of reading. These words probably included those commonly used in formulaic expressions; if so, this would explain why the words in question are comparatively rarely mis-spelt in texts. The written forms of some other words were not taught whole in this way. For the written representation of words whose integral form they had not learnt, scribes had to fall back consciously on a loose piecemeal collection of rules of thumb, probably comprising both sound–letter and syllable–multigraph correspondences. The existence of the latter type of syllabic correspondence seems possible in the light of the fact that the units are syllabic rather than phonemic in the late eleventh-century *Artes Lectoriae* from south-western France (Kneepkens and Reijnders 1979) (and the fact that modern Spanish schoolchildren are often taught that way as well). To make such an analysis, of course, modern investigators need to be able to trust editors to reproduce the textual evidence exactly as it is written. Unfortunately, there are still editors around who aim to 'emend' the spellings of their originals; we still apparently need to beseech them not to do that grotesque and unscholarly disservice to academic advance (Wright 1991d). The particularly interesting cases, in the tenth-century Spanish spellings investigated, are those in which phonological features which had not changed since the days of the Roman Empire, and were thus still broadly speaking isomorphic with the traditional orthography, were none the less often spelt in an incorrect way; in these cases the incorrect spelling can be ascribed not to a phonetic variant (as has been a common reaction of philologists in the field) but to an inappropriate use of those rules of thumb used for writing less common words.

Since teaching people to write always involves some kind of consciously transmitted technique, it is tempting to wonder whether any general language-planning ideas were around in tenth-century Galicia, as they were going to be later in Alfonso the Wise's Castile or the eighteenth-century Academy. Individual monastic centres had their own spelling habits, however, and vary between each other as to which words are liable to be mis-spelt and which are not (cf. Pensado 1991, 199). We can deduce from this that there were teachers, probably monks, who talked to each other, but not the wider standardization that would imply the presence of teacher-training colleges. The situation was thus quite different from that which prevailed in France at the same time. In France, the Carolingian reforms, intended to be uniform over the whole empire, were leading by then to a clear distinction between Latin and Romance (French) as conceptually separate languages. Yet many details remain unclear, even in France. For example, when we consider the relationship between scribal technique and reading aloud in the transitional period of the ninth century, Nelson's (1985) study of Nithard and the Strasbourg Oaths is going to have to lead French philologists back to the drawing-board, for the whole of Nithard's *History*, not just the Oaths, seems (in Nelson's persuasive analysis) to have been intended to be read aloud intelligibly to French-speakers with no great experience of higher education. How was it in fact read, with the new Medieval Latin pronunciation, or as normal Romance? What does this apparent intention imply? It continues to seem appropriate to believe that the reason why the Old French oaths were originally prepared in the way they were (perhaps by Nithard himself, despite Nelson's tolerant scepticism of this suggestion) was in order to aid Germanic speakers who had already become used to reading aloud in the new reformed way (producing a sound for each written letter), to read the text aloud as intelligible vernacular French. For the situation in ninth-century France was confused (and probably into the tenth century as well, in many places); despite the increase in educational levels, the Carolingian Reforms had brought unforeseen complications. Language planning often does. Its effects are often catastrophic. It can be argued that the results of Alcuin's prejudices were almost entirely pernicious (cf. Wright 1991d). On the other hand, further south and west, the contemporary Christian Spaniards, still fortunately unaffected by these reforms, still worked within a metalinguistically monolingual framework, which involved writing a somewhat *ad hoc* mixture of logographic forms and sound-letter correspondences. That makes life difficult for us, the philologists of a thousand years later, but it was a very reasonable attitude for them to take, and in keeping with the versatility, sophistication and flexibility that tenth-century Spanish Romance had in general (Wright 1991e). Philologists of the thirtieth century will have similar problems with texts from twentieth-century France.

Conclusion

Linguists like to think there are linguistic universals. Maybe in the event there is a diachronic universal which we can see at work here, in tenth-century Spain (but not in tenth-century reformed France). Societies that continue to function on a basis of documents generally expected to be intelligible, even when literacy is more restricted than it used to be, and that have inherited traditionally correct and originally phonographic written forms from that much earlier time of wider literacy, may always find it most practical to operate largely logographic systems of reading; and to some extent also of writing. Discovering whether this actually is a universal development is an empirical issue, which I invite specialists in other fields with comparable circumstances to consider. As a consequence of this, it is reasonable to conclude that post-literate societies are different in kind from pre-literate societies even with the same proportion of literate members.

Appendix
52

933, marzo, 1.

Ermildi vende a Nina y a su mujer, Juliana, la heredad de su hija en Ebas y en Lores.

'1 March 933. *Ermildi sells Nina and his wife Juliana her daughter's inheritance in Ebas and Lores.*'

AHN, Clero, Sahagún, carp. 873, núm. 1.

(*Christus*). In Dei nomine Domini.
Ego Ermildi.
Placuit mici bono animo et ispotania nobis benit bolu[m]tas ut binderem tibi Nina et uxori tua[1] Iuliana ereditate de filia mia Sendina in Ebas, in Lores bel in alios lorares binias, terras, pumares bel pumifera in monte, in fonte acesu bel que recre ab omnia intecritate foras una binea que comudabi in Taberneio. Et tu dedisti nobis precium pro ipsa

ereditate duas ceramenes kabiane sirguacata, quartario de cebaria, emina de bino in sub unum in setemedio qua[n]tum nobis bene conplacuit; et de ipso precio abut te debitus non remansit. Ut in ac die bel te[m]pore abeas, teneas ac defendas tum et filis tuis bel progenie tue, tum et filis tuis bel progenie tue belis abere, belis donare.

Si[2] aliquis te inqietarem benerit pro ipsa ereditate aliquis omo de parte mea aut de subrogita persona mea qui in iudicio bindicare non potuero post nomine meo tu[n]c abeas potestate de meo adpre[n]dere ipsa ereditate[3] dupplata qua[n]tum a te[m]pus fuerit meliorata.

Facta karta bendiccioni ipsas kalendas marcas in era DCCCC LXX I.

Regnante[4] domno Rademiro in Legione.

Fredena[n]do Gontesalbes comite in Kastela.

Ego Ermildi in ac karta bendiccionis que relegente audibi manu mea (*signo*) fecit ante testibus mul[tis] tera[di]dit roboranda:

Agane; Dulcidius confirmat manus (*signo*); Argiso testis (*signo*); Dominus testis (*signo*); Ervigius testis (*signo*); Serenus (*signo*); Aragildus (*signo*).

Arias (*signo*) scribsit.

(Mínguez 1976, 84–5)

Notes

[1] Tex.: 'sua'.
[2] Tex.: 'sit'.
[3] Tex.: 'ereditatate'.
[4] Tex.: 'regenate'.

References

Armistead, S. 1986. '*Encore les cantilènes!* Prof. Roger Wright's protoromances', *La Corónica*, 15, 52–66.

Banniard, M. 1976. 'Le lecteur en Espagne wisigothique d'après Isidore de Séville; de ses fonctions à l'état de la langue', *Revue Augustinienne*, 21, 112–44.

Besner, D., Davelaar, E., Alcott, D. and Pairy, P. 1984. 'Wholistic reading of alphabetic print: evidence from the FDM and the FBI', in Henderson, L. (ed.), *Orthographies and Reading*, New Jersey: Lawrence Erlbaum, 121–35.

Bischoff, B. 1990. *Latin Palaeography: Antiquity and Middle Ages*, translated by D. Ó Cróinín and D. Ganz, Cambridge: Cambridge University Press.

Blake, R. 1991. 'Syntactic aspects of Latinate texts of the Early Middle Ages', in Wright (ed.), 1991, 219–32.

Chomsky, N. and Halle, M. 1968. *The Sound Pattern of English*, New York: Harper and Row.

Coulmas, F. 1989. *The Writing Systems of the World*, Oxford: Blackwell.

DeFrancis, J. 1984. *The Chinese Language: Fact and Fantasy*, Honolulu: Hawaii University Press.

Dray, W. H. 1989. *On History and Philosophers of History*, Leiden: Brill.

Emiliano, A. 1991. 'Latin or Romance? Graphemic variation and scripto-linguistic change in medieval Spain', in Wright (ed.), 1991, 233–47.

Frith, U. (ed.). 1980. *Cognitive Processes in Spelling*, London: Academic Press.

—— 1983. Review of Scribner and Cole (1981), *Journal of Pragmatics*, 7, 603–6.

García Leal, A. forthcoming. *El latín de la diplomática asturleonesa (775–1032)*, Oviedo: Universidad.

Ganz, D. and Goffart, W. 1990. 'Charters earlier than 800 from French collections', *Speculum*, 65, 906–32.

Goody, J. 1987. *The Interface between the Written and the Oral*, Cambridge: Cambridge University Press.

Harvey, A. 1990–1. 'Retrieving the pronunciation of early insular Celtic scribes', *Celtica*, 21, 178–90 and 22, 48–63.

Kavanagh, J. F. and Mattingly, I. G. (eds.). 1972. *Language by Ear and by Eye*, Cambridge, Mass.: MIT Press.

Klima, E. S. 1972. 'How alphabets might reflect language', in Kavanagh and Mattingly (eds.), 1972, 57–80.

Kneepkens, C. H. and Reijnders, H. F. 1979. *Magister Siguinus: Ars Lectoria*, Leiden: Brill.

Korhammer, M. 1980. 'Mittelalterliche Konstruktionschilfen und A. E. Wortstellung', *Scriptorium*, 37, 18–58.

McKitterick, R. (ed.). 1990. *The Uses of Literacy in Early Medieval Europe*, Cambridge: Cambridge University Press.

Millares Carlo, A. 1929. *Paleografía Española*, Barcelona: Labor.

Mínguez Fernández, J. M. 1976. *Colección Diplomática del Monasterio de Sahagún (siglos IX y X)*, León: San Isidoro.

Muller, H. F. 1929. *A Chronology of Vulgar Latin*, Halle: *Zeitschrift für Romanische Philologie*.

Nelson, J. 1985. 'Public *Histories* and private history in the work of Nithard', *Speculum*, 60, 251–93.

Pei, M. 1932. *The Language of the Eighth-Century Texts in Northern France*, New York.

Penny, R. 1991. 'Labiodental /f/, aspiration and /h/-dropping in Spanish: the evolving phonemic value of the graphs *f* and *h*' in Hook, D. and Taylor, B. (eds.), *Cultures in Contact in Medieval Spain*, London: King's College, 157–82.

Pensado, C. 1991. 'How was Leonese Vulgar Latin read?', in Wright (ed.), 1991, 190–204.

Riché, P. 1989. *Écoles et enseignement dans le Haut Moyen Age*, 2nd edn., Paris: Picard.

Sampson, G. 1985. *Writing Systems: A Linguistic Introduction*, London: Hutchinson.

Savin, H. B. 1972. 'What the child knows about speech when he starts to learn to read', in Kavanagh and Mattingly (eds.), 1972, 319–26.

Schmandt-Besserat, D. 1991. *Before Writing*, Texas: Texas University Press.

Scribner, S. and Cole, M. 1981. *The Psychology of Literacy*, Cambridge: Harvard University Press.

Stengaard, B. 1991. 'The combination of glosses in the *Códice Emilianense 60* (*Glosas Emilianenses*)', in Wright (ed.), 1991, 177–89.

Stock, B. 1983. *The Implications of Literacy: Written Language and Models of Interpretation in the Eleventh and Twelfth Centuries*, Princeton: Princeton University Press.

Ubieto Arteta, A. 1976. *Cartulario de San Millán de la Cogolla (759–1032)*, Valencia: Anúbar.

Varvaro, A. 1991. 'Latin and Romance: fragmentation or restructuring?', in Wright (ed.), 1991, 44–51.

Veiga Arias, A. 1983. *Algunas calas en los orígenes del gallego*, Vigo: Galaxia.

Wright, R. 1982. *Late Latin and Early Romance in Spain and Carolingian France*, Liverpool: Cairns.

—— 1988. 'La sociolingüística moderna y el romance temprano', in Kremer, D. (ed.), *Actes du XVIIIe congrès international de linguistique et philologie romanes*, V, Tübingen: Niemeyer, 11–18.

—— 1990–1, 'Several ballads, one epic and two chronicles (1100–1250)', *La Corónica*, 18, 21–38 and 19, xiii–xiv.

—— (ed.). 1991a. *Latin and the Romance Languages in the Early Middle Ages*, London: Routledge.

—— 1991b. 'La enseñanza de la ortografía en la Galicia de hace mil años', *Verba*, 18, 5–25.

—— 1991c. 'The conceptual distinction between Latin and Romance: invention or evolution?', in Wright (ed.), 1991, 103–13.

—— 1991d. 'On editing "Latin" texts written by Romance speakers', in Harris-Northall, R. and Cravens, T. D. (eds.), *Linguistic Studies in Medieval Spanish*, Madison: Hispanic Seminary of Medieval Studies, 191–208.

—— 1991e. 'Textos asturianos de los siglos IX y X: ¿latín bárbaro o romance escrito?', *Lletres Asturianes*, 41, 20–34.

—— 1993a. 'Complex monolingualism in Early Romance', in Ashby, W. and Mithun, M. (eds.), *Linguistic Perspectives on the Romance Languages*, Amsterdam: Benjamins, 377–88.

—— 1993b, 'La escritura: ¿foto o disfraz?', in Penny, R. (ed.), *Actas del Primer Congreso Anglo-Hispano*, Vol. I, *Lingüística*, Sevilla: Junta de Andalucía/Castalia.

9

Nominal compounding in the Occitan dialects: influences from French (with an inventory of Occitan compound types)

KATHRYN KLINGEBIEL

Since the thirteenth century, French has been in a position to exert pressure on the Occitan dialects of southern France; lexical items and formations have succumbed to that pressure, as have graphic practice and linguistic structures. The roots of the current diglossic situation can be traced back to 1229, when the political will of the north was definitively imposed on the Midi. Direction of influence has been constant, extending beyond the purely linguistic.[1] The label 'Occitan' is particularly dear to a small but ardently vocal group which has sought linguistic standardization and unification, along with some measure of political autonomy for the Midi. Taken individually, the Occitan dialects include: Provençal in the south-east, Lengadocian in central southern France, Gascon in the south-west, and, abutting French-speaking territories, northernmost Limousin, Auvergnat and the Alpine sub-dialects. Like Catalan in north-east Spain, Occitan is a sub-national language; unlike Catalan, it has enjoyed no lasting renaissance – indeed, despite efforts to shake free of the stranglehold of French, Occitan appears to be in full retreat.

The unrelenting forces arrayed against Occitan have been social in nature. Although the kings of medieval France had no policy of deliberate *francisation*, by the fifteenth century written versions of Occitan had begun to reflect increasing graphic and linguistic influence from French. The mid-sixteenth century saw the beginnings of a permanent split between written and spoken uses of Occitan.[2] During the sixteenth century the lower classes remained solidly occitanophone; a century later Racine still had to use Spanish and Italian in order to make himself understood by the inhabitants of Uzès. Ultimately it was the Revolution, with its insistence on 'one nation, one language', that sealed the fate of the so-called *patois* (a term itself fraught with socio-linguistic implications).

Phonetic, morphological, and lexical variance among the modern-day dialects results from centuries of unchecked differentiation, compounded by the absence of any prestige dialect since the troubadours' literary language. Little satisfaction has resulted from efforts at normalization, which goes beyond individual dialect standardization to aim at supra-dialect unification. Graphic normalization has sought to ensure mutual comprehensibility by adhering to a morphophonemic, rather than phonemic, spelling designed to unite the diachronic and synchronic Occitan communities (Bec 1973, 24). Normalization is predicated upon the dialect of Lengadoc, less sharply characterized, relatively archaic, hence most similar to the troubadour koine. Speakers from areas other than Lengadoc, however, often find the very term *Occitan* unacceptable, refusing what to them appears yet another instance of linguistic imperialism in the guise of imposition of a 'central' norm.[3]

The Occitan nationalist movement itself, after successfully raising the linguistic consciousness of speakers in the Midi, has slowly lost its impetus in the last decade. The political movement has faltered, the dialects are in decline; yet there is evidence of the moral and intellectual victory which Pierre Bec predicted some thirty years ago (Bec 1963, 123), as the language has become a bona fide object of intellectual curiosity, of academic research which can be documented across the world (Klingebiel 1986 and forthcoming).

Diglossic pressures on the Occitan lexicon have begun to receive attention. Decomps (1983) studies the penetration of French technical and scientific terminology into Occitan; Mok (1987) examines the use of suffixal *-eusa* for naming machines in Occitan, as well as the substitution of *-eusa* (from Fr. *-euse*) for native *-airitz*, *-eiritz* to designate female agents; Mok (1991) looks at the competition between prefixal *re-*, restricted in nominal formations, and the verbal phrase *tornar a* 'to repeat an activity'. This paper offers a look at Occitan compounding as it has been influenced by French.

The Romance languages have not been noted for their compositional proclivities, with the major exception of the Verb + Noun (or Verb + Complement) pattern, for example Fr. *garderobe* 'wardrobe'. The present study is based on a corpus of Occitan compounds culled from some eighty-five sources consulted in Paris, Bordeaux, Nice, and in Béziers at the Centre International de Documentation Occitane. These sources, chosen to complement major dictionaries of the four dialects, include hard-to-find materials and works dating back to the mid-eighteenth century: articles, dictionaries both large and small, glossaries, typescripts, manuscripts (Puget 1755), manuals of 'proper' French (Caville 1818, Lascoux 1823), even sixteen boxes of hand-written file cards with vocabulary from the works of Gascon author and ethnologist Félix Arnaudin, which are now being readied for publication.

The corpus numbers approximately 2,500 compounds; presentation and discussion here is limited to nominal patterns, which are arranged in a typological inventory in Appendix B.[4] While the inventory cannot be considered exhaustive, any pattern listed below is attested, at least twice, from different sources. This particular corpus, mixing pre-normalized sources with normalized, offers evidence of compound types new to Occitan since the Middle Ages, whose appearance can be interpreted, if only to a limited degree, in light of diglossic influence from French.

Remembering that Arsène Darmesteter mixed formal and logical criteria in his classic attempt to distinguish 'proper' elliptic compounds from juxtaposed, or syntactic, forms (Klingebiel 1983), I have pre-ferred here analysis by part-of-speech to analysis by function or logical relation. On the basis of straightforward morphological recognizabil-ity, a compound consists of two or more independent lexical items. Such a definition encompasses syntactic compounds, also labelled 'improper' in an earlier, positivistic age. A word such as Niç. *pouorta-panaman* 'towel rack' is analysed here as tripartite VVN, rather than as V + compound N. This definition is extended as well to forms from the medieval language such as *bentenent* 'landowner', *pretzfach* 'flat rate' which some might consider opaque today.

Two major secondary sources provide a diachronic and synchronic overview of Occitan compounding: Edward Adams's study of word formation in Old Provençal, based primarily on dictionaries of the troubadour language by François Raynouard and Emil Levy;[5] and, for modern Occitan, Alibert's *Dictionnaire occitan-français*. Alibert's dic-tionary, based on the sub-dialects of Lengadoc, has served Occitanists to implement lexical normalization as well as elimination of Gallicisms, for example the choice of *decidir, lo metòde, lord* rather than *decidar* (Fr. *décider*, 'to decide'), *la metòda* (Fr. *la méthode*, 'method'), *sale* (Fr. *sale*, 'dirty'), respectively.[6] For his categories and choices, Adams relies heavily on Darmesteter's analysis of French compounds. Alibert's debt to earlier work is less clear, although many of his choices align neatly with the American's study. Adams identifies patterns at two levels: four basic sets of parts-of-speech (noun plus adjective, noun plus verb, noun plus noun, adverb plus noun) for nouns, which break down into a total of twelve patterns. Alibert groups fifteen patterns into eight basic sets, including one catch-all category of complex formations based on syntactic constructions such as prepositional phrases.[7]

Appendix B (Inventory of Occitan Nominal Compounds) follows the two-tiered distribution favoured by both Adams and Alibert, in order to do justice to the richness and variety of Occitan compound structures.[8] Under Noun + Adjective, for example, are found NA, NA*aire*, NA*ador*, NNA, NPresPtc, and NPastPtc. *Pouorta-panaman*, while analysed into three constituents (VVN), figures in the Verb + Noun category. *Baticòr* 'beating of the heart, emotion' is classified as V*i*N, rather than Adams's 'N vocative' or Alibert's 'impersonal V + vocative N'. The inventory in Appendix B below consists of 14 basic patterns at the first level, with a total of 51 patterns at the second. The corpus underlying this inventory invites comments in several areas: orthography, phonology, and lexicon.

The pair *clin d'ues*/*cò d'ues* (Fr. *clin d'oeil*, 'wink of an eye'), taken from a single dictionary of Niçois, is remarkable for the plural noun in both the Occitanized French and the more demonstrably Occitan form. Inconsistent plural marking in compound formations occurs across the Occitan dialects: Niç.-Viv. *lavaman*/Gasc. *lavamans* (Fr. *lave-mains*, 'washbasin'). This -*s*, while generally audible,[9] cannot be said to mark a logical plural, since one is unlikely to wash a single hand (*lavaman*) or wink both eyes (*cò-d'ues*) at the same time. Occitan lexicographers mirror such uncertainties in their French glosses, for example Seuzaret glosses Viv. *pouorto-bouchoun* 'cork-holder' as 'porte-bouchon(s)' (1947, 1401). Eighteenth-century Lang. *cerco-brego* 'argumentative, teasing', flanked by *cerco-reno* 'id.', contrasts with synonymous *cêrco-bregos*, *cerco-rénos* (Mazuc 1899, 260). A close study of French glosses for VN compounds would reveal as much about French compound morphology as it does about Occitan.

While there is no arguable influence from French in the confusion of grammatical and logical plural marking, many orthographical features appear to be closely dependent on French models. Use of punctuation marks in pre-normalized sources for the corpus echoes French in a number of subtle ways: compare Niç. *sauva-conduc* (Fr. *sauf-conduit*, 'safe-conduct') but *sauvagarda* (Fr. *sauvegarde*, 'safeguard'). In normalized Occitan, as in French, *anti-* is never separated from its head noun by a hyphen. Use of the hyphen appears more frequent in twentieth-century works than in earlier sources, where VN compounds appear often as a single unit. On the other hand, Alibert's normalized approach makes a single unit of all VN compounds, reserving hyphens for VV (*vira[-]revira* 'hairpin turn'), VPnInf (*daissa-m'estar* 'laziness, nonchalance'), VArtN, and other two-part and three-part compounds (except NV) in which a verb appears. Apostrophes in the corpus are generally limited to contractions (*d'*, *l'*). Incorrect usage of the apostrophe in French compounds with *grand*, as against correct use of the hyphen, carries through into Niç. *gran'causa* (Fr. [neg.] *grand-chose*, 'nothing much'), *gran'carriero* 'main street'; the apostrophes in these items contrast with Alibert's choice of representation as a single unit, for example, *grandcadiera* 'armchair'.

Spellings in the corpus occasionally reflect French pronunciation, such as Niç *focol* for *faus-couòl* (Fr. *faux-col*, 'celluloid collar'). French orthographic conventions are everywhere in evidence: affricates are occasionally spelled French-fashion ('tch' for [tʃ]). The use of 'ou' for [u] is standard in both Gascon and Provençal, each with its own consecrated graphic system, while the graphy 'u' has been standardized in the spelling of central Lengadocian, upon which Occitan normalized graphies are based. Representation of palatalization is intimately linked to morphological shape, cf. Lim. *chijar* as a variant of *cagar* (Fr. *chier*, 'to defecate'), while the graphy 'ch' in Gasc. *chire-peu* 'hair pulling' represents palatalized [t] (*tirar*). The varied representation of palatals signals the influence of French on Occitan phonology as well; variant forms of *talhar* 'to cut, slice' range through graphies in 'lh' or 'li' (Lim. *talha-*, Viv. *tàlio-*, Gasc. *talhe-*) to Niç. *tàia-*, Pr. *taïo-*, Lang. *tayo-*, the latter echoing post-eighteenth-century French in their simplification of the palatal lateral.

Certain lexical fields have proved susceptible to the influence of French. Occitan kinship terms have shifted into closer alignment with French, forsaking older simplex forms in favour of newer analytic compounds, for example, *bèla-sòrre* for traditional *conhada* 'sister-in-law', *bèla-filha* for *nòra* or *filhastra* 'daughter-in-law', *bèu-pay* for *sògre* 'father-in-law', etc. Even the overwhelmingly NA-structured Occitan variants for 'grandmother' and 'grandfather', for example Pr./Lang. *mairegrand*, Gasc. *may-grane*, *may-boune*, *may bielhe* and Pr./Lang. *pairegrand*, Niç. *paigran*, *peregran*, Gasc. *pay-boû*, show influence of French forms: Gasc. *gran-pay*, *gran-mày* (the hyphens incidentally reflecting standard French usage).

Gallicisms are documented across the corpus, for example, Pr. *bouto-en-trin* (Fr. *boute-en-train*, 'live-wire') or Gasc. *planche à pain* (Fr. *planche à pain* lit. 'bread board', 'tall skinny fellow'). The widespread presence of such borrowings poses a problem: where Alibert shows only *cinta* for 'belt', is Auv. *centura del(h) Bòn Dièu* 'rainbow' to be included in the corpus as Occitan? Does one include or exclude the transposition of Fr. *croc-en-jambe* 'trip, spill' into eighteenth-century Pr. *croc-en-cambo*, or its synonymous reinterpretation as Pr. *crocha-pèd*? Does the presence of *après-sopada* in Alibert's dictionary justify inclusion of Gasc. *après-souper* 'evening (spent in company)' in the corpus or of Gasc. *porte-fruit/porte-fruto* 'fruit server' and *porte-estrie/porte-estrius* 'stirrup holder'? Should *dimèi-fraire* as well as *mita-fraire* 'half-brother' be listed under normalized *'mièg'*? What normalized lemma can serve for multiple compounds beginning with *troubla[r]* (Fr. *troubler*, normalized Occ. *trebolar* 'to trouble') and *traina[r]* (Fr. *traîner*, normalized Occ. *trigossar* 'to drag')?[10] In all the above cases there remains the problem of determining when a borrowing has become fully integrated into native stock of the lexicon.

No influence from French need be argued to account for the continuing success of certain compound patterns in Occitan. The Verb + Noun (VN) pattern reigns unchallenged in Occitan as it does elsewhere in Romance; it continues to attract new formations into its all-pervasive orbit, particularly for names of technical implements, household appliances, and modern products. Lim. *grata-ceu, -ciau* 'skyscraper' parallels Fr. *gratte-ciel*, the English elements themselves transmuted into proto-typical Romance compound shape. In certain instances, the Occitan dialects lean more closely to VN than does French: against Fr. *haut-parleur* 'loud-speaker'(AdvV), the corpus contains synonymous examples of VN-structured *porta-votz* 'loud-speaker' in Limousin, Gascon, and Provençal, the latter with the eighteenth-century designation 'ear trumpet'.[11]

The structural evidence of *malcor*, Pr. *mau-cor*, and Pr. *maudecor* 'sorrow, pain' combines to affirm Adams's claim that some, if not all, Old Provençal NN compounds resulted from an ellipsis of *de*. An additional source for the Noun *de* Noun (N*de*N) pattern is provided by Gasc. *carte-milhas/cart-de-milhas* 'blind man's bluff', with apparently spurious prepositional element. Yet, although Adams and Alibert both fail to include N*de*N in their inventories, the sheer numbers of N*de*N in the corpus of 2,500 compounds (more than 10 per cent of the nouns) argue for inclusion of N*de*N in any listing of basic modern Occitan types.

Finally, the Noun *a* Noun pattern merits attention, although it is mentioned by neither Adams nor Alibert. In the corpus, Auv. *pou a counlévà* 'well' appears to be an outright borrowing of Fr. *puits à bascule*; Gasc. *guarda a mintjar* 'food cupboard' (cf. normalized *garda-manjar*) and Pér. *pensamor* 'dream of love', literally *'pensa a amor'*) represent possible reinterpretations of verb-final and/or prepositional *a*. Ellipsis may be responsible for the form of Gasc. *hiu-cous* 'sewing thread', with infinitival *coùse* (normalized *cóser* 'to sew'), which corresponds otherwise to Fr. *fil à coudre*. Elsewhere, the dialects appear to favour other structures, for example Niç. *bugadiera moutourisada* (Fr. *machine à laver*, 'washing machine'); Niç *pescadou de cane* (Fr. *pêcheur à la ligne*, 'angler'); Niç. *mau d'ouòs* (Fr. *mal aux os*, 'rheumatism'); Gasc. *peira per amorar* and Niç *peira da mola* (Fr. *pierre à aiguiser*, 'whetstone').

Alibert expanded Adams's Old Provençal list to 15 nominal compound types, notably VAdv (*parlo-soulet* 'talkative') and VV (*vira-revira* 'hairpin turn'). The corpus presented here encompasses a total of 51 nominal types, far beyond Alibert's inventory (see Appendix A). The majority of patterns in Appendix B which fail to appear in Appendix A originate in syntactic structures which come to develop lexicalized meanings, for example NA-structured kinship terms or N*de*N compounds. While individual lexical items or entire lexical fields may be subject to borrowing, the process of compound coalescence in Occitan owes no debt to diglossic influence from French. On the other hand, there are so few N*a*N compounds in the modern dialects of the Midi that, in the absence of any medieval evidence, the pattern in Appendix B is labelled a Gallicism.

To the variety of diglossic influences in the lexicon mentioned above, namely; (i) changes of conjugation class in verbs (*decidar* vs. Occ. *decidir*), (ii) changes of gender in nouns (*la mètode* vs. Occ. *lo metòde*), (iii) replacement of individual affixes (*-eusa* vs. Occ. *-airitz*, *-eiritz*), and (iv) borrowing of lexical items (*sale* vs. Occ. *lord*), examination of the present corpus allows us to add one clear example of a borrowed compound pattern, (v) N*a*N. The widely diffused, but merely occasional, evidence of French influence is complemented by the emphasis on correct French which motivated the creation of many of the earliest Occitan dictionaries. For almost two hundred years now, manuals inveighing against *provençalismes*, *périgordismes*, *gasconismes* in French have also allowed us insights into the range of pressures from the national language on the slowly expiring dialects of the Midi. Considered in its historical perspective, the current situation seems all the more fraught with pressures on Occitan lexical features or compound processes which fail to correspond to the structures of French. The actual survival of Occitan is at stake (Mok 1987, 365); as we watch it evolve, Occitan offers a rich domain for study of major and minor Romance compound patterns, both in and for themselves and in relation to each other.

Appendix A
Occitan Compound Noun Patterns in Adams and Alibert

A	Adjective	Pn	Pronoun
Adv	Adverb	PresPtc	Present Participle
G	Genitive	PastPtc	Past Participle
Inf	Infinitive	V	Verb
N	Noun		

Adams (4 basic sets) 12 patterns:

AN, NA, AdvN, NN apposition, NG, GN, VN direct object, VN indirect object, VN vocative, NV, NN by ellipsis, 'abstracts' (including three-part compounds).

Alibert (8 basic sets) 15 patterns:

AN, NA, AdvN, NN apposition, NG, GN, VN direct object, VN indirect object, VN vocative, AA, VV, VAdv, NA elliptic (exocentric), PresPtcN, 'complex' (representing an entire clause).

Appendix B
Inventory of Occitan Nominal Compounds

Auv. (Auvergnat)
Gasc. (Gascon)
Die (city in the northern Occitan Alpine zone)
Lang. (Lengadocian)
Lim. (Limousiñ)
Niç. (Niçois)
Occ. (Occitan, as found in Alibert)
Pér. (Périgourdin)
Pr. (Provençal)
Viv. (Vivarais region, in Lengadocian territory)

Lexical items are shown as listed in individual sources, without any spelling adjustments. Elements in square brackets, in normalized graphy, are taken from Alibert and Taupiac.

1. ADJECTIVE + NOUN
AN	Pér. *malsórt* 'bad luck, misfortune' < [*mal* 'bad'] + [*sòrt* 'fate']
	Lang. *grosso mousco* 'horsefly' < [*gros* 'large'] + [*mosca* 'fly']
NumN	Niç. *catre-temps* 'Lent' < [*quatre* 'four'] + [*temps* 'time']

2. NOUN + ADJECTIVE

NA   Viv. *fere-vuèl* 'scrap iron' < [*fèr* 'iron'] + [*vièlh* 'old']

NA*aire* Gasc. *sizel podaire* 'pruning shears' < [*cisèl* 'scissor'] + [*podaire* 'which prunes']

NA*ador* Gasc. *chèira preishadera* 'pulpit' < [*cadièra* 'chair'] + [*presicadoira* 'for preaching']

NPresPtc Lang. *pei voulant* 'flying fish' < [*peis* 'fish'] + [*volant* 'flying']

NPastPtc Gasc. *pretz-fach* 'flat rate' < [*prètz* 'price'] + [*fach* 'made']

NNA   Gasc. *moune-cu-pelàt* 'female ape' < [*monina* 'she-ape'] + [*cu* 'butt'] + [*pelat* 'bare']

NVN   Pér. *gulha passalana* 'darning needle' < [*agulha* 'needle'] + [*passa* 'pass'] + [*lana* 'wool']

3. NOUN + NOUN

NN   Gasc. *tèrre-hèms* 'compost' < [*tèrra* 'earth'] + [*fems* 'compost']

N[*de*]N Gasc. *taula-marme* 'marble plaque' < [*taula* 'table'] + [*marme* 'marble']

GN   Lim. *fauç-mangle* 'scythe handle' < [*fauç* 'scythe'] + [*margue* 'handle']

NG   Gasc. *piente-lin* 'flax comb' < [*penche* 'comb'] + [*lin* 'flax']

ArtNG   Pr. *lanso-panier* 'basket handle' < [*ansa* 'handle'] + [*panièr* 'basket']

4. NOUN + VERB

NV   Gasc. *aiga-pich* 'small waterfall' < [*aiga* 'water'] + [*pissa* 'piss']

NInf   Gasc. *diu-bedë* 'raising of the Host' < [*diu* 'God'] + [Gasc. *bede* 'to see']

NPresPtc Pr. *bentenent* 'landowner' < [*bèn* 'goods'] + [*tenent* 'holding']

5. NOUN *de* NOUN

NdeN   Niç. *mau de cuor* 'nausea', Pr. *maudecuor* 'nausea, disgust' < [*mal* 'pain'] + [*còr* 'heart']

NdeNplural Niç. *cò d'ues* 'wink of an eye' < [*còp* 'blow'] + [*uèlh* 'eye']

NdeVAdv   Gasc. *culote de piche-biste* 'open underpants for little boys' < [*culote* 'underpants'] + [*pissar* 'to piss'] + [Gasc. *biste* 'fast']

NdeArtN   Niç. *giarra de l'òli* 'oil jar' < [*jarra* 'jar'] + [*òli* 'oil']
            Pr. *mau de la terro* 'epilepsy' < [*mal* 'pain'] + [*tèrra* 'earth']

6. NOUN *a* NOUN, from French Noun *à* Noun, e.g., *tasse à thé* 'teacup'

NaNV   Auv. *pou a counlévà* [cf. Fr. *puits à bascule* 'well'] < [*potz* 'well'] + [*coa* 'tail'] + [*levar* 'to raise']

NaNumN   Niç. *capeu a tré calen* 'three-cornered hat' < ['*capèl* 'hat'] + [*tres* 'three']

7. ADJECTIVE + ADJECTIVE

AA   Pr. *cavafrei* 'chaudfroid' < [*caud* 'warm'] + [*freg* 'cold']

8. VERB + NOUN

VN   Lim. *pòrta-votz* 'loud-speaker' < [*porta* 'carry'] + [*votz* 'voice']

VPn   Gasc. *arrebire-të* 'turning around' < [*re-*] + [*vira* 'turn'] + [*te* 'you']

InfN   Rouergue *pregar-dieu* 'religious service' < [*pregar* 'pray'] + [*Diu* 'God']

VAN   Lang. *galabountan* 'good-time Charlie' < [*gala* 'enjoy'] + [*bon* 'good'] + [*temps* 'time']
           Viv. *monjo-bouon-diéu* 'bigot' < [*manja* 'eat'] + [*bon* 'good'] + [*Diu* 'God']

VArtN   Die *deilobra* 'weak, exhausted [person]' < [*daissa* 'leave'] + [*òbra* 'work']

VVN   Niç *pouorta-panaman* 'towel rack' < [*porta* 'carry'] + [*pana* 'wipe'] + [*man* 'hand']

9. ADVERB + VERB

AdvV   Gasc. *maumarche* 'stumbler' < [*mal* 'poorly'] + [*marcha* 'walk']

AdviV   Lang. *paucival* 'worthless' < [*pauc* 'little'] + [*val* 'is worth']

10. VERB + ADVERB

VAdv   Viv. *parlo-soulet* 'talkative' < [*parla* 'talk'] + [*sol* 'alone'] + [*-et*]

11. VERB + VERB

VV   Pér. *vira-revira* 'hairpin turn' < [*vira* 'turn'] + [*revira* 'turn']

InfInf   Gasc. *dicha-ana* 'casualness, carelessness' < [*daissa* 'let'] + [*anar* 'to go']

VVV   Niç. *etre douna-lèva* 'to be an Indian giver' < [*dona* 'give'] + [*leva* 'take']

VPnInf   *daissa-m'estar* 'laziness, nonchalance' < [*daissa* 'let'] + *me* + [*estar* 'to be']

12. PREP + N

*après*N   Gasc. *après-dinado* 'evening < [*après* 'after'] + [Fr. *dîner* 'dinner']

*arrèire*N   Gasc. *arre-pay* 'grandfather' < [*arrèire* 'behind'] + [*paire* 'father']

*contra*N   Lim. *contra-vermes* 'vermifuge' < [*contra* 'against'] + [*vèrs* 'worm']

*davant*N   Auv. *dant-méidjo* 'morning' < [*davant* 'before'] + [*mièg-jorn* 'noon']

*entre*N   Lang. *entremiech* 'intervening period' < [*entre* 'between'] + [*mitat* 'half']

*fòra*N   Gasc. *horopèt* 'crust, outer skin' < [*fòra* 'outside'] + [*pèl* 'skin']

*sèns*N   Pér. *sanpassinsa* 'impatient, lively' < [*sèns* 'without'] + [*paciéncia* 'patience']

*sota*N   Pr. *souta-terro* 'underground passage' < [*sota* 'under'] + [*tèrra* 'ground']

*subre*N   Gasc. *suberdent* 'protruding tooth' < [*subre* 'above'] + [*dènt* 'tooth']

13. ADVERB + NOUN

AdvInf   Pér. *benestre* 'well-being' < [*bèn* 'well'] + [*estre* 'to be']

AdvPresPtc   Auv. *pauvalent* 'worthless' < [*pauc* 'little'] + [*valent* 'being worth']

AdvPastPtc.   Gasc. *malescaduda* 'failure' < [*mal* 'poorly'] + [*escadut* 'fallen']

14. COMPLEX FORMATIONS

VPnAdv   Niç. *saute-mi-davan* 'untrustworthy' < [*sauta* 'jump'] + [*mi* 'me'] + [*davant* 'before']

V*a*V   Gasc. *pensse a bibe* 'bon vivant' < [*pensa* 'think'] + [*a* 'to'] + [Gasc. *bibe* 'to drink']

Notes

[1] See W. D. Elcock's comment on 'the increasing subservience [of thirteenth-century and fourteenth-century Occitan literature] to models imported from the north' (Elcock 1960, 394).

[2] The edict of Villers-Cotterêts (1539) was apparently intended to impose sole usage of French ('langage maternel françois' 'French mother tongue') for legal and administrative purposes throughout the kingdom.

[3] Gascon, for example, has long enjoyed a consecrated literary norm, as documented in Simin Palay's dictionary of Bearnese-Gascon; for Provençal, Mistral and the Felibrige established a prestige literary norm before the end of the nineteenth century.

[4] See Gross 1988 for a similar typological approach to modern French nominal compound patterns.

[5] Adams (1913, v, note 1) used the portions of Levy's work (1894–1924) that were available when his book went to press.

[6] Taupiac (1977, 17–18) discusses some of the choices facing the Commission de Normalisacion Filologica of the Institut d'Etudes Occitanes, as well as the shortcomings in Alibert's dictionary: (1) lack of names for technological innovations, (2) lack of scientific terminology, and (3) multiple listings for lexical items with widely differing representations across the dialects, for example, *marran/marre, aret, parròt* 'ram'. Since Alibert, others have gone further in the direction of lexical normalization, including Roger Barthe's *Lexique occitan–français* (1972, 3rd edn. 1988).

[7] A number of items cited in the introductory section on word formation unfortunately fail to appear in the body of the dictionary, for example *agulhacosent* (no gloss available). There are other minor inconsistencies: in his introductory analysis of Occitan compounds, Alibert cites *malcòr* 'sorrow, pain' to typify AN, but lists only *mal en còr* (sv. 'mal') in the body of the dictionary.

[8] A fuller version of this compound inventory will appear in the acts of the XXe Congrès International de Philologie et Linguistique Romanes (Zürich, April 1992).

[9] Final *-s* remains pronounced in most Occitan dialects, except in certain regions at the southern tip of the Rhone (Alibert 1966, 17).

[10] Other languages in contact with Occitan provide potential sources of borrowings as well. The dialects of Provence show Italian-inspired forms such as Niç. *sotacopa* (Ital. *sottocoppa*, 'saucer'), *perditemp* (Ital. *perditempo*, 'waste of time'), *fra-tèmp* (Fr. *entre-temps*, 'meanwhile'); and Pr. *(gen de) bassoman* (non-std. Ital. *di bassamano*, 'lower class, of low rank'), *giarra de l'òli* (Ital. *giar[r]a*, 'oil jar'), and *cavaden* (Ital. *cavadenti*, 'dentist').

[11] Despite their VN structure, single attestations of Niç. *escampa-papier* 'toilet-paper holder', Pér. *tetaposca* / Niç. *suerbe-pous* [< *absorbir*] 'vacuum cleaner' (as against suffixal Fr. *aspirateur* 'id.') require further substantiation before they can safely be removed from the realm of lexicographer's coinings.

References

Adams, E. 1913. *Word Formation in Provençal*, New York: Macmillan.

Alibert, L. 1966. *Dictionnaire occitan–français d'après les parlers languedociens*, Toulouse: IEO.

Barthe, R. 1988. *Lexique occitan–français*, 3rd edn., Toulouse: Collège d'Occitanie et Montpellier: Espacesud.

Bec, P. 1963. *La Langue occitane*, Paris: PUF; 5th edn., 1986.

—— 1973. *Manuel pratique d'occitan moderne*, Paris: Picard.

Caville, J.-B. 1818. *Les Périgourdismes corrigés*, Périgueux: J. Danède.

Darmesteter, A. 1894. *Traité de la formation des mots composés dans la langue française*, 2nd edn., Paris: Francke (repr. Paris: Champion, 1967).

Decomps, D. 1983. 'La poussée du français technique et scientifique dans le monde rural occitan moderne et contemporain', *Cahiers d'Etudes Romanes*, 3, Univ. de Toulouse Le Mirail.

Elcock, W. D. 1960. *The Romance Languages*, London: Faber & Faber.

Gross, G. 1988. 'Degré de figement des noms composés', *Langages*, 90, 57–72.

Klingebiel, K. 1983. 'Arsène Darmesteter's *Traité de la formation des mots composés*: 1874, 1894, and beyond', *Romance Philology*, 36, 386–90.

—— 1986. *Bibliographie linguistique (1960–1982) de l'ancien occitan*, Hamburg: Buske, 1986.

—— forthcoming. *Bibliographie linguistique (1983–1990) de l'ancien occitan.*

Lascoux, J.-B. 1823. *Gasconismes corrigés*, Bordeaux (repr. Paris: France Expansion, 1973).

Mazuc, E. 1899. *Grammaire languedocienne. Dialecte de Pézenas*, Toulouse: Privat.

Mok, Q. I. M. 1987. 'La dérivation occitane est-elle encore productive?', in *Actes du premier congrès international de l'AIEO*, ed. Ricketts, P. T., London: Association Internationale des Etudes Occitanes, 359–66.

—— 1991. 'Concurrence de *tornar* + infinitif et *re-* en occitan', in *Actes du XVIIIe congrès international de linguistique et de philologie romanes,* vol. 2, Tübingen: Niemeyer, 104–11.

Puget, P. 1755. 'Dictionnaire provençal et français' (MS, Bibliothèque Municipale d'Aix-en-Provence).

Seuzaret, J. 1947. 'Dictionnaire patois–françois du dialecte du Vivarais et de la région d'Aubenas (Ardèche)' (typescript).

Taupiac, J. 1977. *Pichon diccionari francés–occitan*, Toulouse: IEO.

10

Language status and political aspirations:
the case of northern Spain

JOHN N. GREEN

When the maintenance and revival of minority languages in western Europe first began to attract widespread interest and interventionist concern in the late 1960s, the central issues were: territoriality; the extent of bilingualism; and the shifting definitions of 'language', 'dialect' and 'speech community' (Haugen 1966a, 1966b; Price 1969). A quarter of a century later, when the looser political structures of a rapidly evolving federal Europe give (perhaps spurious) grounds for optimism to language activists, those original issues remain live (see, for instance, Williams 1991), but they have been upstaged by two more insistent research themes: speaker perceptions and attitudes as determinants of language status, and diglossia as a symbol of linguistic conflict. The revaluing of cultural diversity has sharpened awareness both of its vulnerability and of the political commitment required for its preservation, for, as Haugen (1990, 114) reminds us, 'Whenever languages are in contact, they are in competition for users'.

The concept of a 'minority' language has always been problematic, contingent as it must be on non-linguistic factors.[1] Whereas 'minority' is usually understood by English speakers in its straightforward numerical sense, and so need imply nothing more tendentious than that a language is used by less than half of a given population, Romance speakers are more likely to be sensitive to the connotation of relative status embodied in *minor*. Indeed, the concept of diglossia, as redefined in conflictual terms (see, especially, Marcellesi 1981 and Kremnitz 1991), depends crucially on the inequality of status and power relations. In such a framework, a minority language is almost inevitably one that has been subordinated to, or annexed by, a dominant ideology; it has, in other words, been *minorized*.[2] By the same token, its survival may well entail the rejection of this subordinate status and the affirmation of its equality with the dominant code in all functional domains.

My aim in this paper is to examine some of the factors that have led to a revival of interest in minority languages and regional forms of Romance speech in post-Franco Spain, together with their consequences for the social psychology of their speakers and the political stability of the State.[3] Galician is offered as a particularly interesting case study, because its rehabilitation is requiring both corpus and status planning, and because the high incidence of (at least passive) bilingualism in most social groups in Galicia challenges the claim made by conflict theorists that societal bilingualism is always an 'indicateur de crise' (Kremnitz 1987, 211). Elsewhere in Spain, however, I shall argue that there have been attempts to manufacture linguistic identities for dubious motives and certainly without due regard for the likely consequences.

Linguistic minorities in Spain

How many languages are spoken in Spain? Among the many criteria proposed for distinguishing between languages and dialects is that of external recognition: what status educated lay people normally ascribe to a linguistic variety, or what they are taught to believe and find no urgent reason to challenge. On this basis, 'Spanish' and 'Portuguese' have been recognized as independent languages for some five hundred years, at least since the Treaty of Tordesillas of 1494. By contrast, perceptions of the relevant minority languages seem to have undergone some interesting changes within the past quarter century. In his survey of fifteen minority languages of western Europe, Price (1969) mentions only two from Spain: Basque and Catalan. Stephens (1976) devotes a long chapter to linguistic minorities in Spain, with three sections: on Catalan, Basque and Galician. Likewise, Wardhaugh confines his discussion of linguistic competition in post-Franco Spain (1987, 119–27) to Catalan, Basque and Galician – in that order of coverage and apparent importance, though the number of Galician speakers is acknowledged to be much higher than the number of Basque speakers. Most recently, the list of Romance languages published in *The Oxford International Encyclopedia of Linguistics* (see Fleischman 1992) contains, in addition to the Spanish Gypsy language Caló, entries for: Asturian, Catalan, Galician and Valencian.[4]

That Catalan, Basque and Galician should be the three minority languages most often mentioned is in no way surprising, since they were the three most ruthlessly suppressed by the Franco regime in the years following the Civil War, and the first to benefit from the more liberal climate of the 1970s. It is a moot point whether their present vigour is partly owed to the severity of their repression and to the resistance it engendered: in Catalonia at least, the attempt to relegate Catalan to the status of a rural patois was perceived not only as a social injustice but also as an insult to a proud cultural heritage. Claims on behalf of other regional languages are generally more recent, postdating the implementation of the liberal Constitution of 1978, by which they have been facilitated (see Juárez Blanquer 1988 and Herreras 1991). The Constitution, while affirming the indissoluble unity of Spain and the duty of all Spaniards to know and use Castilian as the official language of the State, recognizes the right to regional autonomy and offers official status to any regional language adopted in a Statute of Autonomy. Regional varieties not adopted in this way still qualify for special protection under the title of *modalidades lingüísticas*. Crucially, the powers delegated to an *Autonomía* include: 'The promotion of culture, research and, if appropriate, the teaching of the language of the Autonomous Community' (Article 148, paragraph 17a).[5] With the delegation goes a federal budget to help fulfil the stated aims. There are now seventeen fully approved *autonomías*, each of which may apply to have its regional language declared official. It is under this provision that claims have been made for Asturian, Aragonese and, most recently, Murcian.

Do they have *linguistic* validity? In assessing claims for language status made by, or on behalf of, speakers of minority lects, linguists now typically have recourse to a mix of intrasystemic and external criteria. An important change in recent years has been the recognition that attitudinal factors not only weigh in the decision on status, but also influence judgements of comprehensibility. In turn, the evidence that speakers' expectations can significantly influence their ability to understand a non-native lect, has led to some scepticism about the validity of intrasystemic measures of linguistic distance, which were formerly regarded as more 'objective' and inherently trustworthy. Despite the manifest difficulties, the dialectometric method known as the *méthode globale*, pioneered by Séguy and developed by Guiter, has won credibility by producing results which endorse the broad outlines of received opinion while often revealing discrepancies in the detail of the subgrouping.

Guiter's dialectometric analysis of western Romance (Guiter 1991), for instance, shows (aside from the Basque enclave on both sides of the Pyrenees), one language frontier between French and Iberian Romance, a second between Castilian and Catalan passing just west of

Lérida/Lleida and running almost north–south to Elche/Elx but incomplete in its northernmost stretch, and a third between Galician and Asturo-Leonese, again running north–south approximately along a line joining the mouth of the River Navia to Bragança, so taking in the westernmost parts of Asturias and León – the so-called *franxa*. So far, so relatively uncontroversial. Within Catalan, however, the primary dialect boundary, meandering from La Seu D'Urgell in the north to just south of Tarragona, confirms the traditional split into west and east branches (with the Balearics included in the eastern group), whereas the northern boundary of *valencià* corresponds only to that of a subdialect. In this light, the language frontier separating most of Valencian territory from Castilian symbolizes not the independent status of Valencian, but its membership of the Catalan group, more precisely as one of four equal subdialects of western Catalan. According to Guiter's intrasystemic criteria, then, the distinctiveness of Valencian from its closest linguistic relatives is lower than that of Aragonese and Asturo-Leonese, both of which are demarcated by primary dialect boundaries – a finding that is liable to enrage Valencian activists while still not satisfying those claiming language status for Asturian and Aragonese, who are unlikely to be content with a mere dialect boundary between themselves and Castilian.

If the status of a regional lect can be problematic, so can its name. In Spain, as in most other Romance-speaking territories, the overwhelming majority of regional forms of speech have names derived from geographical adjectives (*bable*, as a designation for the low-status variety spoken in Oviedo and the surrounding district, is one of the few exceptions). Many such names date back to the Reconquest and are now inappropriate, owing to the spread of Castilian and to the redrawing of administrative boundaries. While a territorial mismatch between a lect and the administrative unit whose designation it bears may be condoned – indeed, may pass unnoticed – in the case of a rural dialect perceived to be in gradual decline, it becomes an important factor in any interventionist policy of linguistic rehabilitation. Guiter's map (1991, 359) reminds us that 'Galician' extends beyond the eastern boundary of Galicia into Asturias and that 'Asturian' takes in the northern part of León. 'Aragonese', on the other hand, is shown as restricted to the northern sectors of Huesca and Zaragoza provinces together with a little of Navarre – an area far smaller than the medieval kingdom of Aragón but still more generous than that claimed by modern apologists for the language (Conte *et al.* 1977, 127).

In this context it is obviously instructive to know how native speakers themselves designate their speech. Useful, if patchy, information can be gleaned from the *Atlas lingüístico de la Península Ibérica*

(*ALPI* 1962, Map 4), where /ga'lego/ and near phonological variants are shown solidly throughout Galicia, and /astur'janu/ is found almost as systematically in Asturias and the northern strip of León, whereas in Huesca and Zaragoza /arago'nes/ alternates with names derived from much smaller localities, such as /belse'tan/ < Bielsa.[6] This is confirmed in a recent monograph on the Pyrenean village of Gistaín/Chistáu, whose inhabitants refer to themselves and their speech as /tʃista'vin/ rather than Aragonese (Mott 1989, 217). Valencian activists, however, may take comfort from the fact that *ALPI* shows a good territorial match between province and lect, which is almost universally called /valen'sja/ by its speakers.

Normalization in Galicia

Normalització is the term coined by Catalan and Valencian socio-linguists and later officially adopted by the Catalan Generalitat to refer to the process of raising the social prestige of a language and making its use normal and natural in all functional domains (the process also known as 'status planning'). As such, it represents the antithesis of *diglossia*, redefined by conflict linguists as the subordination of one linguistic code to another and its confinement to non-official and private functions. Since Catalan normalization has generally been viewed as a success (see Bastardas-Boada 1989, Fishman 1991, 287–336, and Strubell i Trueta 1993), it offers an obvious model for Galicia.

Galicia achieved autonomous status under the Spanish Constitution in 1980. Article 5 of the Estatuto de Galicia formally recognizes Galician as the language of Galicia, co-official with Castilian; outlaws linguistic discrimination; and requires the authorities to promote the use of Galician in all spheres of public life, promising them the necess-ary funds to encourage the teaching of the language.[7] There is now a regional government (the Xunta) operating through the medium of Galician, together with municipal administrations and an official body (the Dirección Xeral de Política Lingüística) charged with the im-plementation of the normalization policy and able to draw on signifi-cant funds to do so.[8] Daily newspapers are published in Galician, broadcasts on regional television and radio use the language quite unselfconsciously, and the publishing of both popular and learned books in Galician has been revived. There is a raised consciousness about the language, and a clear awareness of linguistic shibboleths – as attested by the frequent use of red spray paint to 'amend' official signs and place names written monolingually in Castilian. Most valuably for linguists, there are also reliable surveys of linguistic usage and attitudes, and an impressive linguistic atlas (*ALG* 1990–).

In most of the polls taken between 1970 and the present, 85 to 95 per cent of informants claimed to be fluent or fairly fluent in Galician (see Monteagudo and Santamarina 1993, Tables 1–3). Literacy in Galician remains much lower, though self-reported skills in reading and writing have improved markedly over the same period among more highly educated sections of the population; even so, those knowing Castilian tend to have much more balanced proficiency across the linguistic skills (ibid., Tables 4–5). Rates of bilingualism are high, but it is often not balanced bilingualism acquired in childhood: in the late 1980s some 40 per cent of pre-school children in rural hamlets were monolingual in Galician, while over 50 per cent of those from city backgrounds were monolingual in Castilian (ibid., Table 7b). Indeed, locality and social class (which, of course, are often interrelated) are the most important determinants of linguistic usage, followed by age. A poll taken in 1984 found, firstly, that Galician was almost twice as likely to be used for intragenerational interaction among grandparents or among parents as it was among grandchildren; and secondly, that whereas an overall 80 per cent of lower class speakers and 62 per cent of rural speakers would be prepared to initiate a conversation with a friend in Galician, only 35 per cent of those aged below 35 would do so; and in similar proportions 43 per cent of lower class speakers and 37 per cent of rural would speak Galician to their work supervisors, but only 22 per cent of those aged below 35 would do so (ibid., Tables 10 and 12). Interactions between university-educated professionals are almost four times as likely to take place in Castilian as in Galician, whereas over 90 per cent of those between farmers and fisherman will take place in Galician (ibid., Table 8b). Overall, then, Galician emerges as a language of older speakers in low-status employment in rural localities, a combination of factors that elsewhere has led to irreversible decline. There are, nevertheless, some hopeful signs, in the number of young people acquiring fully literate proficiency in Galician at high school or university, and in more positive attitudes towards the language: a poll of priests and seminarists taken in 1989, for instance, shows a massive shift away from Galician as the habitual colloquial language of priests, but a paradoxical increase in preference for Galician as the language of the Church (ibid., Table 16). It follows that the urgent task for status planners is to develop a young, urban middle class, fully proficient in Galician and proud of this ability – and to do so at a faster rate than migration, better education, and higher social aspirations erode the traditional strength of the language in the countryside.

To this extent, the goals of status planning in Galicia are not unlike those in Catalonia, though the Catalan planners started from a much stronger base, with more balanced bilingualism, much higher rates of literacy in Catalan, and an articulate Catalan-speaking urban middle class. In other respects, however, the language situations are not comparable. Catalan enjoys much greater cultural prestige and external recognition than Galician, attributes that tend to go hand in hand with economic power and political influence. But the more decisive factor is that Catalan language planners started out with an acknowledged and fully elaborated standard language – an *Ausbausprache* in Klossian terminology (see Kloss 1987 and Muljačić 1990) – so almost all of their efforts could be directed towards *normalització* and very few towards *normativització*. By contrast, Galician planners inherited serious dialectal fragmentation and a set of competing norms derived from literary models or amateur enthusiasts, none of which enjoyed widespread support. Not surprisingly, a major part of the effort of the planners has had to be directed inwards, towards developing norms for 'common Galician' and countering criticism from diverse groups who espouse fundamentally incompatible views on the future direction that Galician should take.

Corpus planning directed towards a single norm (which need not be the goal, but is often assumed to be) faces major difficulties in Galicia. A few prominent phonological features clearly belong to 'common Galician' and those which differentiate it from Castilian have acquired the status of shibboleths: in particular, the non-diphthongization of proto-Romance stressed /ɛ, ɔ/ (witness *ALPI*, Map 40, *cazuela* 'cooking pot', with /ka'θwela/ found from mid-Asturias eastwards, and /ka'θolə ~ ka'solə/ almost throughout Galicia), and the different outcomes of palatalization processes, with the salient Castilian *jota* /x/ corresponding either to a palatal lateral /ʎ/ (as in *ALPI*, Map 6, *abeja* 'bee' = Cast. /a'βexa/, Gal. /a'βeʎə/, Map 12, *aguja* 'needle = Cast. /a'ɣuxa/, Gal. /a'ɣuʎə/) or to a combination of yod and palato-alveolar fricative /jʃ/ (as in *ALPI*, Map 32, *caja* 'box, cash desk' = Cast. /'kaxa/, Gal. /'kajʃə/, and Map 75, *eje* 'axle' = Cast./'exe/, Gal. /'ejʃə/), although in other contexts Galician laterals are not palatalized (witness *ALPI*, Map 29, *caballo* 'horse' = Cast. /ka'βaʎo/, Gal. /ka'βalo/). Similarly, common Galician is distinguished from Portuguese to the south by the almost universal occurrence of /-aŋ/ as the third person verb ending where Portuguese has the nazalized diphthong /ãw̃/, and by the preservation of syllable-final /-s/ where Portuguese has the palato-alveolar /ʃ/ (witness *ALG*, Map 1, *cantas* 'you sing', pronounced /'kantas̺ /throughout Galicia except for a few localities along the southern frontier which have /'kantɐʃ/, like Portuguese). There are, of course, also many lexical isoglosses which align Galician more closely with Portuguese than with Castilian (as in *ALPI*, Map 20, *ayer* 'yesterday' = Cast. /aˈjɛr/, Gal. /ˈõntə/).

Within Galician dialectology, one of the salient features usually adduced in support of a primary split into western and eastern zones of roughly equal area, is the so-called *gheada*, as a result of which the /g/ phoneme has two voiced allophones in the east, much as in Castilian, while in the west it is realized as a weak voiceless fricative or aspirate (hence *galego* = EGal. [gaˈleɣo], WGal. [xaˈlexo ~ xʰaˈlexʰǫ]; see *ALPI*, Map 4). Elsewhere, phonological isoglosses criss-cross the traditional subgrouping, and the distribution of morphosyntactic variants signally fails to match that of phonological features. By way of phonological illustrations, we may cite: the /θ ~ s/ isogloss, which certainly runs on a north–south line, but far to the west of the main division (hence EGal. /ˈθiŋko/ 'five' and /aˈθero/ 'steel', like Castilian, but WGal. /ˈsiŋko/ and /aˈsero/; *ALPI*, Maps 47 and 9 respectively); the realization of final -*o* as /-o/ in the north and as /-u/ in the south (*ALPI*, Map 33, *camino* 'road' = NGal. /kaˈmiɲo/, SGal. /kaˈmiɲu/, and Map 58, *cuchillo* 'knife' = NGal. /kojˈtelo/, SGal. /kujˈtelu/); and the erratic distribution of /bl- ~ br-/ and /kl- ~ kr-/ (as in *ALPI*, Map 25, *blanco* 'white' = Gal. /ˈblãⁿko ~ ˈblãⁿku ~ ˈbrãⁿko ~ ˈbrãⁿku/, and Map 48, *clavo* 'nail' = Gal. /ˈklaβo ~ ˈklaβu ~ ˈkraβo ~ ˈkraβu/), of which the least inaccurate statement that can be made is that the /l/ variants are more common in the south and the /r/ variants in the north – precisely the opposite of what one might expect from the contiguity of Portuguese.[9] In some important reflexes of verb morphology, however, the isogloss patterns are different again, with a large central zone contrasting with either the western fringe or with a narrow periphery: hence the central zone preserves proto-Romance -T- in second person plural endings while the far west has a syncopated form rather like that of Argentinian Spanish and the far east matches Castilian (see *ALG*, Map 2, 'you (pl.) sing' = CGal. /kanˈtaðeś/, WGal. /kanˈtaś/, EGal. /kanˈtajś/), and the central zone shifts the stress of trisyllabic first person plural endings to the penult, whereas the peripheral areas have proparoxytonic stress like Castilian (see *ALG*, Map 4, 'we used to sing' = CGal. /kantaˈβamoś/ versus WGal., EGal., and Cast. /kanˈtaβamoś/, Map 13, 'we had sung' = CGal. /kantaˈramoś/ versus WGal., EGal., and Cast. /kanˈtaramoś/).

While, individually, none of these variants causes serious difficulties of intelligibility, collectively they do contribute to an impression of irreconcilable diversity. The corpus planners of the Galician Academy and the Instituto da Língua Galega decided to concentrate initially on orthography and morphology, no doubt for the value of a symbolic visual unity, and the reasonably liberal *Norms* they jointly promulgated in 1982 have been adopted for official purposes and primary education without too much controversy. Whether the 1982 *Norms* will hold, and whether other linguistic levels prove so amenable, depends on the outcome of an increasingly acrimonious policy debate between the 'autonomists', who wish to forge a completely independent identity for Galician and its culture, and the so-called 'reintegrationists', who view linguistic reunification with Portuguese as the only viable option for the longer term (for a fair summary of the autonomist position see Monteagudo and Santamarina 1993, and for a strong defence of reintegration, Nolla 1990). Clearly, such divergent underlying persuasions affect almost all decisions on normative detail. For the present, autonomists have been able to present themselves as more moderate and are in the ascendant, aided, no doubt, by widespread ignorance and indifference within Portugal as to the fate of Galician (see Wardhaugh 1987, 126). Their position, as we shall see, carries different dangers.

The social psychology of language planning

Language is a potent symbol of social identity for the individual and of political aspiration for the community. In the social psychological approach to language, individuals are seen as creating their own identity, or acquiescing in the one ascribed to them, by selecting linguistic features from a repertoire of variation; similarly, communities assert their independence within larger social groupings by emphasizing shared properties and accentuating their distinctiveness from 'out' groups (see, for instance, Le Page and Tabouret-Keller 1985). Both processes require a prior awareness of linguistic difference and sensitivity towards the social interpretation likely to be placed upon the linguistic variants. The degree of freedom enjoyed by individuals in establishing their linguistic identity (or, put less positively, the responsibility they must exercise in so doing), clearly depends on the fluidity of the speech community and the pervasiveness of a linguistic standard or of other, looser, norms.

In more traditional accounts of linguistic contact (such as Weinreich 1953, Sala 1988), emphasis is placed on the mechanisms of interference and transfer between the linguistic systems present in the minds of individual speakers; conversely, little attention is paid to the relative status of the codes brought into contact. Trudgill (1986, 39–41) argues persuasively that perceptions of status will certainly affect the diffusion of any linguistic innovation, but also, and more subtly, that innovations arising from a genuine need for accommodation in face-to-face

interaction are perceived differently from those that are merely im-
itated after initially passive reception – as, for instance, from radio or
television broadcasts. Thus, the dichotomy between bilingualism and
bidialectalism, which was largely irrelevant to Weinreich's study of the
systemic effects of contact, becomes crucial to Trudgill's interpretation
of the motivation and sustainability of change. If speakers perceive the
two codes in contact to be separate languages, they may elect to modify
either or both in the interest of fulfilling a communicative need, but if
the speakers are bidialectal and perceive the two codes as variants of
one and the same language, by accommodating to the linguistic behaviour of an interlocutor who has made different choices from the
repertoire, they risk undermining their own linguistic identity. Indeed,
the long-term effects of linguistic accommodation may well go beyond
social perceptions. Until now, it has generally been assumed that
exposure to linguistic variability and the need to accommodate
'merely' add to the repertoire and versatility of individual speakers, so
extending the range of their *performance* without thereby affecting
their underlying *competence*, but recent research by Grosjean and Py
(1991) among Spanish-speaking migrants in the district of Neuchâtel
leads them to conclude that their subjects' first language (their L_1
competence) has indeed been modified as a result of years of contact
and imperfectly understood accommodation.

These points have obvious implications for language planning in a
context of dialectal diversity such as Galicia. A policy of normalization
whose aim is natural bilingualism, with equal facility in two spoken and
two written codes, may be successful within a generation in favoured
urban localities where a koine has already developed and where there is
an unchallenged assumption that vernacular literacy is a prerequisite of
social progress (Siegel 1993). Such a timescale is unrealistic in remote
rural communities where the route to bilingualism must first pass
through a stage of bidialectalism and where the acquisition of literacy
in a koineized – not to say standardized – Galician may well be
perceived both as an educational burden and a cultural alienation.
Paradoxically, the very solidarity of the perception of non-Castilian
'otherness' evinced in the responses to the *ALPI* risks becoming a
liability within an autonomous Galicia, where a policy of normalization necessarily draws attention to the dysfunctionality of dialectal
variation that could previously be overlooked or hailed as a symbol of
vitality. It is far from obvious why rural speakers, whose traditional
loyalty has been focused on the *patria chica* and away from the impersonal Castilian State, should now elect to refocus their linguistic behaviour towards the usage of such metropolitan centres as Vigo, on which
the written norm is inevitably predicated. If economic factors or their

personal aspirations lead them to migrate to urban centres, they will face much greater exposure to koineized Galician but will also come into contact with much larger numbers of monolingual Castilian speakers. Meanwhile, speakers of rural dialect who wish to retain their local identity are being urged to acquire literacy and listen to broadcasts in a Galician which they do not recognize as their own. It is a daily reminder – much more sympathetic and subtle, but no less insistent than that of the Franco regime – that they do not *hablar bien*.

While, therefore, Galician theorists were probably right to analyse the previous linguistic situation as conflictual diglossia between dominant Castilian and oppressed Galician, the normalization policy now runs the risk of creating secondary diglossia, or at least asymmetrical bilingualism, between a newly emergent High form associated with literacy and urban values, and a patchwork of rural varieties whose speakers still constitute the majority of the population. If, as seems distinctly possible, a realigned class structure develops in autonomous Galicia, with secondary diglossia as one of its symptoms, there is little reason to assume that a disadvantaged rural majority will feel more content living under the hegemony of a Galician-speaking urban intelligentsia than under that of a remote Castilian-speaking State. In particular, the chances of conflict are increased if rural speakers feel they are placed in double linguistic jeopardy or denied access, by redefined educational priorities, to the effective instruction in Castilian that would still offer a passport to social mobility.

Conclusion: language and politics

Although the awareness of linguistic variability is attested from the earliest records, its conscious exploitation for political ends seems to be fairly recent: certainly the direct association of language and nationhood was not widespread before the early nineteenth century. The bond was undoubtedly strengthened during the decolonization of the 1960s and 1970s, when emergent states sought to identify and promote a national language as a prime symbol of solidarity and independence. If, as claimed in a provocative but not intentionally political article by Pohl (1988), epithets such as 'Latin', when applied to people, are interpreted first and foremost by reference to language, modern language planners are certainly justified in the priority they attach to status planning. As a corollary, regional or ethnic groups aspiring to political autonomy would do well to raise the profile of their favoured lect and seek its external recognition as a language.

While in theory linguistic intervention could be justified by a range of humanistic considerations, in practice it is rarely undertaken for other than political motives, not least because implementation requires the commitment of much greater resources than are usually to be found in a cultural or folklore budget. In this light, the 1978 Spanish Constitution could conceivably be interpreted as a Machiavellian attempt to divide and rule. All the evidence, however, points in the direction of a genuinely liberal wish to balance the pressures for regional self-determination, fuelled by years of repression, against the imperative of preserving the territorial integrity of the Spanish State. Whether or not the balance can be preserved in the more austere economic conditions of the 1990s must depend on the extent to which political aspirations can be confined to autonomy in everyday domestic administration. About this, there must be doubts. In July 1991, political independence within a federal Europe was adopted as the official policy of the CDC (Convergència Democràtica de Catalunya), the majority party of the Generalitat (as reported in *Diario 16*, 22 July 1991). Even if this gesture was to be interpreted as sabre-rattling, it cannot have been welcome to the authorities in Madrid, where there is a sharp awareness that the effect of the Constitution is to channel large and increasing amounts of federal funds towards regional 'cultural' activities which, in their turn, are fuelling demands for secession. The loss of Catalonia, which is distinguished from other regions both by its independent historical links with Europe and by its growing economic and cultural prestige, would be a major blow to Spanish national pride and would almost certainly spell the end of constitutional liberalism. One can only speculate about the longer-term effects of the ensuing recriminations. Historical precedents certainly do not augur well for troublesome minorities which become too readily identifiable with a territory and with such salient cultural symbols as a distinct language.

What, then, are the likely linguistic consequences of the Spanish experiment with controlled devolution? Any answer must distinguish, firstly, between language maintenance and artificial revival, and secondly, between consensual and conflictual intervention. At one extreme, the future of Catalan has been secured at least for the medium term; at the other, artificial attempts to create 'Murcian' from scattered rural lects which were probably never united, or to revive 'Aragonese' from the attrition and disintegration it has progressively suffered since at least the sixteenth century, are equally doomed to failure – not least because they have so far failed to establish linguistic legitimacy (see, in particular, Monge 1989). An intermediate case is represented by Asturian, whose Academia de la Llingua Asturiana has made strenuous efforts at both status and corpus planning (as witnessed, for instance, by the normative dictionary of Sánchez Vicente (1988)), in the process stirring up a good deal of local resentment while not achieving significant external recognition. Both linguistic and social reasons lie behind this lack of support for linguistic interventionism, for while Asturias is famed for its fierce local loyalty, the 'basilectal' *bable* which might form the basis of an independent language is perceived as coarse and uneducated by many Asturians, and the more acceptable /astur'janu/ is too close to Castilian to gain credibility as a separate language. One cannot create an *Abstandsprache* merely from the wish to be eligible to receive federal development funds.

Catalan *normalització*, in contrast, could count on: the widespread natural use of a fairly homogeneous spoken Catalan, owed in some measure to stubborn resistance in the face of repression; an acknowledged standard, offering the basis for a revival of external recognition; and above all the consent of the majority of Catalonians to the promotion of Catalan as a symbol of their aspirations. In terms of Fishman's GIDS (Graded Intergenerational Disruption Scale; see Fishman 1991, passim), the language shift away from Catalan never fell below the sixth point of his eight-point scale (mother-tongue transmission in the family and neighbourhood), and its revival has attained the second point (use in regional mass media and governmental services); even so, full equality with Spanish in all functional domains remains a distant goal, and Fishman is not wholly convinced that it will ever be reached (1991, 319–24). One of the most significant objectives is to persuade long-established, Spanish-speaking migrants to Catalonia to learn and use the language unselfconsciously; here, according to the surveys conducted by Woolard and Gahng (1990), steady progress is being made.

In assessing the prospects for the survival of Galician – which, incidentally, goes unmentioned by Fishman – we return to the urgency of fostering positive attitudes towards rural lects as a means of arresting their decline. In this respect, the existence of a tradition of naming the lects as /ga'lego/ would be interpreted as a hopeful sign by conflict linguists such as Marcellesi, who argues (1981, 8) that the ability to particularize and reify a language by naming is essential to its preservation (and, one might add, to its repression). It is notable that the *ALPI* question on language name (Map 4) elicited, both from the border of Galicia and Asturias, and from that of Aragón and Catalonia, responses of *chapurrao*, for which the kindest translation is 'medley'. Holmquist's more recent investigation of language loyalty in Cantabria (1988) found that many rural speakers had no noun to designate their speech, and merely contrasted their own *hablar mal* with the *hablar bien* (that is, Castilian) they were fostering in their children.

It is hard to see how any programme of linguistic intervention could counter such negative attitudes.

In conclusion, we should ask whether natural bilingualism is a realistic and effective goal for language planning. It is, after all, the position from which many minority languages have declined calamitously into extinction, sometimes but not always through an intermediate stage of diglossia (see Dorian 1989 for case studies, and Clairis 1991 for a typology of loss). Sometimes the language dies with the more or less active connivance of its speakers, who no longer perceive its practical utility; occasionally, it dies as a result of well-intentioned but misguided governmental intervention aimed at its preservation.[10] Certainly, therefore, the attainment of balanced, non-diglossic bilingualism – however distant that goal may seem in the case of a language such as Galician – cannot be regarded as a guarantee of its survival. Long-term survival is assured not by transient negative polarities, such as the wish to distance oneself from a neighbouring lect or to be rid of an oppressive linguistic 'roof' (see Muljačić 1989), but by the constant usefulness of a language to its speakers and the positive attitudes they harbour towards it. Galician is already recognized as an official regional language within Spain; to attempt more, by the deliberate intertwining of language with nationhood and territoriality, is a sink-or-swim policy courting disaster. Galicia, as 'reintegrationists' realize only too clearly, is too small and economically under-developed to risk complete political independence. That leaves, to say the least, an uncomfortable choice between linguistic reintegration (a misnomer which actually entails seeking the tutelage of what was once the daughter dialect of Galician) and an autonomy which may lead nowhere, while further reducing opportunities for already disadvantaged groups. We linguists tend to be enthusiastic defenders of linguistic diversity and cultural heritage, which is a laudable sentiment, but not one which should be allowed to decide the fate of groups who already consider themselves oppressed. So far, Galician has been nurtured without obvious conflict or detrimental effects, and for that we rejoice. In the long run, as Wardhaugh gloomily says (1987, 127): 'The limited autonomy of the post-Franco years may prove to be largely irrelevant to the future of the language, which is not at all a promising one ...'

Notes

[1] A perspicacious section in the Introduction to Price's pioneering bibliographic survey (1969, 10) reads:

The term 'minority languages' is not perhaps fully satisfactory, as at least two of the languages concerned, Catalan and Faroese, are still spoken by the great majority of the population of the areas with which they are traditionally associated. One can however say in justification of the term that the speakers of each language form a minority within the country or countries of which they are citizens [. . .]. The term 'regional languages' is no better and is indeed open to the further objection that Irish, Romansh, Welsh and perhaps others are in one sense or another 'national' rather than 'regional' languages. The term 'ethnic languages' (*langues ethniques*) recently adopted by some French writers is wholly inappropriate with its misleading implication of an association between language and race.

2 According to Strubell i Trueta (1993, 187), the parent term *minorització* was first coined by the Catalan linguist Enric Montaner. It has now spread well beyond the Catalan and Occitan schools of conflict linguistics to become common currency: see, for instance, the conference papers in Py and Jeanneret 1989.

3 Discussion of bilingualism/bidialectalism will be confined to varieties of Romance, and will not extend to Basque, whose language status has never been in doubt. For information on attitudes and language maintenance in Euskadi, see the excellent survey by Hughes (1992).

4 The relevant entries read:
   Asturian: spoken in Asturias, Spain. Also called Bable. About 80 percent mutually intelligible with Castilian Spanish, the most closely related variety.
   Catalan: around 8,840,000 speakers reported in 1976, with 4,000,000 in northeastern Spain around Barcelona and in Catalonia and Valencia Provinces and the Balearic Islands, 260,000 in France, 12,300 in Andorra, 22,000 in Italy, and 40,000 in the United States. Also called Catalonian. An official regional language in Spain.
   Galician: around 3,170,000 speakers reported in 1986, in Galicia Province, northwest Spain; also spoken in Portugal. Also called Gallego. Portuguese, the most closely related variety, is about 85 percent intelligible to speakers of Galician. An official regional language in Spain.
   Valencian: spoken in Valencia, Spain. Has 90 to 95 percent mutual intelligibility with Catalan, the most closely related variety. (Fleischman 1992, 341–3).

5 The Spanish text of the relevant extracts is:
   Artículo 2
   La Constitución se fundamenta en la indisoluble unidad de la Nación española, patria común e indivisible de todos los españoles, y reconoce y garantiza el derecho a la autonomía de las nacionalidades y regiones que la integran y la solidaridad entre todas ellas.
   Artículo 3
   1. El castellano es la lengua española del Estado. Todos los españoles tienen el deber de conocerla y el derecho de usarla.
   2. Las demás lenguas españolas serán también oficiales en las respectivas Comunidades Autónomas de acuerdo con sus Estatutos.
   3. La riqueza de las distintas modalidades lingüísticas de España es un patrimonio cultural que será objeto de especial respeto y protección.
   Artículo 148
   1. Las Comunidades Autónomas podrán asumir competencias en las siguientes materias: [. . .]
      17.ª El fomento de la cultura, de la investigación y, en su caso, de la enseñanza de la lengua de la Comunidad Autónoma.

6 The well-known problems of timescale and changes of personnel which dogged the *ALPI* detract from the usefulness of Map 4, since the question on language names was asked selectively and at different dates: Galicia, Aragón and most of Catalonia were among the first regions to be surveyed, between 1931 and 1936, whereas Asturias and the rest of Catalonia were not completed until 1947. Linguistic forms enclosed in slashes, in this and the following section, represent broad diasystemic transcriptions, not strict phonemic analyses.

7 The relevant extracts are:
   A lingua propia de Galicia é o galego [...]
   Os idiomas galego e castelán son oficiais en Galicia e todos teñen o direito de os coñecer e de os usar.
   Ninguén poderá ser discriminado por cause da lingua [...]
   Os poderes públicos de Galicia garantizarán o uso normal e oficial dos dous idiomas e potenciarán o emprego do galego en tódolos planos da vida pública, cultural e informativa, e disporán os medios necesarios para facilital-o seu coñecemento.

8 For instance, it runs Summer Schools on Galician language and culture, and offers bursaries to encourage the participation of foreign students.

9 For fuller discussion of the phonological characteristics of Galician and the features which separate it from both Castilian and modern Portuguese, see Álvarez Blanco 1991, Carvalho 1991, and Champion 1990.

10 Hindley (1990) documents how Irish was sent into steep decline in the Gaeltacht when a well-intentioned attempt to encourage its use among young children was interpreted by adult speakers as a pure bribe, and rejected as insulting.

References

ALG. 1990–. *Atlas lingüístico galego*, directed by Constantino García and Antón Santamarina, La Coruña: Fundación Pedro Barrié de la Maza.

ALPI. 1962–. *Atlas lingüístico de la Península Ibérica*, directed by Tomás Navarro Tomás, Madrid: CSIC.

Álvarez Blanco, R. 1991. 'O sistema fonolóxico do galego. Comparación có do portugués', in Kremer 1991, 3, 517–30.

Ammon, U. (ed.). 1989. *Status and Function of Languages and Language Varieties*, Berlin: Mouton de Gruyter.

Ammon, U., Dittmar, N. and Mattheier, K. J. (eds.). 1987–8. *Sociolinguistics. An International Handbook of the Sciences of Language and Society*, Berlin: Walter de Gruyter, 2 vols.

Bastardas-Boada, A. 1989. 'Language-use extension in linguistic normalization processes: general patterns and the Catalan experience', *Catalan Review*, 3, 59–84.

Bright, W. (ed.). 1992. *Oxford International Encyclopedia of Linguistics*, New York: Oxford University Press.

Carvalho, J. Brandão de. 1991. '"Cantabrie" et "mozarabie": de quelques divergences entre espagnol et portugais', *La Linguistique*, 27.2, 61–73.

Champion, J. J. 1990. 'The lateral consonants in Spanish, Portuguese and Catalan', *Romance Notes*, 30, 229–36.

Clairis, C. 1991. 'Le processus de disparition des langues', *La Linguistique*, 27.1, 3–13.

Conte, A., Cortes, Ch., Martínez, A., Nagore, F. and Vázquez, Ch. 1977. *El aragonés: Identidad y problemática de una lengua*, Zaragoza: Librería General.

Dorian, N. C. (ed.). 1989. *Investigating Obsolescence. Studies in Contraction and Death*, Cambridge: Cambridge University Press.

Fishman, J. A. 1991. *Reversing Language Shift. Theoretical and Empirical Foundations of Assistance to Threatened Languages*, Clevedon, Avon: Multilingual Matters.

Fleischman, S. 1992. 'Romance languages', in Bright 1992, 3, 337–43.

Grosjean, F. and Py, B. 1991. 'La restructuration d'une première langue: l'intégration de variantes de contact dans la compétence de migrants bilingues', *La Linguistique*, 27.2, 35–60.

Guiter, H. 1991. 'Applications d'une méthode géolinguistique en galloroman et ibéroroman', in Kremer 1991, 3, 352–61.

Haugen, E. 1966a. *Language Conflict and Language Planning: The Case of Modern Norwegian*, Cambridge, Mass.: Harvard University Press.

——1966b. 'Dialect, language, nation', *Anthropological Linguistics*, 6.8, 922–35.

——1990. 'Language fragmentation in Scandinavia: Revolt of the minorities', in Haugen *et al.*, 2nd edn., 1990, 100–19.

Haugen, E., McClure, J. D. and Thomson, D. S. (eds.). 2nd edn., 1990. *Minority Languages Today. A Selection from the Papers read at the First International Conference on Minority Languages held at Glasgow University from 8 to 13 September 1980*, Edinburgh: Edinburgh University Press, 2nd edn. with corrections and additions (originally published 1981).

Herreras, J. C. 1991. 'Le panorama linguistique espagnol', *La Linguistique*, 27.1, 75–85.

Hindley, R. 1990. *The Death of the Irish Language: A Qualified Obituary*, London: Routledge.

Holmquist, J. C. 1988. *Language Loyalty and Linguistic Variation. A Study in Spanish Cantabria*, Dordrecht: Foris.

Holtus, G. *et al.* (eds.). 1989. *La corona de Aragón y las lenguas románicas. Miscelánea de homenaje para Germán Colón*, Tübingen: Narr.

Hughes, C. 1992. 'Evaluating linguistic competence in a Basque–Castilian speech community', *Bulletin of Hispanic Studies*, 69, 105–26.

Juárez Blanquer, A. (ed.). 1988. *Las lenguas románicas españolas tras la constitución de 1978*, Granada: Tat.

Kloss, H. 1987. 'Abstandsprache und Ausbausprache', in Ammon *et al.* 1987, 1, 302–8.

Kremer, D. (ed.). 1991. *Actes du XVIIIe congrès international de linguistique et philologie romanes*, Tübingen: Niemeyer.

Kremnitz, G. 1987. 'Diglossie, possibilités et limites d'un terme', *Lengas*, 22, 199–213.

——1991. 'Y a-t-il des "diglossies neutres"?', *Lengas*, 30, 29–36.

Le Page, R. B. and Tabouret-Keller, A. 1985. *Acts of Identity. Creole-Based Approaches to Language and Ethnicity*, Cambridge: Cambridge University Press.

Marcellesi, J.-B. 1981. 'Bilinguisme, diglossie, hégémonie: problèmes et tâches', *Langages*, 61, 5–11.

Monge, F. 1989. '¿Una nueva lengua románica?', in Holtus *et al.* 1989, 275–83.

Monteagudo, E. and Santamarina, A. 1993. 'Galician and Castilian in contact: historical, social and linguistic aspects', in Posner and Green 1993, 117–73.

Mott, B. 1989. *El habla de Gistain* (Colección de estudios altoaragoneses, 29), Huesca: Instituto de Estudios Altoaragoneses.

Muljačić, Ž. 1989. 'Über den Begriff *Dachsprache*', in Ammon 1989, 256–77.

——1990. 'Ausbau-Universalien und Quasi-Universalien', *Zeitschrift für Dialektologie und Linguistik*, 57, 167–73.

Nolla, F. Pérez-Barreiro. 1990. 'Which language for Galicia? The status of Galician as an official language and the prospect for its "reintegration" with Portuguese', *Portuguese Studies*, 6, 191–210.

Pohl, J. 1988. 'Qui est latin?', *La Linguistique*, 24.2, 39–73.

Posner, R. and Green, J. N. (eds.). 1993. *Trends in Romance Linguistics and Philology. 5: Bilingualism and Linguistic Conflict in Romance*, Berlin: Mouton de Gruyter.

Price, G. 1969. *The Present Position of Minority Languages in Western Europe. A Selective Bibliography*, Cardiff: University of Wales Press.

Py, B. and Jeanneret, R. (eds.). 1989. *Minorisation linguistique et interaction. Actes du symposium de Neuchâtel, 16–18 septembre 1987*, Neuchâtel: Faculté des Lettres/Genève: Droz.

Sala, M. 1988. *El problema de las lenguas en contacto*, México: Universidad Nacional Autónoma de México.

Sánchez Vicente, X. X. 1988. *Diccionariu de la llingua asturiana, con sinónimos, refranes y frases feches; 30,000 vocablos*, Gijón: G. H.

Siegel, J. (ed.). 1993. 'Koines and koineization'. Special issue of *International Journal of the Sociology of Language*, no. 99.

Stephens, M. 1976. *Linguistic Minorities in Western Europe*, Llandysul: Gomer Press.

Strubell i Trueta, M. 1993. 'Catalan : Castilian', in Posner and Green 1993, 175–207.

Trudgill, P. 1986. *Dialects in Contact*, Oxford: Blackwell.

Wardhaugh, R. 1987. *Languages in Competition: Dominance, Diversity and Decline*, Oxford: Blackwell.

Weinreich, U. 1953. *Languages in Contact. Findings and Problems*, New York: Linguistic Circle of New York.

Williams, C. H. (ed.). 1991. *Linguistic Minorities, Society and Territory*, Clevedon, Avon: Multilingual Matters.

Woolard, K. A. and Gahng, T.-J. 1990. 'Changing language policies and attitudes in autonomous Catalonia', *Language in Society*, 19, 311–30.

11

Ël piemontèis, lenga d'Euròpa

M. MAIR PARRY

The title of this paper occurs in a motion presented at the *VI Rëscontr antërnassional dë studi an sla lenga e la literatura piemontèisa*, held in Alba in Piedmont in 1989 (see Clivio and Pich 1990, 185). Each year participants at the conference vote on a motion, presented in Piedmontese, Italian and French, calling for support, particularly from regional, national and European institutions, for regional and minority languages, and specifically for the Piedmontese language. Neither in common parlance nor in linguistic classifications has Piedmontese traditionally enjoyed the status of 'language'. Like Venetian, Neapolitan and Sicilian, it has been considered one of the many 'dialects' of Italy, cognate with the Florentine dialect, on which the standard language is based. The spread of the standard, a recent phenomenon, since it is only during the present century that it has been acquired by the majority of the Italian population, has inevitably been at the expense of the dialect. Statistics from recent national surveys show that north-west Italy is in the vanguard of the shift to Italian.[1]

The decline of the dialects is a matter of concern to a growing number of Italians who fear the impending loss of their traditions and culture, while separatist political movements such as the northern Leghe have not been slow to capitalize on the symbolic value of the dialects as an expression of regional allegiance in a climate of intense dissatisfaction with the central authorities. Both groups have high expectations of the new more closely integrated Europe, looking to it for recognition and support. This paper presents an overview of the linguistic situation in Piedmont and an analysis of the attitudes of its inhabitants on the eve of a major step towards European political unity, the abolition of border controls within the European Community at the end of 1992. A year previously, on 20 November 1991, a

Bill concerning minority languages had been passed in the Italian Chamber of Deputies, and the discussion it provoked was an unexpected and fruitful source of information about linguistic attitudes towards the dialects in general.

1. The linguistic history of Piedmont

An understanding of contemporary attitudes and developments is impossible without an awareness of Piedmont's linguistic past. Piedmont is Italy's gateway to France and through the ages its linguistic history testifies to pressures from both directions. Until this century the spoken medium was dominated by varieties of Piedmontese, which are also found in written texts, both literary and non-literary, from medieval times. There is evidence, however, of the early circulation of Tuscan literature in Piedmont, while French tended to be the prestige language of court circles as well as being the written medium of many writers.

A particularly important date in the linguistic history of Piedmont is 1560 since in that year Duke Emanuele Filiberto, reinstated after a period of French occupation of Savoy, issued an edict establishing the vernacular as the language of the courts and of legal documents in his French and Italian territories. There has been much discussion as to exactly which vernaculars were intended, as in the case of the edict of Villers-Cotterêts issued by the French king, François I, in 1539. Although Marazzini (1991, 32–4) is of the opinion that French and Italian (that is Tuscan) are intended, Clivio (1970) considers that the reference to an unspecified vernacular must have allowed for the use of Piedmontese, given the declared aim of ensuring maximum comprehension among the duke's subjects. The return to power of the House of Savoy is considered by Clivio (1987) as having provided the necessary conditions for the formation of a Piedmontese 'language', since before then there was no sense of belonging to any particular Piedmontese political community. The growth in political and social preeminence of Turin, the new capital of the Italian territories, conferred on its dialect a prestige that led to its becoming a linguistic model for neighbouring dialects and the basis of a Piedmontese koine (Telmon 1988, 474). However, from the end of the sixteenth century the use of Italian became more and more widespread in Piedmont. Political independence, territorial gains and increased prestige (for example at the peace of Utrecht (1713) Vittorio Amedeo II of Savoy received Sicily with the title of King) brought economic and cultural expansion to

Piedmont, which in turn fostered pride in the native tongue and in some, such as Maurizio Pipino, the dream of a codified, official, national Piedmontese language (Pipino 1783, 132–40; see also Clivio 1987). The French invasion of 1792, however, and the ensuing period of annexation, during which French replaced Italian as the official language, polarized what had been on the whole a harmonious relationship between the two prestige languages, making French a symbol of oppression and Italian by contrast a symbol of resistance to foreign rule.

The reinstatement of Italian after the collapse of the Napoleonic regime, followed in 1861 by the proclamation of Vittorio Emanuele II as King of Italy, swung the pendulum finally towards Italian. The fact that the king preferred to use Piedmontese in conversation, even with his ministers (De Mauro 1970, 32–3), was not, however, destined to alter the fortunes of his native tongue. Demographic changes and compulsory education brought about an increased use of Italian, especially in urban areas of Piedmont, and the spread of the language was further accelerated by Turin's industrial expansion (Fiat was founded in 1899) and the concomitant growth of the working-class population in the first decades of this century. For many, trade union activity constituted their first contact with the national language, whose importance as a weapon in the class struggle was stressed by Antonio Gramsci in his workers' classes in Turin. Nevertheless, in the period before the Second World War, immigrants to Turin normally learnt Piedmontese and the second generation was almost indistinguishable from the native population (Grassi 1964). Since the war, mass immigration of southern workers, together with educational and social pressures in favour of Italian, have dealt severe blows to Piedmontese, in Turin at least.

2. The current sociolinguistic situation

The sociolinguistic survey described in Becchio Galoppo (1978) was aimed at ascertaining the various factors governing choice of code, that is Italian or dialect, by bilingual Turinese, natives or long-resident in the city (significantly the majority of the sample was middle-aged). Of the 39 informants who spoke dialect with their relatives, only five spoke it with their children. The variable that had most influence on the choice of code was that of interlocutor: dialect was used for informal, intimate communication or for addressing people obviously of inferior social status, while Italian was used to show respect to people of

superior social status and in 'transactional' situations.[2] Professed attitudes towards the dialect were positive on the whole, especially towards
the conservative 'torinese illustre'; a few saw the dialect as a 'we' code,
identifying and distinguishing the hard-working Turinese from the
'lazy' immigrants. Many were in favour of Piedmontese being option-
ally offered in schools as part of a more comprehensive cultural course
and 86 per cent thought that their children should know Piedmontese.
Their linguistic behaviour, however, betrayed a lack of confidence and
pride in their mother tongue, and this led them to abandon it in favour
of Italian, perceived as the language of progress and success, for all but
informal situations.

The use of Piedmontese in the region's capital is definitely in decline
(Clivio 1990, 175). Marazzini (1991, 105–7) refers to 'Torino, città nella
quale il dialetto è senz'altro più marginale che in quasi tutte le altre
zone d'Italia' ('Turin, a city in which the dialect is certainly more
marginal than in almost all other areas of Italy') and reveals that, in a
sample group taken from two of the city's middle schools, almost as
many pupils have some knowledge (active or passive) of Sicilian (21 per
cent) as of Piedmontese (22 per cent). The situation in country districts
is rather different, since Piedmontese is still frequently used in the home
and at work, but even there 'l'ecologìa lenghìstica dël Piemont a l'é
pròpi cambià' ('the linguistic ecology of Piedmont has changed completely') (Villata 1988, 2). According to Verdoodt (1989, 516) a small
percentage of monolingual speakers still exists.

3. Questionnaire surveys 1991–1992

3.1 The school survey

My own investigations included a small survey of the linguistic competence and opinions of 36 pupils from Liceo Classico V. Gioberti in
Turin, aged from 14 to 18 years.[3] As in Marazzini's case, the sample is
too small to allow one to draw any firm conclusions, but the results of
the two surveys may be briefly compared, bearing in mind the difference in the age of the pupils and the type of school. Of the 36 pupils, all
but six of whom were natives to the province of Turin, 77 per cent
claimed to understand Piedmontese (Marazzini 22 per cent), although
only 20 per cent were able to speak it (M. 8 per cent). Of those who did
not understand it 43 per cent wished to do so, but only 33 per cent of the
non-speakers wished to speak it. The lower competence in Piedmontese
attested among the middle-school children questioned by Marazzini,

compared to that of the older *liceo* pupils, need not reflect a decline in knowledge of Piedmontese among younger children. Given that the children in both samples were born during the same years, the difference could be due to a gradual acquisition of Piedmontese as the children grow older. It is not unusual, at least in more rural areas, for parents to start speaking dialect to their children once they are confident that they are fluent in Italian, whilst other youngsters may pick it up at work, especially if this is manual labour (see Parry 1989). Further investigations are needed in order to ascertain the extent of this phenomenon. The linguistic attitudes of the schoolchildren, less positive than in Marazzini's survey, will be reviewed in conjunction with those of other groups to whom a questionnaire was sent.

3.2. The adult survey

In addition to the schoolchildren, my survey included a sample of 49 Piedmontese, mostly resident in or near Turin, 19 (9 females and 10 males) under 30 years of age, 22 (12 females, 10 males) between 30 and 60, 8 (6 females, 2 males) over 60, as well as seven linguists of Piedmontese origin, five 'promoters' of the Piedmontese language and three people linked in some way with local government or national politics (all male, save for one female among the 'promoters').[4]

The passing on 20 November 1991 in the Italian Chamber of Deputies of a controversial bill (Bill 612, *Norme in materia di tutela delle minoranze linguistiche*) recognizing the rights of long-established linguistic minorities[5] in Italy (a bill which later lapsed, owing to the dissolution of Parliament in the following March) provided an ideal context for eliciting comments on the status of Piedmontese. In addition to questions concerning competence in and use of Piedmontese, informants were asked whether they were in favour of:

(i) Piedmontese being given the same rights as those which would be granted to the so-called 'minority languages';
(ii) the use of Piedmontese in council meetings at (a) municipal, (b) provincial, (c) regional level;
(iii) the celebration of mass in Piedmontese;
(iv) a Piedmontese-language newspaper;
(v) radio broadcasting of cultural and news programmes in Piedmontese on internationally relevant topics;
(vi) the establishment of a television channel dedicated to or giving priority to programmes in Piedmontese;
(vii) the teaching of Piedmontese in all primary schools, and if so, whether they favoured compulsory or optional classes.

3.3 Questionnaire responses

Table I Linguistic competence and views of different age-groups, expressed as percentages of each group[6]

Group	(a) school	(b) <30	(c) 30–59	(d) 60<
(absolute number of respondents)	(36)	(19)	(22)	(8)
Speak Piedmontese	20	53	71	88
Understand Piedmontese	77	84	100	100
Wish to speak Piedmontese	33	78	33	null
Wish to understand Piedmontese	43	67	NA	NA
In favour of:				
Piedmontese being granted same rights as minority languages	67	79	57	75
the use of Piedmontese in municipal council meetings[7]	10	11	45	75
the use of Piedmontese in provincial council meetings	7	0	32	75
the use of Piedmontese in regional council meetings	7	0	27	75
a Piedmontese language newspaper	57	79	41	50
a Piedmontese radio programmes on general topics	43	47	45	38
a Piedmontese language television channel	60	63	55	50
mass in Piedmontese	7	11	18	38
teaching Piedmontese at primary level	27	47	45	75

Although the sample is not sufficiently objective and representative of the different social strata[8] to provide an accurate picture of the spread of opinion, some interesting points emerged from the data. The most positive response from all the age groups was that regarding the granting of the same rights to Piedmontese as to the 'minority languages'. This reflects the findings of other similar surveys, that is that support in principle for threatened languages (or for the underdog in general) is not hard to come by, whereas support for concrete proposals is less forthcoming and real personal commitment is scarce (for Piedmontese specifically, see Becchio Galoppo 1978 and, for Breton, see Temple, this vol.). The questionnaire did not detail the rights that the Italian state was willing to grant the thirteen minority linguistic groups so that, given the confusion that existed in the Italian press, my informants probably had little idea what rights were intended. For the eligible *comuni* (towns in designated areas in which the minority group constituted at least 15 per cent of the population), these would have included minority language instruction in primary schools (with the possibility of exemption for individuals) and in middle schools, if requested, provided that similar instruction was also guaranteed in Italian; oral use of the language in public offices and in local council and school meetings; written use in council minutes and reports (only the Italian translation, however, would have legal force); bilingual place-name signs and recognition of non-Italian personal names. Provision was also made for broadcasting and for the creation of cultural organizations.

4. The 'minority language' issue

4.1. Reactions to Bill 612 in the press

According to G. Battisti (*La Repubblica*, 22.11.91), approval of the Bill produced 'folgoranti dissensi' ('furious dissent'), not least because it had been misinterpreted by some as applying to the dialects as well. A group of left-wing Piedmontese scholars and journalists wrote a passionate letter to the leaders of the main left-wing parties (PSI and PDS) deploring their support for a law which was 'un vero e proprio attentato all'unità culturale della nazione italiana' ('an out-and-out attack on the cultural unity of the Italian nation'), taking Italy in the direction of strife-ridden Yugoslavia rather than of Europe. The title of a short article written by one of the signatories, G. E. Rusconi, in *La Repubblica*, 24.11.91, betrayed the fear which lay behind their dissent: '*Ma che lingua parlano le leghe?*' ('But what language do the Leagues speak?'). It is true that the question of the cultural and linguistic rights of minorities is being complicated by the fact that the dialects or regional languages are being used as symbols of a distinct identity by separatist groups. Sobrero (1991, 59) writes: 'Nessuno potrà mai calcolare quanto nuoccia alla causa dei dialetti il fatto che costituiscono il cavallo di battaglia della Lega lombarda (e di altre leghe): dialetto diventa agli occhi di molti sinonimo di intolleranza, di movimentismo, di oltranzismo. Tutti caratteri pressoché assente dalla storia della dialettofonia' ('Nobody will ever be able to calculate how harmful to the cause of the dialects is the fact that they are championed by the Lombard League (and other leagues): for many people dialect is becoming a synonym of intolerance, activism, extremism. All features that through the ages have rarely been associated with dialect-speaking'). Similar remarks were made by some of my informants.

In a long article in *La Repubblica*, 28.11.91, entitled '*Niente paura, restiamo italiani*' ('Fear not, we remain Italian'), Tullio De Mauro, one of the linguists consulted in the preparation of the Bill, insisted that the

Bill was not an attempt to win over League supporters and defuse their threat to national unity. He distinguished between the minority languages to which it applied and the dialects to which it did not, stressing that such a law would merely put into effect the guarantee made over forty years ago in the Italian Constitution, Article 6: 'La Repubblica tutela con apposite norme le minoranze linguistiche' ('The Republic protects with suitable legislation linguistic minorities'), thus bringing Italy somewhat tardily into line with many other European states. However, there is disagreement not only among historians concerned about national unity and linguists wishing to preserve threatened languages, but also among the linguists themselves. Certainly De Mauro appears to distinguish clearly between minority languages and dialects but few other linguists are as convinced. In a letter to *La Repubblica*, 9.12.91, Michele Cortelazzo voices the doubts of many of his colleagues: 'con quali argomenti, al di là del puro atto legislativo, si possono porre su piani così diversi sardo e friulano da un lato e ogni altro dialetto italiano dall'altro?' ('what arguments, other than straight legislation, justify making such a clear distinction between Sardinian and Friulian on the one hand and every other Italian dialect on the other?').

4.2 *Questionnaire responses regarding the granting of 'equal rights' to Piedmontese*

Several linguists raise the same doubts as Cortelazzo, for example Grassi calls into question the introduction of a new linguistic category into the Italo-Romance area, namely that of 'lingue minoritarie', to be inserted in the linguistic hierarchy between 'la lingua nazionale e i dialetti'. The distinction between 'dialetti' and 'lingue minoritarie' is 'artificiosa e, al limite, mistificante' ('artificial and, ultimately, misleading'), since the functional relationship of both groups with the standard language is exactly the same. He argues that, while French in the Val d'Aosta, (standard) German in the Alto Adige, and Slovene in Friuli–Venezia Giulia are in a different category from the other languages mentioned in the Bill, insofar as they are manifestations of fully developed national languages from which they are separated for political reasons, the speech of linguistic pockets such as the Serbo-Croat and Greek communities of southern Italy has not developed alongside, and therefore cannot be equated with, the source language. Grassi points out that the process of national standardization, a major criterion for distinguishing 'languages' from 'dialects', is also lacking in many of the other cases, for example Friulian and Sardinian. Responding to my question as to whether Piedmontese should be granted the same rights as the 'minority' languages, Grassi writes, 'risponderei positivamente non perché ritengo che "anche" il piemontese sia una lingua minoritaria, ma perchè *le condizioni d'uso di queste presunte lingue non sono diverse da quelle consuete per tutti i dialetti italoromanzi, ivi comprese le parlate piemontesi'* [his emphasis] ('I would give a positive answer not because I consider Piedmontese "also" to be a minority language, but *because the conditions of use of these presumed languages are no different from those traditionally obtaining for all the Italo-Romance dialects, including the Piedmontese varieties'*). Telmon also believes that Piedmontese should be granted the same rights as proposed for Occitan and Franco-Provençal, for example, since they are genetically equivalent; neither do they differ from the sociolinguistic point of view, insofar as they are:

> (a) privi di standardizzazione; (b) privi, allo stato attuale, di basi letterarie consolidate e divenute *canone*; (c) privi di normativizzazione; (d) totalmente sottomessi, diglossicamente, ad una medesima lingua di cultura (italiano); (e) diatopicamente frammentati; (f) legati quasi esclusivamente a condizioni di vita e di cultura rurale; (g) sottomessi alla tendenza ad eclissarsi in condizioni di vita urbana.
>
> ((a) 'lack an acknowledged standard; (b) lack at present a firm literary basis which has become canonical; (c) lack an agreed codified norm; (d) are completely subordinated in a diglossic relationship to the same language of culture (Italian); (e) are fragmented into many geographical dialects; (f) are associated almost exclusively with rural life and culture; (g) tend to disappear in an urban environment.')

In reality, De Mauro's clear-cut distinction between 'minority languages' and 'dialects' probably rests more on a pragmatic than on a linguistic conviction: for the last twenty years he and others have been working hard (in conjunction with pressure groups on a European level, such as the European Bureau for Lesser Used Languages), to persuade the Italian Parliament to make some provision for minority linguistic groups on a par with those found in other European countries. Any attempt to include all the regional 'dialects' of Italy is bound to be counterproductive. Even as it is, the reaction to the Bill in many intellectual quarters has been particularly hostile, precisely because they believe that granting concessions to the one linguistic category will make it extremely difficult to refuse the other and will in any case increase the sense of injustice, thus causing greater friction with the central authority and fuelling discontent and separatist aspirations.

Not all the linguists contacted believed that Piedmontese should be accorded the same rights as minority languages: Beccaria was against, and Berruto warned of the danger of upsetting the delicate sociolinguistic situation in Italy by introducing by decree into formal contexts a further fifteen or so *linguae minores* (the 'dialects') alongside Italian, itself still imperfectly known to large sections of the population. Supporters of the Piedmontese cause were naturally in favour and were therefore happy to see a bill that did not recognize their 'language' shelved by the dissolution of Parliament. Piedmontese has in fact been included in various lists of minority languages in Europe, for example Verdoodt (1989), and it has been included in 'an official but tentative list' compiled for the European Bureau for Lesser Used Languages by Dr Yvo Peters of the Centre for the Study of Ethnic Group Rights and Federalism. Among my respondents, several noted that the present sociolinguistic situation in Piedmont does not justify differentiating between Piedmontese and Occitan or Franco-Provençal, for example Clivio: 'Sul piano sociologico il piemontese ha certo maggiore importanza dell'occitano e del franco-provenzale di Piemonte' ('From the sociological point of view Piedmontese is definitely more important than Occitan or Franco-Provençal in Piedmont'); and Pich: 'A l'è na lenga con na tradission coltural autërtant e pì amportanta e a l'è 'dcò tant pì parlà' ('It is a language that has an equally and more important cultural tradition and it has a greater number of speakers'). Although the *Assessore alla Cultura e Istruzione* was in favour of the law being extended to include all the Italian dialects, the two PDS respondents were not.

Many respondents from groups (a), (b), (c) and (d) also remarked on what they considered was an unjust distinction between 'lingue' and 'dialetti'. The most common reason given for a positive answer to the question regarding equal rights for Piedmontese was that it was an integral part of the region's culture and therefore should be recognized and supported by the state to prevent the loss of a valuable part of their heritage. A few noted that official recognition would increase the chances of using and learning Piedmontese and one felt that it would serve to distinguish the inhabitants of Piedmont in an increasingly uniform Europe. On the negative side there were fears that support for minorities would create rifts within Italy, just when the general trend within Europe was for greater unity. Others felt that preserving a dialect that no longer served any useful purpose was pointless, for example 'È assolutamente antistorico e inattuale' ('It is completely antihistorical and anachronistic').

5. *Public use of Piedmontese and respondents' views*

A law entitled *Tutela, valorizzazione e promozione della conoscenza dell'originale patrimonio linguistico del Piemonte* ('Protection, enhancement and promotion of the knowledge of Piedmont's indigenous linguistic heritage') was passed in the Piedmontese Regional Assembly on 10 April 1990, establishing an annual Festa del Piemonte (22 May) to mark the anniversary of the promulgation of the Regional Statute (1971) and providing financial support in the following areas: education, diffusion through the press, radio and television, creative arts, publishing, library collections, academic research, and cultural activities.[9] The law makes no specific reference to a 'lenga piemontèisa', to the disappointment of its promoters. Piedmontese has no legal or official status and its use in formal or semi-official contexts is restricted to the domains listed below (see also Verdoodt 1989, 515–25).[10]

5.1 Local politics

As a result of pressure from activists, Piedmontese may be used in the discussions of the Turinese Provincial Council, although a written translation must be provided for the records. Only a few municipal councils have accepted its use, there being often opposition from the Co.re.co (Comitati regionali di controllo) or from council members. The use of the indigenous varieties in official contexts can cause intense resentment, as evidenced in an article in *La Stampa*, 12.9.91, criticizing the decision of a mountain *comune*[11] to allow the use of Piedmontese, 'patois' (Occitan), and French, as well as Italian in council meetings. The writer warned of the danger of excluding non-speakers of these varieties from local politics, of inaccurate translations and cultural isolation. Censin Pich, replying in the name of Ij Brandé, a Piedmontese cultural and literary society, argued that an appeal to national unity as a prerequisite for integration within Europe was misplaced, given the support for regional or minority languages expressed by the European Parliament as well as by the Council of Europe in its *Charter for Regional or Minority Languages*. The use of Piedmontese by another well-known promoter of Piedmontese, Tavu Burat, in a council meeting in Biella in July 1990 caused uproar and dramatic reports in the press (see *Eco di Biella*, 5.7.90).

Answers to my questionnaires also revealed much opposition to the use of Piedmontese in local politics, mainly on the grounds that many people would not understand. Some answers betrayed a disillusionment with political debate in general: 'Già così nelle sedute consiliari non si capisce niente, figuriamoci farle in piemontese' ('As it is, it's impossible to understand what's going on in council meetings, imagine conducting them in Piedmontese'). A few were in favour, provided simultaneous translation was available, but others believed that all official bodies should use Italian, the official language of the state; this was the response of the group involved in public affairs, although the Assessore alla Cultura e Istruzione conceded the possibility of occasional use. The linguists were divided: Beccaria and Berruto were definitely against the use of Piedmontese in formal or official contexts; the rest, while not opposed to it, were sceptical about its practicality, given that few councillors would have the necessary competence and others would lack the confidence to use the language; Grassi added that the use of Piedmontese could have a different effect from that desired; Clivio was in favour, as were the group of 'promoters'.

5.2 The legal domain

While notarial acts may be written in Piedmontese, only the Italian translation is legally binding. In court, Piedmontese may be used by people who cannot speak Italian and the judge will normally have recourse to the services of a translator; all the written reports, including the witnesses' statements, will be recorded in Italian. No specific question on this topic was included in the questionnaire.

5.3 The religious domain

Piedmontese has not been recognized as a liturgical language by the Roman Catholic Church, in which there persists a view (shared by the Protestant Waldensian Church) that the use of dialect diminishes the authority and solemnity of religious services and of the Scriptures (Genre 1988). At the priest's discretion Piedmontese is used for the sermon and for some services, such as mass, marriage, baptism (see also Verdoodt 1989, 518). However, according to Pich, 'a-i va'd preivi coragios e con consiensa étnica e lenghìstica: roba ràira...' ('for this you need brave priests and ones who are ethnically and linguistically aware: rare characteristics'). Most commonly it will be used for special commemorative services (Catholic and Protestant) such as the Festa del Piemonte. The majority of respondents believed that it was essential for everyone to be able to follow the service; as Grassi points out, this was why Latin had been abandoned, a change regretted by some of my respondents. A few felt that the use of Piedmontese in church, in addition to helping those whose understanding of Italian was poor, would give it prestige and induce people to learn it.

5.4 The media

Broadcasting in Piedmontese is scarce on State radio and television; there is some on private local stations, particularly radio (see also

Verdoodt 1989, 522–3), but responses to my questionnaire suggest that the standard of the programmes is low. There is no daily Piedmontese newspaper and the few monthly or quarterly publications are cultural productions. Questionnaire responses regarding provision of a Piedmontese newspaper, radio programmes on internationally relevant topics and a special television channel, show rather greater support for television than for radio programmes, with younger people being more enthusiastic than older ones. Since there was much similarity in the replies to the three questions, they will be considered together.

Many of those in favour felt that such provision would serve Piedmontese speakers with a limited command of Italian, and please the 'nostalgici' and the older generation, but that they themselves would not make use of it. Others believed that it would help maintain the language by encouraging both written and spoken use of the language and by stimulating the local as well as the immigrant population to learn Piedmontese. Only a few observed that people should have the right to such provision in their mother tongue, a point which obviously featured amongst those made by 'promoters' of the language, who were more aware of the crucial role which the media can play in the fortunes of a language under threat. Many noted that such provision would give prestige to Piedmontese, while Villata also stressed the importance of good quality productions: 'Gli utenti dovrebbero ascoltare non perché sono in piemontese, ma perché sono interessanti' ('People should listen not because they are in Piedmontese, but because they are interesting'). Burat is in favour 'per dar forza alla koinè e per far lievitare la coscienza che il piemontese è una lingua, liberata dal ghetto delle tematiche "dialettali" (poesia, satira, teatro...)' ('to give strength to the koine and foster an awareness that Piedmontese is a language, freed from the ghetto of "dialect" themes (poetry, satire, plays...)'). The majority, however, believed that since general interest programmes should be accessible to all, they should be presented in Italian. Some argue in favour of restricting the use of Piedmontese to topics of local interest, but such limitation was unacceptable to others. Some feared that media provision in different languages would be divisive, while others rejected it on economic grounds, doubting its viability or preferring that scarce financial resources be allocated to foreign-language broadcasting.

5.5 Education

Except for a few private courses, Piedmontese is not used as a medium of instruction. A few schools provide some teaching of Piedmontese, but this depends on the local authority and on the teachers involved. Private courses are available in some towns, taught by 'promoters' such as Brero and Burat, who believe that, since most parents no longer speak Piedmontese to their children, transmission must be ensured through education outside the home. Replying to the question regarding Piedmontese instruction in schools, Burat argues that this would give it prestige, eliminating the discrimination between languages that are taught and those which are not; it would develop a greater linguistic sensitivity in the children, freeing them from the monolithism of one language and one inflexible grammatical system; by recognizing their traditional culture and background, it would eliminate any sense of inferiority and it would give immigrants the 'key' to the community, enabling them to become fully integrated: 'perché una lingua senza scuola, oggi, è destinata ad estinguersi rapidamente, con grave danno per il patrimonio culturale di tutti' ('because today a language for which there is no educational provision is destined to fade away quickly, to the detriment of everyone's cultural heritage').

The linguists' response is very varied: Clivio sees educational provisions as the only way ultimately to save the language; Telmon and Genre are in favour but foresee many practical difficulties; Beccaria believes that children's knowledge of Italian is so poor that the time should be devoted instead to improving this; Berruto, while sympathetic, is concerned about the risk of creating 'una sovrapposizione e conflitto di domini fra due varietà che si spartiscono funzionalmente bene il repertorio' ('an overlap and a conflict of domains between two varieties, between which the functions of the repertory are well distributed'); Grassi is particularly worried about possible negative developmental as well as linguistic consequences. Apart from the practical problems of exactly which variety or varieties, and how much, should be taught, and to whom and by whom, Grassi believes that the proposal to teach Piedmontese (a) ignores the risks to a child's normal cognitive and cultural development presented by an imperfectly acquired plurilingualism; (b) does not offer the advantages of a real linguistic education, namely gradual and conscious access to a new conceptual universe, including the sciences, to which everyone has a right; and (c) by selecting Turinese as the regional standard, belittles the culture of other areas (Genre also warns of this last danger). Grassi holds up as a model of good practice the educational policy of the Val d'Aosta, where Franco-Provençal is respected and used with those children who speak it, but no attempt is made to teach it. It must, however, be noted that Piedmontese children, unlike their Val d'Aosta neighbours, do not already have to cope with two official languages at school, although they may, of course, come from homes where a 'dialect' other than Piedmontese is spoken. As for Grassi's second point, the children will have access to new concepts and the sciences through Italian whilst instruction in Piedmontese could open up a 'new' culture or restore to them their traditional culture.[12]

Grassi's last comment raises the far-reaching question of standardization. Not everyone agrees that there is a standard Piedmontese norm (see Telmon above), although there is a literary standard based on Turinese and several grammars and dictionaries of this variety have been produced (Brero 1982, 1989a and b; Brero and Bertodatti 1988; Gribaudo 1983). Most of the 'promoters' believe that if each of the towns and villages of Piedmont is going to insist on gaining recognition for its own local variety of Piedmontese, they will fragment and weaken the campaign against the monolingualism of the state: 'la koinè a rapresenta l'union për difendse da l'italian ch'a veul coatè tut' (Burat 1991, 233) ('the koine represents the common front formed to defend ourselves from Italian which is seeking to engulf everything').[13] On the spoken level, the mutual comprehensibility of the Piedmontese dialects means that conversations are frequently conducted in a number of varieties.[14] It is evident that a coherent language policy needs to be formulated before formal instruction can be introduced into the schools.

Whilst all the 'promoters' and most of the linguists are in favour of some form of educational provision, questionnaire responses from other quarters are rather less positive. Those in favour see it as a crucial factor in maintaining and transmitting their linguistic and cultural heritage both to future generations and to incomers, but none mentions the advantages of early bilingualism. Opponents emphasize the need to improve the level of competence in Italian or the greater utility of learning a foreign language. It is worth noting that the lowest percentage of favourable replies comes from the age group closest to those who would be affected by such provision. Among the factors responsible for their largely negative reaction are presumably the resistance to the idea of increasing schoolchildren's workload, the association of Piedmontese with outmoded ideas and ways of life, and the materialistic outlook of contemporary society which measures everything in financial and utilitarian terms.

6. Linguistic behaviour of respondents

Of particular interest is the fact that in all groups save (c) more respondents speak Piedmontese with their friends than with their relatives. DOXA surveys (see Note 1) have consistently shown the opposite, the expected retreat of the threatened linguistic variety (dialect) into the home.

Table II   Linguistic behaviour of respondents (indicating percentages of each
age-group)[15]

Group	(a) school	(b) <30	(c) 30–59	(d) 60<
(absolute number of respondents)	(36)	(19)	(22)	(8)
At least sometimes speak Piedmontese				
with all or some relatives	10	42	57	75
with all or some friends	23	47	55	88
in some shops	0	11	40	63
in some offices	0	5	21	13
at school/work	9	23	40	71

In the urban environment of Turin it would appear that social pressures have indeed ousted the dialect from its last bastion. The figures for
(c) may be explained by the fact that this group includes more com-
muters from rural areas; also, its older members may well have been
brought up in dialect, which they will still use with parents and older
relatives. Group (d) is too small to be statistically significant: here, the
exception to the otherwise consistent use of Piedmontese with relatives
and friends is provided by an immigrant couple, in which the husband
has learned to speak Piedmontese, which he uses sometimes with
friends.

The wish to learn Piedmontese (see Table I) often derives from a
desire to understand the local language or to speak with older people,
while others are attracted to its 'friendly' or 'colourful' character.
Negative responses concentrate on its 'uselessness'. Most respondents
do not entertain the possibility of incomers learning the local language,
although a few schoolchildren from non-indigenous families say they
wish to learn it.

7. Conclusion

The low figures regarding the use of Piedmontese in the home are
worrying for anyone interested in safeguarding the rich linguistic
diversity of Europe, since the survival of a language depends on
generational transmission. For those who wish to preserve a diglossic
situation, with Piedmontese restricted to informal contexts, this poses a
dilemma. As a linguist in favour of such a policy, Berruto can only
suggest: 'Bisogna soprattutto creare un atteggiamento culturale gener-
alizzato *positivo* e di "language loyalty" in coloro che ancora lo parlano' ('Above all, it is necessary to create a widespread positive cultural
attitude and a feeling of "language loyalty" among those who still
speak it'). Taking into account the historical circumstances that have

led to Italian displacing Piedmontese even as the language of the home, it is difficult to see how the latter can regain prestige without some form of external official intervention. Motivation to learn Piedmontese among the schoolchildren is low and the responses of the others show little evidence of personal commitment towards saving the language. Educational provision of some sort is thus crucial but, as Thomas (1987, 167) points out in the context of Welsh, teaching a language without providing opportunities for using it is pointless. The broadcasting media, especially television which is particularly influential in the case of Welsh and which has contributed so effectively to the diffusion of Italian, could play a vital role in maintaining a bilingual community. There is bound to be opposition on economic grounds especially if the majority remains indifferent. Legislative support will help but, as the Irish case shows, at the end of the day, survival will depend on the will of the people: 'Ma, për salvé na lenga, a basta nen mach fé 'd lej ch'a la difendo e ch'a stabilisso ch'as dev parlela e ch'as dev ëstudiela a scòla. Për salvé na lenga a-i va 'dco la volontà 'd tuta la popolassion che a séguita a parlela' (Villata 1991, 277) ('But, to save a language, it is not enough to make laws to protect it and to decree that it must be spoken and studied at school. To save a language it is essential also that the whole population continue to speak it').

Notes

1 See the following publications of DOXA (*Istituto per le Ricerche Statistiche e L'Analisi dell'Opinione Pubblica*) and ISTAT (*Istituto Centrale di Statistica*): *Bolletino della* DOXA, 23–4 (1974); 10 (1982); 6–7 (1988); *Notiziario* ISTAT, s.4, 41 (1989).

2 This functional separation of codes according to a distinction based on the variable *formality/informality* may be considered diglossic in the wider acceptation of the term. Berruto (1989, 14) has proposed the term 'dilalia' to describe the Italian situation.

3 The school survey was conducted with the much-appreciated co-operation of the teacher, A. M. Billi (for further details, see Parry 1993). Later, questionnaires were also distributed to friends and relatives by M. Danieli and S. Molfetta and, in addition, were sent directly to a number of Italian linguists as well as to individuals who could be deemed to be interested in the issues raised. I am sincerely grateful to all for their collaboration.

4 The following linguists returned questionnaires: Gian Luigi Beccaria (Turin), Gaetano Berruto (Zurich), Gianrenzo P. Clivio (Toronto), Arturo Genre (Turin), Corrado Grassi (Vienna), Tullio Telmon (Chieti), Bruno Villata (Montreal). Clivio and Villata may also be considered 'promoters' (that is involved in cultural activities whose aim is to foster and promote the use of Piedmontese), the rest of this group being composed of Camillo Brero (writer), Sergio Gilardino (university lecturer in Italian literature, Montreal), Tavu Burat (Gustavo Buratti, teacher and writer), Albina Malerba (Director of the

Ca dë Studi Piemontèis) and Censin Pich (writer). The three 'public figures' were Giuseppe Fulcheri, *Assessore Regionale alla Cultura e Istruzione* of the *Regione Piemonte* (the person responsible for cultural and educational matters), Sergio Chiamperino, Partito Democratico della Sinistra (PDS) leader for the Province of Turin, and Gian Giacomo Migone, university lecturer and PDS candidate, recently elected to the Italian Senate.

5 Albanian, Catalan, Franco-Provençal, French, Friulian, German, Greek, Ladin, Occitan, Romani, Sardinian, Slovene and Serbo-Croat.

6 All percentages are calculated on the number of valid responses; 'null' = no response to the question; NA = 'not applicable'. In order to obtain as objective a picture as possible of the views of the population in general, the linguists, 'promoters' and public figures were not included in these age-groups.

7 Some respondents were in favour of the use of Piedmontese in council meetings only if it was not compulsory.

8 The majority of those in groups (b) and (c) were either students or white-collar employees.

9 I am grateful to G. Fulcheri for the information that, so far, support has been granted in 174 instances, in the following domains: Piedmontese education (22); the media (7); creative arts (24); publishing (51); library collections (10); academic research in conjunction with the University of Turin (3); other cultural activities (51); reinstatement of traditional place-names (6).

10 Some of the figures and judgements given in Verdoodt need to be considered with caution, especially when compared to the far less generous ones given, for example, in the same volume for Welsh.

11 Inverso Pinasco lies between Pinerolo and Perosa Argentina, to the west of Turin.

12 There is in any case no reason in principle why any speech variety cannot, through the process of elaboration, become the vehicle for all human communicative and conceptual needs (as Clivio's articles in Piedmontese on linguistic topics seek to demonstrate, e.g. Clivio 1990).

13 'An ëscrivend e an parland èdco an koinè, noi i voroma nen crasé gnun-a forma local, ma fortì la consiensa d'avèj na lenga, ël piemontèis, con ij sò dialèt (monfrin, canavzan, langareul, bielèis e valsesian)' (Burat 1990, 231) ('By writing and speaking also in koine, our intention is not to crush local varieties, but to strengthen the awareness of having a language, Piedmontese, with its own dialects (Monferrino, Canavesano, Langarolo, Biellese, Valsesiano,...)').

14 Telmon refers to conversations between himself and the local pharmacist in Susa, in which 'la comunicazione è praticamente bilingue perchè io parlo il torinese di Susa e lui l'albese, di cui giustamente non modifica una parola, né un accento, né un fonema, né un sintagma' ('communication is practically bilingual because I speak the Susa variety of Turinese and he speaks Albese, which quite rightly he does not modify in any way, not a word, not an accent, phoneme or syntagm').

15 For reasons of space it is not possible to include here more detailed information such as frequency of use and identity of the relatives.

References

Becchio Galoppo, C. 1978. 'Prime annotazioni in margine ad una indagine sull'uso di italiano e dialetto nella comunità urbana torinese', in Clivio and Gasca Queirazza 1978, 116–26.

Berruto, G. 1989. 'Main topics and findings in Italian sociolinguistics', *International Journal of the Sociology of Language*, 76, 7–30.

Brero, C. 1982. *Vocabolario piemontese italiano*, Turin: Piemonte in Bancarella.

——1989a (reprint). *Vocabolario italiano piemontese*, Turin: Piemonte in Bancarella.

——1989b. *Sintassi dla lenga piemontèisa*, Turin: Ij Brandé.

Brero, C. and Bertodatti, R. 1988. *Grammatica della lingua piemontese*, Turin: Piemont/Europa.

Burat, T. 1991. 'Lenga piemontèisa e parlada local ant la literatura bielèisa', in Clivio and Pich 1991, 181–235.

Clivio, G. P. 1970. 'The *volgare* in Piedmont from the Middle Ages to the end of the sixteenth century', *Romanische Forschungen*, 82, 65–9.

——1987. 'Passà, present e avnì dla lenga piemontèisa,' in Clivio and Pich 1987, 175–84.

——1990. 'Ël piemontèis parlà, ël piemontèis literari e 'l dissionari stòrich-etimològich ëd la lenga piemontèisa', in Clivio and Pich 1990, 175–84.

Clivio, G. P. and Gasca Queirazza, G. (eds.). 1978. *Lingue e dialetti nell'arco alpino occidentale. Atti del Convegno internazionale di Torino (10–14 aprile 1976)*, Turin: Ca dë Studi Piemontèis.

Clivio, G. P. and Pich, C. (eds.). 1987. *At dël III Rëscontr antërnassional dë studi an sla lenga e la literatura piemontèisa, Alba 10–11 magg 1986*, Alba: Famija Albèisa.

——1990. *At dël VI Rëscontr antërnassional dë studi an sla lenga e la literatura piemontèisa, Alba 6–7 magg 1989*, Alba: Famija Albèisa, 175–84.

——1991. *At dël VII Rëscontr antërnassional dë studi an sla lenga e la literatura piemontèisa, Alba 12–13 magg 1990*, Alba: Famija Albèisa.

De Mauro, T. 1970. *Storia linguistica dell'Italia unita*, Bari: Laterza.

Genre, A. 1988. 'Comunità religiose e minoranze linguistiche: Chiese e occitano cisalpino', *La Valaddo*, 59, 3–5.

Grassi, C. 1964. 'Comportamento linguistico e comportamento sociologico (a proposito di una recente pubblicazione)', *Archivio Glottologico Italiano*, 49, 40–66.

Gribaudo, G. 1983. *Dissionari piemontèis*, Turin: Editip, A l'ansëgna dij Brandé.

Holtus, G., Metzeltin, M. and Schmitt, C. (eds.). 1988. *Lexikon der Romanistischen Linguistik, IV, Italienisch, Korsisch, Sardisch*, Tübingen: Niemeyer.

Jenkins, J. R. G. 1987. *Indigenous Minority Groups in Multinational Democracies in the Year 2000: Problems and Prospects*, Canada, Interdisciplinary Research Committee, Wilfred Laurier University.

Marazzini, C. 1991. *Il Piemonte e la Valle d'Aosta*, Turin: UTET.

Parry, M. M. 1989. 'Language and dialect in a small industrial town of North-west Italy', *Italian Studies*, 44, 102–37.

——1993. 'L'avvenire della lingua piemontese', *L'Arvista dl'Academia dla lenga piemontèisa*, 1, 27–42.

Pipino, M. 1783. *Gramatica piemontese*, Turin: Reale Stamperia.

Sobrero, A. A. 1991. 'Immagine e percezione dei dialetti', *Lettera dall'Italia*, 24, 59.

Telmon, T. 1988. 'Aree linguistiche II. Piemonte', in Holtus, Metzeltin and Schmitt 1988, 469–85.

Temple, R.A.M. (this vol.) 'Great Expectations? Hopes and fears about the implications of political developments in Western Europe for the future of France's regional languages.'

Thomas, N. 1987. 'Wales in the balance', in Jenkins 1987, 159–79.

Verdoodt, A. 1989. *The Written Languages of the World: A Survey of the Degree and Modes of Use. 3. Western Europe*, Les Presses de l'Université de Laval.

Villata, B. 1988. 'Considerassion d'un "Canadèis" an sl'usagi dla lenga piemontèisa', *Musicalbrandé*, 119, 2–3.

——1991. 'L'avnì dle lenghe regionaj e dël piemontèis an particolar', in Clivio and Pich 1991, 263–82.

12

Great Expectations? Hopes and fears about the implications of political developments in Western Europe for the future of France's regional languages[1]

ROSALIND A. M. TEMPLE

The issue I intend to examine in this paper is the effect of political developments at national-government level and at international level on the state and status of France's regional languages, and how these effects are perceived. I shall focus on the latter aspect, that is, the expectations and fears of interested parties concerning the implications of greater European unity, in the light of their reactions to previous legislation at national and EC level. It hardly needs saying that the nature of Europe post-1993 will not be the same as had been expected when the idea for this paper was originally conceived, and when most of the questionnaire responses were returned.

The opinions discussed in the paper were collected by sending questionnaires by post to various individuals and bodies in France who may be deemed to be concerned, albeit indirectly in some cases, with the fate of minority languages. The only language groups targeted were those speaking an indigenous language associated with a particular region. Thus, linguistic groups such as immigrants from North Africa and elsewhere, and Romanis, who have their own pressing concerns (which often overlap with those of the regional-language groups), were not included, on the grounds that if any group is to benefit from EC policies, the most hopeful candidates are the geographically identifiable ones.[2] The addressees included those whose role is to support one or more of the regional languages of France (for example the Association des Parents d'Élèves pour l'Enseignement du Breton, head-teachers of private Roman Catholic schools where Breton is taught), representatives of the Establishment (for example Rectors of all

Académies[3] where a regional language is spoken), academics and a small selection of organizations committed to the defence of the French language. This is a notoriously unsatisfactory research method: a total of 130 questionnaires were sent out originally, the vast majority to Brittany, and 23 replies (approximately 18 per cent) have so far been received, the majority of which, not surprisingly, were from Brittany. Therefore, although this paper addresses issues pertinent to the situation of all the lesser-used languages of France, and makes reference to other areas, it is essentially about Breton.

1. Government policy and lesser-used languages within France

The regional languages of France were essentially left to their own devices until the Revolution. There were hopes at that time that the downtrodden masses of the provinces would benefit from new freedoms, but these were soon dashed, with the French language being considered by the authorities to be the key to bringing the whole population of the new Republic into line. By the beginning of the nineteenth century, the abbé Grégoire was preparing his report on the necessity of stamping out *patois* and by the end of that century, Jules Ferry had introduced his compulsory French-speaking primary schools, where children were educated out of speaking their native tongues by continuous exposure to French and the threat of the humiliating punishments meted out to those caught speaking anything else.[4]

The period since the Great War can perhaps best be categorized as one of benign neglect by the government, with some less benign exceptions, for example the infamous statement by President Georges Pompidou that 'Il n'y a pas de place pour les langues minoritaires dans une France destinée à marquer l'Europe de son sceau' ('There is no place for minority languages in a France which is destined to make its mark in Europe'). But this is because there has been little offensive action left to be taken, with the regional languages having been dealt severe blows by the population migration which accompanied industrialization and the two World Wars, and the national language being universally used in administration, education and the legal system and effortlessly winning the prestige battle.

There are some uncanny underlying parallels between the progression from hope to fear through the Revolutionary period and that surrounding the coming to power of the great 'liberator' for the 1980s, a socialist president. There was much talk in the run-up to the

1981 presidential election of 'le droit à la différence' ('the right to be different'); my first question[5] sought to discover to what extent this noble sentiment of Mitterrand's had succeeded in flying in the face of the Jacobin ideal of a unified, 'egalitarian' and monolingual France, and indeed how strongly the will to succeed in doing so existed.

There are many examples to be found of measures taken by the government since 1981 in favour of regional languages. These include:

– in 1982 the provisions of the 'loi Deixonne' (a law originally passed in 1951, which permitted a limited amount of teaching of Breton, Basque, Catalan and Occitan in state schools) were extended to Corsican;
– also in 1982, the State broadcasting authorities (Radio France and FR3) were charged with promoting all aspects of regional identities, including the linguistic aspect;
– the 'loi du 26 janvier, 1984' declared one of the missions (Fr. *missions*) of higher education to be the promotion and enrichment of regional languages and cultures;
– in August 1985 Jack Lang, Minister of Culture, announced that the CAPES[6] teaching qualification would be available for students of Breton.

Richard Grau (1987) is, however, cynical about these measures: 'La démarche de l'État français ne réside pas, comme il est d'usage d'affirmer, dans un refus systématique de [la] diversité. Elle est bien plus subtile' (p.143) ('The tactics of the French State do not amount, as is usually stated, to a systematic rejection of diversity. They are far more subtle'). The approach is different from Grégoire, nearly two centuries ago, but the underlying attitude has not changed so greatly. As Grau points out (ibid., 147), most of the measures introduced have been introduced through ministerial circulars and have therefore been internal to the branch of the administration concerned (for example, the education system), rather than creating statutory rights. The position is thus relatively easily reversed, as, one might argue, has happened with education minister Jospin's recent deletion of Breton from the list of languages admissible towards the *baccalauréat*. Those measures which have been passed as laws by parliament[7] are couched in very general terms. Again Grau is cynical: 'doit-on y voir la mise à la charge de l'État d'une réelle obligation de promouvoir et d'enrichir les langues et cultures... régionales... ou la simple proclamation, une fois de plus, d'une liberté formelle?' (ibid., 151) ('should we see the State here being charged with a real obligation to promote and enrich the regional languages and cultures, or, once again, the mere declaration of freedom only in principle?').

This cynicism is shared by the majority of my respondents. When asked whether Mitterrand's 'droit à la différence' promises had been put into practice in their region, their overwhelming response was 'no'. For fifteen of the twenty-two the 'no' was categorical, and sometimes accompanied by remarks bordering on the vitriolic, for example: 'NON. De belles paroles, au moment où il était important de gagner des voix . . . Mais restées depuis INEFFICACES' ('NO. There were fine words when it was important to gain votes. But they have since remained INEFFECTUAL').[8] Many wrote of a lack of political will, and a lack of concrete evidence of the promises having been put into action. Again, the wording was sometimes very strong: 'Ce slogan n'a aucune application en Bretagne et révèle l'hypocrisie de son auteur' ('This slogan has in no respect been applied in Brittany, and it betrays the hypocrisy of its author'); or 'NON . . . Le discours politique de nos gouvernements berce d'illusions le peuple et l'endort comme l'opium, car les moyens concrets ne suivent pas' ('No . . . The political discourse of our governments lulls the people with illusions and drugs them like opium, for it is not followed by concrete measures'). Details are given by some: the paucity of regional language time on the radio, the fact that there is only an hour-and-a-half per week of Breton on the television, the problems faced by children wanting to study the language at school, despite the 'loi Deixonne'.

Five respondents gave a qualified negative answer. Per Denez, Professor of Breton at the University of Rennes, and a long-standing campaigner for Breton, defends François Mitterrand, pointing out that it was the latter's personal intervention which enabled the *licence de breton* to become available in 1981, the CAPES in 1985 and the DEUG[9] in 1989, but he stresses that these were personal moves, and goes on to say that 'la décision présidentielle a été suivie de discussions très dures avec les services de l'Éducation nationale' ('the presidential decision was followed by extremely tough discussions with the Education Ministry'). In answer to the second part of the question, which refers to evidence of action at departmental and municipal levels, he reiterates the point that the implementation of those government decisions which do favour the regional languages is retarded and sometimes effectively reversed by lower levels of officialdom: 'l'administration cherche toujours à reprendre dans la pratique ce qui a été officiellement autorisé ou consenti' ('the bureaucrats are always looking for ways to water down in practice concessions which have been officially authorized or agreed to').

There were no categorically positive answers to the question, although three respondents gave a qualified 'yes'. Two of these were from the Réctorats of the Académies of Rennes (where the Rector himself replied) and of Corsica. One would of course expect them to reflect the official line more closely, but even their replies were not unqualified.

Answers were more varied to the second half of the question, which related to the implementation of 'droit à la différence' principles at the more localized levels of the *département* and the municipality. There were only three categorically negative answers, and there was even one unqualified 'yes' (from a Catholic headteacher in Brittany), but the overall picture which emerged indicated that the level of support depended very much on the goodwill of the local governmental bodies (*Conseil général* and *Conseil municipal*, and thus could not be directly attributed to government action.

The *Conseil général* which received the most praise was that of the Département du Finistère, the westernmost of the four Breton *départements*, where Brest and Quimper are situated. It pays the salary of a Breton teacher at one of the Catholic schools, provides a range of subsidies for bilingual schools, recognizes Breton as a language for official purposes, and has begun to provide bilingual roadsigns. Respondents from the neighbouring *départements* of Morbihan and the Côtes d'Armor also sing its praises while lamenting the slowness of their own Conseils généraux. But even where there is possible support at departmental level, the pattern of blockage at lower levels discussed above is repeated when it comes to the municipalities. Some do show their support for the language – one even has bilingual headed notepaper, and one mayor was sent a photocopy of the questionnaire by another respondent and filled it in in great detail; others pay lip-service in the form of, for example, a bilingual sign at the entrance to the town, or a grant of 500F[10] per year to the local DIWAN school; others are indifferent and verge on the hostile:

> Plouvien, un exemple, parmi d'autres sans doute, de municipalité pour qui le droit à la différence, en ce qui concerne le breton, n'existe pas. Par exemple, l'association Skolig-al-Louarn qui pourtant travaille sur le département et même la Bretagne est considérée 'sans intérêt pour la communauté de Plouvien', communauté bretonnante de 60%...
>
> ('Plouvien, one example among many, no doubt, of a municipality for whom the "right to be different", as far as Breton is concerned, does not exist. For example, the Skolig-al-Louarn association, which works throughout the *département* and all over Brittany, is considered to be "irrelevant to the community of Plouvien", 60 per cent of whose inhabitants are Breton speakers...')

Moreover, several respondents expressed concern that action taken by local authorities (for example, in the field of education) does not rightfully fall within the bounds of their responsibilities, and they receive no government funding in support of it. In the words of another Catholic headteacher from the Département du Finistère: 'Le conseil général fait un gros effort, mais ce n'est pas son rôle, à vrai dire' ('The conseil général is trying hard, but it is not really its responsibility'). Coupled with this are several calls for a greater degree of decentralization, including of the budget: 'le pouvoir est à Paris. La France est trop centralisée et les régions n'ont pas assez d'autonomie. Je ne sais pas ce qu'il va advenir, dans ces conditions, de la langue bretonne' ('the power is all in Paris. France is too centralized and the regions do not have enough autonomy. I do not know what will become of the Breton language under these circumstances'). And: 'L'État devrait transférer à la Région (aux Régions) tout ce qui concerne "les langues et les cultures de la République française" (. . .) les crédits seraient aussi décentralisés' ('The State should transfer to the Region (to the Regions) everything concerning "the languages and cultures of the French Republic" (. . .) funding should also be decentralized').

   A second general point to emerge is that there has been an increased consciousness of the value of a regional identity and language at all levels, down to that of the individual. The Rector of Rennes refers to '[une] prise de conscience par les collectivités locales de la nécessité de préserver, d'enrichir et de transmettre l'héritage patrimonial sous toutes ses formes' ('a heightened awareness on the part of local communities of the need to preserve, enrich and pass on their ancestral heritage in all its forms'). And one of the headteachers says that 'il n'y a jamais eu autant de doléances et de manifestations en faveur de la langue bretonne et des minorités' ('there have never been so many complaints and demonstrations in support of the Breton language and the minorities'). But one wonders how much this 'prise de conscience' is the result of government action and how much the result of that of local activists. One of the DIWAN[11] respondents claims, 'Tout est dû aux militants bretons qui vont de l'avant ... et font parfois plier le gouvernement, mais ce n'est pas sans mal' ('The credit should all go to the Breton activists who lead the way ... and sometimes succeed in making the government give way, but not without great difficulty').

2. Response to EC policies on lesser-used languages

The EC is today perceived as having a benevolent attitude towards marginal and/or disadvantaged regions, but its existence has not always been to their advantage. Martel (1987, 129) points out that the post-1957 shaping of the Community actually boosted the importance to the French government of the 'mythe français' of centralization and unification because the removal of trade barriers meant that it was subject to the same sort of competition with other states as had existed hitherto between its own regions, with the added perceived danger of its (then) peripheral geographical position. Inhabitants of Corsica, Brittany, Catalonia and the Basque country would no doubt relish the irony there, if not the consequences ... The reaction was to concentrate resources in the better-developed, more competitive regions of the country, which of course had direct and indirect effects for the regional-language-speaking populations, the most significant being the acceleration of migration away from southern and western France and the further confirmation in people's minds that their languages were useless for those wanting to 'get on in life'. Clearly, France has not been thus marginalized in the EC. It is no longer even geographically peripheral. Perhaps this has been one reason for the relaxation of attitudes towards the regions and the (limited) measure of devolution of power. This seems to have done little to halt the decline of the regional languages, but at least the way is clear for the EC to be seen to be a potentially positive rather than a negative factor.

As Florian Coulmas points out in his lengthy and detailed article on EC language policy (Coulmas, 1991), there is further irony to be found in parallels between the situations of the State and of its regions, in this case in the fact that the relatively positive attitude of the Community towards linguistic and cultural plurality is '...a corollary of the member states' general hostility towards multilingualism, that is, the nation states' tendency to favour cultural and linguistic homogeneity. It is precisely the great importance the European states attach to their national languages which motivates their backing of linguistic pluralism in the Community context (if only as a means of protecting the national languages). A strong commitment to monolingualism, if multiplied, necessarily results in support for multilingualism' (ibid., 14).

2.1 The 'Arfé Resolution'

Whatever the motivation, there have been positive consequences in the form of declarations by various European bodies of support for cultural diversity and multilingualism. The first major EC pronouncement was the 1981 Resolution number C287/106 by the European Parliament 'on a community charter of rights of ethnic minorities', known as the Arfé Resolution. The Resolution, whose full text appears as an appendix to Coulmas (1991), recognized the importance of the identities of ethnic and linguistic minorities within Europe and their value for Europe, made various specific requests to governments of member states, and recommended the use of Community finances (via a Regional Fund) for the promotion of regional languages and cultures. It was chosen as the focus for the second question on the present questionnaire because of its call for action from state governments, and because the date when it appeared coincides with the year of Mitterrand's election to the French presidency. The coincidence of dates introduces complications into the analysis, since it is not always possible to tell which government actions are attributable to the 'droit à la différence' 'policies' and which to EC pressure, and this is reflected below. However, it does allow for comparison between the effects of Community and government policies over the same period of time. The question centres on the calls for government action in section 2 of the Resolution.

Only one respondent (Office de tourisme de Strasbourg) said that yes, the government had responded positively to Arfé. Two gave more qualified 'no' answers to that part of the question, one of them mentioning that 'il y a toutefois des évolutions positives' ('there have, however, been some positive developments') without specifying what they were. The other, the Rector of Rennes, was evasive, but his answer amounts to a 'no' to the specific question. He points out that those who speak no French have the right to an interpreter in court and in dealing with the authorities, but admits that the right has not been extended to speakers who are bilingual in French and another language. Municipalities and private organizations such as banks, he says, are free to use the languages in certain circumtances.[12]

But again, the overwhelming response was unequivocally negative, for example: 'Seuls les militants culturels ont su qu'il y avait un rapport Arfé. L'administration a superbement ignoré ses recommandations' ('Only the cultural activists knew that there was an Arfé Report. The Administration has succeeded spectacularly in ignoring its recommendations'). The familiar note of cynicism is present in one respondent's 'Je ne suis pas sûr que cela soit possible' ('I am not convinced that that is possible'), and in the reiterated claims of others that high-sounding words have not been matched by action: 'Oui dans le discours théorique. NON dans les faits et la pratique quotidienne' ('Yes, in theory. No in everyday reality'). Various details are cited in support of these negative answers, again many of them familiar from answers to Question 1: the removal of Breton from the *baccalauréat* list, the minimal radio and television time given to regional languages. Other details are less familiar, and specific to the recommendations of Arfé: the lack of bilingual official forms or notices, the refusal to admit evidence given through an interpreter. Three respondents mention obstacles put in the way of attempts to increase the number of bilingual classes by all levels of the Administration, from the government's claim that it has insufficient funds to train the teachers to the 'barrage systématique et draconien à l'Inspection Académique de Quimper et au Rectorat de Rennes' ('systematic and draconian obstruction by the Inspectorate of the Académie at Quimper, and by the authorities in Rennes'), and similar action from the authorities responsible for the private Catholic schools.[13] In contrast, the Rector of Rennes, in his answers to part (b), seems proud of the initiative to set up a bilingual stream in state schools (29 primary classes and eight at secondary level) and of the fact that since 1983 numerous nursery and primary schools, one *collège* out of two and two *lycées* out of three have a member of staff responsible for teaching Breton.[14] He also mentions under 2 b) the assumption of responsibility by the education ministry for fifty primary-level DIWAN classes. This refers to an agreement whereby the ministry took fifty DIWAN teachers onto its payroll.[15]

Much of the detailed comment, then, was about education. On general issues, answers to part (b) of the question again stress that positive action is usually the result of initiatives by individuals, private associations or a sympathetic local authority, or in response to protests by activists. Thus, one DIWAN respondent reports that there is an ever-increasing number of bilingual placename signs, but that this is more a consequence of 'barbouillages nocturnes' ('nocturnal daubings') than of action by the politicians.

The corollary of this, of course, is that where the goodwill does not exist, the regional languages suffer. We have already seen the accusations of blocking tactics in educational matters by Quimper and Rennes, and, earlier, of the hostility of the municipality of Plouvien. (The latter Académie is accused by one respondent of still being at the stage of 'défense de cracher par terre et de parler breton' ('No spitting and no speaking Breton'), an allusion to the title of a 1960s book, itself alluding to a public notice on a wall which forbade the speaking of Flemish in those terms.) In the private domain, one respondent reports that it is possible to write cheques in Breton, but that only one bank provides bilingual cheque books and it is almost impossible to have cheques accepted when drafted in Breton. Not surprisingly, then, there are again calls for more action at higher levels: 'Mais le département [Finistère] ne peut pas, ne doit pas suppléer à l'ETAT qui doit RE-CONNAITRE OFFICIELLEMENT SES LANGUES RÉGIO-NALES' ('But the *département* [Finistère] cannot and should not be doing the work of the STATE which must OFFICIALLY RECOGNIZE ITS REGIONAL LANGUAGES'), together with more devolution of power and money, particularly within the education system (with, one supposes, legal safeguards to ensure that support for languages is not dependent on the whims of local bodies). It is, however, noteworthy that these responses are directed at *l'Etat* ('the State') rather than at the EC, the subject of the question.

Some do call for an enhanced EC role. The comments of a professor from the university of Montpellier suggest that there is a need for more pressure from the EC on the French government: 'il faut comprendre qu'en France une loi peut être votée en faveur de l'occitan etc. Ainsi la France est en règle avec l'UNESCO, le Parlement Européen etc., mais les décrets d'application de la loi ne sont pas promulgués et le génocide culturel se poursuit.'[16] But the Arfé Resolution contains a proviso 'having due regard for the independence' enjoyed by national governments, which is symptomatic, according to Coulmas, of the 'balancing act' of a European Parliament 'juggling to defend minority interests, on the one hand, and to respect national interests, on the other' (1992, 15). In addition, although he reports a greater degree of sympathy towards regional languages and more specific calls for action from the European Parliament than from the Commission (including one concerning regional languages which was addressed to the French government), the very reason that these attitudes are possible resides in the facts that: (a) decisions are taken by majority vote in the Parliament and not by unanimous agreement, and, more significantly, (b) the European Parliament passes resolutions calling for action by member governments but does not have the power to impose anything on those governments, unlike the Commission, which can issue Regulations and Directives which do have legal consequences for the member states. What is more, the effect of the Arfé Resolution on the authorities has not been enhanced by the lack of awareness on the part of the general public that it exists, as mentioned above, and by what a few of the respondents report as a general apathy on their part.

A few silver linings are to be found, including more comments about consciousness-raising at individual and administrative levels, and the report in the Lorient edition of the newspaper *Ouest-France* of 29 January 1992 that it will soon be possible to be married in Breton in Lorient.[17] But on the whole it seems that the Arfé Resolution has failed to have any impact on official practice or public consciousness and has not even managed to equal the rhetorical reverberations of 'droit à la différence'. In the words of the other DIWAN respondent, 'La vie linguistique reste ce qu'elle était, comme si Arfé n'existait pas' ('Our linguistic life is the same as ever, as though Arfé did not exist').

2.2 Expectations of the future

EC action did not end with Arfé, however. Amongst subsequent
measures have been the following: in 1982 the European Commission
commissioned the Istituto della Enciclopedia Italiana to produce a
report on the situation of regional languages in the Community; in
1983 the Parliament reiterated the calls made in the Arfé Resolution
and this was followed by the setting up of the European Bureau for
Lesser Used Languages which, although an independent body, receives
substantial funding from the EC; also in 1983, the Parliament initiated
a fund allowing the Commission to aid publications, research programmes, and conferences in support of regional languages and cultures; in 1987 the MERCATOR network for documentation on
indigenous regional languages was set up by the Commission. A summary of related issues addressed by the European Parliament can be
found in the 1987 report by W. Kuijpers.

The next question on the questionnaire looked to the future and
asked whether the then expected political rapprochement of the EC
states would have positive consequences for France's regional
languages and why. Respondents were then asked whether, even in
favourable political circumstances, there were enough speakers to
ensure the survival of the languages, and to what extent public opinion
was optimistic, pessimistic or indifferent concerning the languages and
the EC. Answers to this set of questions were more evenly distributed
between positive, negative and non-committal and there was greater
variety of detail than before, which is hardly surprising since the
respondents were being asked to speculate. I shall concentrate on
factors which were mentioned several times.

Of those who thought EC development would have positive consequences, many placed their hopes in greater co-operation between
minority language communities across the EC. Some envisaged co-
ordinated campaigns to achieve legislative changes, whilst others saw
the links more as a source of mutual encouragement, or provocation to
action; for example: 'Il est nécessaire de reconnaître dans l'Europe, la
force des régions' ('We must recognize the power of the regions within
Europe'). 'Oui, nous comptons beaucoup sur l'expérience et l'exemple
du bilinguisme des autres pays de la CEE' ('Yes, we gain much encouragement from the experiences and examples of bilingualism in other
EC countries'). But most of these had reservations about whether
the French government would allow itself to be bound by EC legislation on the subject and most of the negative answers gave this as a
reason for this pessimism: 'd'aucuns comptent sur une réglementation

européenne pour "contraindre" l'administration à des actions mais trop peu de décideurs et d'hommes politiques affichent une réelle volonté de voir les choses évoluer' ('there are those who are counting on European legislation to "force" the Administration to act, but too few of the decision-makers and politicians demonstrate a real desire to see things change'). 'Je suis très sceptique: les gouvernements français se sont toujours montrés jacobins, donc hostiles à toute force visant à maintenir ou à accroître les différences entre Paris et les régions à forte personnalité culturelle' ('I am very sceptical: French governments have always been Jacobin, and so hostile to any force which would aim to maintain or increase the differences between Paris and those regions which have a strong cultural identity'). This pessimism seems more valid than ever in the light of recent developments. The Danish people's rejection of the so-called Maastricht Treaty set the European boat rocking violently, and at the time of writing it is still rocking.[18] When the economic shock-waves from the upheaval in the EMS have died down, and discussions embrace the broader issues to be salvaged from Maastricht, no doubt the much-discussed principle of *subsidiarity* will return to the limelight. Although subsidiarity taken to its logical conclusion might have helped some regional languages, the interpretation favoured by the British government (that is, the 'devolution' of power to member-state governments) and which is no doubt supported by a number of the other member governments, could have serious consequences for the languages spoken in states such as France, where the government is not particularly sympathetic to their lot.

Other reasons given by respondents for pessimism included fear generated by observation of the consequences of destructive nationalism in Eastern Europe and the fact that increasing economic and political interdependence in the EC would be an incentive for students to learn major languages of other member states and thus a disincentive for them to waste energy on an apparently economically useless language.

Nevertheless, there were marginally more optimistic answers than pessimistic ones – twelve 'yes's' (some of them qualified) versus eight 'no's'. But, whatever may be achieved on the political plane through the EC, a language will not survive without speakers, and many of the respondents who had given positive answers to the question 3(a) were among those who did not think that there were enough speakers to ensure the survival of the regional language(s). The demographic evidence shows that there are more Breton speakers dying than being born and the task of not only encouraging more to learn the language but also encouraging children who speak it to take it seriously is hampered by the lack of facilities to study it and use it as a medium for education. Even if these facilities were more readily available, as some respondents point out, the economic motivation is absent: 'tant qu'il n'y a pas un intérêt économique à savoir le breton (pour gagner sa vie) il n'y aura pas de revendication forte pour son enseignement' ('so long as there is no economic incentive to know Breton (in order to earn a living) public opinion will not demand that it be taught').

Much was made throughout answers to question 3 of the apathy of the general public, both speakers and non-speakers of regional languages, and this was obviously painful for some respondents to watch: 'la population assiste, passive, à l'agonie de la langue – Pour elle, cette langue appartient au passé, à une époque révolue: elle n'est bonne que pour les personnes âgées' ('The people look on passively at the death-throes of the language – For them, this language belongs to the past, to a bygone age: it's no good to anyone but the old'). Perhaps surprisingly the majority of respondents reported public opinion about the fate of the languages to be indifferent, but there were six who reported it to be favourable. However, several of the latter added comments to the effect that this positive attitude is nevertheless a passive one. The Rector of Rennes even hazards a (restrained) joke on the subject: 'L'opinion publique (. . .) semble être devenue favorable à son maintien et optimiste quant à son avenir. Il faut toutefois remarquer qu'il s'agit d'une sensibilité générale plus que d'un engagement individuel (on compte sur le voisin pour sauver la langue!)' ('Public opinion seems to have become favourable regarding the maintenance [of Breton] and optimistic as to its future. One should note, however, that this represents a vague feeling rather than concrete commitment on the part of individuals (it's up to the next man to save the language!)').

Even some of the 'yes' answers were tinged with hopelessness – yes, the languages might survive, but that they would be living languages was doubtful, and several defenders of the language stated that there would be little point in that. However, one respondent thinks that, although in present circumstances there is little hope, the tide could even now be turned: 'Dans les circonstances actuelles NON, car les bretonnants sentent très fort la non-reconnaissance actuelle de leur langue. Mais il suffirait, nous semble-t-il, de bien peu de choses pour leur faire retrouver la fierté de leur originalité et de leur langue. ... Qu'on donne au 500,000[19] bretonnants cette "reconnaissance" et on aurait là un levier extraordinaire pour assurer la survie du breton.'[20] Another reminds us, '. . . mais qui eût pensé, il y a 15 ans, que DIWAN arriverait à ouvrir un collège? Il faut donc continuer à travailler ... Travailler toujours, n'importe ce qui arrivera...' ('. . . but who would have thought, 15 years ago, that DIWAN would manage to open a secondary school? So we have to keep working ... Work, work, work, whatever happens'). Yet another thinks that the number of Breton speakers will fall to below 100,000, but that all will not be lost: 'La chute quotidienne du nombre des bretonnants va continuer. Nous descendrons au-dessous de 100,000. C'est évident! Mais il existe des Forces de renouveau. En premier lieu DIWAN. [...] Je suis plutôt optimiste à long terme (2050!)' ('The daily fall in the number of Breton speakers will continue. We will fall below 100,000. That's obvious! But there are rejuvenating Forces. First, DIWAN. [...] I am fairly optimistic in the long term (2050!)').

3. Conclusions

The intention of this paper has been to survey opinions. The very fact that the respondents discussed bothered to return the questionnaires suggests that they have in common varying degrees of sympathy for the regional languages. They give a fairly consistent factual picture of the state of the languages, the most depressing component of which is the demographic trends which are familiar to anyone concerned with minority languages. But they are divided in their interpretations of the implications of these facts and their expectations for the future.

So far as the status of the Breton language is concerned, the general picture that emerges of the French authorities suggests an inability and unwillingness to break from the Jacobin mould. Legislation in favour of the regions has failed to have much effect on the state of the languages: words are not matched by deeds and when political will does appear to exist at the centre, change is blocked lower down the administrative scale, or by a lack of financial support. As for the EC, the Arfé Resolution is not perceived as having had a positive effect either; indeed, as some respondents mention, most Bretons are unaware that it exists. The non-binding nature of European Parliament Resolutions means that the pattern is likely to continue. Developments since the return of the questionnaires, not least the narrow margin of victory of the 'Yes' vote in the recent referendum on the Maastricht Treaty in France, are symptomatic of increasingly strong resistance by member states and their inhabitants to perceived 'interference' in their internal affairs. And well before the referendum, the French government had brought to fulfilment 500 years of pro-French linguistic policy by writing the French language into Article 2 of the Constitution, placing it with the Marseillaise and the *Tricolore* flag as an essential part of the Republic. As Henri Giordan points out (1992, 4), this runs directly contrary to the position of the European Community and the Council of Europe who have consistently supported the principles of respect and promotion of the diverse linguistic and cultural heritage of Europe, principles which are enshrined in article 128 of the Maastricht Treaty.[21] Where the EC can help, in the view of some, is in the economic and cultural domains, bringing economic assistance which may halt the drain of speakers away from lesser-used language regions and the facilitation of cultural links which would (and already do) provide inspiration and support for the defenders of the languages. The pessimists, however, doubt the effectiveness of the economic intervention and see the cultural measures as mere window dressing which does not go to the heart of the problem.

It is difficult, then, to extract a clear picture of the future from the questionnaire responses. Reason pushes one towards the view of the pessimists who see little future for the regional languages of France and no hope under the Vth Republic of salvation through national or European legislation. And yet a great deal is being done to try to ensure the survival of the languages, not least by many of these pessimists. The cliché 'where there's life, there's hope' springs to mind, and one is in the end drawn irresistibly towards the optimists' view, as expressed by Professor Per Denez, who has spent most of his life in the thick of the fight: 'Aucune langue, grande ou petite, n'échappera à l'obligation de lutter pour sa vie. Le combat pour le breton affirme tous les jours son importance. La survie ne nous intéresse pas: ce qui nous intéresse c'est le développement' ('No language, large or small, can escape from the obligation to fight for its life. The fight for Breton gains in strength daily. We are not interested in survival, what we want is progress').

Great expectations, indeed.

Appendix

Questionnaire sur le futur des langues minorisées en France [sample – translation follows]

(1) Un des slogans de François Mitterrand lors de sa première campagne électorale parlait du 'droit à la différence'. Est-ce que cette politique a été mise en pratique de façon efficace en Bretagne?

    Et dans votre département/municipalité?

(2) En 1981, en réponse au Rapport Arfé, le Parlement européen a invité les gouvernements nationaux et les pouvoirs régionaux et locaux à autoriser et à promouvoir l'enseignement des langues et des cultures régionales; et à garantir aux minorités, en ce qui concerne la vie publique et les rapports sociaux, la possibilité de s'exprimer dans leur propre langue, notamment dans leurs relations avec les représentants des pouvoirs publics et devant les organes judiciaires.

(a) A votre avis, le gouvernement français a-t-il répondu de façon positive à ces recommandations?

(b) Quelles ont été les conséquences pour votre région?

    Et pour votre département/municipalité?

(3) Certaines organisations et certains individus se sont montrés optimistes à propos du futur des communautés minoritaires dans la CEE.

(a) Est-ce que vous croyez que le rapprochement des pays de la CEE, qui est censé avoir lieu en 1992/93, aura des conséquences positives pour la langue bretonne?

    Pourquoi?/Pourquoi pas?

(b) Même si du côté politique les perspectives sont favorables, est-ce que cela laisse prévoir un avenir meilleur pour la langue? C'est-à-dire, quoi qu'en fasse les autorités, est-ce qu'il y a assez de gens qui sont prêts à utiliser la langue dans la vie quotidienne pour assurer sa survie?

(c) A votre avis, est-ce que l'opinion publique dans votre département/municipalité à propos du futur de la langue au sein de la CEE se montre plutôt optimiste, pessimiste ou indifférente?

(4) Dans le cas du catalan, le parlement européen a recommandé l'utilisation de la langue pour la publication des traités européens, pour la dissemination d'information concernant la CEE et dans les bureaux

de la commission européenne. Croyez-vous que ceci serait nécessaire ou désirable pour la langue bretonne?

(5) Si vous désirez ajouter d'autres renseignements ou commentaires, ils seront reçus avec reconnaissance.

Questionnaire on the future of minority languages in France

(1) One of François Mitterrand's slogans during his first electoral campaign talked of the 'right to be different'. Has this policy been put into practice effectively in Brittany?

And in your *département*/municipality?

(2) In 1981, in response to the Arfé Report, the European Parliament invited national governments and regional authorities to authorize and promote the teaching of regional languages and cultures; and to guarantee for minorities the opportunity to express themselves in their own language in public life, and in particular in their encounters with representatives of public authorities and before legal bodies.

(a) In your opinion, has the French government reacted in a positive fashion to these recommendations?

(b) What have the consequences been for your region?

And for your *département*/municipality?

(3) Some organizations and some individuals have expressed optimism about the future of minority communities within the EEC.

(a) Do you believe that the closer ties between the EEC countries which are supposed to be formalized in 1992/93 will have positive consequences for the Breton language?

Why?/Why not?

(b) Even if the political outlook is good, does that mean a better future for the language? In other words, whatever the authorities do, are there enough people who are prepared to use the language in everyday life for it to survive?

(c) In your opinion, is public opinion in your *département*/municipality optimistic, pessimistic or indifferent when it comes to the future of the language within the EEC?

(4) In the case of Catalan, the European Parliament has recommended the use of the language for the publication of European treaties, for the dissemination of information concerning the EEC, and in the offices of the European Commission. Do you think that this is necessary or desirable for the Breton language?

(5) Any other information or comments you would like to add would be gratefully received.

Notes

1 I should like to thank David Livesy for his invaluable help in supplying addresses in Brittany.

2 Which is not to say that the EC has not addressed itself to the linguistic problems of other groups.

3 Administrative (geographical) division within the education system, headed by a *Recteur* ('Rector').

4 Welsh children were similarly punished for speaking Welsh rather than English in school well into the twentieth century.

5 A sample questionnaire is provided in the Appendix.

6 Certificat d'aptitude pédagogique à l'enseignement secondaire.

7 It should be noted that support for the regional languages comes from right across the political spectrum, as does opposition to them.

8 Throughout, the quotations from questionnaire responses are provided with the capitalization, punctuation and emphasis used by their authors, and nothing added by myself.

9 Diplôme d'études universitaires générales.

10 Approximately £50!

11 DIWAN is an association of independent, privately-funded Breton-medium schools.

12 The Rector of Corsica, on the other hand, is in line with the majority of informants, who give a definite 'no'.

13 The accusation that the Catholic schools are also obstructive is surprising. Head teachers of Catholic schools were the group with one of the highest response rates (9/35 compared with only 2/23 from directors of DIWAN schools) and were for the most part pro-Breton, some passionately so, as we have already seen. One writes of his personal struggle to keep the teaching of Breton on the timetable, and of his struggle against the authorities and the apathy of even his teachers of Breton to bring to fruition his plans for bilingual classes.

14 The Rector does not mention whether these individuals are also responsible for teaching other subjects. I have been told about cases where teachers have been employed to teach Breton and English and ended up hardly teaching any Breton at all.

15 I had understood from personal contacts that the ministry had suddenly pulled out of the deal before the beginning of the 1991/92 academic year. At the time of writing, the situation was still not resolved, hence the mayor of Plougastel's response to the same question: 'La question des écoles DIWAN n'est toujours pas réglée, hélas!' ('Alas! the DIWAN school problem has still not been resolved').

16 'You must understand that in France a law in favour of Occitan etc. can be passed. France is therefore complying with the requirements of UNESCO, the European Parliament and so on, but the decrees enforcing the law are not promulgated and the cultural genocide continues.'

[17] The respondent who sent me the cutting did not say whether he thought this had anything to do with Arfé.

[18] Since the paper was written, the boat has come very close to sinking, with the extremely narrow margin of victory of the supporters of the treaty in France, repeated crises in the ERM, and the bitter political battles in Britain over ratification of the treaty.

[19] The number more frequently cited for Breton speakers in the questionnaire returns is 300,000.

[20] 'In present circumstances, NO, for Breton speakers are deeply hurt by the present non-recognition of their language. But we believe that it would take very little to make them re-discover their pride in their originality and their language... If the 500,000[19] Breton speakers were given this "recognition" we would have an extraordinarily powerful lever with which to ensure the survival of Breton.'

[21] Further gloom was cast over the outlook for France's minority languages at the beginning of October 1992 with the refusal of the French government (amongst others, including the British) to ratify the Council of Europe's European Charter for Regional or Minority Languages.

References

Coulmas, F. (ed.). 1991. *A Language Policy for the European Community. Prospects and Quandaries*, Berlin: Mouton de Gruyter.

Coulmas, F. 1991. 'European integration and the idea of the national language. Ideological roots and economic consequences', in Coulmas (ed.), 1–44.

Giordan, H. 1992. 'The language of the Republic is French', *Contact Bulletin*, 9(2), 4.

Grau, R. 1987. 'Les langues face aux institutions et aux juridictions', in Vermes and Boutet (eds.), I, 143–62.

Kuijpers, W. 1987. European Parliament Session Documents, Doc. A 2–150/87.

Martel, P. 1987. '25 ans de luttes identitaires', in Vermes and Boutet (eds.), I. 125–42.

Neville, G. 1987. 'Regional languages in contemporary France', in *Proceedings of the Third International Conference on Regional Languages* (Galway, June 1986).

Plaid Cymru 1992. *Tuag at 200. Rhaglen Plaid Cymru ar gyfer Cymru yn Ewrop* (= Plaid Cymru election manifesto).

Vermes, G. and Boutet, J. 1987. *France, pays multilingue*. 2 vols. Paris: l'Harmattan.

13

Breton speakers in Brittany, France and Europe: constraints on the search for an identity*

J. IAN PRESS

The journalist Mark Frankland wrote of the fragmentation of central and eastern Europe that 'when a totalitarian system collapses what people need to know most is who they are'.[1] The need to know who one is also applies to the tendency to integration, which is claimed for western Europe. Both tendencies are unsettling in that they bring inequalities among ethnic groups to the surface; the analysis of linguistic identity might help us understand the conflictual situations which arise.

By linguistic identity I mean that a community may seek to mark its sense of identity through its language. A standardized, but flexible, language emerges, to be used in all or almost all areas of communication. The community's attachment to its language will be enhanced by the language being given some worthy and ancient history. The community will need to maintain its identification with and pride in its language. This is close to the humanistic *Questione della lingua* of the fourteenth to sixteenth centuries, with its concepts of *dignitas*, or the appropriateness of a particular linguistic medium to serve as the official language of a community, and *norma*, namely the selection of models to serve as a linguistic example within the community. So a linguistic community will seek to have a worthy and ordered oral and written medium, with which it can associate itself, which expresses its culture,

* This paper has developed out of papers given to the International Conference on Language Revival, SOAS, University of London, 7–8 June, 1990 (publication forthcoming) and the Romance Linguistics Seminar, Trinity Hall, University of Cambridge, January 1991. It formed a component of my Inaugural Lecture, 'The Forging of European Linguistic Identities – Reality and Myth', QMW, University of London, 20 February 1992. I am very grateful to Serj Richard and Lenora A. Timm for their help.

and which is desirable for speakers of the community in which it is used. Needless to say, this cannot be applied in any straightforward way to Breton.

Some linguistic identities may not be positive, and Breton seems, from the perspective of the concerned outsider, to be a case of a negative identity imposed upon a language and its speakers by the presence of a dominant community. This negative identity may be reflected in the educational means used to spread the dominant language and in the character of the modern, urban, anonymous power-base which is needed to keep the enlarged, largely dominant community together.

In Europe we have had well over a century of mythical national states, a century or more of monolingualist supremacy. The multilingual, and multiethnic, reality was suppressed, something which has distorted our perceptions of the world.[2]

In the case of Breton, a lesser-used language locked entirely within a highly centralized state, we may see the problem of a negative identity.[3] Like 1917 in Imperial Russia, 1789 in France was seen as heralding a new, egalitarian, era. In both cases, state multilingualism was at first treasured, no doubt in part for reasons of political expediency; then, and very quickly and officially in France, monolingualism became the aim, to protect the fragile nascent national unity.

Awareness of multilingual states leads to awareness of language shift and loss. Can – indeed should – shift and loss be prevented? Breton, which has had quite viable speaker resources, may be a case where the community overall no longer perceives a need for its language, at least in a meaningful range of uses. Language shift is rarely a phenomenon which suddenly emerges. The mental attitude shaping it is ancient and may be irreversible. And in twentieth-century Europe it may have been accelerated to unstoppable speeds by improved communications (which favour national languages), industrialization, the media, and migration (including where other linguistic communities move into minority areas and these new communities cannot be expected to use the local language). Shift is something feared even by the French language. Once French writers welcomed foreign influence: 'Ce n'est point chose vicieuse, mais grandement louable: emprunter d'une langue étrangère les sentences et les mots pour les approprier à la sienne' (Du Bellay, 1549); 'Prenons de tous côtés ce qu'il nous faut pour rendre notre langue plus claire, plus précise, plus courte et plus harmonieuse' (Fénelon, 1716).[4]

By the eighteenth century a fear of English began to emerge. Thus we have Fougeret de Monbron's *Préservatif contre l'anglomanie* (1757). Does this intimation of insecurity indicate that dominant peoples or communities like the French lack identity? Are they stricken with anonymity? Do they lose their naturalness once we give them a name? The Russians themselves are for perhaps the first time trying to come to grips with their own lack of identity.[5]

The era of fragile, fearful nation-states brushed aside the potential of bilingualism. We have had the association of one language with one national state, reflecting a political and economic reality, but probably nowhere socially or linguistically valid. This mythical association, consolidated through education and the exercise of centralized power, has had its effect, to the extent that more than half the population of France may be asserted to have changed language, to French, since 1789.

The mentalities forged by history[6] were aggravated by oppression and subsequent urbanization, industrialization, improved communications, the development of tourism, and the emptying of rural areas. Efforts by intellectuals to revive dying languages would be looked on with suspicion by the native speakers, themselves unable to see any value in their language. After the excesses of the desire to spread civilization, enlightenment, and education of the post-Revolution period, there is now a need, and not only in France, for a promotion of bilingualism. There is no risk to French, which the Bretons and Basques in any case need in order to communicate with the outside world; and the French realize that, like the English and the Russians, their language is in fact not their own.[7]

The pressure is considerable on a language like Breton, confined as a lesser-used language within one state. It needs help, but the help it needs does not have to be linguistic. Having an urban cultural centre where the language is used in as many areas of life as possible is invaluable, and creating enough jobs in a threatened linguistic community to prevent emigration for ten years will guarantee a new generation of speakers. Other reasons for emigration have to be tackled: the individual's feeling of being second-rate, the stigma of having a language 'unsuited to the modern world', and poverty. Any local improvement has for a while to be truly local. A government's help is needed, but the local people are the core of the effort. Given the will to survive, a community needs a solid infrastructure, institutions, and financial means.[8] In modern Europe, the priority is stable bilingualism, and not only as regards speakers of minority languages. All this probably implies the creation of standard languages. But who speaks them, or indeed writes them? To some extent no one but the very formal and pedantic does. Language is not only communication, but also emotion: Breton is largely home-based and rural. For the sake of education, the norm needs to be relatively stable. Codification, in such cases, needs to include the colloquial, in order the better to reflect the daily reality of the language users. There is a need to identify with the language; otherwise, one identifies with the dominant one. For Breton, this demands careful objective study of how the remaining native speakers actually use their language alongside French, the slipping from one to the other depending upon a myriad of variables.[9] After all, Mathesius defined a literary language as having a 'flexible stability'. But we still ignore at our peril the views of such people as the Great-Russian nationalist Struve who felt that the presence of Ukrainian in education would be 'an artificial and unjustifiable waste of the psychological force of the population' (1911) and represent a 'nationalist multiplication of cultures'.[10]

Looking back to 'origins', Breton may well be the continuation of the speech of 'Celtic' emigrants from the British Isles around the fourth-fifth centuries AD, but it is important to bear in mind that the peoples of Armorica could not have existed in a vacuum. Whether or not there were still Celtic speakers in what is modern Brittany will remain controversial. Are the Bretons essentially 'British', or do they reflect the Gaulish 'essence' of France? This problem is unlikely ever to be solved. What of contemporary migration, travel, and commerce? Perhaps Gaulish *had* died out there by the time there was real British settlement, but we must accept that there were cross-Channel contacts over hundreds of years, something which could have helped keep Gaulish going.[11] Briefly, roots can be a myth. We accept the term 'Breton' as one manifestation of that rich variety which has survived nineteenth-century Europe.

No one knows how many speakers of Breton there are, or the type of speakers they are. Research may show that they actually speak in a complex interplay of varieties of French and Breton. Recent guesstimates range from 50,000 to 1,200,000, with Morvannou's 500,000 probably reflecting the most common-sense figure:[12]

How many people speak Breton?

Year	Number	Type of speakers	Source
1977	1,200,000	'Know Breton'	Le Menn
1977	300,000	'Can use Breton'	Le Menn
1980	500,000	'Speakers'	Morvannou
1986	50–100,000	'Habitual speakers'	Press
1987–	250,000	'Breton speakers'	Broudic
1989	50,000	(as Press)	Abalain

The fact is that Breton is in decline. The question is whether this decline is irreversible.

The decline of Breton is not a twentieth-century phenomenon, although it has accelerated tremendously during this period. The major long-term cause is that its speakers have belonged to a relatively disadvantaged community. Its own early apparently successful expansion eastwards may have contributed to its eventual weakening. A situation arose where there was strong Breton–French bilingualism and a concentration of the biggest towns, namely Rennes and Nantes, in the eastern area, where Breton was not indigenous. In Lower Brittany, where the language was indigenous, its retreat from urban areas was well underway by the sixteenth century.

By the seventeenth to eighteenth centuries the first steps were being taken towards a standardization of the language, without the distorting puristic tendency of more recent times; but the sense that 'French' was 'more desirable' was already well established. By 1850 the language was largely lost in the towns and further undermined by the rise of school education in French, industry, migration, the railways, and military service. In the First World War around 120,000 Bretons died, at times allegedly because they could not understand orders or were even assumed to be the enemy because of their language. Associated with the Second World War is the stigma of collaboration, no more deserved in Brittany than anywhere else in France, but in Brittany associated with nationalism and the related language question.

The dialectal fragmentation of the language has led to mixed feelings about Breton on the part of the speakers. Overall, native-speaker linguistic attitudes have been seen to represent a sort of denial of the language, since the spoken standard language seems artificial or alien, the dialects have low prestige, and only French is felt worthy of public use. For example, 'Le breton n'aurait jamais dû exister, j'aurais préféré être mort plutôt que de vivre cette honte, nous étions comme une portée de poulets sans défense, on disait que cette langue était réservée aux vaches at aux cochons' ('Breton should never have existed. I'd have preferred being dead to living this shame. We were like a brood of defenceless "chickens"; people said this language was reserved for cows and pigs') (cited by Kress (no year), 45–63 (5)).

French competes with standard and vernacular Breton in all areas of oral communication. For Carhaix it has been shown that standard Breton is very little used, namely in non-agricultural work, town hall, education, and oral media. The vernacular is present in all areas of communication except education and the oral media. French is present in all areas, and predominant in all but cafés and agricultural work.[13] French overall has the role of lingua franca or 'Standard "Breton" Language', both for out-of-house communication and in writing. Vernacular Breton is in lively informal use, interplaying in a complex way with French, but almost certainly fading with the passing generations.

The struggle for a majority, even exclusive place for Breton in education and the media is concerned with reducing and reversing this, and creating a relatively uniform Breton language.[14] The Breton may overall be viewed negatively, as 'têtu, plouc, arriéré, passéiste, réaction-naire, conservateur, mystique, triste' ('stubborn, a country bumpkin, retarded, backward-looking, reactionary, conservative, mystical, sad'); positive references, such as 'courageux, travailleur, honnête, persévérant' ('courageous, hard-working, decent, persevering'), strike one as condescending.[15] But the language has survived, and the question arises as to whether one associates this with a deep emotional attachment or with the backwardness and poverty of the region, or with both.

Real pressure on the regional languages of France began soon after 1789. Immediately after the Revolution, however, there was much more support for the multilingual and multicultural character of France. On 14 January 1790 it was decreed that all documents of the National Constituent Assembly would be translated into the various idioms of the Republic and distributed to the appropriate regions. In May of that year the salaries of teachers using two languages in Brittany, Alsace, and the Basque Country were increased. And in November it was made clear that all haste should be employed in translating documents into the other languages of the country. With the declaration of the Republic in July 1792 the situation seemed to change: the 'other languages' were referred to as 'still' spoken in France. It is from this point that attitudes hardened, first in the Barère report (27 January 1794), and secondly in the more considered and informed but ultimately more political and damning Grégoire report (6 June 1794).

Grégoire was told in no uncertain terms of the beauty of the *patois*, something repeated at least in 1834.[16] He stated that around fifty per cent of the population had a language other than French as their first language, from which he concluded that as part of breaking down all obstacles to the creation of the new state, French had to be made the language of all its citizens. He had some quaint ideas, for example, that the national language was indispensable to the perfection of agriculture. Later, in 1831, it was explicitly stated that the Breton language had to be fragmented, and, in 1845, that it was the teachers' duty to kill it:[17]

> [il faut] par tous les moyens possibles, favoriser l'appauvrissement, la corruption du breton, jusqu'au point où, d'une commune à l'autre, on ne puisse pas s'entendre ... Car alors la nécessité de communication obligera le

paysan d'apprendre le français. Il faut absolument détruire le langage breton' (advice from the préfets of the Côtes-du-Nord and Finistère to the Minister of Public Education, Montalivet (who was favourable to the regional languages), 1831).

'Surtout rappelez-vous, messieurs, que vous n'êtes établis que pour tuer la langue bretonne' (1845, a sous-préfet of Finistère, to school teachers).

All this reflected and reinforced the deepening stigmatization of Breton and 'Bretonness': it was regional, backward, and rural, and this must have had its impact on the psychology of Breton speakers, even if many of them might be argued to be eager to jettison Breton and 'join the modern world'. Breton's situation is also weakened by its lack of an accepted written standard. Traditional standard Breton is not everywhere accepted, understood, or used, and has no agreed orthography. The orthographical controversy is one of the most vehement and suicidal controversies of the last fifty years, strengthening the arguments of those opposed to granting a greater place to Breton within French education and life.[18]

The education of the young was the key to the centralization of France. The introduction of obligatory and free primary state education by the Jules Ferry laws of the 1880s meant more and more children learned French, which meant that regional languages such as Breton became a handicap. The effect was not as dramatic as it might have been, since most Breton-speaking children had left school by the age of fourteen; but it reinforced the undermining of Breton which was already underway. The greater mobility of labour brought by industrialization, and the experience of the First World War, meant that French became even more positively charged: it offered advancement, power, and the opportunity for escape from what was perceived as a backward environment.

The inculcation of a negative attitude to Breton within the minds of schoolchildren began with the presentation by the school of an alternative model for life. At the beginning of the nineteenth century the Breton language was still a most important factor in the transmission of 'Bretonness'. Being Breton and a peasant became a social and cultural handicap within the context of French society and culture – it created an identity crisis. The effects of the crisis differed – some people welcomed the new model, but it was still a crisis, even for them. This situation still persists: 'On était arriérés quand on arrivait à l'école – on parlait tous breton' ('We were backward when we started school – we all spoke Breton') (b. 1938).[19]

In school, the method of learning French was basically that of total immersion supplemented by threats and punishments. The teachers' attitude was not always very strict with the youngest children, whom they would permit to speak Breton in the playground. When it came to the older children, there was no such leniency. Teachers would play the children off against each other, using mockery and thereby ridiculing the language.[20] 'L'instituteur avait demandé comment s'appelle la femelle du cochon et M. avait répondu la "wiz". Toute la classe était pilée de rire' (1943; *gwiz* = 'sow'). It was the language, the intimate life of the children, which was targeted. Punishments were typical, but also included writing lines ('Je ne parlerai plus breton' ('I shall no longer speak Breton')) and conjugating verbs (especially 'dactylographier' ('to type')). A favoured tactic would be 'divide and rule': mockery, using tell-tales. Another phenomenon was the so-called 'symbole', an object which would be given to anyone caught speaking Breton, and which that person would try to pass on to whoever he or she heard speaking Breton. The object was always negative or trivializing: a stone, a cork, a button, a rough wooden clog (it might even, in a small community, have been made by the child's father), a piece of paper attached to the child's back, declaring 'Défense de parler breton' ('No speaking Breton'), a potato, a tin of shoe polish, a metal ring, an animal bone. The person became the object. All that was closest to the children (their family, their environment) was devalued; they felt stupid, backward, and ashamed of their parents. If they were stuck with the 'symbole' at lunchtime or at the end of the school day, they had to carry the shame into the community.[21] Some teachers, however, did later have reservations about what they had done: 'Pourtant je commence à penser qu'il n'était pas nécessaire d'interdire le breton pour apprendre le français' (retired school teacher); 'Depuis une dizaine d'années il me semble qu'on aurait dû laisser les élèves apprendre les deux langues puisque c'est profitable. Je me souviens que lorsque j'étais à l'école, au CEG de Rostrenen, j'avais 16 ans, les meilleurs élèves venaient de la campagne. Peut-être justement parce qu'ils savaient deux langues' (school teacher from Rostrenen, born 1935).[22]

The 'symbole' had its effect: the last traditionally brought-up monoglot child (but brought up by its grandparents) from the central area of Brittany is recorded for 1973; monoglot children have begun to reappear, but in almost all cases they are monoglot because the parents have chosen a Breton-language upbringing for them; such children are often a source of wonderment and admiration for local native speakers – or of dirtiness and indiscipline. It is important to note that the children very often make little of the effects on them of the 'symbole' or of the forced learning of French; one might argue that they have hidden the humiliation away in their subconscious, or that the humiliation was just one more of the trials of childhood.

None the less, the overall consequence was humiliation inside and outside school, the refusal to transmit the language, the devaluation of the language, something they yet profess to love, the devaluation of themselves and consequent serious inferiority complex, and the rejection of their *bretonnité*, the withdrawal of the language 'into the closet', or into the most isolated, intimate, situations, ones which represented part of the linguistic impasse, a dead end which closed off the language to the modern world. Reactions may be varied, but the common denominator seems to be a negative self-definition, or a positive definition of something else; one is different, and inferior in one's difference (militants would stress the difference).[23]

Nowadays, many parents are bemused by the rise of some teaching of Breton. Some realize that the imposition of French impaired the spontaneity and richness of the children's life and of their own, most are hostile. In the Lower Brittany context, French was simply not their language. Certainly there were teachers who allowed some use of Breton, as easing the way towards the learning of French. But this was rare. The most common approach seems to have been that of punishment and the total imposition of French.

Inspectors' reports were extraordinarily blunt and condescending. It never occurs to them that Breton might have been used.

> 'L'usage courant de la langue bretonne en 23 de nos cantons est toujours un obstacle puissant à l'enseignement de la langue française. Néanmoins les exercices de langage [...] auront pour résultats de délier la langue de nos petits Bretons, de les amener à entendre et à parler plus tôt et avec moins d'hésitation la langue nationale, de développer plus rapidement leur intelligence et leur instruction' (Inspecteur Lucas, 1890).[24]

Breton is seen as a foreign language. It is even claimed that the parents sabotaged the children's future and the school's work by speaking Breton to their children.

During the second decade of this century, however, we get instances of two inspectors recommending the teaching of Breton. They are still in a minority, but reflect some evolution in thinking: 'Pour ce qui est de la langue bretonne, on a trop dit que la connaissance et la pratique de cet idiome nuisaient chez les enfants à l'intelligence de la langue française. Ce n'est jamais un malheur de SAVOIR deux langues' (Inspecteur d'Académie Léon Giusticci, 1911–12).[25] They also began to realize that there was not the time to teach most of the curriculum successfully. They were locked into the conviction that only French could possibly be used, and that to be a good patriot one had to know French. This fits in with Gellner's characterization of nationalism as a very distinctive species of patriotism, with homogeneity, literacy, and anonymity as its distinguishing features, whether aspired to or attained.[26] The miracle, perhaps, is that the language has hung on against such a hostile background.

Agitation has helped over the years since the Second World War. Soon the whole of primary and secondary education will be covered by the Breton-medium schools of DIWAN.[27] The signs, too, are that the obligation to teach French in addition to Breton has not at all impeded the children's progress: examination results indicate that the children's French is at least on a par with that of children in French-medium schools, and that their French and Breton are equally good. Brittany without DIWAN is unimaginable, though the movement is still new, rather suspect for many people, financially insecure, and caters for a minuscule number of children. I tend to trust DIWAN's recent claims that it is moderate, and that its aims are pragmatic: materials and text-books are being developed, and various working groups have been set up to make sure that the practical side of Breton-medium education can be achieved; and moreover there is an acceptance of the need to work within the official, national, French programme. Militants, insistent on being different and on not compromising in any way, would not find this acceptable.

Breton classes have also been extended within the state system, even though, again, on an extremely small scale. This was marked by the Savary circular of June 1982 and an earlier speech.[28] By 1990–1 there were 509 children in such classes. The aim is 10,000 such children by the year 2000. Altogether, there are over 1,250 children receiving education involving Breton as an academic subject or as the language of instruction.[29]

The pressure continues. Yves Dollo, *député* for the Côtes-d'Armor, made clear in a speech in 1990 that people now expected minority rights to be recognized, and that France should not be the last west European country to refuse its citizens basic cultural rights which it itself had recognized in international agreements. He declared his love for French, but bewailed the years of blind centralism and the policy of destruction of the regional languages.[30]

Did the process of decline of Breton begin so long ago that reversal is impossible? One has to hope that times and mentalities are changing in its favour, and in that of many other lesser-used languages too. Breton's future remains highly uncertain, given the loss of a generation of native speakers, the long process of linguistic attrition, and the particular situation in France. All the more reason for us to note Hagège's words:

> [...] il appartient à l'État de respecter, et d'aider à se développer, les langues minoritaires. Il est révélateur que, dans la France d'aujourd'hui, leurs

défenseurs se répartissent sur tout l'échiquier politique, alors qu'autrefois seules les tendances les plus conservatrices prenaient en charge les patois. Encouragé par ce consensus, le pouvoir devrait, d'autre part, prendre en considération l'intérêt pédagogique qui peut être celui des patois: le bilinguisme des patoisants est aussi une richesse, et l'enseignement peut y gagner. [...] Il faut aider les langues menacées d'extinction: [...]: la disparition d'une langue est une perte pour toute l'humanité.[31]

Nationality may be a myth, and in its perversion as nationalism it is a most dangerous one, since it means we play into the hands of the powerful myth or nation makers. Bretons need to be told that their identity is as positive, as negative, as complex, and as complicated, as everyone else's. The constraints on their search for an identity have over the last two hundred years been born of the fear manifested by that fragile, mythical nation called France and to some extent of the resistance of the Bretons themselves. They, their language, and their culture, are the equal of all other peoples, languages, and cultures. A whole convergence of circumstances has made them resist help, in case that help lock them into their perceived backwardness or make them more like their alleged oppressor. It may have caused them to be denied help by occasionally even well-meaning oppressors. They do need help, though 'help' is almost certainly not the right word. The constraints will be loosened when the right word is found. In the meantime, Breton-language education, television, and the like represent the practical way forward.

Notes

1 The *Guardian*, 17.11.91, 13.
2 The Czarist empire, the Habsburg empire, the Ottoman empire within Europe, Belgium, Switzerland, Spain, the United Kingdom, France, and so on have never ceased to be multi-ethnic states. There was, of course, a relation of domination: through conquest (Austria–Hungary, Russia), through majority group (Italy, France), and through cultural superiority (perhaps the Germans in Austria–Hungary). See Citron 1987.
3 Note Meillet's words on Breton: 'Par rapport au français le breton est un outil si grossier, si peu utile qu'aucun Breton sensé ne peut songer à l'employer de préférence. [...] [Les langues régionales] ne concurrencent pas réellement les grandes langues. Elles n'en sont que les parents pauvres qui n'ont pas réussi' ('In comparison with French, Breton is so crude and so useless an instrument that no sensible Breton can think of preferring to use it. [...] [The regional languages] are not really rivals of the great languages. They are merely their poor relations which have not succeeded') (cited from Breton 1976 by an Du 1991, 236, which is a valuable complement to McDonald 1989 (see Note 9 below)).
4 'It is by no means incorrect, but much to be lauded if one borrows from a foreign language phrases and words in order to assimilate them to one's own',

and 'Let us take from all sides what we need in order that we may render our language more clear, more precise, more concise, and more harmonious' (cited from Hagège 1987, 18–19).

5   Pool 1980, 237–48 (237, 239).

6   My rendering of Hagège's phrase, 'les mentalités forgées par l'histoire', 1987, 198.

7   But note the problems: Abalain 1989, 222–3, cites the French declaration to the UN (30.3.1977), and anxieties may be expressed in the media and national assembly regarding the position of French, e.g. Lagorce in *Le Figaro*, 11.3.1982.

8   Prattis 1981/1990, 21–31.

9   McDonald 1989, 279, 281, 300–2, presents the case for this.

10   Shevelov 1986, 71–163 (109), and 1987, 118–224.

11   MacDonald 1986, 333–47 (335–7).

12   See Press, note 29 below.

13   Timm 1980, 29–41 (34).

14   Hélias 1990, 351–2 confirms this but denies the stigmatization which has been linked to use of the Breton language.

15   an Du 1991, 7.

16   Cited from Kergoat (no year). Also Grillo 1989, who gives a fine presentation of the situation in all its complexity.

17   '[We must] by every means possible further the impoverishment and corruption of Breton, to the point where, from one commune to another, the people cannot understand one another ... Because then the need to communicate will oblige the peasant to learn French. It is absolutely necessary to destroy the Breton language', and 'Particularly bear in mind, gentlemen, that the only reason your posts have been established is to kill the Breton language.' See also Press, note 29 below.

18   Perhaps more people are reading and writing Breton, with books said to be published in runs of 2,000. However, Direzon states in *Bremañ* 116 (May 1991), 15, that, though 15,000 readers of Breton are claimed, only 500–1,000 copies of each book are published. It is the *zedacheg* orthography which seems to be emerging as the standard.

19   an Du 1991, 8.

20   'The schoolteacher had asked what a female pig was called, and M. had replied "*wiz*". The whole class collapsed with laughter' (cited from an Du 1991, 35–6).

21   an Du 1991, 39–55.

22   'Yet I begin to think that it was not necessary to prohibit Breton in order to learn French', and 'For some ten years now I've thought one ought to have let the pupils learn the two languages, since it's a good thing. I remember that, when I was at school, at the CEG in Rostrenen, I was sixteen, the best pupils came from the countryside. Perhaps they were the best precisely because they knew two languages' (cited from an Du 1991, 66).

23   an Du 1991, 77–9, citing Bourdieu and Passeron 1985, and Camielleri and Émerique-Cohen 1986.

24   'The everyday use of the Breton language in 23 of our *cantons* is still a powerful obstacle to the teaching of the French language. Nonetheless, language exercises [...] will have the result of loosening the tongues of our little Bretons, bringing them to understand and speak sooner and with less hesitation the national language, of enlarging more rapidly their intelligence and their education' (cited from an Du 1991, 159).

25 'So far as the Breton language is concerned, it has been said too often that the knowledge and practice of this "idiom" by children damaged their understanding of the French language. It is never a misfortune to KNOW two languages' (cited from an Du 1991, 174).

26 Gellner 1983, 53, 138.

27 See McDonald 1989, 175–202.

28 Cited from an Du, 1991, 240–55.

29 For more information see McDonald 1989 and Press 1992, 407–26.

30 See an Du 1991, 263–71, citing also Dollo's claim that 98 per cent of communes in Finistère are in favour of some official status for regional languages and cultures.

31 'It is for the State to respect minority languages, and to help them develop. It is revealing that in modern France, their defenders are to be found over the whole political spectrum, whereas formerly it was only the most conservative tendencies which concerned themselves with the *patois*. Those in power, encouraged by this consensus, ought to take account of the pedagogical usefulness of the *patois*: the speakers' bilingualism is also a boon, and teaching can gain from it. [. . .] One must help languages threatened by extinction [. . .]: the disappearance of a language is a loss for the whole of humanity' (Hagège 1987, 199–200).

References

Abalain, H. 1989. *Destin des langues celtiques*, Paris: Ophrys.

Allworth, E. 1980. *Ethnic Russia: The Dilemma of Dominance*, New York–Oxford: Pergamon.

an Du, K. 1991. *Histoire d'un interdit: le breton à l'école*, Lesneven: Hor Yezh.

Bourdieu, P. and Passeron, J. C. 1985. *Les héritiers*, Paris: Les éditions de minuit.

Bremañ, Rennes/Roazhon.

Breton, R. 1976. *Géographie des langues*, Paris: PUF.

Camielleri, C. and Émerique-Cohen, M. 1986. *Chocs de cultures*, Paris: Payot.

Carrer, Ph., *et al.* (no year). *Permanence de la langue bretonne. De la linguistique à la psychanalyse*, Rennes: Institut Culturel de Bretagne.

Citron, S. 1987. *Le mythe national*, Paris: Éditions ouvrières.

Gellner, E. 1983. *Nations and Nationalism*, Oxford: Blackwell.

Grillo, R. D. 1989. *Dominant Languages. Language and Hierarchy in Britain and France*, Cambridge: Cambridge University Press.

Hagège, C. 1987. *Le français et les siècles*, Paris: Éditions Odile Jacob.

Haugen, E., McClure, J. D., and Thomson, D. S. (eds.). 1981/1990. *Minority Languages Today*, Edinburgh: Edinburgh University Press (2nd revised edn., 1990).

Hélias, P. J. 1990. *Le quêteur de mémoire. Quarante ans de recherche sur les mythes et la civilisation bretonne*, Paris: Plon.

Kergoat, L. (no year). *Problèmes modernes des pays celtiques*, Université de Rennes 2 Haute Bretagne, Stagadenn I, Stagadenn II, and *passim*.

Kress, J. J. 'Incidences subjectives des changements de langue régionale', in Carrer *et al.* (no year), 45–63.

McDonald, M. 1986. 'Celtic ethnic kinship and the problem of being English', *Current Anthropology*, 27/4, 333–47.

McDonald, M. 1989. *'We are not French!' Language, Culture and Identity in Brittany*, London and New York: Routledge.

Pool, J. 1980. 'Whose Russian language? Problems in the definition of linguistic identity', in Allworth 1980, 237–48.

Prattis, J. I. 1981/1990. 'Industrialisation and minority-language loyalty: the example of Lewis', in Haugen, McClure, and Thomson 1981/1990, 21–31.

Press, J. I. 1992. 'The situation of the Breton language in Brittany', *Multilingua*, 11–4, 407–26.

Shevelov, G. Y. 1986–7. 'The language question in the Ukraine in the twentieth century (1900–1941)', *Harvard Ukrainian Studies*, X, 1/2, 71–163, and XI, 1/2, 118–224.

Timm, L. A. 1980. 'Bilingualism, diglossia, and language shift in Brittany', *International Journal of the Sociology of Language*, 25, 29–41.

14

Attitudes to linguistic change in Gaelic Scotland

DERICK S. THOMSON

A very brief account of the historical position of Gaelic in Scotland may be necessary to establish some perspectives in this discussion. The language arrived, from Ireland, in an ancient form, from the third century AD onwards, but there was a significant escalation of speakers of it from the fifth and sixth centuries. In other words, Gaelic became established in Scotland while it was still in the language's Archaic period. It is common to talk of Archaic and of Old Irish – strictly speaking Archaic and Old Gaelic is more accurate. That ancient language changed radically, to give eventually the languages we know as Modern Irish and Modern Scottish Gaelic.

On its arrival in Scotland, Gaelic would have had to co-exist with British, or Welsh as we would now refer to it, and Pictish, and perhaps with remnants of other pre-Indo-European languages. And within two or three centuries it would have established frontiers with the advancing Teutonic language which in due course was to produce such variants as Scots, Scottish English, and Highland English, and one form or another was to colonize almost the whole of Scotland.

But first, Gaelic was to achieve its own extensive colonization, gradually replacing Pictish and Welsh in wide areas of western and central Scotland, in the south-west, in the east (north of the Firth of Forth) including the north-east, and in the northern parts of the country. There was to be a counter-colonization, by Norse, in the north and west, especially in the islands, starting significantly in the late eighth century and lasting until at least the thirteenth.

By this time Gaelic, although winning the linguistic battle with Norse, was beginning to lose it with Inglis. The Gaelic royal court was becoming Anglicized in this sense, progressively from the twelfth century, so that the elements of Gaelic ritual still retained in the coronation of Alexander III (in 1249) may probably be regarded as survivals. By this time English/Scots was being progressively extended in usage in commercial and in legal transactions, and Gaelic was being edged into a more subordinate role, except in some powerful Gaelic clan courts, most notably that of the MacDonalds of the Isles.

The history of Gaelic from the thirteenth century onwards is one of slow but steady attrition in large areas of Scotland, and in the twentieth century we have seen the final disappearance of the native Gaelic of such areas as Donside and Braemar in Aberdeenshire, Cowal in Argyll, areas of Speyside, Forfar, and South Perthshire, while other areas such as Kintyre and Arran are near that end of the road that was reached in Ayrshire in the eighteenth century, Fife perhaps in the sixteenth, and so on.

The history, the pace, and the geographical pattern of this growth and decline of Gaelic are relevant to the attitudes to the language and the patterns of survival and resistance that emerge. Some sort of national consciousness has survived that Gaelic is the oldest language to be continuously spoken in Scotland, and it is sometimes referred to as the 'national language', although it is now spoken by only 65,000 of the population (according to the 1991 Census figures). It is treated with respect by a significant proportion of Scottish people, although there is another section of the population that prefers to offer jibes. In the past there have been many examples of antagonistic and contemptuous attitudes to Gaelic and its speakers, and some of the modern supportive attitudes flow from a desire to make amends for these.

There is quite a range of ways of reacting to linguistic colonization. We may look briefly at two extremes of this range. The first of these is withdrawal, perhaps with the setting up of barriers, or the creation of a ghetto. Remoteness can give a degree of protection, and we can see clear evidence of this in the strong survival, until quite recent times, of Gaelic in the remoter areas of Scotland. The pattern is a familiar one in Wales, as in Ireland and Brittany, and as in many other situations where the conflict between majority and minority language develops. In Scotland we see surviving Gaelic communities in the fringe areas of the Highland mainland, remote in terms of transport, the end of the road rather than passing-through places. The islands offer clear examples, with those nearer the mainland becoming bilingual earlier and losing Gaelic to a more significant degree: Gaelic thins out in Mull earlier than in Tiree, in Skye sooner than in Harris, in Benbecula (with its airport and army camp) sooner than in South Uist. Regular transport communications become a threat to the minority language, and improved radio and television communications accentuate that threat.

Also remoteness, while offering some sort of defence, leaves other defences weak, as it encourages parochial reactions.

Withdrawal can also lead to the setting up of ghettos, or partial ghettos, and we have some experience of that in Scotland, especially in the cities. Glasgow is a prime example. With a Gaelic population earlier in the century of some 16,000 to 17,000, now shrunk to under 10,000, Glasgow developed a wide range of territorial associations, clubs and churches with a strong Gaelic bias. These were extremely popular as social centres, with Gaelic in common use, and predominantly Gaelic entertainment, or debate, or religious observance. But the ghetto was only one side of the Gaels' life in Glasgow, for they were also part of the more general social fabric, acting as servants in Lowland houses, as nurses in hospitals, policemen on the streets, teachers in the schools, welders in the shipyards and so on. Sometimes this wider experience produced dividends for Gaelic too, as in the noticeable surge in Gaelic publishing in Glasgow, from the second half of the nineteenth century on, and the later development of Gaelic drama, and the recent growth of television activity in Gaelic.

We have in these instances moved away from the ghetto syndrome. The other extreme, contrasting with withdrawal, is strong assertion of language loyalty in spite of the majority culture. This can take separate forms. There can be ethnic assertion (with its attendant dangers), or political assertion, or religious separateness, or indeed combinations of these. We have had these various reactions in Gaelic Scotland. The eighteenth-century poet Alasdair Mac Mhaighstir Alasdair wrote of 'mì-rùn mòr nan Gall' 'the Lowlanders' great ill-will' (to the Gael, that is), and the phrase is still quoted with approval. Sometimes it is used in a political context to cast doubt on the Nationalist solution, to suggest that for the Gaels Edinburgh would not be a great improvement on London. This is sometimes a Labour Party stance, which seems to go easily with the 'little Highlander' position, a concentration on the Highland Gaelic community – so that here we can see the pendulum swinging back to the ghetto situation. In contrast, there is a Nationalist view that would place Gaelic much closer to the centre in an independent Scotland. And it is fair to say that there are also Labour and Tory lobbies that give some encouragement to a wider accessibility for Gaelic, for example in schools and on television. But in neither the Nationalist nor the other parties does Gaelic get much beyond the fringe of serious discussion.

We can see a similar ambivalence in the Churches. There was a time, only a generation or so ago, when the Churches, and particularly the Free Church, had an extremely strong Gaelic identity in the Gaelic areas. The Church of Scotland had begun rather earlier to infiltrate occasional English services into its schedule. Now there is a serious dilution of Gaelic-only congregations, and either a shortage of Gaelic-speaking ministers or a readiness on their part to move to a bilingual or English-dominant pattern. The effect of this movement is already very clear in younger people's linguistic range. The 'high' church register is foreign to most young speakers now, and this has helped to dilute not only an understanding of theological vocabulary but also a whole range of grammatical and syntactical and idiomatic usages.

We can bring educational change into this discussion too, illustrating the ambivalencies that are endemic to the present situation of Gaelic. On the one hand, there is a significant movement promoting Gaelic nursery education and Gaelic-medium education, with a strong emphasis on everyday fluency in Gaelic, and on the other hand a strong tendency to dilute Gaelic studies, for example by restricting the range of literature studied. When we add to these tendencies the powerful attraction of popular culture (such as television and pop music), with its inevitable English preponderance, it is not surprising that there is a serious decline in the range and depth of Gaelic usage in younger age-groups. Unfortunately some of this has spilled into the Gaelic media, reinforcing the decline.

I have the impression that Wales has achieved a more effective combination of ethnic, religious and cultural consciousness linked to the Welsh language, and that when the religious impulse weakened, a political dimension has been substituted for it. Scotland has had a stronger nationalist movement, but it has for the most part been rather divorced from language activism. This is something of a puzzle, but it is an old puzzle in Scottish life. We may remember David Hume's concern over Scotticisms in the eighteenth century, and the side-lining of Scots in official discourse over the last century and a half at least. In spite of Burns, and the Scottish literary renaissance of this century, Scots is still struggling as a language of literacy: acceptable for poetry, but distinctly awkward as a language of fiction, and not to be thought of as a language of business or public affairs. By contrast, Gaelic is much more developed as a contemporary language, with high and low registers, full credibility as a language of poetry, fiction, current affairs and so on, though restricted in various scientific and philosophical and other specialized registers.

As part of this development there has been a degree of public recognition of Gaelic which is in marked contrast to the state of affairs in the first half of the twentieth century. There is no problem, for example, over getting banks to print bilingual cheque-books, or, in Gaelic areas at least, to use Gaelic signs and names on their premises. Various local authorities use Gaelic or bilingual letter-heads.

University student organizations such as Students' Representative Councils in some cases have this sort of Gaelic profile, usually through the intervention of Nationalist officials. The Nature Conservancy body in Scotland uses Gaelic in this way and in some of its literature. The Western Isles Council conducts some parts of its business bilingually or wholly in Gaelic. But in many of these instances one is forced to conclude that there is a fair degree of window-dressing.

And although Gaelic has achieved a degree of range and credibility, it has been achieved by a restricted sector of the Gaelic population. It would probably be fair to say that only a very small minority is familiar with, or can confidently handle, a wide range of Gaelic usage. An imbalance of this kind is no doubt normal in most societies. So the majority of Gaelic speakers use the language for everyday chat and gossip, household purposes, telling jokes and stories, perhaps talking of crops and sheep and fishing, and would think of it as a natural language for fank-day (a communal gathering for shearing and dipping sheep), for a visit to the pub, for church in some areas, basically for rather local and parochial purposes, and they would easily turn to a more mixed discourse, with a high degree of code-switching, if the conversation turned to politics, or consumer topics, or dress and fashion etc. Even a visit to the local shop would be likely to result in some code-switching, for example in the naming of certain products and in price references.

Gaelic writers in the main tend to ignore this code-switching, and to restore Gaelic to some sort of grammatical and lexical respectability in the utterances of a range of characters. But a few writers have reported in the course of their writing the situation that exists, at least in some contexts. This emerges in the plays of Alasdair Caimbeul, and in one sequence of poems by Iain Crichton Smith. There is an element of caricature here, which adds to the fun and interest, but it is an actual situation which is reflected. Here are two short passages from the sequence 'The Island'. In the first a Lewis lady is telling how her son works with computers, was in New York and is now in Germany, where she visited him:

> ... Nothing but the best anns a' Ghearmailt. Ach tha rudan gu math dear. Wine, coffee, tha iad sin exorbitant. Tha mo mhac a' handligeadh com-puters. Bha e ann a New York ach chuir employers a-null a Germany e ... Tha iad gu math spotless over there. Na gardens aca cho clean, na pave-ments as well. I liked it very much. In fact I would go back there. I went by plane, tha thu tuigsinn (Mac a' Ghobhainn 1987, 41).[1]

Or from another conversation in a pub:

> Aig Christmas bha mi fhìn is Sheila ann a Minorca. I'll tell you something, no more peats for me. Am faca tu a' video 'I was alone in New York'? Bha

mi bruidhinn ri Sasannach, 's *caomh* leis a bhith buain na mònach (ibid., 43).[2]

Probably only the last line needs translation: 'I was talking to an Englishman, he *likes* cutting peats'.

Only a small minority would tend to insist on using Gaelic for a wide range of speaking and writing, and they would be regarded, often, as somewhat élitist or eccentric: their Gaelic might be referred to as 'deep' or 'difficult', or occasionally as 'artificial'. Even within this minority, there is a fair range of attitudes and competencies: from the easy, assured, natural style to the laboured, over-anxious style that can sometimes produce an unattractive strained 'correctness'.

This range of speakers, thinking now of both the majority and the minority, throws up a wide range of language attitudes and practices, and we can try to set these out in some sort of progression, taking into consideration both spoken and written forms of Gaelic:

(1) There is still a fairly strong core of indigenous, idiomatic, lexically-rich Gaelic, with regional varieties or dialects. Its exponents will tend to be middle-aged or older.

(2) A similar category can be distinguished in writers of the language. These will tend to be conservative, to retain separate case-forms for nouns, reproduce historical syntax and idioms, and use borrowings sparingly. Some of these will want no change in spelling conventions.

(3) Different attitudes can be shown both by speakers and writers who are prepared to make reasonable compromises, for example to borrow sensibly, allow a degree of grammatical change, admit some calques, and reform spelling.

We should look more closely at the circumstances that dictate these approaches. Gaelic, unlike Welsh, has retained a case system, with separate forms for the genitive singular of practically all nouns, for the vocative singular of masculine nouns, the dative singular of feminine nouns, and the genitive and dative plural of certain nouns. But in some dialects this system has been breaking down for generations, and it is showing signs of shakiness more widely, for example in the dative forms. Also, the stronger and the older the bilingual condition is in a locality, the more likely is the Gaelic of the area to be affected by borrowing, calques and code-switching.

(4) Another group, especially of *speakers* rather than writers, is lax and innovative, usually in a totally unthinking, casual way, not bothering about mixing both Gaelic and English, mutilating gender and case distinction.

(5) A small class of Gaelic users, often coming to the language from outside, has developed a kind of jargon which uses Gaelic vocabulary most of the time, but with a semi-understood syntax. We are likely to get more of this as Gaelic arts and Gaelic television are pounced on by ambitious outsiders.

I have listened to some speakers of this kind, and while understanding every separate word uttered, had little idea of what was being said.

You will see from that range of instances that we are in the midst of change and turmoil. Some of that change has been going on for a hundred years, some has shown up in the last ten years. The smallness of the Gaelic minority, and its scattered distribution, raise difficult problems. A larger or a more cohesive community would reduce such problems, for example by allowing a greater volume of language usage either in publication or communication. The actual situation seems to force more difficult choices on the community. It must bear in mind the economic imperatives that have so often in the past forced its members to go outside the Gaelic area for work. Cultural and linguistic idealism can hardly be expected to have a wide appeal unless clearly linked with some social and economic realism. For these reasons the advocates of stronger, purer, more wide-ranging Gaelic usage can be seen as a minority within a minority.

It may be that a different situation could be created by a resolute policy of Gaelic-based education. What some would regard as the last realistic opportunity for that was missed by the Western Isles in the mid-1970s, when they opted for a bilingual policy instead of a Gaelic-based one. There have been serious attempts to replace this, in recent years, with a Gaelic-medium educational approach, though the community's scepticism still shows. The lack of a comprehensive Gaelic-medium policy in the secondary school also undermines the whole concept, and makes further advances difficult. One kind of ideal situation might be to base education in the Gaelic areas firmly and completely on Gaelic (even accepting the premise that non-Gaelic children would simply have to adjust), introducing English as a second language later in the curriculum, and continuing with that sort of balance throughout the educational process. This would imply a special set of examinations throughout, and to make it work there would need to be a whole range of Gaelic material available in all subjects. But at the end of the day such a system would be judged by its practicability: its products would have to be seen to find their useful roles in society for the rest of their lives. Short of large-scale conversion within Scottish society to Gaelic usage it is difficult to see such an outcome.

The alternative is to make a less ambitious choice, which may still be an honourable one. This would still require the strongest kind of Gaelic educational foundation, achieving Gaelic literacy first, but would then move to a frankly bilingual scenario, with some subjects studied through Gaelic and some through English. It would not be easy to preserve the full integrity of such a scheme against the pressure of media exposure. The success of such a scheme would probably depend on a very positive input of attitudes and materials, on both the Gaelic and the English sides, in schools, in the media, and in the whole life of communities. All this calls for a very strong political and emotional drive, which has been known in other societies to produce the desired results.

You can appreciate that this is not an optimistic report. It is, in my judgement, an honest one. I could have emphasized more strongly some more positive aspects of the Gaelic situation, such as the continuing drive to develop Gaelic usage for contemporary purposes, the palpable surge in interest in, and learning of, the language, the positive advances in Gaelic publishing, and the new excitement and power that has informed Gaelic creative writing in the last half century. It is true that such positive achievements have happened in parallel with language decline, but even in the worst scenario some of these will survive. In a more favourable scenario these positive achievements might be gradually built into a new structure that gave Gaelic a secure and dynamic place in some sort of bilingual or multi-cultural world.

Notes

1 '... Nothing but the best in Germany. But things are pretty dear. Wine, coffee, they are exorbitant. My son handles computers. He was in New York but his employers sent him over to Germany ... They are pretty spotless over there. Their gardens are so clean, the pavements as well. I liked it very much. In fact I would go back there. I went by plane, you understand.'
2 'At Christmas Sheila and I were in Minorca. I'll tell you something, no more peats for me. Did you see the video "I was alone in New York"? I was talking to an Englishman, he *likes* cutting peats.'

References

(These are intended to provide basic reading suggestions as well as references to texts referred to above.)
Caimbeul, A. 1990. *Trì Dealbhan Cluiche*, Skye: Clò Ostaig.
Calder, G. 1980. *A Gaelic Grammar*, Glasgow: Gairm Publications.
Gaelic Books Council Catalogue of Gaelic Books in Print, 1992. Department of Celtic, University of Glasgow.

Mac a' Ghobhainn, I. 1987. *An t-Eilean agus an Cànan*, Glasgow: Department of Celtic, University of Glasgow.

MacAulay, D. 1976. *Nua Bhàrdachd Ghàidhlig. Modern Scottish Gaelic Poems*, Edinburgh: Canongate.

Thomson, D. S. 1990. *An Introduction to Gaelic Poetry*, Edinburgh: Edinburgh University Press.

——1994. *The Companion to Gaelic Scotland*, Glasgow: Gairm Publications.

Watson, W. J. 1926. *History of the Celtic Place-Names of Scotland*, Edinburgh: Blackwood.

Withers, C. W. J. 1988. *Gaelic Scotland. The Transformation of a Culture Region*, London: Routledge.

15

The poetry of speech in a lesser-used language

BEDWYR LEWIS JONES*

Linguistic geographers can describe the retreat of a minority language such as Welsh. They can map the stages in the break-up of an extensive territorial continuum with 70 per cent and more Welsh speakers into a number of small discrete areas of pervading Welsh usage. To borrow Professors Bowen and Carter's figurative comparison from 1974, geographers can show us a lake drying, the unbroken expanse of water disappearing, leaving behind a number of separate patchy and uneven pools. Geographers can also plot on a map areas where there is a marked variance between the numbers who claim to speak Welsh and the numbers who are able to read and write the language, thereby indicating communities vulnerable to language shift.

Yes, geographers can, and do, tell us a great deal about minority language change. So too can linguists. By analysing the speech patterns of young speakers, they can chart lexical and syntactical change brought about by linguistic interference. They can quantify the indiscriminate use of English words and phrases in Welsh utterance, especially in informal speech situations, by speakers who are unaware that they are using two distinct languages. They can note the use of prepositions to support the meaning of verbs in expressions such as *rhoi esgidiau ar* 'to put one's shoes on', *ble ti'n dod o* 'where do you come from', usages which go beyond the acceptable extension of existing patterns in Welsh. Of all this, and of its connection with registers, with domains, with compound rather than co-ordinate bilingualism, etc., much has been written and said. It is another aspect of language change

* It was with great sorrow that we learnt of the sudden death of Professor Lewis Jones only a few weeks after the Colloquium, where his fascinating paper and characteristically inspiring delivery were much appreciated by all the participants.

which concerns me here. Put simply, it is what happens to the poetic creativity of speech in a lesser-used minority language such as Welsh.

Since 1536 and until very recently Welsh has been denied official prestige status, except in religion. It has never been the language of commerce or manufacture or of urban life. It has been a language of restricted domains. It has survived and evolved as the habitual tongue of close-knit rural and semi-rural communities. Its strength has lain in the speech of these communities. To a much greater degree than a major language like English, its base has been an oral one, with some support from religious writing and to a lesser extent from other litera-ture. The language's oral base, however, has been strikingly exuberant and rich; it still is.

Gleaning in the speech of Welsh speakers has become a compulsive hobby of mine. I listen for words, idioms, figurative usages which are new to me. I am continuously surprised by what I hear. Words which dictionaries list as archaic turn up splendidly alive in ordinary, un-educated talk. One of the earliest poems in Welsh is a series of heroic elegies believed to have been composed in the Edinburgh area around AD 600 and preserved in a thirteenth-century manuscript, elegies which praise and mourn a troop of warriors who rode out on a disastrously unsuccessful expedition to try to recapture Catraeth, or Catterick in Yorkshire, from Anglo-Saxon control. One stanza describes a young warrior riding forth. It mentions, in bold impressionistic strokes, his swift, long-maned horse; his light broad shield; his shining blue sword. Then comes a line, *ethy eur aphan*, which has attracted more than a little interpretative commentary. Kenneth Jackson in his English version of the poem – a version fraudulently called 'The Oldest Scottish Poem' – translates *ethy eur aphan* as 'fringes of worked (?) gold', a rendering which conveys little to me. But ten or so years ago a chance remark made by a farmer from Penllyn (near Bala) revealed for me the image intended by the early poet, or at least so I think. The farmer was talking about a mountain stream in summer and about the strands of growth attached to stones in the water – a kind of algae – which sway with the flow. His word for these strands was *eddi* – *eddi yn yr afon*, '*eddi* in the stream', a particular usage of *eddi* which is defined in dictionaries as 'thrums, fringes or end of thread remaining on the loom'. I too had seen what he described. I had noticed how they lay submerged in the water, a deep, dark colour on a clouded day but when the sun shone they danced and weaved in a mixture of gold and green. The poet of the Gododdin was conveying something similar. That young warrior on horseback wore a mantle or cloak, probably of green. It was embroidered with gold. The gold on his cloak, the *eddi*, undulated and shone as he rode out in the morning light just like *eddi* in a stream.

My example is a very special one, I admit, but I could refer to a score and more words in medieval texts whose full meaning and range of reference has been enriched for me by hearing them used in living speech: the word *llory* in a seventh to eighth-century child's hunting song from Cumbria used by coracle fishermen at Cilgerran in West Wales for a cudgel to stun salmon; *sangar* used by an Anglesey man for the instep of the foot which helps to explain *sangarwy* for a stirrup, a *rwy* or ring around the instep, in a late eleventh-century prose text. Oral tradition includes words and idioms just as much as story elements, memorates, and weather lore. In a settled, fairly stable community, where a language's base is primarily oral, lexical items can live on, often within a very localized area, with remarkable tenacity. It happens where that language, in this case Welsh, has been and still is over-whelmingly dominant, that is with 80 per cent and more Welsh speakers, and where there is a core, possibly a hidden core, of virtually monolingual users of Welsh.

Another feature of speech in such a community is its ability to borrow extensively to enrich its lexicon without in any way destabiliz-ing its own distinctiveness. Kate Roberts is regarded, rightly, as the foremost prose author in Welsh. A quality in her writing often com-mended by critics is the untainted raciness of her Welsh. One of her best works is her novel *Traed Mewn Cyffion* ('Feet in Chains') published in 1936, a short novel about the impact of the First World War on a rural community in north Wales. Because the publisher saw the possibility of *Traed Mewn Cyffion* becoming a school set-book, a glossary was added of distinctive local words and idioms which, it was felt, needed expla-nation. It lists seventy-five or so items. Of these a third are borrowings from English. That the domineering aged mother in the novel should be left to stand on her own feet is conveyed by *ar 'i liwt 'i hun*, 'on her own lute' – that is, she should survive on what she earned playing a lute. A young woman is described unfavourably as *hen gyrbiban bach lartsh*, with the borrowed English *large* retaining one of its old meanings of 'vain, haughty, cocky'. A young town lad is referred to disparagingly as a *dili-do*. Kate Roberts would have been shocked had she realized that *dili-do* is English *dildo*, a word defined in the *Concise Oxford Dictionary* as an 'artificial penis used by women for sexual pleasure'.

The high incidence of 'good Welsh words' which are really English borrowings is not unique to Kate Roberts. Another classic of Welsh prose is Ellis Wynne's early eighteenth-century *Gweledigaetheu y Bardd Cwsc* ('Visions of the Sleeping Bard'), a fairly free adaptation of Sir Robert L'Estrange's English version of Quevedo's *Los Sueños*. Again the raciness of Ellis Wynne's Welsh is a feature applauded by critics. John Morris-Jones's 1898 edition of the 'Visions' contains notes on some 300 lexical items. Almost a third of these are again borrowings. The proportion of borrowed items is roughly similar in two small collections which I have published of distinctive words and idioms I have heard in Anglesey and in Llŷn and Eifionydd in north Wales. An example is *Howtluwch hi odd'ma*, which I heard from Mynydd Mechell in Anglesey and which can be translated as 'Away with you!' *Howtleuwch, howtleuo* is in origin English *(to) outlaw*, almost certainly a medieval borrowing which to my knowledge does not occur in any Welsh text or dictionary. *Criwtio* is a similar example, used of someone getting better after illness. It is English *recruit* in its old sense of seeking to recover one's health.

Borrowings like this account for a larger proportion of the Welsh lexicon than we care to admit, and the same, I suspect, is true of other minority languages. The borrowings are oral. They are often old. The imported items were absorbed into the speech of monolinguals, becoming an indistinguishable ingredient in their language. There, once naturalized, a borrowed item could germinate and grow, generating new grammatical forms, acquiring different semantic tones. For a lesser-used language like Welsh, a language of limited domains, such oral borrowing has been a vital source of enrichment. Welsh poetry proves as much. Poets find themselves seeking to renew poetic diction continuously. In their attempt to do this, Welsh poets, the more important ones, turn to the spoken language; naturalized borrowings are an important aspect of the linguistic freshness which they take up. Dafydd ap Gwilym in the fourteenth century did this, even if it was to a considerably lesser extent than the eighteenth-century neo-classicist Goronwy Owen claimed when he accused Dafydd of almost killing Welsh through his over-fondness of filching English words. Parry-Williams, the later Williams Parry, and Gwenallt in our century have all done the same. Let me repeat, however, that the borrowing I am talking about was borrowing into Welsh speech communities where Welsh was dominant, where Welsh monolingualism was strong. Today that kind of stable linguistic heartland barely exists.

Wealth of words is one aspect of the speech of Welsh-speaking communities which repeatedly surprises me. Another is the richness of idiom and metaphor in everyday talk. In Welsh it is common to refer to an east wind as *gwynt traed y meirw* 'the wind of dead men's feet', referring to the Christian practice of burying the dead with their feet pointing to the east. It was from a farmer from the eastern border of Montgomeryshire that I heard a synonymous noun-phrase which sent a shudder down my back. He referred to the east wind as *gwynt o'r Hen Bengwern* 'the wind from Old Pengwern'. Pengwern was the name of one of the royal courts of a politically independent Powys, possibly near the Wrekin. It was captured and destroyed by the men of Mercia sometime in the mid-seventh century, a defeat which became the subject of memorable ninth-century saga verse in Welsh. 'The wind from Old Pengwern', never recorded in writing as far as I know, carries within it historical echoes reaching back thirteen centuries and more. My example is again special, but far from unique. Speaking to a friend one day, he referred to an untrustworthy woman as *Siwan o hen beth* 'a real Joan'. Siwan, the Welsh form of Joan, was the name of the daughter of King John of England who married Llywelyn the Great of Gwynedd in 1205. I asked the friend where he had heard *Siwan o hen beth*. 'From my grandmother in Dolwyddelan', he replied. Dolwydde-lan was one of the courts of Llywelyn, possibly his birthplace. One can imagine Joan visiting Dolwyddelan accompanied by her Norman-French attendants; one recalls too that Joan was caught in adultery with the Norman baron William de Breos in 1229: William was sub-sequently hanged. Joan/Siwan was not much liked amongst her hus-band's subjects. Her name lived on orally in parts of Gwynedd as a synonym for a female person whom one cannot trust. In *Siwan o hen beth*, as in *gwynt o'r hen Bengwern*, a phrase used in speech preserves vestiges of collective memory from a distant past. They are a facet of unconscious handing down of cultural inheritance, an aspect of *tradi-tio*, which at the same time give colour and character to commonplace conversational remarks. 'Languages', as George Steiner remarked, 'are the instruments of storage and of transmission of legacies of experience and imaginative construction particular to a given community.'

I could go on adding examples. One more will suffice. It has to do with conveying illegitimacy. But before the example, a brief prologue *digressio*. Some of you may recall how on a farm in spring, when hens used to roam free, one hen would insist on laying its eggs in some hidden overgrown corner. One searched for her nest in vain. Then one day she would turn up in the yard at feeding time with one or two chicks. End of *digressio*. I was talking to an elderly lady in Llŷn whom I did not know well. She wanted to convey that there was some doubt about a certain person's paternity. She dropped her voice slightly and said, 'His mother brooded out of doors', *gori allan wnaeth 'i fam o. Gori allan* 'to brood out of doors' as an expression for having a child before marriage is not recorded in any dictionary. It was not a phrase the person I was talking to had coined. She had acquired it in her com-munity. It had been minted by 'some mute inglorious Milton', it had caught on and become part of local speech. The linguistic creativity which produces expressions of this kind, the circumstances for trans-mitting them, these things belong to the same oral linguistic base that was able to absorb and digest borrowing and retain lexical items which in terms of standard literary usage are considered archaic. It is this oral richness and the imaginative potential of speech which is the strength of a lesser used language with limited institutional support, like Welsh.

Is this oral base still there? To a certain degree, yes. I was pleased recently to add to my collection of expressions which convey thinness a saying I picked up from a young man in Anglesey who observed that someone looked *yn dena fel dipstic* 'as thin as a dipstick'. I was more delighted to hear another young person in a village pub one Wednesday night asking a friend for the loan of five pounds. 'You'll get it back on Friday', he said, adding jokingly, *Dydd Gwener mae'r gog yn galw* 'on Friday the cuckoo drops by'. A community where a young unemployed person can refer to a social benefit giro slip as a cuckoo's egg retains its linguistic creativity. But both of my last examples come from communities where Welsh is still dominant, with over 70 per cent using the language habitually as a mother tongue. Such areas are today few. Increased physical mobility, the homogenizing influence of contemporary mass culture and mass market, cultural fragmentation, in-migration of non-Welsh speakers into areas which have hitherto been predominantly Welsh, these and other factors inevitably reduce the percentage of speech-events which are carried on normally in Welsh; they work to destabilize the language in what has been its traditional heartland. It is a fact that all the examples of lexical raciness which I quoted earlier on, all apart from the last two, come from the speech of elderly persons.

Preliminary results of the 1991 population census for Wales are beginning to appear.[1] They seem to indicate a fall in the rate of decline in the overall number of people able to speak Welsh. Percentages of Welsh speakers amongst school children and in the younger age groups are increasing. Bilingualism, it appears, is being stabilized. There is a proven capability, mainly through education, to generate an increasing number of potential Welsh speakers. A question remains, however, about the richness and creativeness of a lesser-used minority language like Welsh which is being promoted through education and other conscious means today. But then should one ask about the quality of a minority language or is such a question nothing more than nostalgic yearning for a world that has passed?

Note

[1] The census results confirm what Professor Lewis Jones writes: the proportion of children aged 3–15 able to speak Welsh has risen from 18 per cent (1981) to 24.9 per cent (1991), cf. Janet Davies, *The Welsh Language* (Cardiff University of Wales Press 1983), 67. [Editors].

16

A Tale of Two Dialects: standardization in modern spoken Welsh

MARI C. JONES

Introduction

It is at best rare for the same language to be spoken in the same way throughout an entire speech community. Factors such as substrata or relative isolation – both geographical and political – inevitably result in its fragmentation into a number of dialects which, as in the case of Italy, are sometimes so different from each other as to be mutually incomprehensible. This may pose problems for inter-regional communication or for the establishment of public institutions, such as legislative administration or media, which aim to serve the whole of the speech-community, and often precipitates linguistic standardization – a process whereby the speech community is once again reunited by the adoption of one dialect as the standard.

Selection as an appropriate candidate for standardization has very little to do with a variety's linguistic features. Most sociolinguists (see, for example, Leith 1983) tend to reduce the process to four separate stages. First, there is the selection of one form as a prestige variety. The successful candidate is usually chosen for cultural or socio-political reasons (Scaglione 1984, 13; Joseph 1987, 132) such as political centralization, with the language of the powerbase often being considered as a prestige variety due to the fact that it is commonly used in most political transactions and commercial dealings. Once selected, the variety will undergo a process of codification during which it is systematized by dictionaries and grammars. This provides a fixed means of reference, a model of what is deemed to be correct and a goal to be aimed for by those learning the language. When this has been accomplished, the new, codified language will start to oust the other dialects from many of their domains and will take over all functions associated with, for example, law, education, religion, literature, government and so forth. In such cases the standard may have to start expressing concepts in domains with which it has previously had little or no contact. This inevitably leads to the creation or borrowing of vocabulary and new grammatical conventions. Standardization is complete when the speech community starts to identify with the selected variety. At this point, the standardized dialect often becomes synonymous with the concept of a national language and serves as a strong unifying force within a region, a powerful marker of national identity.

However, despite its occurrence in many of the world's languages, elevating dialects such as East Midland and Francien to, respectively, standard English and French, the above formula is not the sole path to linguistic standardization, as I will now demonstrate with reference to Welsh.

The standardization of written Welsh

The written standardization of Welsh took place many centuries ago. Given the fact that we have written evidence that the language has been spoken for at least 1,400 years, it is not surprising that widespread dialectal fragmentation has occurred due to a mixture of historical, geographical and political factors resulting in major dialect areas, roughly corresponding to the old kingdoms of Gwynedd, Powys, Dyfed and Gwent.

Bowen (1964, 14, cited in Thomas 1987, 101) observes that, because of the nature of its terrain, Wales has historically never had a single natural focal point and 'in consequence, the salient element which is seen in the history over the ages is centrifugal rather than centripetal development' (Thomas's translation). Bowen sees this as having been an impediment to the development of the nation as a political unit, but another result of the lack of an easily recognizable powerbase was that there was no prestige dialect immediately available as a candidate for elevation as the standard, so that when it did occur, the process of standardization differed from the conventional pattern, outlined above.

By the twelfth century, the country's literature was based firmly on the bardic tradition. All bards served their apprenticeship in bardic schools whose strict regulations led to the development of a highly specialized, poetic language which was far removed from the spoken language of the day. No dialectal features appeared in their work, which was composed of language that had been consciously divested of all regional idiosyncrasies in an attempt to arrive at a 'common core'. Thus, on the basis of language alone, it was extremely difficult to tell from which part of Wales a poet came – in other words, by the sixteenth century, Wales possessed a literary standard, common to all regions.

The dissolution of the bardic schools brought in its wake a relaxation .in the implementation of the rigorous poetic conventions and there began to appear texts which abounded in dialect forms and colloquialisms; but although the standard fell largely into disuse during this period its existence was not forgotten, and when called upon in 1563 to undertake a translation of the New Testament into a Welsh which would be understood by the whole of the country, William Salesbury turned to the old bardic language as the only literary standard available. A similar policy was adopted by William Morgan who, in 1588, produced the first complete Welsh Bible. Standard literary Welsh then underwent the usual process of codification by means of grammars and the process was completed when the rules and general principles of Welsh were laid down in a report, *Orgraff yr Iaith Gymraeg* ('The Orthography of the Welsh Language') published in 1928 by the University of Wales Press, which was subsequently accepted as the authoritative norm.

The example of written Welsh, therefore, provides us with an alternative formula for linguistic standardization, involving the proliferation of an a-regional variety produced by 'factoring out' all localized features to arrive at a 'common core' variety.

The standardization of spoken Welsh

The matter of a *spoken* standard has never really been satisfactorily resolved. There exists no codified model of standard pronunciation for Welsh (Thomas 1987, 105). In order to avoid any possible etymological or phonological controversy in the matter of orthography, it had been determined in the late nineteenth century (Lewis 1987, 16) that literary pronunciation would be decided according to a word's history yet, this apart, there existed no prescribed norms for spoken usage and during the Middle Ages, the Welsh language had been in a state of quite marked dialectal fragmentation. The standard of the Bible had given rise to a uniform oral language which was used by preachers travelling around different parts of the country, but its literary overtones made it far too formal for everyday colloquial usage. Thus, for many years, there existed a dichotomy in Wales with the existence of a nationally accepted written standard, but no corresponding spoken variety.

The passing of the Welsh Language Act in 1967, which greatly increased the status of the language in domains such as legislation and education, brought with it a rapid curtailment of the state of diglossia that had previously existed in the country and highlighted the need for some form of standard, national Welsh to be available for both written and spoken purposes and for second-language teaching. As Lewis (1982, 231) states, the costs involved in these enterprises made it impossible to cater individually for every dialect.

An attempt to alleviate the problem resulted in the creation of *Cymraeg Byw* in 1976. This was an effort to suggest modifications to the different dialect forms in order to bring about a possible compromise between them. The work has, however, never been fully accepted by Welsh academia and has provoked a great deal of controversy, and accusations of being over-simplistic.

Standardization in two Welsh communities

The twenty-five years since the passing of the Welsh Language Act have witnessed a huge growth in the spread of the language to other domains, with the creation of S4C, the Welsh-language television channel, and the massive expansion of the Welsh-medium education sector. The language is now much more high-profile, with the widespread availability of bilingual forms and pamphlets. It has its own youth culture, popular music and 'pulp' literature and is no longer confined to the world of the chapel and *penillion* singing and their associated images. In order to determine whether or not the above sociological factors were influencing spoken Welsh, I carried out a detailed investigation of the varieties used by two Welsh communities: Rhymney in south-east Wales, and Rhosllannerchrugog in the north-east of the country. This involved tape-recording informants who had been chosen in accordance with the 'friend-of-a-friend' technique[1] in an environment which was as conducive as possible to the elicitation of casual speech (Trudgill 1974, 50–2). The communities chosen paralleled each other from a sociological point of view – both were former mining communities of similar populations, located relatively near to the English border – yet contrasted in terms of their number of Welsh speakers: the 1981 Census puts the Welsh-speaking population of Rhymney at 9.45 per cent and that of Rhosllannerchrugog at 48.87 per cent. If standardization was found to be occurring, therefore, it would be possible to determine whether or not the linguistic environment was having any bearing on the process.

The informants selected fell into three broad age-groups: school-children and young adults (seven to twenty-five years of age); middle-aged people (twenty-five to sixty-five years of age) and elderly people (sixty-five and over).[2] The variables examined were phonological in nature and were chosen from works such as Griffith (1902) and Middleton (1965) for Rhymney, and G. D. Jones (1962) for Rhosllan-nerchrugog, which gave quite comprehensive inventories of the dialects in question.

In analysing the data for each variable, I noted three things:

(a) the total number of contexts (T) in which a variable could occur
(b) the number of times the dialect variable (D) occurred
(c) the number of times the standard variable (S) occurred.

Speakers scored one for a standard variable and zero for a dialect variable and the data were analysed for one variable at a time. The results were then plotted onto a bar graph. I made a separate analysis of the data for the younger, middle-aged and older generations and was therefore able to represent the three groups of results side by side, thus allowing easy inter-group comparison.

I had initially considered converting the scores obtained for each variable into percentages, the maximum score being one hundred and the minimum zero. However, due to the varying lengths of my inter-views there was a possibility that a speaker who made very marked use of either standard or dialect could bias the group results. I therefore decided to use the following formula: after having calculated T for each speaker, I proceeded to calculate S and converted this figure into a proportion of T. By taking an average of all the S/T proportions in the group I obtained a figure which gave an accurate representation of the use of the standard within that group. In the case of the plural suffixes, where a three-way variable was introduced, I applied the above for-mula to each of the three variants in turn. In the interests of greater accuracy, I then calculated the standard deviation and standard error for each age-group and have represented the latter on the bar graphs as a series of error bars. Finally, I made a cross-variable comparison of standardization in modern spoken Welsh by calculating the average of all the S scores for the different variables.

Results

1. Rhymney
Analysis of my data revealed two main patterns, namely standardiz-ation involving the decline of dialect features and standardization involving the disappearance of dialect features.

(a) Standardization involving the decline of dialect features
The most common trend was for there to be a progressive decline in the occurrence of dialectal features through the generations, the older generation maintaining a relatively high percentage of local traits, the middle-aged speakers gradually starting to divest their speech of such features and the schoolchildren retaining very few regionalisms indeed. This trend may be illustrated by discussion of two variables – /h/ insertion and retention of the diphthong [jɔ].

The most notable difference between the phonological inventories of the Gwenhwyseg dialect of the Rhymney area and of standard Welsh is the absence of an /h/ phoneme from the former: /h/ does not occur in Gwenhwyseg in any context. Analysis of the data, however, showed clear evidence of the progressive introduction of /h/ in all contexts[3] with the younger generation using the phoneme in 71.3 per cent of possible contexts, compared to the 33.9 per cent scored by my elderly informants. The middle-aged speakers, at 44.82 per cent, proved to be a form of intermediate link between the other groups, introducing fewer /h/'s than the younger generation but more than my elderly informants.

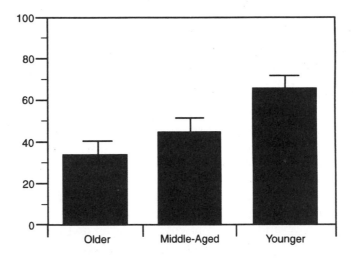

Figure 1. Insertion of /h/.

The group *-io*, whether part of a verbal ending *peidio, gweithio* or a noun *cinio* is reduced to *-o* in Gwenhwyseg. Hence, Gw. ['pidɔ] 'to stop', Gw. ['guiθɔ] 'to work', Gw. ['kɪnɔ] 'dinner'. The results obtained for the [jɔ] variable demonstrated quite dramatically the extent of the standardization that has taken place over just three generations. Whilst there is a 75.34 per cent instance of [jɔ] > [ɔ] in the speech of the older generation, the phenomenon only occurs in 7.63 per cent of cases involving the younger informants, with the middle-aged group falling once again between the other groups at 64.29 per cent.

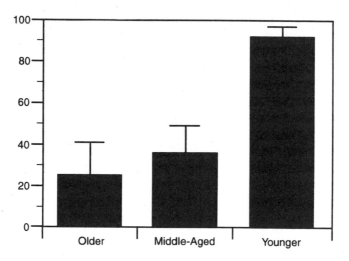

Figure 2. Retention of [jɔ]

(b) Standardization involving the disappearance of dialect features
The second pattern that emerged was a situation where the process of standardization was so well advanced that it had resulted in the disappearance of the dialect feature from the speech of my younger informants, as in the case of provection.

It is a characteristic of Welsh that voiced consonants are never fully voiced, even intervocalically.[4] However, in south-east Wales, a development occurs whereby phonologically voiced stops are actually fully devoiced in certain contexts. This medial devoicing is known as provection, defined by G. E. Jones (1988, 100) as the 'neutralization of the contrast between voiced and voiceless plosives in the penultimate syllable'. As a rule, then, this provection only occurs after the tonic vowel. The provected consonant may thus belong to the tonic syllable, as in ['ɛt|van] 'to fly', ['ɛk|lʊs] 'church' or to the countertonic syllable, as in ['ka|tu] 'to keep' or ['we:|tɪn] 'then'.[5] However, the phenomenon is largely idiosyncratic and is not always constant so that individuals may show pairs such as ['rʊpaθ] / ['rʊbaθ] 'something', although there are no apparent phonetic or phonological reasons for non-provection in words which provide the appropriate context for the phenomenon to occur.

Provection has been eliminated from the speech of the younger generation, who did not reveal any evidence of the phenomenon in the three words studied (compared with respective scores of 10.84 per cent, 79.17 per cent and 33.33 per cent, and 67.01 per cent, 88.84 per cent and 53.17 per cent for the same words in the case of the middle-aged and elderly informants – see Figures 3, 4 and 5).

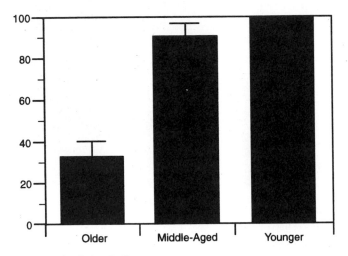

Figure 3. Non-provection in 'gwybod'.

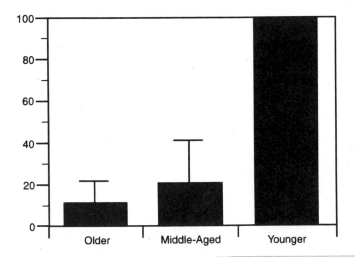

Figure 4. Non-provection in 'rhywbeth'.

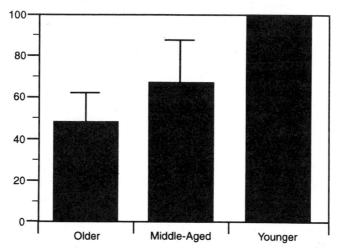

Figure 5. Non-provection in 'ydw' / 'ydy'.

2. Rhosllannerchrugog

My fieldwork in Rhosllannerchrugog was conducted so as to provide as close a parallel as possible to that carried out in Rhymney. Once again, the same two main trends were revealed.

(a) Standardization involving the decline of dialect features

In the dialect of Rhosllannerchrugog, final consonant clusters may be modified by the insertion of an epenthetic vowel – thus St. ['aml] 'often' – Rh. ['amal]; St. ['pɔbl] 'people' – Rh. ['pɔbɔl]; St. ['ɬʊɪbr] 'path' – Rh. ['ɬʊɪbɪr].

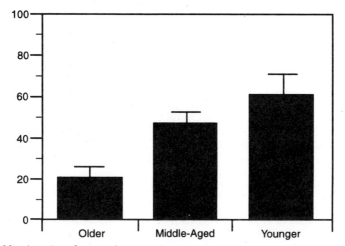

Figure 6. Non-insertion of an epenthetic vowel.

The results obtained from examining such clusters displayed a clear tendency towards standardization. Whereas such vowels were inserted by the older generation in 78.96 per cent of cases, the phenomenon only occurred 37.74 per cent of the time in the speech of my younger informants (see Figure 6).

(b) Standardization involving the disappearance of dialect features
Unlike Gwenhwyseg, the dialect of Rhosllannerchrugog has a /h/ phoneme and like all /h/ dialects it shares a development that was not incorporated into the standard, whereby certain phonemes become aspirated and voiceless in the context of the aspirate mutation. This extended mutation is triggered by the pronouns *ei* 'her' and *eu* 'their' and affects the phonemes /m/, /n/, /l/, /r/, /w/, and /j/ so that, for example St. [mam] 'mother' – Rh. [i'mam] 'her/their mother'; St. [jar] 'hen' – Rh. [i'jar] 'her/their hen'.

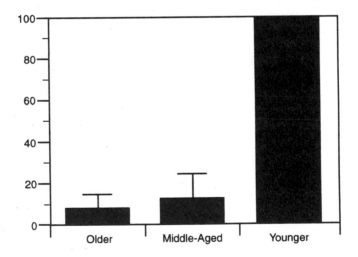

Figure 7. Non-occurrence of the additional aspirate mutation after 'ei' (f.).

As Figure 7 clearly indicates, this extended aspirate mutation, present in 92.86 per cent and 87.5 per cent of the speech of my older and middle-aged informants respectively, was completely absent from that of my younger informants. This is probably due to the fact that it is not a feature of written Welsh and, therefore, not taught alongside the other mutations in school.

The averaging of the scores obtained for each variable enabled me to make a cross-variable, inter-group comparison of standardization in both communities which revealed its progressive introduction over the past sixty years or so.

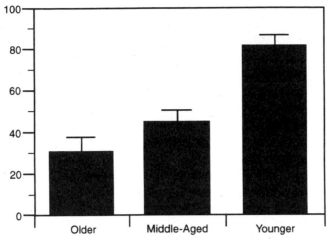

Figure 8. A cross-variable, inter-group comparison of standardization (Rhymney).

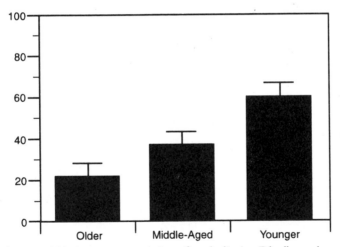

Figure 9. A cross-variable, inter-group comparison of standardization (Rhosllannerchrugog).

As Figures 8 and 9 indicate, there appeared a definite correlation between the results obtained in Rhosllannerchrugog – a relatively strongly Welsh-speaking community, and those obtained in Rhymney – a relatively anglicized community. Such results confirm the view of Professor Edward Anwyl, the eminent Welsh academic, who is cited by C. M. Jones (1989, 64) as stating that where society is undergoing a severe cultural change or is characterized by a considerable amount of contact with other speech communities, one can also find a significant language change which is correlated with the age of the speaker.

Marked inter-generational differences have also been found in Done-gal Irish (O'Dochartaigh 1982), with these differences having increased significantly in the course of the past twenty or thirty years.

The fact that similar results have been obtained from two linguisti-cally diverse parts of Wales leads me to suggest that this phenomenon could also be under way in other parts of the country. If future projects were to reveal that this were so, then the future of the Welsh dialects might indeed be uncertain.

3. Dialect mixing – the plural suffixes

Welsh has a variety of plural suffixes, one of which is *-au*. Gwenhwyseg is one of the dialects where this [ai] suffix is realized as [a] so that, for example *pethau* St. ['peθai] 'things' – Gw. ['peθa]. However, in the dialect of Rhosllannerchrugog, the [ai] suffix of the standard is realized as [ɛ]. I therefore decided to make my examination of this suffix into a three-way variable: this would enable me to measure not only move-ment towards the standard but also whether the dialect forms of a particular area were being generalized to other parts of the country.

In the case of Rhymney, although there was the already established pattern of decrease of the dialect feature [a] down the generations (51.94 per cent – 19.97 per cent – 4.65 per cent), accompanied by an increase in the use of the standard suffix [ai] (12.16 per cent – 68.5 per cent – 71.63 per cent), there was also evidence of the proliferation of the [ɛ] suffix, which is more characteristic of the south-west and north-east of the country (see Figure 10).

At first, it seems strange that [ɛ] should be more common in the speech of the older generation than in that of both the younger and

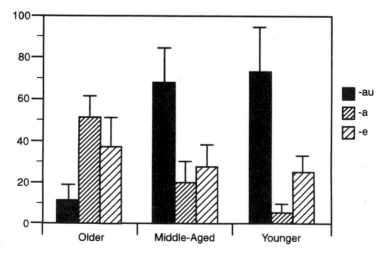

Figure 10. Plural suffixes (Rhymney).

middle-aged informants; however, more detailed consideration of the inter-variant relationship within each age-group yielded the following results:

In the case of the older generation, the Gwenhwyseg form *-a* registered the highest score, at 51.94 per cent; next came the form in *-e* which, as stated, is more characteristic of the south-west and north-east of the country (37.91 per cent), with standard *-au* registering the lowest score at 12.16 per cent.

With my middle-aged informants, we can see the beginning of standardization, the standard plural suffix *-au* increasing significantly with a score of 68.5 per cent. Moreover, the *-e* suffix, at 27.23 per cent, has overtaken the *-a* suffix (19.97 per cent) – revealing evidence of dialect mixing.

Examination of the results recorded for the younger generation indicates the supremacy of the standard form in modern spoken Welsh, which was used in more than two-thirds of all possible contexts (71.63 per cent). Moreover, the *-e* suffix, at 25.4 per cent, has clearly established itself over the *-a* suffix (4.65 per cent). This confirms that the speech of the younger generation is displaying evidence of quite marked dialect mixing.

The results yielded by my Rhosllannerchrugog data showed a similar trend to those obtained for Gwenhwyseg (see Figure 11). Once again, the progressive emergence of the standard [ai] suffix is clear, together with the accompanying decline of the dialect suffix [ɛ] through the generations. It is also possible to witness the appearance of the [a] suffix, characteristic of other dialects in south-east and north-west Wales.

Figure 11. Plural suffixes (Rhosllannerchrugog).

Considering each group individually, we find that the older informants almost exclusively use the dialect suffix, with a mere 1.64 per cent
instance of standard [ai]. The middle-aged group also favour the use of
[ɛ], although the use of [ai] has increased to 2.2 per cent. However, the
most striking result is that of the younger informants, whose [ɛ] score of
56.3 per cent indicates that while this is still the most commonly chosen
of the suffixes, it is not used as frequently by this generation; the
standard [ai] suffix now being used in 34.63 per cent of all possible
contexts. Moreover, with this generation come the first major signs of
dialect mixing, with the [a] suffix used 8.1 per cent of the time.

This set of results shows that although standardization and dialect
mixing may be occurring at a slower rate than in Gwenhwyseg, their
existence can by no means be denied. The fact that only a very small
degree of standardization was present among the older and middle-
aged generations demonstrates the continued use of Welsh in the home
and the community. It is significant that such a leap in standardization
and dialect mixing should occur in the Welsh of the first generation to
have Welsh-medium media and a complete system of Welsh-medium
education.

4. Dialect mixing in the lexicon

Although not an integral part of the progression towards a non-
regional 'common core', this tendency towards a dialect amalgam
seems to be happening as a corollary to standardization and contrasts
with the maintenance of a high degree of region-specific dialectal
features in the speech of the older generation. I decided therefore to
look for further evidence of this phenomenon with regard to the
lexicon, since the use of terms which were historically considered to be
geographically restricted in locations other than their 'native' regions
would provide readily available confirmation or disproof of its occurrence. Moreover, since the choice of a particular word is arguably a
more conscious process than the selection of a particular realization of
an underlying 'target' suffix, any such amalgamating of the lexicon
would suggest that spoken Welsh was becoming so uniform that dialect
words were losing their geographical connotations and being increasingly regarded as synonymous alternatives.

My data yielded the following results:

(a) Mamgu/Nain (see Map 1)

Welsh has two words for 'grandmother', namely *mamgu* and *nain*. The
Linguistic Geography of Wales (Thomas 1973, 307) tells us that *mamgu*
is a feature of southern Welsh, while *nain* is used exclusively to the
north of a line drawn from the Dyfi estuary to the source of the Wye.

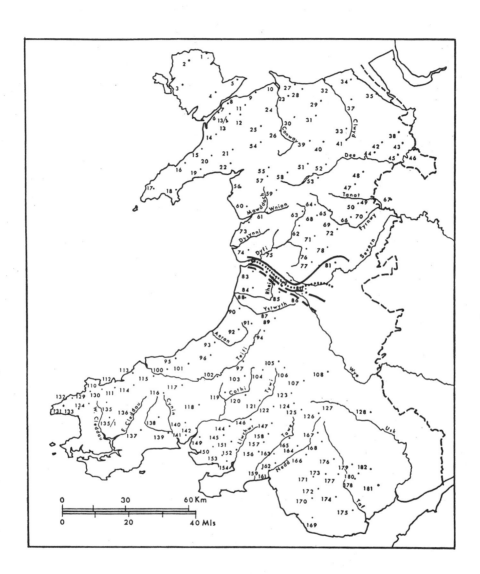

Map 1
Isogloss showing the northernmost limit of MAMGU
(Source: Thomas 1973, Fig. 7)

The fact that I recorded four examples of *nain* from four different younger-generation informants, none of whom had ever lived anywhere other than Rhymney, during the course of a few relatively short interviews suggests that the term is starting to become established in south Welsh. I also obtained an example of southern *mamgu* from a six-year-old who had lived all his life in Rhosllannerchrugog. This is probably due to the influence of the media, Welsh books and teachers working in the schools located outside the confines of their native dialect.[6]

(b) Efo (see Map 2)

Efo is the north Welsh equivalent of south Welsh *gyda* 'with'. Although *efo* is described in the *Linguistic Geography of Wales* (fig. 286) as characteristic of the area north of the Dyfi–Wye line, I recorded examples of *efo* in the speech of three of my informants in Rhymney, two of whom were middle-aged and the other a schoolchild.

(c) Arian

I also obtained four examples of *arian* (lit. 'silver' but used to mean 'money') from my north Walian informants, one of which came from a man in his eighties. Thomas and Thomas (1989, 95) describe this word as southern, and also as the form used in standard Welsh. *Pres* (lit. 'brass') is the more commonly used term in north Wales.

(d) Nene

The most salient lexical feature of the dialect spoken in Rhosllannerchrugog is the demonstrative *nene* 'that over there'. Although the forms

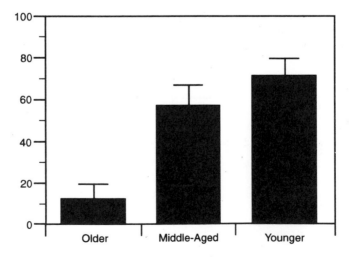

Figure 12. Non-occurrence of *nene*.

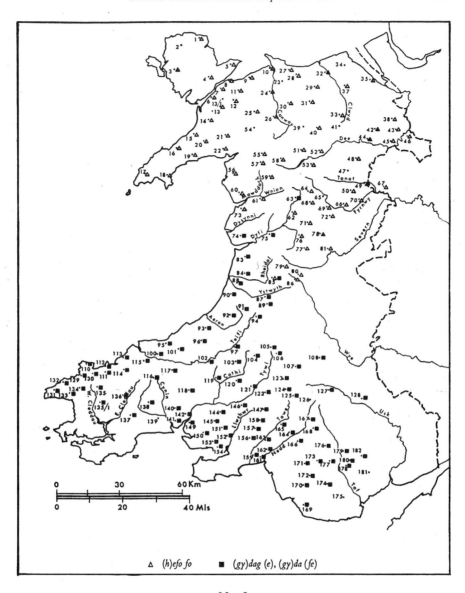

△ *(h)efo fo*   ■ *(gy)dag (e), (gy)da (fe)*

Map 2

Distribution of EFO and GYDA ('with') [Rhymney near Point 182] [Rhosllannerchrugog at Point 46]

(Source: Thomas 1973, Fig. 286)

ene 'that' and *dene* 'there [personal pronoun/noun] is' are found elsewhere in north-east Wales, *nene* seems to be restricted to the Rhosllannerchrugog region. The people of the village feel it to be such a symbol of their identity that it was chosen as the name for the local newspaper. My results, however, gave clear indication of the systematic elimination of *nene* and its replacement by standard *hwnna* or *hynny* (see Figure 12).

Conclusion

Analysis of the data collected clearly illustrates that the Welsh spoken in the historical territories of both the dialects of Rhymney and Rhosllannerchrugog is undergoing a series of related processes of linguistic change. My apparent-time study shows that this change has become more prevalent during the past sixty years or so, with the speech of my younger informants displaying innovations that were largely, if not totally, alien to that of their grandparents.

Where varieties in contact are related and similar there is often a process of linguistic levelling; in other words they may retain what they have in common and lose what is different. This is clearly reminiscent of the definition of language suicide,[7] the process akin to decreolization whereby a variety gradually disappears as it progressively submerges itself with features pertaining to another, related, variety. However, my data illustrate that in Rhymney and Rhosllannerchrugog (and, I would posit, several other areas of Wales) we are witnessing an instance of language suicide which is markedly different from most of the documented cases of this phenomenon. It differs in that it has nothing to do with decreolization or a return to the superstrate language but is, rather, a process whereby the dialects of Wales are becoming progressively divested of some of their phonetic regional features and idiosyncratic lexical items in a way which resembles the standardization that occurred centuries ago in the written language.

As mentioned above, the process of standardization displayed by Welsh differs from the more conventional pattern of prestige-variety proliferation which has been noted for varieties such as English and French. The model has been discussed by Pulgram (1958, 54) who likens 'the ... peeling off, as it were, (of) dialectal vagaries' to the removal of 'the petals of an artichoke until there remains the small but delicate heart'. 'But', he continues, 'if viewed realistically, flaws appear to the critical eye of the linguist ... as the heart of the artichoke is not a whole artichoke, so a de-dialectalized language, incorporating only the common denominator of all related dialects of a nation, would be a poor thing indeed.'

What then, are the implications of all this for modern Welsh? The Census figures for 1981 and 1991 indicate that, after a long period of decline, the number of Welsh speakers is stabilizing, at around 19 per cent. This stabilization is occurring against a backdrop of increased status and functional expansion for the language. As mentioned at the beginning of this paper, functional expansion is usually associated with linguistic standardization since it is extremely difficult for any variety to achieve the former on a national level without being fully comprehensible to a significant proportion of the relevant speech community. If Welsh is to be at all successful in its battle for survival, then, it is essential that standardization should take place, for its present number of speakers – some 500,000 in total – is already so low that continued dialectal fragmentation will merely hinder any further elaboration of its functions.

What, then, of Pulgram's description of this method of standardization, whose end-product he defines as a 'poor thing indeed'? Pulgram's argument seems to revolve around a notion that by eliminating all the idiosyncratic, regional traits of a language, we are divesting it of vitality. While this may indeed be the case, it should not be forgotten that whether the selected variety is a synthetic creation or not, from the moment it is standardized it becomes subject to rigid codification and strict monitoring which artificially constrain the language's natural tendency towards innovation.

The rise of any form of standard is mainly a result of socio-political and cultural factors. These, in turn, influence the mechanism of its linguistic development in an attempt to combine a 'minimal variation in form' with a 'maximal variation in function' (Haugen, cited in Joseph 1987, 14). Thus, I would argue that the 'heart of the artichoke' variety is no less 'vital' or 'colourful' than a standard which has been established via the proliferation of a so-called 'prestige' variety since, ultimately, the hallmark of human intervention is always prevalent. It could, perhaps, be argued that the former is more drastic in its elimination of regional features for the elevation of one variety usually leaves the others intact, albeit stigmatized, whereas in the 'heart of the artichoke' method of standardization all but one composite variety vanish. However, as far as the *nature* of the standardized variety itself is concerned, in purely linguistic terms there is very little difference between the end-products of either process.

Furthermore, I would argue that this model of standardization may even be advantageous in that it avoids any rivalry that might surround the selection of the variety to be elevated. Given the dissatisfaction in Eire at the proliferation of so-called 'Dublin Irish' as the language of administration and education, standard oral Welsh's lack of an indigenous historical territory must undoubtedly be in its interest. People from all parts of Wales are content to learn and teach this variety, whereas north Walians might resent being forced to foster a variety of southern Welsh as 'superior' to their own and vice versa. Having a non-regional standard precludes all the problems involved in the selection of an appropriate variety. It is foreseeable that, as the dialect of the powerbase, the variety of Welsh spoken in Cardiff would have a strong claim to this position. However, the areas with most Welsh speakers might well claim that their dialects were most suitable since they represent an area where, unlike Cardiff, Welsh is actively used on a daily basis. Such conflict has already been witnessed in Eire regarding the selection of a standard Gaelic: Nua Ghaeilge or 'Dublin Irish' is often denigrated by native speakers in the Gaeltacht regions who frequently have problems in understanding this variety and who feel resentful that the variety spoken in predominantly anglicized Dublin should be considered a more worthy candidate for elevation than their own varieties which, if nothing else, are at least living means of communication. Put another way, why should they, as speakers of living dialects, be forced to learn what is largely an unspoken variety? When a language is undergoing a dramatic decline in speakers, such squabbling is counterproductive and the existence of a non-geographically locatable, 'neutral' standard may therefore be beneficial.

In view of what has been said, I would disagree with Pulgram's description of a de-dialectalized language as a 'poor thing.' Modern Welsh may indeed have overtones of Nua Ghaeilge, described by Breatnach (1964, 20) as 'an artificial standardized amalgam of dialects, purged of grammatical irregularity ... (and) designed originally for official use' but it can be no accident that the huge increase in the use of this variety has coincided with a stemming of the decline in Welsh speakers.

The fieldwork undertaken in the communities of Rhymney and Rhosllannerchrugog might profitably be extended to other areas of Wales in an attempt to investigate a possible correlation between dialect death and language maintenance in Wales. This could have interesting implications for the field of language planning for it may be possible to demonstrate that, to extend the metaphor of language death, a dialect suicide pact on a subordinate level may be instrumental in staving off the impending threat of superordinate language murder.

Notes

[1] See Milroy (1980).
[2] I am aware that my middle-aged category covers a very broad age-range.

However, since the main purpose of my study was to observe trends rather than obtain precise numerical information, I did not feel that a further sub-division of my informant groups would be of any additional profit since the trend towards standardization was readily apparent from the three existing groups. Moreover, my use of statistical analysis has prevented any individual from biasing the data. I am therefore confident that the results obtained give an accurate representation of the situation in Rhymney and Rhosllannerchrugog.

3 That is, cases where the speakers of other dialects and/or the standard would have /h/. For example St. ['he:n] – Gw. ['e:n]; St. ['hɔfi] – Gw. ['ɔfi].

4 See Jones, G. E. (1984, 41).

5 Where | marks a syllable boundary.

6 Another possible explanation could, of course, be due to the fact that the children in question still have two grandmothers, one of whom they refer to as *mamgu* and the other as *nain* in order to distinguish between them. However, whilst this may be true for some of the cases, I am reluctant to believe that it would occur in all four of them. Moreover, even if this were so, the fact that both terms were being used as synonyms (since it is unlikely that in all four cases one grandmother came from the north and the other from the south) is confirmation of the levelling of dialect terms, with the elimination of regional connotations. The other terms cited in this section, however, have no such tentative alternative explanations and can only be interpreted as instances of dialect mixing.

7 Aitchison (1991, 198).

References

Aitchison, J. 1991. *Language Change, Progress or Decay?* 2nd edn., Cambridge: CUP.

Breatnach, R. A. 1964. 'The Irish revival reconsidered', *Studies*, 53, 18–30.

Griffith, J. 1902. *Y Wenhwyseg: A Key to the Phonology of the Gwentian Dialect*, Newport: Southall.

Jones, C. M. 1989. 'Cydberthynas nodweddion cymdeithasol ag amrywiadau'r Gymraeg yn y Mot, Sir Benfro', *Bulletin of the Board of Celtic Studies*, 36, 64–83.

Jones, G. D. 1962. 'Astudiaeth eirfaol o Gymraeg Rhosllannerchrugog', Univ. of Wales unpublished MA thesis.

Jones, G. E. 1984. 'The distinctive vowels and consonants of Welsh', in Ball, M. J. and Jones, G. E. (eds.), *Welsh Phonology*, Cardiff: University of Wales Press, 40–64.

——1988. 'Some features of the Welsh of Breconshire', in Ball, M. J. (ed.), *The Use of Welsh*, Clevedon: Multilingual Matters, 97–103.

Joseph, J. E. 1987. *Eloquence and Power: The Rise of Language Standards and Standard Languages*, London: Frances Pinter.

Leith, D. A. 1983. *A Social History of English*, London: Routledge & Kegan Paul Ltd.

Lewis, E. G. 1982. 'Movements and agencies of language spread: Wales and the Soviet Union compared', in Cooper, R. (ed.), *Language Spread*, Bloomington: Indiana University Press, 214–59.

——1987. 'Attitudes to the planned development of Welsh', *International Journal of the Sociology of Language*, 66, 11–26.

Middleton, M. 1965. 'Astudiaeth seinyddol gan gynnwys geirfa o Gymraeg llafar ardal Tafarnau Bach', Univ. of Wales unpublished MA thesis.

Milroy, L. 1980. *Language and Social Networks*, Blackwell: Oxford.

O'Dochartaigh, C. 1982. 'Generational differences in Donegal Irish', *Belfast Working Papers in Language and Linguistics*, 6, 67–103. Cited in O'Dochartaigh 1984.

——1984. 'Irish', in Trudgill, P. (ed.), *Language in the British Isles*, Cambridge: CUP, 289–305.

Pulgram, E. 1958. *The Tongues of Italy*, Cambridge Mass.: Harvard University Press. Cited in Joseph 1987.

Scaglione, A. 1984. 'The rise of national languages: east and west', in Scaglione, A. (ed.), *The Emergence of National Languages*, Ravenna: Longo Editore, 9–49.

Thomas, A. R. 1973. *The Linguistic Geography of Wales. A Contribution to Welsh Dialectology*, Published on behalf of the Board of Celtic Studies, Cardiff: University of Wales Press.

——1987. 'A spoken standard for Welsh', *International Journal of the Sociology of Language*, 66, 99–113.

Thomas, B. and Thomas, P. W. 1989. *Cymraeg, Cymrâg, Cymrêg: Cyflwyno'r Tafodieithoedd*, Caerdydd: Gwasg Tâf.

Trudgill, P. 1974. *The Social Differentiation of English in Norwich*, Cambridge: C.U.P.

Uned Iaith Genedlaethol Cymru. 1976. *Gramadeg Cymraeg Cyfoes: Contemporary Welsh Grammar*, Y Bontfaen: D. Brown a'i Feibion.

17

'Tafodieithoedd Datguddiad Duw': the change in the voice of the Welsh Bible

DAVID THORNE

Welsh has a literary and linguistic history spanning nearly 1,500 years, but it is only during the latter part of the present century that it has been recognized, in the modern period, as a language of law, public administration, formal state education and the professions. These facts between them have decided the character of modern standard literary Welsh, which has its origins in the language of the Welsh translation of the Bible, first published in 1588 and revised in 1620. Professor Henry Lewis (1889–1968) was responsible for the orthographic revision of the 1620 Bible: the New Testament in 1936, the Bible (excluding the Apocrypha) in 1955 and the Apocrypha in 1959. Lewis's revision remained the only standard Welsh Bible in general use until a new translation of the New Testament appeared in 1975. To celebrate the fourth centenary of Bishop William Morgan's work, a new translation of the complete Bible was published in 1988. Biblical texts quoted in this paper are from the 1955 and 1988 editions, representing respectively the voice of the past and the voice of the present in Welsh biblical language.

When the Bible first appeared in Welsh, the language had already experienced a thousand years of intense literary activity, during which the main creative interest focused on poetry. And Welsh poetry was a learned and scholarly art, suggestive, allusive, very much aware of an ancient and honourable tradition. It enjoyed a substantial measure of linguistic uniformity as it had been targeted over the centuries at a select aristocratic or squirearchal audience throughout the length and breadth of Wales. By the fifteenth century there had been finalized a sophisticated system of alliteration known as 'cynghanedd' and 24 strict poetical metres such as 'Cywydd Deuair Hirion', 'Englyn', 'Hir a Thoddaid' etc. The language used by the 'strict metre' poets was highly cultivated and rigorously taught in the medieval bardic schools. Unlike the free verse of the sixteenth century and the prose of the later Middle Ages it excluded regional and dialectal forms and above all possessed the copiousness and dignity, the resources – 'amlder Cymraeg' ('the amplitude of Welsh'), which was a fundamental requirement of good poetry according to the Welsh bardic grammars: it was no less essential to express the imaginative, the literary, the historical passages of the Bible and explore its homiletic, moral and philosophical themes. These latter themes extended the register range of the language into areas not previously encountered in Welsh writing.

Solicitude for the language was part and parcel of the training and *raison d'être* of the professional poets: and their language was a vehicle which had been refined and developed in the bardic schools since the earliest of times to celebrate in eulogy and elegy the virtues deemed necessary to maintain civilized society. This traditional function developed traditional forms and a traditional language and its adoption as the language of the Welsh Bible ensured that it became the keystone for modern standard literary Welsh. 'Penseiri yr iaith' ('architects of the language'), and 'vetustae linguae custodes' are the accolades accorded to the strict metre poets by the Welsh Protestant humanists William Salesbury (1520?–89) and John Davies (*c.* 1547–1644). Welsh bardic ideals and humanist linguistic models shared considerable common ground: uniformity, amplitude and eloquence were, after all, the basic requirements of any vehicle of learning, together with good dictionaries and grammars. And bards and humanists had an interest in lexicography. It was bardic custom to fashion and commit to memory lengthy word-lists and Salesbury published *A Dictionary in Englyshe and Welshe* in 1547, and John Davies his *Antiquae Linguae Britannicae ... Dictionarium Duplex* in 1632. Salesbury's *A brief and playne introduction, teaching how to pronounce the letters in the British tong* which also included an elementary discussion of the Latin element in Welsh was published in 1550, and John Davies's important grammar *Antiquae Linguae Britannicae ... Rudimentae* in 1621. Three centuries later Sir John Morris-Jones (1864–1919) said of the latter work: '... the author's analysis of the literary language is final: he has left to his successors only the correction and amplification of detail.'[1]

Naturally the Welsh Bible also inherited patterns from the prose literature of the medieval and early modern period such as the construction called the abnormal sentence by Welsh grammarians. This feature in which an unemphatic subject or adverbial phrase precedes the verb in a declarative clause, does occur in strict metre poetry but it is one of the main characteristics of Biblical prose. For example:

A Job atebodd ac a ddywedodd (1955)
'And Job answered and said'

(Job, 12:1)

A'i ddisgyblion a ddaethant ato (1955)
'And his disciples came to him'

(Matt., 8:25)

am hynny y digiais wrth y genhedlaeth honno (1955)
'because of that I was indignant with that generation'
(Heb., 3:10)

The influence of the Welsh Bible over the centuries that followed cannot be overestimated, for Wales in the sixteenth century and for centuries afterwards had no capital city, university or cultural institutions to act as centres of learning or literary life. Moreover the bardic tradition was entering on a period of decline, as a result of social and political pressures, from which it would never recover. 'Mae'n darfod y glod, y glêr – ni cherir' ('Eulogy is ceasing, the bards are unloved'), complained Simwnt Fychan (*c*. 1530–1606), and Edward Dafydd (*fl.* 1623–25) lamented a little later: 'Nid yw'r byd hwn gyda'r beirdd' ('This age is not with the bards'). They were correct because by the middle of the seventeenth century the language had to all intents and purposes lost its place of honour, lost its former patronage, in the homes of the Welsh gentry. Had the function of the professional poet as guardian of the literary language disappeared leaving no structure or institution in its place, it would have signalled the beginning of the end of Welsh as a literary medium. But the Welsh Bible, by adopting the linguistic standards of the strict metre poets and prose writers of the Middle Ages, retained the language of that tradition as the basis of all literary Welsh down to the present day. It saved the language from suffering a similar fate to that of other Celtic languages such as Irish and Breton, namely disintegrating into a number of dialects mutually difficult to understand, with no one dialect possessing the authority or the means to acquire the status necessary for it to be adopted as the standard language and thence developing as the literary medium. William Salesbury realized the need for urgent action and spelled it out bluntly:

A ydych chwi yn tybieit nat rait amgenach eirieu, na mwy amryw ar amadroddion y draythy dysceidaeth, ac y adrodd athrawiaeth a chelfyddo-deu, nag sydd genwch chwi yn arveredig wrth siarad beunydd yn pryny a gwerthy a bwyta ac yfed? Ac od ych chwi yn tybyeit hynny voch twyller. A chymerwch hyn yn lle rybydd y cenyf vi: a nyd achubwch chwi a chyweirio a pherfeithio r iaith kyn daruod am y to ys ydd heddio, y bydd ryhwyr y gwaith gwedy. Ac a ny bydd dysc, gwybodaeth, doethineb, a dywolwch mewn iaith, pa well hi na sirmwnt adar gwylltion, ne ruat aniueilieit a bwystviloedd?[2]

Welsh at best could have continued as a vulgar *patois* possessing neither dignity nor uniformity. But Salesbury's warning was heeded and the Welsh lexicon was enriched and enlarged and standardized during this period. The link with the future had been successfully forged, and Welsh alone amongst the Celtic languages succeeded in bridging the gap between the oral and manuscript traditions of the Middle Ages and the printed word of the modern period.

From the 1520s onwards there is evidence that copies of the Scriptures in English were circulating in Wales and that some could read them without difficulty. But there was also a desire to see the Bible translated into Welsh and made available to the monolingual majority in a total population estimated to be in the region of a quarter of a million. Most of the Welsh Protestant humanists had been educated at Oxford and Cambridge. As humanists they were dismayed that their native language, unlike other vernaculars, was not the subject of intensive study. As Protestants they were sad that the Scriptures were incomprehensible to the vast majority of their fellow countrymen by being presented in a language which most of them could not understand. Sir John Prys (1502–55) in *Yny lhyvyr hwn . . . (1546)* – one of the three in competition for the honour of being the earliest Welsh printed book – urged his fellow countrymen to seize the opportunity offered by the advent of the printing press to spread the word of God:

> gweddys yw rhoi yngymraec beth o'r yscrythur lan, o herwydd bod llawer o gymry a vedair darllein kymraeg, heb vedru darllein vn gair saesnec na lladin . . . Ac yr awr y rhoes duw y prynt yn mysk ni er amylhau gwybodaeth y eireu bendigedic ef[3]
>
> ('it is fitting to put parts of holy scripture into Welsh because there are many Welsh people who are able to read Welsh [but] unable to read one word of English or Latin . . . And now God has given us print in our midst in order to spread knowledge of his holy word').

The Welsh Protestant humanists responded positively and enthusiastically to the challenge. Throughout Protestant Europe translations of the scriptures had become the tools that ensured salvation. Having the Bible in Welsh gave the language the prestige and dignity that had been conferred on other vernaculars in Europe by this time – French, English, Spanish, Danish, Polish, Icelandic, etc. Any additional impetus necessary was provided by the belief that the faith of the Reformed religion was the faith of the old British-Welsh Church; the first of the 'isles of the Gentiles' (Gen., 10:5) to be selected by divine intervention to receive the faith and God's word. The theme is taken up by Bishop Richard Davies (?1501–81) and Dr John Davies in their writings. Siôn

Dafydd Rhys (1534–1609), a Catholic humanist, wrote in the introduction to his *Cambrobrytannicae Cymraecaeve Linguae Institutiones et Rudimenta* (1592):

> Nid oes nemor o iaith (hyd y gwnn i) ynn Eurôpa a'i hynysoedd, nas cafas ei hymgelêddu a'i choledd gan ei Ieithyddion a'i Gwladwyr 'ihûn o amser i gilydd; onyd eyn hiaith ni y Cymry. Yr honn ynawr yn hwyr ac o fraidd, a ddechreuodd gaphael pêth gwrtaith gann wyrda dyscêdic o'n hamser ni; a hynny yn enwêdic o ran cymreic-háu corph yr yscrythur lân.[4]

The adoption of the language of the Welsh bardic tradition as canon meant that Welsh, like these other European languages, had an approved standard. And Welsh was the only Celtic language in which the translation of the Bible became a classic. When the Bible did appear, it was praised not only for content but also for the presentation of content: it conferred status and authority on the language and made the scriptures accessible to the people of Wales, areas of Herefordshire and other border counties. Owain Gwynedd (*c.* 1545–1601), one of the last representatives of the old bardic tradition, readily acknowledged the achievement:

> ... Doctor Morgan,
> E wnaeth, wrth drin doethineb,
> I'n hiaith ni hyn ni wnaeth neb.
> ('Dr Morgan, by discussing wisdom, did for our language what no one else did').

Prose-writers like Huw Lewys (1562–1634) in *Perl Mewn Adfyd* (1595) also warmly welcomed the translation and in a number of prose works produced soon after the publication of the Bible there is a deliberate attempt to develop and nurture a standard literary language based on bardic canon. As Rowland Vaughan (*c.* 1590–1667), a translator of devotional works, states unequivocally in *Yr Ymarfer o Dduwioldeb* (1630):

> Eithr deall, mai wrth fwrw fy serch ar gywyddau cymraeg y cefais i y gyfarwyddyd wan sydd gennif, ac yr wyf yn gobeithio i mi arfer y geiriau sathredig a arferodd hên Athrawon o'm blaen i, ac na chyfeiliornais o athrawiaeth Doctor Dauis ynghyfieithiad y Bibl, yr hwn yw'r vnig Plato ardderchawg o'n haith ni.[5]

Had the Bible not been translated into Welsh, English would eventually have become the language of public worship, preaching and religious life in general thus creating a powerful and permanent infrastructure undermining the language.

As it transpired the Bible had a profound influence on the religious and literary life of Wales. In the sixteenth century priests were the only educated class with an important professional interest in Welsh language and literature. There were, of course, the poets, but the tradition had been for the most part oral. The vast majority of the significant authors of the next two or three centuries were drawn from the ranks of the parsons of the established Church and Nonconformist ministers – Morgan Llwyd (1619–59), Charles Edwards (1628–91), Ellis Wyn (1670/1–1734), Theophilus Evans (1693–1767), Goronwy Owen (1723–69), Evan Evans, Ieuan Brydydd Hir (1731–88), William Williams, Pantycelyn (1717–91). It is true that the literature that they produced was restricted in scope and theme, much of it being written from a religious, moral or linguistic standpoint. But it was lively, sometimes brilliant and dressed in a language well able to meet the demand placed upon it by the Renaissance and its aftermath.

And the secular history of the Welsh Bible was no less important in maintaining and nurturing the language. Robert Llwyd (1565–1655), an Anglican cleric and author of several devotional works, asked in 1629: 'Pa fodd y gwasanaethi di Dduw gan na fedri ddarllain ei air ef?[6] ('How can you serve God since you cannot read his word?'). From the end of the seventeenth century onwards the Welsh Bible was used as a textbook to teach reading to a deprived peasantry. Between 1737 and 1779 it is claimed that 327,075 had attended the circulating schools of Griffith Jones (1683–1761) and Madam Bridget Bevan (1698–1779). Throughout the nineteenth century it was the reading of the adult population of Wales in Sunday school and religious service. The population of Wales in 1905 was just over 2 million and 836,343 scholars attended 5,375 Sunday schools. Between 1800 and 1899, 203 editions of the complete Bible were published and in addition 148 editions of the New Testament.

Formal spoken Welsh also has its origin in biblical Welsh, although dialectal influence is frequently evident. It was conceived to meet the needs of itinerant preachers in religious services the length and breadth of Wales, particularly in the wake of the Methodist revival of the eighteenth century and the growth of Nonconformity. And the earlier translation of the Welsh Bible is not free of dialectal and regional characteristics. I will note just one example: in Matt. 13:51 (1955) the question and reply reflect northern usage: *A ddarfu i chwi ddeall hyn oll? Hwythau a ddywedasant wrtho, Do.* 'Have you understood all these things? They replied, "Yes".' The new translation has adopted the standard (and southern) form of question and response: *A ydych wedi deall yr holl bethau hyn? Dywedasant wrtho, Ydym.* The formal spoken register is not confined to the pulpit but serves as the natural vehicle for formal public discussion, formal lecturing and formal broadcasting. When it exemplifies the spoken mode at its most formal, there is little to choose between it and the literary register.

The Welsh Bible always provided a dependable linguistic standard for literature, scholarly writing, teaching and discussion and at the turn of the present century, the distinguished Welsh scholar Sir John Morris-Jones (1864–1929) made an unambiguous call for a return to the traditional bardic standards in order to rescue the language from the inanities of William Owen Pughe (1759–1835). Pughe's theory of language was based on his belief that Welsh had been constructed by the druids from a set of monosyllabic roots and he set about reforming Welsh orthography and grammar with devastating effect. Pughe's romantic linguistic ideas coloured a substantial part of Welsh writing in the latter part of the nineteenth century and Morris-Jones's contemporaries responded positively to his appeal. Morris-Jones believed that it was his task to describe and defend the cultivated language of the Welsh literary tradition, to re-create the standard literary language. Academic scholars like Morris-Jones himself, Owen M. Edwards (1858–1920), T. Gwynn Jones (1871–1949), T. H. Parry Williams (1887–1975), R. Williams Parry (1884–1956), W. J. Gruffydd (1881–1954), Saunders Lewis (1893–1985) delivered the desiderata and set in motion the literary revival of the present century. Despite the linguistic authority of the Welsh Bible, twentieth-century literary Welsh has no inclination to fossilize and differs in many ways from its predecessor not least by the almost total absence in modern literary Welsh of the abnormal sentence structure. It is a construction entirely abandoned in the 1988 translation of the Bible where the former abnormal sentence is realized by the normal construction:

> *Atebodd Job* (1988)
> (Job, 12:1)

> *Daethant ato* (1988)
> (Matt., 8:25)

> *Dyna pam y digiais wrth y genhedlaeth honno* (1988)
> (Heb., 3:10).

Archaic or obsolete vocabulary and many regional forms have been replaced by current or standard usage in the new translation; for example *esgeiriau* 'legs' (1955) in John 13:9 is replaced by *coesau* (1988); *hoenyn* 'snare, cord' (1955) in Job 18:10 is replaced by *cortyn* (1988); *goglud* 'trust' (1955) is replaced by *ymddiried* (1988) in Prov. 11:28. Similarly *gorsingau* 'posts, thresholds' (1955) in Amos 9:1 is rendered *rhiniogau* (1988).

In the earlier translation the preposition *gan* precedes a verb-noun to translate a Hebraism which intensifies the action of the main verb. The Hebrew idiom is rejected in the new translation:

Gan farw y byddi farw (1955)
Byddi'n sicr o farw (1988)
'You will surely die'
(Gen., 2:17)

Yn ddiau gan fendithio y'th fendithiaf,
a chan amlhau y'th amlhaf (1955)
Yn wir, bendithiaf di, ac yn ddiau, amlhaf di (1988)
'I vow that I will bless you abundantly and multiply your descendants'
(Heb., 6:14)

In contemporary Welsh the vowel change $a > e$ in the second-person plural present indicative and the second-person plural imperative is often ignored in speech and in informal texts. The short *i* which once occurred before the personal ending and triggered the affection had disappeared by the medieval period. In the standard literary register, however, the change is normally realized, but is ignored in the new translation of the Bible:

Cenwch i'r Arglwydd ganiad newydd (1955)
Canwch i'r Arglwydd gân newydd (1988)
'Sing to the Lord a new song'
(Ps., 98:1)

Cerwch y brawdoliaeth (1955)
Carwch y frawdoliaeth (1988)
'Love the brotherhood'
(1 Pet., 2:17)

Other conservative characteristics, however, have been retained: the pronouns *chwi, hwy, myfi,* the final *-nt* in the third-person plural suffixes of verbs and prepositions as in *maent, arnynt*; the bound morphemes *-au,-ai, -oedd, -af* as in *pethau* 'things', *gwelai* 'would see', *cannoedd* 'hundreds', *gwelaf* 'see', all of which have for centuries, except in the most formal of texts, been realized as *chi, nhw, yfi, -n,* as in *maen, arnyn,* and *-a* or *-e, -odd, -ad* as in *pethe/petha, gwele/gwela, cannodd, gwela*. In the prose tradition transmitted by the early translation of the Welsh Bible standard literary usage triumphed and they are the only forms that occur in the new translation, for example:

Y maent hwy'n hoffi gweddïo ar eu sefyll
'They love to say their prayers standing up'
(Matt., 6:5)

Yr oedd arnynt ofn y dyrfa
'They were afraid of the crowd'
(Mark, 12:12)

Yn y pethau hyn i gyd yr ydym yn ennill buddugoliaeth
'In all of these things we are victorious'
(Rom., 8:37)

Y miloedd a'r cannoedd, a oedd wedi dychwelyd
'The thousands and the hundreds that had returned'
(Num., 31:14)

Similarly the informal and dialectal affix *-iff/-ith* in the third-person singular present-future tense of the simple verb does not occur in the new translation. Like its predecessor and standard literary Welsh, the 1988 version selects either zero affix: *etyb, gall, ffy, syrth, cyfyd*, or *-a: llwydda, parha*.

The General Introduction to the New Welsh Bible states:

Nid diogelu urddas yr Ysgrythyrau ar gyfer darllen cyhoeddus yw'r unig amcan wrth gyfieithu fel y gwnaed yma, ond hefyd (ac yn bennaf efallai) cadw cyswllt rhwng y Beibl a'n llenyddiaeth gyfoes.

('Safeguarding the dignity of the scriptures for the purpose of public reading was not the sole aim in translating in this fashion but also (and chiefly perhaps) to preserve a link between the Bible and our contemporary [Welsh] literature.')

This statement partially explains why the standard literary and the less formal occur side by side in the new translation. I will merely note a few examples.

The highly literary *yr wyf fi* 'I am' occurs with the less formal *'rwy(f)*:

Trwy fys Duw yr wyf fi'n bwrw allan gythreuliaid
'It is by the finger of God that I drive out devils'
(Luke, 11:19)

'Rwyn dweud wrthych
'I tell you'
(Matt., 11:11)

'Rwyf wedi prynu pum pâr o ychen
'I have bought five pairs of oxen'
(Luke, 14:19)

The standard *nad yw* and the less formal *sy(dd) ddim* introduce negative relative clauses:

Gwyliwch y rhai sy ddim ond yn gwaedu'r cnawd
'Beware of those who only bleed the flesh'
(Phil., 3:2)

Pam y gwariwch arian ar yr hyn nad yw'n fara?
'Why do you spend money on that which is not bread?'
(Isa., 55:2)

The standard *na(c)* and the less formal *paid â* are used to negate imperatives:

> *Na chuddia fy ngwaed*
> 'Cover not my blood'
> 			(Job, 16:18)

> *Nac anghofia'r anghenus*
> 'Forget not the needy'
> 			(Ps., 10:12)

> *Paid â gwneud dim niwed i ti dy hun*
> 'Do yourself no harm'
> 				(Acts, 16:27)

The standard *oni(d)* and the less formal *os na(d)* introduce conditional clauses:

> *Oni fyddwch yn sefydlog ni'ch sefydlogir*
> 'Unless you will be established you will not be established'
> 				(Isa., 7:9)

> *Os nad yw dyn yn medru rheoli ei dŷ ei hun, sut y mae'n mynd i ofalu am*
> 	*eglwys Dduw*
> 'Unless a man is able to control his own family, how is he going to
> 	look after God's church'.
> 				(1 Tim., 3:5)

The standard *yn unig* and the less formal *dim ond* are selected in the new translation:

> *Ef yn unig a wasanaethi*
> 'You shall serve him alone'
> 			(Luke, 4:8)

> *Dim ond imi gyffwrdd â'i fantell, fe gaf fy iacháu*
> 'If I can only touch his cloak, I shall be cured'
> 				(Matt., 9:21)

The subjunctive mood in the earlier translation is frequently replaced by the indicative in the new:

> *Ni frysia yr hwn a gredo* (1955)
> *Ni frysia'r sawl sy'n credu* (1988)
> 'He who believes shall not make haste'
> 			(Isa., 28:16)

> *Y mae'r gwynt yn chwythu lle y mynno* (1955)
> *Y mae'r gwynt yn chwythu lle y myn* (1988)
> 'The wind blows where it wills'
> 			(John, 3:8)

In contemporary Welsh the subjunctive is restricted to a few constructions, fossilized expressions and idioms. Its functions have been
assumed by the indicative and the imperative.

The functions of the present-future tense of the simple verb are more
extensive in standard literary Welsh than in other registers. In standard
literary Welsh the present-future verb form may realize a universal
present and an iterative present as well as the future, whereas it realizes
future only in other registers. In the new translation the compound
verb is selected to express the present and the simple verb is used to
express the future.

In Welsh the choice of response is dependent on the clause structure
of the interrogative sentence. When the simple verb predicator is
realized by a tense other than the preterite, the response in the highly
literary register consists of a repetition, in part, of the verbal form
realizing the predicator in the interrogative sentence, that is the verbal
form of the response has the same time referent as the verbal form in the
interrogative sentence, but makes relevant adjustments as regards
person and number:

> *A ddihengi di yn ddigerydd? na ddihengi* (1955)
> 'Will you escape unpunished? no'
> > (Jer., 49:12)

In less formal registers and in varieties of spoken Welsh the inflected
form of *gwneud* 'to do' is selected regardless of the item realizing the
verb in the interrogative. The latter practice is followed in the new
translation:

> *A ddihengi di yn ddigerydd? Na wnei* (1988)

In less formal texts the preposition *â* is frequently omitted following
peidio 'cease', *methu* 'fail', *arfer* 'be accustomed', *priodi* 'marry'; in the
new translation *â* is omitted following *methu* and *priodi*:

> *Methodd Joseff ymatal yn̄g ngŵydd ei weision*
> 'Joseph could not refrain himself before his servants'
> > (Gen., 45:1)

> *Fe all ddigwydd iddo osod y sylfaen ac wedyn fethu gorffen*
> 'He may lay the foundations and then fail to complete'
> > (Luke, 14:29)

> *Y mae'r sawl sy'n priodi gwraig a ysgarwyd yn godinebu*
> 'The one who marries a divorced woman commits adultery'
> > (Matt., 5:32)

Contracted morphological forms such as *pam?* 'why?', *ple?* 'where?',
prun? 'which one?', *mynd* 'go', *dweud* 'tell', *gwneud* 'do', *rhoi* 'give', *dŵr*

'water', *gweld* 'see', have been selected throughout the new translation rather than the old standard forms, *paham, pa le, pa un, myned, dywedyd, gwneuthur, rhoddi, dwfr, gweled.* For example:

> *Pa un o'r ddau a wnaeth ewyllys y tad?* (1955)
> *Prun o'r ddau a gyflawnodd ewyllys y tad?* (1988)
> 'Which of the two did as the father wished?'
>
> > (Matt., 21:31)

> *I ba le yr aeth dy anwylyd?* (1955)
> *Ple'r aeth dy gariad?* (1988)
> 'Where has your beloved gone?'
>
> > (S. of S., 6:1)

Paham y gwnei i mi weled anwiredd ac y peri i mi edrych ar flinder? (1955)
Pam y peri imi edrych ar ddrygioni, a gwneud imi weld blinder? (1988)
'Why do you show me iniquity and cause me to see grievance?'

> > (Hab., 1:3)

These varying forms and the examples of contracted usage are not context sensitive in the new translation; standard literary Welsh will frequently make the highly literary selection, the conservative selection, but there is abundant evidence of all of the less formal forms noted, in the contemporary 'literary language' – a variety of Welsh which, especially since the thirties, has been widely used as a written medium for a whole series of functions including creative literature, official, liturgical and educational purposes.

The new translation has recognized the discernible difference that has evolved between the grammar of the standard literary language on the one hand and that of the contemporary literary language and spoken Welsh on the other. Certain morphological and syntactical features linked exclusively with standard literary usage have been retained, whilst other morphological and syntactical features that are extensively used in the contemporary literary language and in the spoken language have been adopted, often side by side with the features of the standard literary language. This had led inevitably to a definite 'destandardization', that is the adoption of forms current in less formal texts and in varieties of spoken Welsh in the new translation.

Soon after its inception, Morris-Jones's re-created literary Welsh was felt to be removed from the language of non-academic writing. Edward Anwyl (1866–1914), a colleague of Morris-Jones, noted in 1906:

> Gallwn ddysgu llawer ynghylch teithi ac anianawd yr iaith oddiwrth ein hen awduron godidog; ond ni thalai ini wneuthur eu rheolau ieithyddol hwy, yn eu cyfanrwydd, yn rheolau i ni.[7]

('We can learn a lot about the characteristics and nature of the language from our splendid authors of the past; but it would be unwise of us to adopt their linguistic standards, unreservedly, as our standards.')

A similar chord is struck by Hugh Evans (1854–1934), an author and publisher, in the foreword to the second edition (1933) of *Cwm Eithin*, a popular description of Welsh rural life and customs that first appeared in 1931. He writes:

Un peth arall a'm cymhellai i gyhoeddi'r llyfr oedd fy nghred mai trychineb i'r iaith Gymraeg fyddai i lenorion gwerin ddarfod o'r tir; fe gadwant ddolen gysylltiol rhwng ein dysgedigion a'r darllenwr cyffredin. Credaf i'n dysgedigion ddechrau'r ganrif hon, wrth wneuthur y gwaith ardderchog o buro'r iaith, fod yn rhy lawdrwm ar y gwerinwyr ac eraill na allent ysgrifennu Cymraeg cywir, er y gallent ysgrifennu Cymraeg dealladwy a diddorol ... Rhaid i'r gwerinwr gael llonydd i ysgrifennu Cymraeg orau y medro...[8]

Much to the author's surprise the language of *Cwm Eithin* was applauded by W. J. Gruffydd as 'y Gymraeg yn ei dillad gorau' ('Welsh in her best garb').

By the thirties the process of 'destandardization' was well under way and it was a process seen as inevitable by John Morris-Jones himself in an article on 'Cymraeg [Yr Iaith]' in *Y Gwyddoniadur Cymreig* (second edition, 1889–96, Vol. 31, 68).

The voice of the earlier translation had been based, in the main, on the language of the Welsh bardic tradition adapted and interpreted by the Renaissance grammarians. It introduced to Welsh prose 'cyfraith yr iaith iawn', the standardized and cultivated language which previously belonged only to strict metre poetry; it also laid a firm foundation for the Welsh literary register. The voice of the new translation adopts the literary register but tempers that register by introducing less formal usage current in contemporary Welsh writing and in contemporary formal spoken Welsh. The new translation also occasionally selects forms and expressions that normally occur only in the most informal of texts and informal speech: *ddim o gwbl* 'not at all' (Rom., 3:9; 3:31), *ddim ar unrhyw gyfrif* 'not on any account' (Rom., 6:15), *dim byth* 'never' (1 Cor., 6:15), *cwpl o deisennau* 'a couple of cakes' (II Sam., 13:6), *penci* 'fool' (II Sam., 3:8).

It is far too early to speculate at present whether some or all of these 'destandardized' and informal forms will eventually acquire prestige status and themselves develop as standard forms. What is abundantly clear, however, is that the two translations consciously select different voices. We can, therefore, with justification, adopt the words of the Welsh poet Gwenallt (1899–1968), quoted in the title to this paper, and, in the context of the translations of the Welsh Bible, refer quite properly to 'tafodieithoedd Datguddiad Duw' ('the dialects of Divine Revelation').

Notes

1 Morris-Jones, 1913, V.
2 Hughes (1952, 10–11): 'Do you suppose that there is no need for more fitting words, and a greater variety of phrase, to set out learning, and to converse on doctrine and science, than that which you use in your daily conversation, buying and selling, eating and drinking? If you think that, you are deceived. And you may take this by way of a warning from me: unless you safeguard and repair and perfect the language before the present generation is out, it will be too late for the work [to be done]. And unless there is learning, knowledge, wisdom, and godliness in a language, how much better is it than the chatter of wild birds, or the roaring of animals and beasts?'
3 Ibid., 3.
4 Ibid., 63: 'There is not (to my knowledge) a language in Europe and its outlying regions which has not, from time to time, been protected and nurtured by its own grammarians and countrymen, other than our own Welsh language: which now, tardily and incompletely, has begun to receive succour from learned gentlemen in our own time, particularly as regards putting into Welsh the whole of holy scripture.'
5 Ibid., 120: 'But understand that it is by being attracted to Welsh cywyddau that I obtained the scant knowledge that I have, and I hope that I have used the well-worn words used by the old Masters before me, and that I have not erred from Doctor Davis's teaching in the translation of the Bible, the only eminent Plato in our language.'
6 Ibid., 129.
7 Anwyl, 1906, 24.
8 'I was impelled to publish this book by one other consideration. To my mind it would be a disaster if the folk writers were to disappear; they constitute a vital link between our scholars and the ordinary reader. I believe that our scholars at the beginning of this century, while fulfilling excellent work in purifying the language, were too severe on all who could not write Welsh correctly (i.e. according to the canon of the re-created literary language), although they could write easily understood and interesting Welsh ... The man in the street must be left alone to write Welsh as best he can. . .'

References

Anwyl, E. 1906. 'Safonau yr iaith Gymraeg', *Y Geninen* 24, 44–9.
Bowen, D. J. 1981. 'Y Cywyddwyr a'r Dirywiad', *Bulletin of the Board of Celtic Studies* 29, 453–96.
Evans, D. S. 1964. *A Grammar of Middle Welsh*, Dublin: Institute of Advanced Studies.
Evans, O. E. 1976. *Cyfieithu'r Testament Newydd i Gymraeg yn yr Ugeinfed Ganrif*, Darlith Goffa Henry Lewis, Coleg y Brifysgol, Abertawe.
——1988. 'Y Beibl Cymraeg Newydd', *Taliesin*, 64, 8–19.

Gruffydd, R. G. 1988a. *William Morgan: Dyneiddiwr*, Darlith Goffa Henry Lewis, Coleg y Brifysgol Abertawe.

——1988b. *Y Gair ar Waith*, Caerdydd: Gwasg Prifysgol Cymru.

——1988c. *Y Beibl a Droes i'w Bobl Draw*, Y Gorfforaeth Ddarlledu Brydeinig Llundain.

Gruffydd, W. J. 1931. 'Cwm Eithin gan Huw Evans', *Y Llenor*, 10, 25–55.

Hughes, G. H. 1952. *Rhagymadroddion 1547–1659*, Caerdydd: Gwasg Prifysgol Cymru.

Jones, G. H. 1988. *Newydd a Hen yng Nghymraeg y Beibl*, Darlith Goffa Flynyddol Syr John Morris-Jones.

Jones, J. G. 1988. 'Cefndir William Morgan a'i gyfraniad i Brotestaniaeth yng Nghymru', *Trafodion Cymdeithas Hanes Sir Gaernarfon* 49, 27–86.

Morgan, D. Ll. 1988. 'The Welsh Biblical heritage', *Trafodion Cymdeithas Hanes Sir Gaernarfon* 49, 7–25.

Morgan, P. 1988. *Beibl i Gymru*, Pwllgor Dathlu Pedwarcanmlwyddiant Cyfieithu'r Beibl, Aberystwyth: Gwasg Cambria.

Morris-Jones, J. 1913. *A Welsh Grammar Historical and Comparative*, Oxford: Oxford University Press.

Thomas, C. H. 1975. 'Y Beibl Cymraeg: Y Testament Newydd', *Diwinyddiaeth* 26, 34–41.

Williams, G. 1988. 'Yr Esgob William Morgan a'i Feibl', *Diwinyddiaeth* 39, 1–17.

Williams, G. 1991. *The Welsh and their Religion*, Cardiff: University of Wales Press.

Williams, T. H. 1902. 'Vox Populi – a plea for the vulgar tongue', *Transactions of the Guild of Graduates of the University of Wales*, 21–33.

18

The survival of Arabic in Malta:

the Sicilian centuries

JOSEPH CREMONA

Lil Glanville, b'rahan ta' qima.

It is only quite recently that the survival of Arabic in Malta has attracted the attention of scholars and shown itself to be something requiring an explanation. Interest in Maltese has generally tended to focus on other topics and when considering the relations between Maltese and two of the most important languages with which Maltese has come into contact, Sicilian and Italian, scholars have generally concentrated their attention on examining the Romance element and on measuring or explaining the depth of its penetration. A recent illustration of this approach is Brincat's 1991 study on 'Language and Demography in Malta'. What needs to be examined more fully is in fact the reverse of the medal, the vitality shown by the local language in its contacts with the languages of Malta's rulers. When we consider the very considerable social and demographic changes undergone by the islands in medieval times and subsequently, it is surprising to find that the islands still speak a language so very different from the highly prestigious ones that have dominated the political, social and cultural middle and upper class life of the Maltese islands over the last eight or nine centuries. It is indeed a remarkable case of linguistic conservatism.

Two scholars in particular have written on this topic during the last few years and they are both Sicilianists. The first, Alberto Varvaro, a philologist, drew attention to the phenomenon in his linguistic history of Sicily, when comparing the fate of Arabic in Sicily and Pantelleria with its fate in Malta (Varvaro 1981, 170). Varvaro later expanded his analysis in a study contrasting the linguistic history of Sicily with that of Malta and Gozo and offering explanations for their divergence

(Varvaro 1988). The second was the historian Henri Bresc who, in a monumental work on the Sicily of the fourteenth and fifteenth centuries, devoted several pages to what he called 'la résistance maltaise à la latinisation' ('the Maltese resistance to latinization' Bresc 1986, II, 624–8). Both scholars are medievalists: it is only during the medieval centuries that Arabic was spoken in Sicily and that a parallel could therefore be drawn with Malta's linguistic history. The pressures that had worked against the survival of Maltese Arabic during the middle Ages went on being exerted during the modern period, however, so that the resistance shown by the local vernacular to these pressures needs to be explained for the successive centuries too. In this short paper I have space only to examine the conditions that have led to the survival of Arabic in its Maltese form during the late medieval centuries and make some reference to the disappearance of Arabic in Sicily to the north and Pantelleria to the west.

The history of Malta both in antiquity and in medieval times has frequently echoed the history of its larger and close neighbour, Sicily (Varvaro 1981, 169; Varvaro 1988, 1; Bresc 1986, II, 622). Half-way through the thirteenth century, however, the history of the Maltese islands begins to diverge from that of Sicily and it does so most markedly at the linguistic level. The pressure for linguistic change away from Arabic appears to have been less in Malta than in the major island. This is seen by Varvaro to be a consequence of the marginal position of the Maltese islands in medieval times compared with that of Sicily (Varvaro 1988, 4; a more qualified position is taken by Bresc 1991, 48). Those who have studied the period have to agree with Anthony Luttrell when he writes in this context that 'confusions of race, religion, residence and language seem inescapable' (Luttrell 1991, 38), although the complexity of the social structure in Malta cannot have matched that pictured by Varvaro for Sicily during the same period (Varvaro 1979, especially 153–6). In Sicily, Arabic peters out after the expulsion of the Muslims (Varvaro 1979, 157).[1] In Malta, the language not only went on being used by the native inhabitants, but it was sooner or later taken up by the several waves of settlers from the larger island and elsewhere, if not at the first, at the second or third generation, whether they were nobles, knights, notaries or artisans.

We know very little about the inhabitants of Malta and Gozo between the date of the Norman conquest (AD 1091) and the expulsion of the Muslims in 1249. During this period, Maltese and Gozitans tend to be referred to as 'Saracens' by visiting travellers.[2] After 1249, the information becomes less scanty and easier to interpret. From a census taken in 1241, it is possible to work out a population of about 10,000 for the two islands, over half of which were Christian and the rest either Muslims or Jews.[3] The figure for Christians must have included immigrants from Sicily and elsewhere (some of whom may have been Arabic-speaking), and also recent converts to Christianity. These converts shed their religion but not their language and, together with the descendants of earlier converts, must have been numerous enough to have kept the balance of languages numerically in favour of Arabic.

The immigration movement, started under the Norman and Hohenstaufen administrations, was continued under the Angevins and, after the Sicilian Vespers of 1282, under the Aragonese (Luttrell 1975, 40–1). In the 1270s, 'for the first time a European, Latin, Christian style of government and society is clearly visible on Malta and Gozo' (Luttrell 1975, 41). In addition to administrators and troops, Bresc records the arrival of merchants and usurers from Tuscany, Pisa and Amalfi (as in contemporary Sicily), and of 'specialists': notaries (for example one Tuscan and two Sicilian notaries are mentioned in a will of 1299) and what Bresc calls 'siciliani colti' ('educated Sicilians'), often referred to as 'notaries' (Bresc 1974, 314). Bresc argues for the presence of a 'civic nobility' of knights and notaries, of mixed Maltese and immigrant origin, from the first quarter of the fourteenth century (Bresc 1974, 314; 1991, 52). Although the ruling classes in the fifteenth century appear to have been mainly of foreign origin,[4] there are indications that Maltese indigenous families were coming to the fore in Maltese urban society and beginning to play some part in the administrative, religious and intellectual life of the islands (such as it was) (Bresc 1986, II, 627; Luttrell 1991, 38). During the fifteenth century, the 'official' written language in use on the islands was Latin, frequently interspersed with phrases in Sicilian (Wettinger 1993, 151). Population figures appear to oscillate between 10,000 and 20,000 until we reach the end of the fifteenth century, but the early fifteenth century saw a marked fall, largely the result of disastrous North-African raids (Blouet 1957, 46–7).

The peasantry remained solidly Maltese. The poverty of the islands did not attract farmers or labourers, only soldiers and administrators (Bresc 1986, II, 625). The immigrants appear to have resided mainly in the fortified urban areas of the two islands (the capital Mdina and its suburb Rabat, the Castellammare on the shores of the main harbour and its suburb Birgu and the Citadel of Gozo). Bresc gives the attachment of the Maltese to the land and their resistance to urbanization as one of the reasons for the survival of Arabic.[5] We would expect, therefore, that, at this stage, the countryside spoke Arabic while the urban districts spoke also Sicilian (in the case of the Jewish population in Mdina and Gozo, Judaeo-Arabic). Luttrell has suggested that certain classes of native Maltese that were resistant to latinization 'perhaps even used [Maltese] as a secret speech which excluded foreigners' (Luttrell 1991, 39).

The position of Pantelleria, superficially similar to that of Malta, was in fact different in a number of important respects.[6] It is a smaller island (about the size of Gozo) and is situated much closer to the coast of Africa. Captured early by the Arabs (circa AD 750), it was not firmly held by Sicily until 1221, after the Norman period. The small population appears to have remained largely Arab-speaking and Muslim throughout the period that concerns us, for the Muslims were not expelled from the island until the end of the fifteenth century. The inhabitants retained a measure of independence in the management of their own affairs and were in close contact with their North-African brethren. It is significant that the rulers of Sicily shared equally with the rulers of Tunis the tribute paid by the islanders. The dichotomy between a mainly immigrant town population and a native rural population that we found in Malta and Gozo also occurred in Pantelleria, although it appears that foreign immigrants were quick to absorb Arab culture (Bresc 1986, II, 623). There is thus no indication that the position of Arabic on Pantelleria had weakened in any significant way until we come to the expulsion of the Muslims around 1480.[7]

To return to Malta, it is perhaps time to stop talking of Arabic and begin to speak of Maltese when referring to the local vernacular as we enter the fifteenth century. A change appears to take place in contemporary local consciousness about the language spoken on the islands. A will of 1426 speaks of *lingua arabica* (Bresc 1986, II, 625, n. 189), but ten years later a will of 1436 contains the expression *in lingua maltensi* (Wettinger and Fsadni 1983, 31). A search through fifteenth-century Maltese notarial documents (a collection of which is soon to be published by Godfrey Wettinger) will doubtless reveal a considerable chronological overlap between the use of the two terms to represent the same reality (see now Wettinger 1993, 159–60). Nevertheless, the use of *maltensis* in referring to the language is highly significant.[8] Similarly, it is during the fifteenth century that a distinct Maltese nation is coming to be recognized in Sicily, as suggested by Bresc (1986, II, 627), who adds: '...à Trapani, vers 1440, l'expression *maltensis natione* est de règle: elle précise l'originalité linguistique et sous-entend une coutume particulière ... un complexe culturel et juridique, des solidarités que la "naturalité" sicilienne n'assume pas complètement' ('At Trapani, towards 1440, the expression *maltensis natione* is regularly used: it makes explicit the linguistic originality [of the islands] and implies a special body of customary law ... a cultural and juridical complex, and close solidarities which the Sicilian "naturality" does not wholly cover.')

During this period, the role played by the Church in the survival of Arabic is not known but is likely to have been considerable. For most of the fourteenth and fifteenth centuries, only part of the higher clergy was of Maltese origin. The higher dignitaries appear to have been mainly Sicilian and all the bishops either Sicilian or Catalan.[9] The religious orders came to Malta relatively late, towards the end of the fourteenth century (Luttrell 1975, 63). Nevertheless, Bresc considers that the Church was beginning to offer the possibility for social and political advancement to the local bourgeoisie: 'Le chapitre offre enfin une possibilité d'ascension sociale aux fils des familles de la bourgeoisie de Mdina' ('the [cathedral] chapter finally provides the opportunity for social climbing to the sons of the Mdina middle class': Bresc 1986, II, 627). Moreover Bresc does not rule out the possibility of a connection between the resistance to latinization and an attempt on the part of the Maltese upper-class families to recapture, through the Church and its prestigious offices, the social and political positions occupied by the Sicilians (ibid.).

On a less worldly plane, it may not be excessively anachronistic to suggest that the role known to have been played by the Church in later centuries in fostering the use of local vernaculars in daily religious exercises and communication may have possibly already started taking place in the fifteenth century.[10] What is certain is that by the beginning of the sixteenth century the use of the vernacular for religious purposes was being pressed from on high in the secular hierarchy, seemingly because of complaints against the appointment of clergy that could not speak Maltese.[11] Wettinger and Fsadni quote a letter, dated 10 May 1514, from King Ferdinand II of Spain to his ambassador in Rome requesting him to ask the Pope to appoint in future only Maltese clerics to benefices in Malta, giving as one of the reasons the need for priests to know the language so as to be able to hear confessions (Wettinger and Fsadni 1983, 29).

An unexpected witness to the vitality of Maltese in the fifteenth century is the existence of a text, a recently discovered poem of some twenty lines (some of which repeat earlier material), known as the *Cantilena* and composed between 1450 and 1485 by a fifteenth-century judge, Petro de Caxaro. The version we possess was written down around 1533 by one of the author's relations, the notary Brandano de Caxario.[12] The language is highly metaphorical and the contents of a philosophical, moralizing nature, but we shall have to limit our attention to points of linguistic interest. The language is accessible, albeit with some difficulty, to one equipped with a sound knowledge of modern Maltese. It is written in a Roman script with ambiguous renderings of the consonants so typical of Arabic dialects.[13] The fact that the graphy shows no signs of standardization makes it unlikely that the *Cantilena* represents more than a one-off attempt at recording a Maltese composition in writing, although the possibility of it having been written down from memory and not copied weakens the soundness of this conclusion.[14]

The literary interests of Petro de Caxaro are highly suggestive. A native of Mdina, he is described as 'poet, orator and philosopher' by Brandano, his relative, and is known to have played a part in the political life of the Malta of his time. Luttrell sees behind his poem 'a minor world of provincial culture' (Luttrell 1975, 66), but to add with Bresc (1986, II, 627) 'c'est le notariat qui manifeste son attachement à la culture arabe littéraire' ('it is the body of notaries manifesting its attachment to Arab literary culture') may be going too far.

The language of the poem is, as might be expected, an archaic form of Maltese, showing many of the features typical of the north-west-African Arabic colloquials. It gives several indications of the state reached by the language in its passage to modern Maltese.[15] It is remarkably free of Romance traits, especially in its vocabulary, but this may be due more to the nature of the contents than to an attempt on the part of the author to keep to words with a Semitic structure and origin, predating the *Malti safi* ('pure Maltese') movement by some four centuries.

That fifteenth-century Maltese was full of words of Romance origin, however, is demonstrated by the presence of Romance words (most of which survive today) in a number of Judaeo-Arabic texts in Hebrew characters found some twenty-five years ago in the Malta Cathedral Archives and Museum by that redoubtable pair, Wettinger and Fsadni, and studied in part by G. Wettinger in a monographic study *The Jews of Malta in the Late Middle Ages* (Wettinger 1985). The published texts consist of orders or acknowledgements of payments and records of financial or property transactions. As in the case of Judaeo-Arabic texts found in neighbouring parts of the medieval world (for example Sicily and Tunisia), the language is strongly influenced lexically by the local vernaculars. In the case of the Maltese texts, Wettinger writes that they 'could almost just as correctly be called Judaeo-Maltese as Judaeo-Arabic' (Wettinger 1985, 3, 155), warning us, however, that it would be 'misleading to consider [them] as a pure recording of Medieval Maltese' (Wettinger 1985, 156).[16] Two of the contrasts between the language of these texts and the language of the *Cantilena* are of interest to us here. First, the Judaeo-Arabic texts contain many everyday words of Romance origin (but belonging to semantic areas different from those of the *Cantilena*); examples include *xurin* 'florin', *qawza* 'court case', *qumandamint* 'order', *aquzani* 'he accused me'.[17] Their presence in these texts shows that words of this type must have been widespread in everyday spoken Maltese. Secondly, the grammatical words of literary origin present in Judaeo-Arabic texts but absent from the spoken language are also absent from the *Cantilena*. The latter difference seems to disprove Bresc's statement that some of the Christian notaries were still attached to Arabic literary culture (see above, p. 286).[18]

The word 'survival' can be ambiguous when it refers to language. It may refer to the survival of enough of its elements and rules for it to maintain its identity, or it may refer to the number of speakers, or, better, to the social viability of the group formed by its speakers. The new contacts of Maltese Arabic with Romance, the virtual loss of contact with other Arabic-speaking peoples and, especially, the total lack of contact with literary (Classical) Arabic meant that, from about 1250 onwards, Maltese was bound to develop away from the other Arabic colloquials. Nevertheless, at the close of the fifteenth century, the differences are likely to have been almost wholly lexical in character. Caxaro's *Cantilena* shows that Maltese possessed at the time essentially the same linguistic structures (phonological and grammatical) as those featured today by the Arabic colloquials spoken across the Mediterranean. It is still too early to speak of the interpenetration of two linguistic systems. When Varvaro wrote, with reference to Maltese:

> The close contact between two different linguistic systems, the Arabic and the Sicilian, and the disparity of prestige between the two, at that time wholly to the advantage of Sicilian (that also enjoyed the advantage of being the official language of administration in the Kingdom of Sicily), brought about a marked permeability of the socially weaker system, that of Arabic, to the advantage of the stronger, that of Sicilian (Varvaro 1988, 4; my translation, slightly adapted)

he ran the danger of overstating the case. What evidence we possess down to 1530 appears to restrict the effect of Varvaro's 'permeability' to a process of absorption of Sicilian words (and phrases) into Maltese. Varvaro is closer to the mark when he contrasts the fate of Arabic in Sicily with its fate in Malta in his 1981 study *Lingua e Storia in Sicilia*. The gist of his argument is worth repeating. The author asks himself whether the cause of the disappearance of Arabic in Sicily may not have been due to the collapse of the Arabic linguistic system because of the rapidly growing infiltration of Romance elements. Infiltration is dismissed as a likely cause, however, because of the testimony of modern Maltese, and also of English and Rumanian. In these languages, the large number of loanwords (and, in the case of modern Maltese, encroachments into the morphology) did cause a crisis but it was a crisis that was overcome, whereas in Sicily and Pantelleria, Arabic did not just become 'sclerotic'[19] but was wholly abandoned. There is a great difference, Varvaro adds, between infiltration and sclerosis on the one hand and collapse on the other. In a stable social context, articulated into well-differentiated classes and with little mobility, whether social or spatial, infiltration and sclerosis need not compromise the vitality of a language. In Sicily, those who spoke Arabic but belonged to the Jewish religion kept their Arabic to the end, whereas those who were Moslem or Christian abandoned it. The conclusion arrived at by our author is that the difference can only derive from differences in the socio-cultural (and perhaps economic) identity of the groups (Varvaro 1981, 170).

The borrowing of lexical items, even in substantial numbers, need not constitute change of structure unless accompanied by changes of a phonological or grammatical nature.[20] This appears to be so even with a Semitic language, where derivation by means of root and vowel patterns is an integral part of the linguistic structure. What evidence we have tends to show that Maltese medieval borrowings from Sicilian became morphologically well adapted to the structure of Maltese.[21] These adaptations have survived for the most part till the present day and seem to have limited substantially the consequences of the permeability referred to by Varvaro. To this limited extent, then, Maltese was being latinized during the medieval centuries, but it was also imprinting its mark on what it was absorbing. In other words, the linguistic system of Maltese appears to have been only very marginally affected.

It is to be expected too that some measure of dialectalization had started to take place by the end of the fifteenth century among speakers of Maltese, differentiating those who lived in close contact with the 'Sicilians' in the urban areas from those, probably more numerous, who lived in the country and had little or no contact with non-Maltese speakers. The permeability of the urban Maltese must have been clearly more marked than that of their rural brethren. This differentiation, still very much alive today, was to play an increasingly important role in later centuries in the debates concerning the choice of a linguistic model to be used for literary purposes.

Not only did Maltese stand its ground relatively well linguistically, but it also seems to have done so sociolinguistically, since by this time it probably had started its slow spread upwards and established a number of bridgeheads among the 'Sicilian' strata of Maltese society. This was a task which it was to complete in later centuries. In the early 1500s, there was still some way to go before it could be said that the language was spoken and understood at the top. In a letter dated 3 September 1522, for instance, the Viceroy of Sicily instructs the Syndics visiting Malta to choose an interpreter from among the best men of Mdina so that they would be able to understand fully the complaints against public officials (Wettinger and Fsadni 1983, 28; see also Wettinger 1993, 155). Similarly, on 2 December 1522, one of the Syndics, John Aloysius Carbuni, accepted the notary James Bondin as an interpreter to help those who could not speak Sicilian (Wettinger and Fsadni 1983, 28). In other words, both Sicilian and Maltese were being spoken in Malta at the beginning of the sixteenth century, but the use of both languages, bilingualism, appears to have been limited to some of the circles constituting urban society.

The fate of Maltese appears thus to have been still in the balance, sociolinguistically at least, at the time of the arrival of the Knights of St John in 1530. However, the coming of the Knights, accompanied by a comparatively numerous retinue, radically altered the situation, socially and linguistically. Among the consequences of the great upheaval was a weakening of the prestige of Sicilian *vis-à-vis* Maltese, the result of bringing other rivals into a dominant position, notably Italian, as pointed out by Varvaro (Varvaro 1988, 4). But at this point we enter a new and better documented period in the linguistic history of Malta.

Notes

[1] An exact date can be given for the disappearance of Arabic in Sicily: 1492, the year of the expulsion of the Jews, for the Jews of Sicily spoke a form of Arabic (Judaeo-Arabic). Non-Jewish speakers of Arabic seem to have disappeared from about the second half of the thirteenth century, after the expulsion of the Muslims by Frederick II (Varvaro 1981, 166–7).

I would like to thank Professor G. Wettinger and Dr M. Mifsud for several helpful suggestions made to an earlier draft of this paper. Unfortunately, it has not been possible to make full use of Professor Wettinger's 1993 article, as it was published well after this paper was composed.

[2] For example, by Master Burchard of Strasburg in 1175 (Pertusi 1977, 275). For an up-to-date statement on medieval Malta, see Luttrell 1975, complemented by Luttrell 1991, 33–9.

[3] The figures are based on a report by the Royal Governor, Giliberto Abbate, as interpreted by Luttrell (1975, 38–9), an interpretation accepted by most specialists (Wettinger 1985, 6; Bresc 1986, II, 624; Abulafia 1990, 116).

[4] 'During the fifteenth century a class of notables or oligarchs, most of whom were more or less recently established in Malta, came to dominate the island's affairs...' (Luttrell 1974, 322). Also: 'Le sicilien apparaît ... comme la langue de la classe dominante: sur 48 personnes qui composent le Conseil élargi entre décembre 1453 et août 1454, et qui appartiennent à 31 familles, trois seulement portent un patronyme de matrice arabe' ('Sicilian appears ... to be the language of the dominant class: of the 48 persons who constitute the enlarged Council

between December 1453 and August 1454 and who belong to 31 families, only three carry a surname of Arabic origin': Bresc 1986, II, 625). By the mid-fifteenth century, however, many of the non-Arabic surnames referred to by Bresc had been established in Malta for several generations (Wettinger, private communication).

5 'L'attachement à la terre et à l'habitat dispersé protégeait la population maltaise du contact, dans le creuset de Mdina, avec les éléments d'origine sicilienne ou hispanique' ('Their attachment to the land and to a scattered habitat protected the Maltese population from having contact, in the Mdina melting pot, with elements of Sicilian and Spanish origin': Bresc 1986, II, 626). A similar opinion is expressed by Varvaro when he includes 'la consistenza e la compattezza della società rurale maltese, ben maggiore che non a Pantelleria' ('the density and compactness of Maltese rural society, much greater than at Pantelleria') among his reasons for the survival of Arabic on Malta (Varvaro 1988, 4).

6 My information on Pantelleria is derived from 'Abd el Wahab 1951, Bresc 1971 and Bresc 1986, II, 622–4. A useful comparative account of Malta and Pantelleria with respect to Sicily in late medieval times is given in Bresc 1991, 47–56.

7 There is some uncertainty as to when Arabic ceased to be spoken on Pantelleria. It seems that Arabic or a form of Arabic was still spoken there during the second half of the seventeenth century: a French merchant from Cassis, escaping from captivity in Tunisia via Pantelleria in 1670, said he needed a Maltese interpreter on Pantelleria 'parce qu'on parle la même langue à Malte et à la Pantalarie' ('because the same language is spoken in Malta and in Pantelleria': Galland 157, a source cited by 'Abd el Wahab (1951, 72) and by Bresc (1986, II, 623)). Varvaro (1981, 170; 1988, 3) cites Amari (1933–9, 3iii, 895) who writes: 'ma fino al XVI secolo, ancorchè gli abitatori professassero già il Cristianesimo, "avean comune co' Saraceni l'abito e la favella", al dir del Fazzello (*Deca I*, Lib. I, Cap. I.)' ('but up to the sixteenth century, although the inhabitants already professed Christianity, "they had in common with the Saracens their style of dress and their speech" according to Fazzello (*Deca I*, Book 1, Chap. I)'). Varvaro, however, understands this to mean that the inhabitants of Pantelleria stopped speaking Arabic in the sixteenth century. The words used by Tommaso Fazello, a sixteenth-century Sicilian historian, are: 'habitatores Christiani sunt, Hispanorum regum parentes Imperio: idiomate tamen, & habitu Sarracenorum utuntur' ('the inhabitants are Christian and owe allegiance to the kings of Spain; nevertheless they use the language and style of dress of the Saracens': Fazello 1560, 10).

8 Note too *in lingua nostra maltensi* in a contract of 1496 (Wettinger and Fsadni 1983, 31) and *lingua melitea* in a text of around 1533 by Brandano de Caxario (Wettinger and Fsadni 1983, 12 and 47), for whom, see below. Note the contrast between the latinized Sicilian *maltensis* and the classical-sounding quasi-humanistic *meliteus* of the sixteenth-century lawyer.

9 Bresc 1986, II, 627; the basis for the calculation is an analysis of patronymics for the period 1330 to 1467.

10 'Peut-on avancer que les prêtres ont, après l'entreprise réussie de déracinement de l'Islam, joué un rôle protecteur des particularismes culturels?' ('May we suggest that the priests, after succeeding in uprooting Islam, played a protective role with regard to cultural particularisms?') writes Bresc (1986, II, 627). For the following centuries, we may expect that, *mutatis mutandis*, the use of the vernacular was being conserved by the Church in Malta in the same way as in Sicily the Sicilian vernacular was being conserved against the encroachments of

Tuscan. This is how Franco Lo Piparo comments on the linguistic situation in Sicily towards the end of the sixteenth century: 'Scomparso nella seconda metà del Cinquencento dai documenti ufficiali dello Stato, il Siciliano continua ad essere praticato e incoraggiato nella Chiesa fino a tutto il Settecento e, in tono minore, anche in epoca successiva. Alla lunga durata dell'idioma siciliano (dialetto? lingua?) nell'organizzazione del consenso religioso storici della lingua e della cultura non hanno finora dedicato l'attenzione che il fenomeno meriterebbe' ('Although its use had disappeared during the second half of the sixteenth century from all official state documents, Sicilian continues to be used and encouraged by the Church until the end of the eighteenth century and, though in muted fashion, even later. Historians of language and culture have not yet given the long life the Sicilian idiom (dialect? language?) has had in the organization of the religious consensus the attention that the phenomenon deserves': Lo Piparo 1987, 751). In this context, we should keep in mind that from 1154 the bishops of Malta, together with the bishops of Girgenti and Mazzara in Sicily, were suffragans of the Archbishops of Palermo (Bonnici 1967–8, I, 66).

[11] One such complaint had been made on 28 January 1481 by the Town Council of Mdina against the appointment by the bishop of Malta of a parish priest who did not know Maltese (Wettinger and Fsadni 1983, 29).

[12] The MS was discovered in the Valletta Notarial Archives in 1966 and edited by the finders, G. Wettinger and M. Fsadni (Wettinger and Fsadni 1968, 2nd edn. 1983). The near repetition of three and a half lines may be due to a faulty first draft of the middle section of the poem: see Brincat 1986, 11–14.

[13] Arabic /q/ (Modern Maltese /ʔ/), for instance, is rendered by the graph *c* four times, by the graph *k* three times and by the digraph *ck* twice. At the same time, the graph *c* also represents the Arabic and Maltese phoneme /k/ four times while the same phoneme /k/ is represented by the graph *k* three times (see Cohen and Vanhove 1984–6, 178; Wettinger and Fsadni 1983, 45).

[14] We are discounting here the writing down of Maltese place-names and nick-names in notarial records and similar documents. Efforts at discovering further examples of fifteenth- or sixteenth-century Maltese have proved fruitless: see Wettinger 1985, 154. The next text of any substance written in Maltese that we possess is a sonnet composed some 200 years later by G. F. Bonamico (*circa* 1675).

[15] The following notes on the language of the *Cantilena* may be found useful. The phonology appears conservative: some, but not all, of the phonemic distinctions made by Old Arabic, preserved in most 'core' Arabic colloquials but lost in modern Maltese, are retained, as far as it is possible to tell from the unsystematic script (see Borg 1978, 47–50; Wettinger 1985, 188 note 24 and 189 note 28; and especially Cohen and Vanhove 1984–6, 179–83). There is little to say on the morphology and syntax within our context beyond stating that it is free of Romance traits. It is also free of those grammatical words and phrases of Classical origin which did not form part of the spoken language but were common in written Arabic and found also in contemporary Judaeo-Arabic texts of Maltese origin (for example hād[i]h[ī], u[a] ḏāl[i]k[a] [']an[na], al[la]ḏi, l[i']an: see Wettinger 1985, 165). As for lexis, there is unexpectedly only one non-Semitic word, the Sicilian *vintura* ('fortune'), which, ironically, is no longer current in modern Maltese.

[16] The author adds in a note: 'The main difficulty in speaking of Judaeo-Maltese rather than of Judaeo-Arabic of Maltese origin arises from the presence of

conventional Classical Arabic elements which might lead to a serious mis-
understanding of the true character of the Maltese vernacular in the later
fifteenth century' (Wettinger 1985, 188 note 12). In a later note: 'It is unlikely
that the speech of the Maltese and Gozitan Jews differed much from that of
their Christian compatriots because they did not live in separate ghettos'
(Wettinger 1985, 188 note 16), adding, however, that 'they [the Jews] had much
closer contact with foreign cultural influences.'

17 Wettinger 1985, 164. Only some of the vowels have had to be supplied by the
    editor. The Judaeo-Arabic texts generally tend to use the *scriptio plena*, that is
    to write down the short vowels, particularly when transcribing words of
    Romance origin (Wettinger 1985, 157).

18 This does not rule out, of course, attachment to oral forms of culture repre-
    sented by folk-tales, proverbs, and so on: see Bresc 1986, II, 626. There is the
    possibility, to my knowledge not yet explored, that the *Cantilena* may have
    started life as oral literature.

19 I take this to be equivalent to 'linguistically non-productive'. In other words,
    the language no longer grows by following its own word-formation rules. New
    items in the lexicon cease to be formed through internal means but are
    borrowed from some prestigious language. That this is invariably the case in all
    dialects of modern Maltese needs to be established.

20 In this connection, we should remember that the great majority of borrowed
    items are likely to have belonged to peripheral areas of the vocabulary and not
    to the central core. This is the case in modern Maltese (see Cremona 1990, 168)
    and is thus all the more likely to have been the case in medieval Maltese,
    although there are some notable exceptions.

21 In the language of the Judaeo-Arabic texts published by Wettinger, for in-
    stance, the plural of *xurin* 'florin' is *xrunjat*, that of *qrlin* 'carlino', an old Italian
    coin, is *qrniat*. Both plurals are formed by adding the sound feminine plural
    suffix *-at*, usual for words of foreign origin in Classical Arabic (Wright 1896–8,
    II, 198; Wettinger 1985, 166–7). *qrniat* appears to have had a continuous history
    in Malta in the modern Maltese expression *tliet-karnijiet* 'tuppence-halfpenny',
    literally 'three carlini', showing the modern form of the *-at* suffix featured in the
    medieval word; in the sense of the coin, on the other hand, the plural of *karlin* is
    karlini, featuring the plural suffix *-i*, of Siculo-Italian origin. (A broken plural
    form *kranel*, given in De Soldanis's eighteenth-century manuscript lexicon and
    quoted in Aquilina's *Maltese-English Dictionary*, is unreliable.) The word for
    'florin', on the other hand, appears to have been reborrowed from Italian
    fiorino as modern Maltese *fjorin*, with only one plural form *fjorini*. Similarly, the
    modern *xelin* 'shilling' from the Italian *scellino*, has only the one plural form
    xelini. It can be seen from the foregoing that the study of modern Maltese does
    show the existence of some correlation between date of borrowing and
    thoroughness of adaptation to the morphology of Arabic. The correlation is
    unreliable as a method of dating, however, since there are many examples of
    comparatively recent loans that have been fully adapted. One of the factors
    determining the degree of adaptation to Semitic morphological patterns
    appears to be the phonological pattern into which a word falls (see Mifsud,
    forthcoming). The examples of *xurin* and *xelin* are thus particularly interesting
    because of the similarity of their phonological patterns.

References

'Abd el Wahab, H. 1951, 'Pantellaria, île arabe', *Proceedings de la Société Royale Égyptienne d'Études Historiques*, I, 57–78.

Abulafia, D. S. H. 1990. 'The end of Muslim Sicily', in Powell, J. M. (ed.), *Muslims under Latin Rule*, 1100–1300, Princeton, NJ: Princeton University Press, 103–33.

Amari, M. 1933–9. *Storia dei Musulmani di Sicilia*, 2nd edn., edited by Nallino, C., 3 parts, Catania: Prampolini.

Aquilina, J. 1987–90. *Maltese-English Dictionary*, 2 vols., Malta: Midsea Books.

Blouet, B. 1957. *The Story of Malta*, London: Faber.

Bonnici, A. 1967–8. *History of the Church in Malta*, 2 vols., Malta: Empire Press – Catholic Institute.

Borg, A. 1978. *A Historical and Comparative Phonology and Morphology of Maltese*, Jerusalem: The Author.

Bresc, H. 1971. 'Pantelleria entre l'Islam et la Chrétienté', *Cahiers de Tunisie*, XIX No. 75/76, 105–27.

—— 1974. 'Malta dopo il Vespro Siciliano', *Melita Historica*, VI No. 3, 313–21.

—— 1986. *Un monde méditerranéen: Economie et société en Sicile (1300–1450)*, 2 vols., Paris-Rome-Palermo: Bibliothèques des Écoles françaises d'Athènes et de Rome, fasc. 262.

—— 1991. 'Sicile, Malte et monde musulman', in Fiorini and Mallia-Milanes 1991, 47–79.

Brincat, G. 1986. 'Critica testuale della Cantilena di Pietro Caxaro', *Journal of Maltese Studies*, 16, 1–21.

Brincat, J. M. 1991. 'Language and demography in Malta: the social foundations of the symbiosis between Semitic and Romance in Standard Maltese', in Fiorini and Mallia-Milanes 1991, 91–110.

Cohen, D. and Vanhove, M. 1984–6. 'La cantilène maltaise du XVème siècle: remarques linguistiques', *Comptes Rendus du Groupe Linguistique d'Études Chamito-Sémitiques*, XXIX–XXX, Paris: Librairie Paul Geuthner, 177–200.

Cremona, J. 1990. 'The Romance element in Maltese', *Transactions of the Philological Society*, 88 No. 2, 163–99.

Fazello, T. 1560. *De rebus siculis decades duae*, Palermo: I. M. Mayda and F. Carrara.

Fiorini, S. and Mallia-Milanes, V. (eds.). 1991. *Malta: A Case Study in International Cross-Currents*, Malta University Publications.

Galland, A. (ed.). 1810. *Relation de l'esclavage d'un marchand de la ville de Cassis, à Tunis*, Paris: Ferra.

Lo Piparo, F. 1987. 'Sicilia linguistica', in Aymard, M. and Giarrizzo, G. (eds.), *La Sicilia*, Turin: Einaudi, 733–807.

Luttrell, A. T. 1974. 'A Maltese casale: 1436 (1),' in *Melita Historica*, VI–3, 322–4.

—— 1975. 'Approaches to medieval Malta', in Luttrell, A. T. (ed.), *Medieval*

Malta: Studies on Malta before the Knights, London: The British School at Rome, 1–70.

—— 1991. 'Medieval Malta: the non-written and the written evidence', in Fiorini and Mallia-Milanes 1991, 33–45.

Mifsud, M. forthcoming. *The Non-Semitic Element in the Morphology of the Maltese Verb*, dissertation for the Ph.D. degree at the University of Malta.

Pertusi, A. 1977. 'Le isole maltesi dall'epoca bizantina al periodo normanno e svevo (secc. VI–XIII) e descrizioni di esse dal sec. XII al sec. XVI', *Byzantinische Forschungen*, V, 253–306.

Varvaro, A. 1979. 'La situazione linguistica della Sicilia nel basso Medioevo', reprinted in Varvaro, A., *La parola nel tempo*, Bologna: Il Mulino, 1984, 145–74.

—— 1981. *Lingua e storia in Sicilia*, I, Palermo: Sellerio.

—— 1988. 'La lingua in Sicilia e a Malta nel Medioevo', *Journal of Maltese Studies*, 17–18, 1–5.

Wettinger, G. 1985. *The Jews of Malta in the Late Middle Ages*, Malta: Midsea Books.

—— 1993. 'Plurilingualism and cultural change in medieval Malta', *Mediterranean Language Review*, 6–7, 1990–3, 144–60.

Wettinger, G. and Fsadni, M. 1983. *L-Ghanja ta' Pietru Caxaru*, Malta: The Authors.

Wright, W. 1896–8. *A Grammar of the Arabic Language*, 2 vols., 3rd edn., Cambridge University Press, 1981 reprint.

19

Dialect and standard in speakers' perceptions: delayed reactions to linguistic reality in a German city

WINIFRED V. DAVIES

Until the nineteenth century the linguistic situation in Germany could be described as diglossic with standard German and dialect having their own clearly delimited domains. The former was normally used only when reading out from a text or for writing, whilst the local dialects were used in less formal situations. Over the last 150 years, several social developments have played a major role in changing the nature of the relationship between the standard and the dialects. These developments include the unification of most of the German-speaking territory in 1871, the forced migrations of the post-second-war period, the growth of transport and mass communications and the rapid urbanization of Germany. Amongst the linguistic developments that have followed in the wake of such social developments is the tendency for the formerly clearly distinct and autonomous norms of the standard language and the dialects to become less clear-cut (cf. Durrell 1992). In central and southern Germany and in Austria, especially in urban centres, the local varieties and the standard are not as clearly delimited from each other as they are in northern Germany or Switzerland and we are faced with what Keller calls 'an extremely complicated gradualism' (1978, 516). The norms that govern use have also become less clear-cut and subject to more individual interpretation (cf. Keller 1978, 517–18 and Durrell 1992). However, as will be shown in this paper, the perception of the relationship is still in terms of two autonomous polar norms *Hochdeutsch* ('High German') and *Dialekt* ('dialect').

This paper focuses on some findings of an investigation into linguistic variation in Neckarau, a suburb of the German city of Mannheim, concentrating on an analysis of attitudes expressed towards this variation. Attitudes are generally assumed to contribute towards an explanation of patterns of linguistic variation, for example: '(...)

linguistic attitudes and stereotypes can be a powerful force in influencing linguistic behaviour and, ultimately, linguistic forms themselves' (Trudgill, Labov and Fasold 1979, viii–ix). One has to bear in mind, however, that speakers are quite capable of saying one thing and doing another. As Omdal (forthcoming) says: 'It is not at all easy to make straightforward statements about the strength of the relationship between expressed attitudes and behaviour.' Nevertheless, it is clear that language attitudes are worthy of study because they form part of the communicative competence of the speech community.

Mannheim-Neckarau

Mannheim (population 301,770) is an important urban centre in the Rhine-Neckar area of Germany and is the second largest city in the Rhine Franconian dialect area. Neckarau was incorporated into Mannheim in 1899. Until then it had been one of the largest villages in Baden. Historically it is, therefore, a *gewachsener Vorort* ('a suburb that has gradually evolved') and not a *Stadtteil* ('district of the city'), a distinction that is very much alive in the consciousness of the community. It had a long agricultural tradition which was broken with the advent of industry around the middle of the last century. The inhabitants regard the break with the agricultural tradition as having been completed long ago, and the change in the economic structure of the suburb is seen as being reflected in the local linguistic variety: 'mir redde nimmer de gands alde dialegt, de baierlische' ('we no longer speak the really old dialect, the peasant variety').[1]

Today Neckarau has a population of 27,000. Industry no longer provides the main source of employment and many Neckarauer work in service industries in the suburbs or in the city centre. The population is fairly mixed: it cannot be categorized as an *Arbeiterviertel* ('working-class district') or a *Beamtenviertel* ('civil servants' district') in the same way as some other suburbs.

The linguistic situation in central Germany

I have already referred to Keller's description of the linguistic situation in central Germany as one of 'an extremely complicated gradualism' (1978, 516). The most satisfactory way of describing the situation is to see it in terms of a continuum (cf. Barbour and Stevenson 1990, chapter 5), ranging from the narrowest local forms to standard. Linguistic features can be arranged along this scale; variants which occupy roughly the same position on the scale are more likely to co-occur than are variants from opposite ends of the continuum, for example, in Neckarau a speaker who uses *kumme* (past participle of *kommen* 'to come') relatively consistently in a discourse is likely to use *gedenkt* (past participle of *denken* 'to think') more often than *gedacht* in the same discourse.[2] At each end of the continuum there will be more consistency in the use of either local forms or of standard forms, and this is reflected in the speakers' perception of the two varieties as discrete, classifying them as either *Dialegt, Blatt, Neggarauerisch, Mannemerisch*[3] or *Schriftdeutsch*.[4] In the questionnaires used for data collection the terms *Hochdeutsch* and *Dialekt* were used as labels for the two poles between which speakers apparently move. The informants had no difficulties with the two terms, qualifying them where necessary, for example, 'gemäßigter, gehobener Dialekt' ('moderate, elevated dialect'), 'das, was man hier Hochdeutsch nennt' ('what we call High German here'). As we shall see, informants are aware of intermediate levels, but as basically either dialect or standard with an admixture of the other variety: 'gemischt', 'Mischmasch', 'n paar Brogge komme jo immer noi' ('mixed', 'mixture', 'a few bits always get in'). In Le Page's terms we have two 'focused' varieties; he says: 'A language variety is described as focused when speakers perceive it in some sense as a discrete entity' (Milroy 1982, 141).

The two poles 'standard' and 'most local variety' cannot be seen as absolutes, defined in the same way for every community. Communities, and even individuals, may divide the continuum up in different ways: for some the point at which a linguistic variety is regarded as standard may come relatively low down on the scale (that is, close to the local end), whereas others may dismiss as dialect any but the topmost stratum of the continuum; as Mattheier says:

> Untersuchungen über die Fähigkeit von Mitgliedern einer örtlichen Sprachgemeinschaft, das sie umgebende sprachliche Kontinuum in verschiedene unterschiedliche Sprachlagen zu differenzieren haben gezeigt, daß nicht einmal innerhalb eines kleinen Dorfes alle Ortsbewohner die gleichen Auffassungen darüber haben, was Dialekt ist, was Halbmundart und was regionale Umgangssprache (1980, 198).[5]

One thing I hope to show in this paper is that there is substantial agreement amongst informants in Neckarau with regard to their expressed opinions on the breaks in the continuum and in their evaluations of the varieties thus distinguished.

If one were to assume that one pole of the continuum in Neckarau was the codified standard and that the other was the local variety, one would find considerable linguistic distance between the two. This assumption, however, gives a false picture of the true linguistic situation in Neckarau. For many Neckarauer the linguistic variety that they refer to as *Schriftdeutsch* is not synonymous with the standard language of the prescriptive manuals. As we shall see below, there is much less linguistic distance between the variety accepted as *Schriftdeutsch* or standard in Neckarau and the local variety than there is between the latter and the codified standard.

Given the fact that the linguistic distance between the local variety and what I shall for the time being call provincial standard is not particularly large, what is interesting amongst other things is why the local variety is being maintained and kept distinct from this standard. It is unlikely that considerations of intelligibility have anything to do with the matter since most speakers of the local variety can be assumed to have some competence in the standard, and communication, at least on the referential level, could take place in that variety. The answer must lie, rather, in what Blom and Gumperz, in their account of code-switching in Norway, call the 'social meaning' of the variety. They see social factors as playing an important role in the maintenance of linguistic separateness between the dialect and the standard, *Bokmål* (Blom and Gumperz 1972, 416–17). Social meaning attaches both to the local variety and to the variety seen as the alternative – in our case *Schriftdeutsch*. One needs to establish the social meaning of both varieties in order to discover why both can be used within the community, and why one is not redundant.

Data collection

In order to obtain data a questionnaire was formulated with questions on social background, linguistic usage, attitudes towards linguistic varieties, and on the linguistic biography of the informants, and it was used in a face-to-face interview, that is, I asked the questions and wrote down the answers rather than allowing the informants to fill in the questionnaire in their own time, and the interview was taped. Where possible the interview was carried out by two people, myself and an employee of the Institut für deutsche Sprache in Mannheim. He was already known personally to most of the informants and he knew friends or acquaintances of all of them. I, on the other hand, knew no one personally.

Twenty-eight informants were interviewed, twelve males and sixteen females. The sample lacks representativeness, but whereas statistically significant correlations between linguistic usage and attitudes and basic social structures across the community as a whole can be established by working with large numbers of speakers, valuable insights into the nature of linguistic variation and its relation to factors such as degree of integration into local networks, loyalty to the community, adherence to vernacular culture and social ambition can be gained by small-scale studies, as shown by Milroy (1980), Douglas-Cowie (1979) and Cheshire (1978, 1982) amongst others. Romaine obviously thinks that this is a respectable approach since she refers to Le Page's view of speech as 'an act of identity' as having 'validated the individual as a respectable starting point for sociolinguistic analysis' (Romaine 1982, 7).

Seventeen of the informants were natives of Neckarau (henceforth referred to as locals); three had moved to Neckarau from other suburbs of Mannheim; eight had moved to Neckarau from outside Mannheim. One informant was still at school (age group A), two were classified as younger generation, but not at school (age group B), eleven were between 30 and 50 (age group C), fourteen were over 60 (age group D). In terms of educational achievement, one of the most important constituents of status in contemporary Germany, the group was fairly homogeneous. None of the locals and only three incomers (Haw, Chw and Har) had been to university, and only four persons (Haw, Chw, Har and Güh) had passed the *Abitur* (rough equivalent of 'A'-levels). Most of the informants who were in employment were in white-collar, skilled jobs. In socio-economic terms they were fairly typical of the majority of Germans.

Various means of establishing the attitudes of the speakers towards the variation that exists were used. In the section of the interview that will be described here the informants were requested to listen to recordings of three different Neckarauer and were then asked 'Wer von den drei redet, wie man heute in Neckarau redet?' ('Which of these three speaks as people do in Neckarau today?'). It must be stressed that this technique only enables one to describe expressed attitudes and it is quite possible that there are discrepancies between the attitudes expressed in the interview situation and actual linguistic usage. In addition to evaluating and commenting on the replies given in answer to the direct question, I shall be attempting an evaluation of the many comments that informants made almost 'by the way' while listening to the recordings or afterwards, since I believe that their incidental and spontaneous nature can provide us with interesting and relevant insights.

The recordings are extracts from authentic discourse. The first speaker, a male in his late twenties, was recorded during an informal conversation in a pub; the second, a female in her thirties, was taped during an interview with a member of the project group *Kommunikation in der Stadt* (Communication in the City) based at the *Institut für deutsche Sprache* (as was the third, but as none of the informants considered that his speech was similar to his or her own I shall be disregarding him for the purposes of this discussion). Because there are different speakers involved, there is always a danger that informants will react to the voices rather than to linguistic features. One speaker could have been asked to produce more than one variety, but if the varieties are not produced spontaneously it is highly likely that they will come across as unnatural, and this could influence informants' reactions. In fact, as Barbour and Stevenson (1990, 123) point out, with reference to the matched guise technique of eliciting reactions to speech varieties: 'In practice however it is extremely difficult to design tests in such a way that evaluations really can be attributed to a single factor.'

Linguistic characteristics of the recorded samples

Speaker I is typical of the most local variety. He has examples of [u] for [o] before nasals; lenition of voiced stops even in initial position; [w] for [b] intervocalically; [p] in final position rather than the standard affricate; monophthongizations (for example *eens, aa* for standard *eins, auch*); reduction of inflectional ending [-ən] to [-ə]; [ʃ] for [ç]; unrounding of vowels; *verzählen* for standard *erzählen* 'to tell stories'; conditional with *tun*, rather than standard *werden*.

Speaker II also has some characteristic features of the local variety: [ʃ] for [ç]; [ʃt] for [st]; regular reduction of [-ən]; short vowels (for example *habbe* for standard *haben* 'have'); *kegle* for standard *kegeln* 'to play skittles', but there are no examples of qualitative vowel changes or of initial lenition.

Responses to the recorded samples

In what follows the figures are given first in absolute terms, for example, 22 speakers out of 26, and then as a percentage. Attention has already been drawn to the small size of the sample, in which case percentages could be misleading. Nevertheless, it was decided to include the percentage figure in order to express what are felt to be valid generalizations.

Speaker I was chosen by most informants: 22/26 (85 per cent). (The responses of two informants, one from age-group A and one from age-group B, were disregarded for various reasons.) Men and women showed a large measure of agreement: 9/12 (83 per cent) men and 11/14 (86 per cent) women chose this speaker. The agreement amongst local men and women (that is, excluding those from other suburbs) was even more striking: all the men (9) and all the women (8) agreed. All those who had moved to Neckarau from within Mannheim (3) agreed with the real locals. If we look at the reaction of different age groups to the recordings, we find that the only person in age group B (20 years old) chose I, as did over half (7/11 or 64 per cent) of those in age group C (30–50) and all (14) of those in age group D (60 +). Thus all age groups are represented, but it would appear that there is not the same degree of agreement amongst the younger and the older informants (that is, amongst age groups B and C on the one hand, and age group D on the other). However, if we compare the younger with the older locals the picture changes: 100 per cent of the younger locals picked speaker I as did 100 per cent of the older locals. In the younger age group it was the inclusion of informants from outside Mannheim that led to the low percentage figure. Including those informants who had moved to Neckarau from other suburbs within Mannheim made no difference at all to the figures.

If we compare the locals with the incomers we see that 100 per cent of the locals picked I, whilst only 56 per cent of incomers picked him. Again, it is the incomers from outside Mannheim that account for this large measure of disagreement: if we include the incomers from other parts of Mannheim with the locals, we find that the percentage of locals agreeing on I stays at 100 per cent, whilst the percentage of incomers who chose I shoots down to 33 per cent. The two incomers who picked speaker I are Hec and Vol; both are Germans who were expelled from Czechoslovakia after 1945, have lived in Mannheim for many years and know Mannheim and Neckarau well. Both mix with Neckarauer in informal situations.

I shall now consider those informants who disagreed with the majority verdict and chose speaker II. Four of the nine incomers picked II (44 per cent, or 67 per cent if we disregard those incomers from within Mannheim). Let us concentrate on those from outside Mannheim. They are Dijw, Har, Chw and Haw. The numbers are very small, but we can see that there is no major disagreement between men and women. All four are from the same age group (30–50); this means that all the incomers to Mannheim in this age group chose speaker II, whereas all the locals in the same age group chose speaker I.

Some reasons why these informants should have replied as they did might be suggested. First of all, we need to consider the reactions of some locals to speaker I. Many commented to the effect that this was how Neckarauer would talk in certain situations. Typical comments were: 'Bekannte unter sich, die geben sich keine Mühe', 'Wenn so im Verein so ne Klicke zusammensitzt am Stammtisch oder so dann würd ich sagen, spricht man so wie der erste', 'Das typische, wenn man untereinander ist, ist der erste' ('Friends with each other, they're making no special effort', 'When a group is sitting together in a club or a pub then they'd talk like the first, I'd say', 'The first is typical of the way we speak to each other'). It may be surmised that this is seen as a variety that is typical of informal, private situations. Of the incomers, Har (who is Japanese) didn't understand it; Chw thought that it was broader than typical Mannheimerisch ('ausgeprägter wie hier in Mannheim'); Haw made no comment.

I would suggest that if this is the variety that Neckarauer believe that they speak amongst themselves, then it is not very surprising that Har, Chw and Haw are not familiar with it. Considerations of intelligibility, if nothing else, demand that Neckarauer speak more supraregionally with Har. Chw and Haw, for all the goodwill towards the place shown in the course of their interview and their desire to be integrated, were far from being so. They had not been living in Neckarau for very long (eight months) and as yet their interactions with the locals were restricted to formal or semi-formal situations where one would not expect the most local variety to be used.

Dijw is a more difficult case to explain. One would have expected, if this variety really is typical of informal, private exchanges between Neckarauer, that she would be aware of this: after all, although she herself is not from Neckarau and does not speak the local variety, she has lived there for fifteen years, is married to someone who regards himself as an *Urneckarauer* ('genuine Neckarauer') and who speaks the local variety (as do her parents-in-law and her son), and she has plenty of opportunity to hear the local variety since she is a member of a club that meets in Neckarau. Her reaction to speaker I is: 'n urneggarauer is des nit, er schbrischt mehr wie jetz' ('That isn't a real Neckarauer. He speaks more like now') and to speaker II: 'sie bemüht sisch, so wie isch' ('She's making an effort, like me'), so it seems clear that she does not regard speaker II's speech as the latter's vernacular, and yet she claims that it is typical of the way people speak in Neckarau. She may possibly be saying that there are some, like her, for example, who try to avoid the most local variety. Her reaction to speaker I is puzzling: obviously she recognizes the variety, and yet refuses to say that it is typical. Either she is unaware of the linguistic reality of some domains of Neckarauer life, or those people who describe speaker I as typical are refusing to admit that the local variety is no longer as dominant as it used to be.

Whatever the reality behind the claims expressed about speaker I, what is clear is that most locals wish to believe that there still exists a variety that is clearly marked for locality and is used in informal situations amongst Neckarauer.

The locals regard the variety spoken by speaker II as typical of certain situations or certain people: 'sie gibt nen inderview' ('She's giving an interview'), 'so könnte in jeder Elternversammlung eine das Wort ergriffen haben' ('That's how anyone could have spoken in a parents' evening'), 'ne Zugeschlupfte' ('a newcomer'), that is, either she was local and in a formal situation, or she must be from outside Neckarau/Mannheim, since the stated belief is that it would not be normal for a local to talk like that in an informal situation: 'so redet bei uns niemand' ('No one talks like that here'), 'die würde also normaler-weise nie so schbreschen, wenn sie mit ihresgleichen zusammen gewe-sen wäre' ('She would never talk like that normally when she was with her peers'). There are many references to the fact that this kind of German is seen as unspontaneous: 'bemüht', 'sie gibt sich mühe', 'sie versucht, hochdeutsch zu reden', 'gekünstelt' ('strained', 'she's making an effort', 'she's trying to speak High German', 'artificial').

No one rejects speaker II out of hand as being completely untypical of Neckarau: the levels of German spoken by speakers I and II are real to the informants, but are clearly subject to differing evaluations and are not regarded as being situatively equivalent, that is they would not both be used in the same situations. This reflects a differentiated view of linguistic usage (and the reality of linguistic usage in Neckarau, of course): people do not speak in the same style all the time. One has to be able to switch; as one informant said: 'das keert zum flair, is er-ziehungssache, isch muß misch verschdändige könne' ('that's part of one's *savoir faire*, it's a question of education, I have to be able to make myself understood').

There were several comments to the effect that the variety used by speaker II was not 'pure' dialect or 'pure' standard. Not everyone made a comment, but the comments that were made can be put into four main groups.

Group 1

These comments describe the variety with reference to the local variety, but not in favourable terms: 'kein reiner Dialekt' ('not pure dialect'); 'nie mehr das echte' ('no longer the genuine dialect'); 'verfälscht' ('falsified'); 'abgeändert' ('changed').

Group 2

These comments, too, describe the variety with reference to the local variety, but in more favourable terms: 'gemäßigter' ('more moderate'); 'gehobener' ('more elevated'); 'n bissel besser' ('a bit better'); 'net so arger Dialekt' ('not such broad dialect').

The comments in groups 1 and 2 imply that there is a belief in a level of language that can be called dialect, but the attitudes towards it differ: group 1 regard it as an ideal form of language, whereas group 2 are less favourably disposed towards it.

Group 3

These comments describe the variety with reference to the standard, in unfavourable terms: 'sie versucht, hochdeutsch zu sprechen' ('She's trying to speak High German'); 'die hat versucht, hochdeutsch zu sprechen' ('She tried to speak High German').

Group 4

These comments describe the variety as a mixture: 'gemischt, Dialekt und Hochdeutsch' ('mixed, dialect and High German'); 'gemischt' ('mixed', twice); 'da hört man noch den Dialekt durch' ('one can still hear the dialect'); 'Hochsprache n bissel mehr debei' ('There is a bit more High German in it'); 'Hochdeutsch is debei' ('There is some High German in it'). Most of the comments fall into this group.

To sum up: the comments in these groups show that the informants categorize this speaker and her speech style in terms of either *Dialekt* or *Hochdeutsch* with most of those who made any comment regarding it as a mixture of standard and local variety. None of them, therefore, regarded this as an autonomous level of language. This shows, in my opinion, the reality of the bipolar points of evaluation referred to and suggests that, in the minds of Neckarauer at least, these two varieties exist as separate entities.

The Karch extract

In addition to the three recordings of speakers from Neckarau, the informants were also played an extract from a recording made by the *Deutsches Spracharchiv* (German Linguistic Archive) and analysed by Karch in his monograph on the Mannheim *Umgangssprache* 'colloquial speech' (Karch 1975). Karch posits three levels of *Umgangssprache*, ranging from close to the standard to close to the *Stadtmundart* 'city dialect' as described by Bräutigam in his dissertation of 1934. The extract used was in the variety classed by Karch, taking Siebs and Duden[6] as his guides, as furthest from the standard.

The extract has the following linguistic characteristics: initial and medial lenition; [ʃ] and [ç] for standard [ç]; [x] for [k] after back vowels;

[w] for [b]; [-ən] twice reduced to [-ə] in dative plural; monophthongs (for example, *uff* for standard *auf*), but there is very little reduction of [-ən] to [-ə] and no qualitative vowel changes with the exception of *uff*. We even find final devoicing of [g] in the pronunciation of *Freiburg*.

The informants were asked: 'Muß man in Neckarau so hochdeutsch reden, wenn man es mit einem Fremden zu tun hat oder in einer öffentlichen Situation, z.B. auf der Behörde?' ('Must one speak such High German in Neckarau when one is dealing with a stranger or is in a public situation, e.g. when dealing with officialdom?') Only one person disputed the labelling of this variety as *Hochdeutsch*, despite Karch's classification of it as *mundartnahe Umgangssprache* 'colloquial non-standard'. Bas (a local) objected to it on the grounds that as it contained three 'Orthographiefehler' ('spelling mistakes') 'des is immer noch dialegt. Wenn er sacht mit meine alte Kegelbrüder des is kei hochdeutsch ... unter hochdeutsch dann mein isch, daß ma vollkommenes schriftdeutsch und net irgend ne Endung, die mannemer is, dranhängt' ('That is still dialect. When he says "with my old skittle-playing friends" [without the dative -*n* that standard German requires after the preposition *mit*] that is not High German. By High German I mean that one [should speak] perfect written German without adding on any Mannheimer endings'). None of the others was quite so fussy. More than one called it 'ein schönes Hochdeutsch' ('a beautiful High German'). Not every informant made an evaluative comment on this speaker. Of those who did, most were favourable, for example, 'verständlich', 'kultiviert', 'n bissel besser', 'n gutes hochdeutsch', 'absolut hochdeutsch', 'gut ausgesprochen', 's versteht sich besser' ('comprehensible', 'cultivated', 'a bit better', 'good High German', 'well pronounced', 'more easily comprehensible'). The unfavourable comments are: Bas's comment mentioned above, 'gezwungen', 'krampfhaft' (twice), 'arg übertrieben', 'hochgestochen' ('forced', 'stiff', 'totally exaggerated', 'posh'). Whether the comments are favourable or not, they all show that the informants rate this variety higher than Karch does. The perceived distance of this variety from the local variety would seem to be greater than the actual distance, given its classification by Karch as furthest from the standard. This might help to explain why two distinct varieties are being maintained in the community when the linguistic distance between them is 'objectively' small.

All recognized the speaker as a Mannheimer (the characteristics mentioned were apocope, [ʃ] for [ç], *nix* for *nichts* 'nothing'), but this local colouring did not affect their evaluation of the variety as *Hochdeutsch* or standard. This tolerance of local colouring in phonology and intonation, which is characteristic of central and south Germany in general (cf. Schlieben-Lange 1978, 75), would seem to support

Hudson's suggestion that 'Pronunciation seems to differ from other types of [linguistic] item in its social function' (1980, 44). Regional accents are likely to persist even when speakers no longer use regionally restricted vocabulary and syntax.

Conclusion

By looking at comments made in response to three different speakers I have attempted to give some indication of the social meaning of the local variety and of the regionally coloured standard. The local variety is associated with Neckarau and with private or informal situations. It is not clear which of the two criteria, 'private' or 'informal', is more important: theoretically they need not both be present.[7] It is not clear how informants define informality or privateness but impressions gained during the interviews and from informal observations suggest that the interlocutor's identity is a major factor. However the situation is defined, what is important is that there is an awareness of the situative adequacy of the local variety in certain situations.

The reactions to the variety that is located between the local variety and the regionally coloured standard throw some light on the way in which the community comes to terms with the complex linguistic reality that surrounds it, and which can 'objectively' best be described as a continuum. My informants apparently think in terms of two varieties (the two poles of the continuum for many of them) and this would seem to support the maintenance of a clear distinction between the two.

The Karch speaker was generally perceived to be speaking an acceptable form of standard German, and no one (with the exception of Bas) appeared to be irritated by the clearly non-standard phonological features. The comments on this speaker testify to the acceptability of this variety in certain situations, for example 'wenn man einen Vortrag hält' ('when one is making a speech'), 'wenn man den Jahresbericht vorliest, vorm Verein' ('when one is reading out the annual report in an AGM'), and underline its perceived distance from the local vernacular.

These three factors, which were revealed in the attitudes expressed by my informants, would therefore appear to offer some explanation of the relationship between different linguistic varieties in Neckarau and why the local variety is being maintained and kept distinct from the standard.

Appendix

Note: = indicates that an unstressed pronoun, article, etc., is reduced and fused with the preceding word.

Speaker I

un = e noch = n ungkel von mir der is der ungkel schorsch der is eens gebore des is der is dreieachzisch un der is aa fit un wenn der verzehlt do kann ich schdundelang zuheere wenn mei oma noch lewe dät die alde von dem was frieher gewese is also ganz frieher da hawwe die so sache im kopp die kenne die kleenschde kleenischkeite des neiere des kenne se nimmehr so phalte awwer die frieher die kleenschde – die wisse noch wo = se em verzehnte krieg in = nere wettschaft ware do un wees de daifel was doch wirklisch was = se do gesse hawwe un alles möglische...

Speaker II

ging der kleine hin und da habbe sisch halt die mütter getroffe beim kinderabhole wie = s üblisch is und eine kam dann auf die idee ach gott man könnt ja mal ging da jemand kegeln von dene mütter man könnt eigentlich n kegelklub gründe und das war so = n zulauf daß wir da zwölf dreizehn fraue ware die also ihre kinder im kegelklub äh im kindergatte gehabt habbe un da haben da vorne in so = nem alten lokal also uralt e bahn bekomme jeden donnerschtag und seit der zeit isch glaub das besteht jetz seit vier jahre gehen wir alle virrzen tage donner-schtags kegle...

Karch speaker

ja sie woldn nun wissn was man en glein bissl was man an schbord gedriebn had nun ja ich hab in meine ganz junge jahre schon mid sechdsen un sibdsen jahren gerudrd bis isd mir soldad wurde im jahr neundsenhundedundswölf da mußd = ich = s nadürlisch aufschdegn – weida kond = ich nicht mehr rudern ... da war isch in freiburk un da ka = ma högschdns uff = m sant rudern un nit uff = m wassa – dserüge-komme nach mannheim da waa = s ... rudern auch widda nigs – na da wurd man se langsam doch dsum rudern – um nen rischidschen schbord dsu dreiwe dsu alt – had ma = s noch sonndachs mal ab = n dsu gedriebn...

The last transcription is based on the transcription in Karch, 1975.

The following table shows how the informants who chose Speaker I are distributed by sex, age and geographical provenance:

All	22/26 (85%)
Males	9/12 (83%)
Females	11/14 (86%)
Local Males	9/9 (100%)
Local Females	8/8 (100%)
Age group B (20 years old)	1/1 (100%)
Age group C (30–50)	7/11 (64%)
Age group D (60+)	14/14 (100%)
Locals	17/17 (100%)
Incomers	5/9 (56%)
Locals with incomers from Ma suburbs	20/20 (100%)
Incomers from outside Ma	2/6 (33%)

Notes

[1] Quotations are from interviews carried out by the author in Neckarau in 1985 and 1986. Modified orthography is used where phonetic detail is irrelevant in order to make the reader's task as simple as possible.

[2] *Kumme* and *gedenkt* are typical of the most locally restricted variety, cf. Bräutigam, 1934, 104.

[3] These are the terms normally used to refer to the most locally restricted variety and they are given here in a form approximating to the usual pronunciation in Neckarau.

[4] This literally means written German, but it is the local term for standard German, written or spoken.

[5] 'Investigations into the ability of members of a rural speech community to divide the linguistic continuum that surrounds them into different linguistic varieties have shown that, even within a small village, not all inhabitants share the same opinion about what is dialect, what is semi-dialect and what is regional colloquial speech.'

[6] Formal standard German has been codified in works such as *Siebs Deutsche Aussprache*, *Duden Aussprachewörterbuch*, *Duden Wörterbuch*, and *Duden Grammatik*.

[7] Cf. Mattheier (1980, 105–6): 'Auch fallen die Faktoren >Formalität< und >Öffentlichkeit< keinesfalls zusammen, wie das in manchen dialektsoziologischen Untersuchungen den Anschein hat' ('Neither do the factors "formal" and "public" always coincide, although some dialect-sociological surveys give that impression.')

References

Barbour, S. and Stevenson, P. 1990. *Variation in German*, Cambridge: CUP.
Blom, J.-P. and Gumperz, J. 1972. 'Social meaning in linguistic structures: code-switching in Norway', in Gumperz, J. and Hymes, D., *Directions in*

Sociolinguistics. The Ethnography of Communication, New York: Holt, Rinehart and Winston, 407–54.

Bräutigam, K. 1934. *Die Mannheimer Mundart*, Heidelberg: Fr. Lamade.

Cheshire, J. 1978. 'Present tense verbs in Reading English', in Trudgill, P. (ed.), 1978, 52–69.

——1982. 'Linguistic variation and social function', in Romaine, S. (ed.), 1982, 153–66.

Douglas-Cowie, E. 1979. 'Linguistic code-switching in a Northern Irish village: social interaction and social ambition', in Trudgill, P. (ed.), 1978, 37–51.

Durrell, M. 1992. 'Pygmalion Deutsch: attitudes to language in England and Germany', *London German Studies IV*, 1–26. London: University of London Institute of Germanic Studies.

Hudson, R. A. 1980. *Sociolinguistics*, Cambridge: CUP.

Karch, D. 1975. *Mannheim – Umgangssprache. Phonai Bd.* 16, Tübingen: Niemeyer.

Keller, R. E. 1978. *The German Language*, London: Faber and Faber.

Mattheier, K. 1980. *Pragmatik und Soziologie der Dialekte*, Heidelberg: Quelle and Meyer.

Milroy, L. 1980. *Language and Social Networks*, Oxford: Blackwell.

—— 1982. 'Social network and linguistic focusing', in Romaine, S. (ed.), 1982, 141–52.

Omdal, H. forthcoming. 'From the valley to the city: language modification and language attitudes', in Nordberg, B. (ed.), *The Sociolinguistics of Urbanization: The Case of the Nordic Countries*, Berlin: Mouton de Gruyter.

Romaine, S. (ed.). 1982. *Sociolinguistic Variation in Speech Communities*, London: Arnold.

Schlieben-Lange, B. 1978. *Soziolinguistik. Eine Einführung*, 2nd edn., Stuttgart, Berlin, Cologne, Mainz: Kohlhammer.

Trudgill, P. (ed.). 1978. *Sociolinguistic Patterns in British English*. London: Arnold. (Reprinted with corrections 1979.)

Trudgill, P., Labov, W. and Fasold, R. 1979. 'Editor's Preface', in Giles, H. and St Clair, R. (eds.), *Language and Social Psychology*, vii–ix. Oxford: Blackwell.

20

Language loss and language recovery: the case of the *Rußlanddeutsche*[1]

CHARLOTTE HOFFMANN

Introduction

Ethnic Germans have a long history of settlement in various parts of the former Soviet Union. They also represent the largest German minority anywhere in the world, accounting for almost two million people. A succession of turbulent political events spanning the period from Stalin to Glasnost have affected them deeply, resulting in loss of territory and language decline. What makes the Russian Germans special as a linguistic minority is that a sizeable number of them now find themselves in a position where they are recovering their language and adjusting their identity from being minority Germans in Russia to being members of the dominant majority society in Germany.

I shall first present an outline of the sociocultural and linguistic factors that have contributed towards language shift among ethnic Germans in the former Soviet Union. This will involve a brief look at the past and present situation of Russian Germans and their language, as well as examining Soviet language policies. The second part is concerned with the *Rußlanddeutsche* in Germany and the issues involved in their linguistic adaptation. Of particular interest is the observation of contact between different varieties: Russian, Russian German, standard German and German regional dialects, and the linguistic responses to cultural and emotional pressures that are beginning to emerge. In both parts, the underlying theme is that of replacive bilingualism – in the former Soviet Union German is being replaced by Russian, but in the case of the *Rußlanddeutsche* German is now being substituted for Russian.

German minorities in Russia

Several waves of immigration had brought German settlers to different parts of Russia.[2] From the fifteenth century onwards colonization was generally encouraged by the authorities, particularly during the reigns of Peter I (1689–1725) and Catherine II (1762–96) and in the early nineteenth century. Often settlers were given certain rights and guarantees that enabled them to maintain their German culture and language. They came from different social and geographical backgrounds (from Germany, Austria and Alsace), and for a variety of reasons (economic, political and religious). Their settlement areas varied in size and geographical homogeneity, and the German communities they formed differed as to the extent of their social and cultural cohesion and the degree of autonomy in cultural matters that they enjoyed. Until 1940 the Ukraine and the Volga Basin contained some 50 per cent of all Russian Germans, and with the establishment of the Autonomous Socialist Republic of the Volga in 1924 the group reached the peak of their cultural and political autonomy. Notwithstanding some degree of assimilation and widespread bilingualism or multilingualism, until the Second World War German communities remained, on the whole, distinct cultural groupings who used German not only in private domains but at work, in education and in church life.

The war and its aftermath brought dramatic changes to all German minorities. Expulsion from their traditional settlement areas led many to flee the Soviet Union altogether, whereas others were resettled in Siberia and other non-European regions of the Soviet Union. The Germans thus became a dispersed minority without a homeland, and until their official rehabilitation in 1955 all manifestations of cultural identity were suppressed. Today, the largest number of ethnic Germans is to be found in Kazakhstan, where they constitute the third largest ethnic group – some 1,150,000 according to the 1989 census (Hilkes 1989). Other areas of high German settlement are Kirgizia, Tadzhikistan and Moldavia. In the 1979 Soviet census almost two million had registered as German nationals (the figure given in Born and Dickgießer (1989) is 1,936,214, amounting to 0.74 per cent of the total Soviet population at the time). Because of their high birth rate, the overall number of ethnic Germans has remained relatively stable over the years, although emigration has been intense since the late 1980s. It has affected, in particular, the rural settlements in some parts of the former Soviet Union.

Soviet language policies and language provision for German minorities

The Soviet Constitution formed the basis for language policies. Article 36 dealt with the rights of the different races and nationalities of the people of the Union, including the right to use one's mother tongue. In reality the 130 languages involved did not receive equal treatment, as many of those without national or regional official status have seen long periods of suppression and/or neglect. It has been suggested (Kreindler 1982, Haarmann 1992) that Soviet language policies in the field of status planning never really attempted to put into practice Lenin's principle of guaranteeing complete (including linguistic) equality to all nationalities, but instead aimed at promoting the social and political pre-eminence of Russian. Many measures taken during the Stalinist era showed quite openly the regime's distrust of minorities, such as the elimination of the intelligentsia among non-Russian nationality groups, the destruction of their national and cultural institutions (such as closing churches and schools) and the dispersal and resettlement of linguistic groups. Other measures, notably in the field of education, had the effect of favouring Russian *vis-à-vis* other languages.

Bilingual education programmes became the object of attention for Soviet language planners from 1960 onwards. A growing number of Russian-medium schools and pre-school establishments were set up, and Russian increasingly became portrayed as the language of scientific and technological progress as well as the best means of international communication. Kreindler (1982, 27) emphasizes the political aspect when she speaks of the promotion of Russian as 'a forger of common supranational identity', while Haarmann (1992) points out that the encouragement of collective bilingualism had the ultimate aim of spreading Russian at the cost of the Union's other national languages.

In April 1990 a new, more liberal language law was passed, giving the various republics of the Union a greater degree of linguistic autonomy (Schröter 1990). But the former Soviet Union broke up early in 1991. I have not been able to find out what linguistic rights, if any, the German minorities now enjoy in the newly independent republics where they are settled.

In the decade after the end of the Second World War language rights were non-existent for the German minorities. Official rehabilitation in 1955 brought, apart from recognition, no significant improvements. In 1957 the first German mother-tongue classes were started in Russia, Kazakhstan, Uzbekistan and Tadzhikistan. But from the outset they suffered problems – some of which (like inadequate resources) still remain today, while additional ones have been caused by the emigration of families with children. The study by Hilkes (1988) into mother-tongue teaching among German minorities makes rather depressing reading. Initial problems involving the setting up of 'German schools' (a label used for classes rather than establishments) and training for teachers have, to some extent, been solved. But the acute shortage of resources and, most importantly, of suitable material and meaningful syllabuses[3] is still impeding progress. Centres may be sited far away from the children who need to attend them, and often classes are offered only outside normal teaching hours, which makes attendance less attractive.

Other factors, too, have had a demotivating effect on both teachers and the taught, such as decades of isolation from Germany, the absence of modern audio-visual teaching materials, and the lack of course-books designed specifically for bilingual learners – as well as the particular linguistic situation in which the German minorities find themselves. The latter is probably a crucial factor. Most ethnic Germans are dialect speakers with little or no competence in standard German. Yet mother-tongue teaching has tended to be concerned mainly with imparting knowledge of the spoken and written standard, so children have to learn a new variety instead of having their mother tongue (that is the dialect variety of their community) reinforced.

The role of the German media in the former Soviet Union was similarly insignificant in maintaining or promoting German. Whereas in 1937 there were over seventy different publications, today fewer than a handful are to be found. State interference and editorial restrictions have influenced both the form and the content of the published German newspapers and yearbooks, and they have generally kept to a minimum minority issues which could reinforce the German identity of their readers. The media have also experienced difficulties as the result of a number of other negative factors – for example, the multilingualism of their readers, which allows them to turn to non-German publications for local, national and topical news rather than having to rely on the German-language press. Rather disparagingly, Ritter (1985, 9) refers to the German media in the former Soviet Union as 'one-sided and artificially impoverished literature aimed at a homogeneous socialist readership who happen to speak German'. He also suggests that as the readership of the German media is neither educationally nor linguistically sophisticated, the general standard of these publications is not very high and their role with respect to the German minorities is a conservative rather than a progressive one.

Russian Germans and their language

The specific linguistic features of Russian German dialects stem from the fact that they developed as a result of contact with other German dialects, often in isolation from both literary and public standard varieties. Other languages spoken around them, particularly Russian, have added two further characteristics: lexical borrowing, and grammatical and stylistic interference. For many of the ethnic Germans who are German-speaking, German is essentially a spoken variety.

The distribution of German mother-tongue speakers varies considerably. The highest number of those who declared themselves to be German mother-tongue speakers can be found in Kazakhstan (almost two-thirds of all ethnic Germans there), whereas the lowest number (somewhat less than 50 per cent) is to be found in the Russian Republic. Urban areas are more russified than rural ones, and virtually all ethnic Germans know Russian: 42.59 per cent as a first language and 51.71 per cent as a second language; the rest may well know it as a third language. (All figures, from Born and Dickgießer (1989), are based on the 1979 census.) These numbers demonstrate that in terms of language assimilation the Germans have tended to adapt to Russian rather than to the other national languages spoken around them. Data supplied by successive censuses indicate that the number of German mother-tongue speakers is rapidly declining. But the interpretation of census material with regard to German nationality and use of German is difficult, as people may have given different answers to census questions at different times, depending on what they considered to be politically opportune (Fleischauer and Pinkus (1986) elaborate this point). A further problem is posed by the term 'mother tongue', which is not clearly defined in census instructions. If it is taken to be 'first language learnt' then it may not say much about the speakers or their proficiency. The census also included questions on knowledge of 'other languages of the Soviet people'. As German was not recognized as a language in that category there are no statistics showing to what extent German was known as a second language.

Language shift among Germans in the Soviet Union

Haarmann's (1992) discussion of Soviet language policies points towards covert language spread of Russian which resulted in language shift among many linguistic minorities. Language shift represented a social factor of considerable relevance, as 16.3 million non-Russians had shifted to Russian as their first language by 1979. This process was described in the Soviet literature in positive terms, and the new first language of those who had shifted (i.e. Russian) was labelled 'second mother tongue'. Thus someone who had shifted to Russian as second mother tongue was described as monolingual Russian, whereas a person who had adopted Russian as a second language was a bilingual with a non-Russian first language.

Language shift therefore followed a pattern whereby Russian became a second language during a transitional period, while for the younger generations Russian increasingly became the first (and dominant) language. A comparison of three sets of census figures may help to illustrate this: in the 1970 census 68.8 per cent of Russian Germans said that their mother tongue was German; in 1979 the number had been reduced by over one-sixth to 57 per cent; and by 1989 the number of German mother-tongue speakers was down to 54.4 per cent (Hilkes 1989, Berend 1992). It seems that, whereas collective bilingualism served many of the needs of communication within the community, it nevertheless often led to a situation where the minority language was not passed on to the younger generations.

To sum up, a number of factors have combined to speed up language loss:

(a) Dispersal and resettlement of ethnic Germans after the Second World War broke up long-established communities and destroyed their cultural ties with their traditional geographic regions. In the new mixed communities in which they found themselves, German was no longer the language shared by all.

(b) With the closure of cultural, religious and community institutions, German could no longer be used as a language for public communication.

(c) The ban on publishing in German in the post-war period, and later editorial restrictions on German publishing, seriously undermined any meaningful role that the media might have played. If books and newspapers cannot reflect on issues of ethnic identity and common concerns, using the minority's language as a vehicle for conveying a feeling of common identity, there is little else that can reinforce or maintain cultural identity. In the case of the Germans, it also weakened their knowledge of standard German, thereby further undermining language competence.

(d) The continued lack of contact with the 'mother country' (*Mutterland* is the term used by ethnic Germans to refer to Germany) deprived the minority of sorely needed contacts with spoken and written forms of German.

(e) With the closure of all educational establishments the younger generations' access to German became seriously curtailed during the post-war years. Mother-tongue classes set up after 1957 met with many obstacles; their contribution to language maintenance was therefore of limited value.

(f) The increase in mixed marriages, particularly in urban areas, meant that in many families German was replaced by Russian as the home language.

(g) Parents who did not want their children to be discriminated against on the grounds of ethnic background often encouraged the use of Russian in the home alongside German. Language maintenance is more successful if the majority language can be kept away from the home, thus establishing clearly defined contexts for the use of each (Hoffmann 1991a).

(h) The continued exodus of many Russian Germans to Germany, particularly families with young children, weakened communities numerically and also structurally as the viability of social and educational institutions was threatened.

(i) In addition, language shift was accelerated as a result of industrialization, urbanization and greater mobility – processes which generally weaken closely-knit rural communities.

In general, then, overt and covert pressures led to a situation where successive generations perceived less need, or had fewer opportunities, to use the minority language than their elders. Language maintenance is always an uphill struggle when there is little outside help available to underpin the 'cultural core values' (Pütz 1991), that is, those values that are associated with cultural content and meaning, and which help maintain ethnic identity through the vehicle of the minority language. All too often, language choice patterns within particular role-relationships (such as among friends, between partners or parents and children or siblings) in bilingual communities gradually become undermined by increased use of the dominant language, until real choice disappears because the speakers no longer have fluency in the two different codes. But among Russian Germans, German continued to be seen as an all-important symbol of ethnic identity, even among those who no longer used it (Hoffmann 1991b).

Language competence of the Rußlanddeutsche in Germany

The term 'replacive bilingualism' is used to describe a linguistic configuration where the dominant language is in the process of superseding, and eventually replacing, the mother tongue. The discussion so far indicates that the linguistic situation of ethnic Germans in the former Soviet Union can be described as one of replacive bilingualism.

I now turn my attention to those for whom the process of language replacement is being reversed, namely the *Aussiedler* from the former Soviet Union.[4] For many of them emigration is something of a dream come true: the desire to leave the land of their ancestors goes far beyond economic considerations and is most often expressed as the wish 'to live as Germans among Germans'. For them language recovery is essential. They need to be fluent in German so that they can achieve full integration in their new environment. In linguistic terms this requires developing the skills necessary to communicate effectively and confidently. In emotional and sociocultural terms it also implies adapting to mainstream society and moving from minority status to that of indigenous majority. This process is fraught with difficulties and frustrations that many *Aussiedler* are unprepared for; for a time at least, it looks as though many run the risk of becoming a new marginalized minority of 'Germans among Germans' (Projektgruppe EVA-A 1991).

Their position is affected negatively by the fact that, over the years, Germany has seen a large influx of immigrants and asylum-seekers, who have added to the numbers of non-German migrant workers already in the country, and it is an unfortunate fact that, both in public discussion and in the minds of many Germans, the *Aussiedler* are often grouped together with the various communities of *Ausländer* ('foreigners'). To be sure, they come from another country and they often do not speak German or they speak it in a way that is considered odd. But they are German in that they have German nationality (they hold German passports) and in that they identify themselves as Germans. And many of them are also competent in a dialect of German.

Mother tongue according to year of birth (percentages)

year	standard German	dialect	non-German
1905–1935	27.9	67.4	2.6
1936–1955	28.9	52.9	14.7
1956–1965	21.9	40.6	37.5
Total	28.0	58.2	11.1

(adapted from Hilkes 1989, 5)

The Munich Project,[5] which used a sample of 450 Russian German *Aussiedler* informants, showed that there was a correlation between proficiency in German and age of the informants: the younger the informants, the less likely it was that they knew German.

It is interesting to note that there is, in comparison with the other sets, much less change in the figures relating to knowledge of standard German. This seems to indicate that those who had contact with the written language were more inclined to pass it on to their children than those who knew a spoken dialect only.

When asked about their own linguistic competence, only 8.5 per cent of those interviewed said that German was their best language; the vast majority said that Russian was their strongest language or that they were proficient in both. Another subjective measurement of their linguistic competence took the shape of an evaluation by the interviewers, who judged 62 per cent of the sample to have good, or very good, proficiency in German. Linguistic competence was not measured objectively in the Munich project, so we have to rely on the subjective data that is available. On this basis we can come only to tentative conclusions about actual language use. For instance, most of the *Aussiedler* claimed that they spoke German mainly to their parents (82.2 per cent). Otherwise communication within the family was either bilingual or, for about half the sample, in Russian. More than half used Russian when talking to their friends and 91.5 per cent said they used Russian only at their workplace. In other words, the communicative contexts and functions of German, and therefore competence in the language, were very limited.

In the EVA-A Project, which is a sociological study covering a smaller number of *Aussiedler* from different eastern European countries, a question on language use which was included produced the following figures (based on interviews with seventeen Russian German families): 28 per cent said that they had always used German at home, 50 per cent that they had sometimes used German, and 22 per cent never. In this project, 82 per cent claimed that they had no problems with the language – and the same proportion said that they had attended a German language course in Germany. However, the report does not make clear whether the absence of problems in the language can be attributed to the fact of having attended such a course.

To sum up, there is little detailed information about language competence among *Rußlanddeutsche*, but we do have a good deal of anecdotal evidence (for example from social workers, teachers, administrators) that most of them lack fluency in the language, specific linguistic knowledge such as various technical registers, and the grammar of standard German. Many experience difficulties making themselves understood when talking to Germans. The dialects they speak are, of course, old established German varieties, but German listeners are not used to them, nor are they able to understand the various Russian borrowings, switches or loan translations that they contain. *Rußlanddeutsch* is seen as 'outmoded, preserved, Slavonic German'

(Berend 1992), and it is looked down upon by many Germans. As fluency in German is seen by the latter as an indispensable marker of group identity, failure to 'speak German properly' may be equated with 'not really being German like us'. Such attitudes by the majority may lead to marginalization of the *Aussiedler* which, in turn, makes linguistic integration more difficult.

Language recovery among Rußlanddeutsche

There is now a growing body of literature outlining the measures that must be (or are being) taken to further language maintenance, or recovery, in countries such as Spain, Wales or Ireland, to name just a few western European cases. Language recovery in these contexts is promoted by language policies formulated by either majority govern- ments or newly autonomous minority administrations, and they are aimed at stemming the decline of the minority language or promoting the status of the minority by expanding the use of their language.

As far as the *Rußlanddeutsche* are concerned, language recovery is purely a question of individual or family effort. The enterprise varies in complexity depending on the amount of linguistic and pragmatic knowledge that needs to be acquired, and also according to the social and cultural pressures each individual speaker finds herself or himself under. Whereas linguistic adaptation is generally accepted as being a necessary prerequisite for full integration into mainstream society, few *Rußlanddeutsche* were fully prepared at the outset for its implications. Many have found that becoming fully German goes hand in hand with losing ties with the language which hitherto was their strongest, Russian, and with their bilingual and bicultural identity. Whereas in Russia they may have been considered German, in Germany they are often seen as being Russian, and this fact stands in the way of their becoming fully integrated. In most other minority contexts language recovery has usually taken the form of additive social bilingualism, but in the case of the *Aussiedler* we find the opposite, that is, a form of replacive bilingualism, as there is no institutional support for one of their languages.[6]

Linguistically, language recovery presents three concrete challenges:

(i) *Rußlanddeutsche* need to acquire the standard forms of written and spoken German;
(ii) they have to adapt to a local and regional variety which is new to them;
(iii) they need to adapt their own dialect in such a way that they are understood by the Germans around them.

'Recovering the language of their forebears' is a rather general expression for a number of quite specific tasks that involve learning new forms of the language and developing linguistic sensitivity and knowledge of pragmatic choices.

Nina Berend (1991), herself a *Rußlanddeutsche* working on the linguistic integration of the *Rußlanddeutsche* in the Mannheim region, has reported on their rapidly increasing language awareness. But she also observed the 'language confusion' (*Sprachverwirrung*) resulting from conflicting expectations and realities encountered upon arrival in Germany. For many *Rußlanddeutsche* their variety of German used to epitomize their 'Germanness', and more often than not they had only a vague idea about notions of, and differences between, standard and dialect. They knew they had to learn to speak 'proper German', and they thought that this could be achieved just by adding new words and expressions to their existing knowledge. But frustration sets in when they arrive in Germany and realize that the German they know is of limited use for communication with Germans, and that it can even hinder them in their acquisition of standard German grammar. They also notice that not everybody around them speaks standard German, which they recognize as the prestige variety, and that the local dialect is different from their own – and difficult to understand.

Most of their linguistic efforts are now geared towards learning standard German, usually by attending language courses which are offered to *Aussiedler* as well as foreigners. Language recovery, however, goes well beyond learning more complex grammatical structures and new words and idioms. For those who speak a Russian German dialect it means making their language more easily understood. This may involve the suppression of Russian influences in their speech or the relexification of their dialect.[7] Berend describes how, under the influence of standard German, a new Russian German spoken variety is emerging, a 'rußlanddeutsche Umgangssprache' as she calls it, in which Russian lexical elements are replaced by standard German (not local dialect) ones and only phonological and morphological features remain Russian German. For example:

Russian German:	ich sin in de bolnitze gwest
becomes:	ich sin im Krankenhaus gwest
(standard German:	ich bin im Krankenhaus gewesen)
	('I've been in hospital')
Russian German:	noch e ostanoffka, no ge:me raus
becomes:	noch e haltestelle, no ge:me raus
(standard German:	noch eine Haltestelle, dann steigen wir aus)
	('one more stop and we get off' [the bus/tram])
	(Berend 1992)

Berend further remarks on the development of another variety, which she terms 'angestrebtes Hochdeutsch', which results from increased exposure to standard German and is the outcome of attempting (not always successfully) to speak standard German.

There is no doubt that eventually the *Rußlanddeutsche* will adapt themselves linguistically, most easily of course the members of the younger generations, who have entered the education system in Germany. But neither the children nor the older *Aussiedler* receive help that is specifically geared to their needs. Integration becomes a battle that most of them have to fight alone. Perhaps it is not surprising that, in response to the many outside pressures and in recognition of their bilingualism, many now rely on Russian as their home language, even if in Russia or Kazakhstan they used to employ German in this domain. For many, Russian is the language they know best, and for all it is the language that represents the other half of their identity – which they are only now becoming fully aware of.

Conclusion

Over the past fifty years or so the Russian German minority in the former Soviet Union has undergone widespread language shift. Generally speaking, there was among them widespread monolingualism in German before the Second World War, and over the next half century many became monolingual in Russian, with a period of transitional bilingualism in between. In the case of the *Rußlanddeutsche* now in Germany, language change has gone a step further as they are having to learn, or relearn, German. In the cases of both the Russian Germans and the *Rußlanddeutsche* it could be argued that language shift foreshadows the end of a minority, even if this need not be a sudden-death phenomenon.

But language is not the only marker of ethnic identity. Ethnic Germans in Russia and the other former Soviet republics may well continue to see themselves as Germans. The changed political climate may enable them to reinforce their German culture through new contacts and exchanges – and here the *Rußlanddeutsche* could play an important part.

And what about the *Rußlanddeutsche*? By emigrating they have, of course, ceased to be a linguistic minority, although it is to be feared that, for the time being at least, they may constitute a new social minority. When they arrive in Germany they find that 'being German' is not quite what they had imagined it to be. They are 'also German' in a monolingual majority context, whereas formerly they may have seen themselves as 'just German'. It will be interesting to see for how long they will maintain the Russian element of their linguistic and cultural make-up, and whether or not acceptance by the majority will depend on their shedding the Russian component of their identity.

Notes

[1] *Rußlanddeutsche* is the German term used in the literature to refer to those ethnic Germans who originally settled in Russia (but are now found in various parts of the former Soviet Union), as well as those who have emigrated to Germany since the Second World War. The English term has been 'Soviet Germans'. In view of the changed political circumstances I have adopted a loan translation so that I refer to ethnic Germans in the former Soviet Union as 'Russian Germans'. I use *Rußlanddeutsche* when talking about those Russian Germans who have emigrated to Germany. I employ the term *Aussiedler* when referring to ethnic Germans from various eastern European countries who have recently moved to Germany; there is no suitable English equivalent.

[2] The biggest settlement areas were around St Petersburg, in the Ukraine and the Crimea, in Georgia, Belorussia and Moldavia.

[3] Hilkes (1988) mentions the widespread use of the Soviet German press for teaching purposes and comments on its unsuitability as regards language, interest and topicality.

[4] Numbers have increased markedly in recent years. In the period 1950–86 approximately 95,000 Germans emigrated; the figure for the two years 1987–89 alone was 160,000, and this trend is continuing (Projektsgruppe EVA-A 1991).

[5] The Osteuropa-Institut in Munich is engaged in a major study of German minorities in the former Soviet Union, using information provided by *Aussiedler*.

[6] In contrast, for many foreigners, mainly migrant workers and their families, some form of provision (albeit insufficient) in their own languages is offered.

[7] In the absence of an all-embracing German standard, Russian exercised a strong influence on Russian German dialects. Berend (1992) has an example where all nouns have been replaced by Russian ones:
hol die banke mit warenje, uff de polke im tschulan
(Standard German: hol das Glasgefäß mit Marmelade auf dem Regal in der Kammer, 'get the jam-pot from the shelf in the larder')

References

Berend, N. 1991. '"Alles ist anders...". Rußlanddeutsche in Mannheim', *Sprachreport* 3/91.
——1992. 'Sprachdrill oder kommunikative Integration: zur Situation der Rußlanddeutschen in der Bundesrepublik', in *Proceedings of GAL Conference 1991* (to be published by Brockmeyer).
Born, J. and Dickgießer, S. 1989. *Deutschsprachige Minderheiten*, Mannheim: Institut für deutsche Sprache.
Fleischauer, I. and Pinkus, B. 1986. *The Soviet Germans: Past and Present*, London: Hurst and Co.

Haarmann, H. 1992. 'Measures to increase the importance of Russian within and outside the Soviet Union – a case of covert language-spread policy', *International Journal of the Sociology of Language*, 95, 109–29.

Hilkes, P. 1988. 'Unterricht in der Muttersprache bei den Deutschen in der Sowjetunion', *Osteuropa*, (2) 38, 931–49.

——1989. 'Deutsche in der Sowjetunion: Sprachkompetenz und Sprach-verhalten. Forschungsprojekt "Deutsche in der Sowjetgesellschaft"', *Arbeitsbericht* Nr. 10. Osteuropa-Institut München.

Hoffmann, C. 1991a. *An Introduction to Bilingualism*, London: Longman.

——1991b. 'Language and identity: the case of the German Aussiedler', in Meara, P. and Ryan, A. (eds.), *Language and Nation*, British Studies in Applied Linguistics 6, London: CILT.

Kreindler, I. 1982. 'The changing status of Russian in the Soviet Union', *International Journal of the Sociology of Language* 33, 7–39.

Projektsgruppe EVA-A 1991. 'Erfolg und Verlauf der Aneignung neuer Um-welten durch Aussiedler.' Phase I: Pilot-Studie.

Pütz, M. 1991. 'Language maintenance and language shift in the speech behaviour of German-Australian migrants in Canberra', *Journal of Multilingual and Multicultural Development*, 12, 6, 477–89.

Ritter, A. 1985. 'Zur Problematik der Medien bei den deutschsprachigen Minderheiten', *Germanistische Mitteilungen*, 22, 3–21.

Schröter, K. 1990. 'Zur Sprachenproblematik in der Sowjetunion', *Fremdsprachenunterricht*, 34/43, 12, 586–8.

21

Language and nationalism: Britain and Ireland, and the German-speaking area[1]

STEPHEN BARBOUR

Most of the inhabitants of Greece are Greeks and they speak Greek; most of the inhabitants of Norway are Norwegians and they speak Norwegian; most of the inhabitants of Spain are Spaniards (or Spanish) and they speak Spanish. In every part of Europe we find modern nation-states where names for the state, the national language and the majority ethnic group are etymologically clearly related, not only in English, but also in the local language, and in other languages. There are, of course, awkward exceptions: the Dutch speak Dutch and live in the Netherlands or Holland, the Belgians live in Belgium and speak French or Dutch, and the Swiss live in Switzerland and speak German, French, Italian or Romansh. While the last two mentioned are clear exceptions to the pattern, the Dutch case is not nowadays usually exceptional in the usage of the Dutch language itself, which usually has *Nederlanders* living in *Nederland* and speaking *Nederlands*. Until very recently Yugoslavia and the Soviet Union provided very clear exceptions, but with the disintegration of those states we now find Slovenes living in Slovenia and speaking Slovene, Ukrainians living in Ukraine and speaking Ukrainian, and so on.

What we have reflected here is, of course, the familiar phenomenon of the ethnically and linguistically relatively homogeneous nation-state, where a particular ethnic group has become dominant in a particular area, coinciding roughly with the geographical extent of its language, has achieved sovereignty and independence for that area, and has very often succeeded in weakening or removing rival languages from the territory. Of course linguists do not need to be reminded that this picture of the phenomenon is considerably over-simplified; frequently ethnic groups have given their speech the status of an independent language, where an outside observer might well have concluded, on the basis of linguistic criteria such as structural similarity, that it was a dialect of some more widely spoken language (see Haugen 1976 and, for a discussion of the now highly topical eastern European nations, Gustavsson 1990). A superficial view of the ethnic composition of Europe might lead one to suppose that speaking a particular language was the most important determinant of ethnic group membership, but in fact it is usually only one of a number of criteria; the ethnic group delimited entirely by language probably does not exist (see Hobsbawm 1990, 51–63). In addition political scientists do not need to be reminded that the majority population of a modern European nation-state is often a very different kind of entity from the ethnic groups which one might delimit in other times and other parts of the world (see Smith 1991, 19–70).

Despite all the complexities of the phenomenon, there is no doubt that in Europe the monolingual, mono-ethnic nation-state is the norm. This does not, of course, mean that such states are entirely monolingual or mono-ethnic, and almost all of them contain sizeable ethnic and linguistic minorities, either indigenous or of more recent immigrant origin; what it does mean, however, is that a very clear majority belong to the dominant ethnic and linguistic group, and that members of other groups are under varying degrees of pressure – cultural, economic, political or even military – to abandon their minority culture or language, ranging from the economic pressure on many Irish speakers in Ireland to use only English, to the enforced assimilation of Turks in Bulgaria.

It is relatively easy to take a moral stance on enforced assimilation, but should we not just accept the gradual attrition of languages and cultures as an inevitable, if unfortunate, aspect of modern life? If the Irish of the Gaeltacht have jobs and houses, why should anyone think twice about the loss of their traditional language and culture? In *The Languages of Britain* (1984) Glanville Price charts the decline of the indigenous minority languages of Britain with a vivid sense of loss, which I certainly share. The sheer excitement of diversity in language, as in any area of human experience, can never be offset by some ill-defined and dubious gain in efficiency which a monolingual society might experience. The loss of any language, almost like the loss of a species, represents an impoverishment of the world, the loss of a unique means of expression, which can never be regained.

If we can agree that the spread of monolingualism represents a loss, then we should accept that to combat or even restrict it might be easier if we understood it better. I hence propose to look at the spread within Europe of two of the major languages, English and German. I choose these two because, while there are similarities between the ways in which they have spread, there are very significant differences which can illuminate the entire phenomenon of the spread of monolingualism.

My approach will be multidisciplinary, combining linguistics with insights from the work of historians, and political and social scientists. Linguistics alone cannot explain why some languages die out and others survive. Typological dissimilarity, or lack of obvious historical relationship between a majority and a minority language, may increase the threat to a minority language: the closely related Catalan is less threatened by Castilian Spanish than is the linguistically distant Basque (Clare Mar-Molinero, and Max Wheeler, personal communications), but this is far from the whole story; in Britain Scots, closely related to Anglo-English, is every bit as threatened as the linguistically remote Celtic languages, yet among the Celtic languages, all equally linguistically distant from English, Welsh is in an appreciably stronger position than the others (Price 1984, 39–154, 186–93). To attempt explanations of these phenomena, linguistics needs social and political science and history; in other words it needs to become sociolinguistics, and even go beyond sociolinguistics as it is often understood.

Social and political science, and history, have noted the persistence of ethnic and national identities, socio-cultural phenomena, despite profound changes in the factors which constitute those identities; for example in the eighteenth century many felt that to be truly English one had to be Protestant, while this view is now uncommon (Smith 1991, 84–5). Linguistics may be able to illuminate this persistence in the face of change, since it studies languages, in many respects socio-cultural phenomena, which are frequently regarded as remaining the same, in the sense of remaining German or English or Greek or whatever, over centuries, even millennia, while undergoing profound changes in many aspects of the structure and lexicon.

Turning now to the German-speaking and English-speaking areas of Europe, we notice strong parallels in the spread of the majority language over the last thousand years. A thousand years ago English was largely restricted to England; it has since become dominant throughout Britain and Ireland, but without the wholesale displacement of speakers of other languages. More common has probably been the gradual spread of English through language shift, with of course some population movement as well (Price 1984, *passim*).

A thousand years ago German was largely confined to what is now the western part of Germany and of Austria;[2] the spread of German to areas east of the Elbe has usually been seen as a result of wholesale population movement, but even conventional accounts such as Grundmann (1973, 261–5) imply language shift in a remaining population as an important process, while the overwhelming number of place-names of Slavonic origin in eastern Germany is strong evidence for a gradual shift to German in an existing Slavonic-speaking population, taking place alongside the immigration of German-speakers (see Lockwood 1976, 166–74).

What is clearly different between the spread of English and the spread of German is that, in the case of English, the language has not become the symbol of an English national identity, coterminous with its speakers; speakers of English in Britain and Ireland variously consider their national identity in the twentieth century to be Welsh, Scottish, Irish, English or British, the last two being conflated by many inhabitants of England, but not by others.

In contrast the German language is the prime symbol of German national identity. Apart from the Swiss, Alsatians and Luxemburgers, a numerically tiny proportion of the total, speakers of German consider that they have a German national identity; a distinct Austrian (in the sense of non-German) national identity does not predate the Second World War (see Hobsbawm 1990, 32, 40, 92), and even the French (in Alsace), Swiss-German and Luxemburgish national identities of some German speakers have only become absolutely clear since the Nazi period made a German identity undesirable (for the Swiss case see Russ 1987, 104).

While there have been links between the spread of English in Britain and Ireland and the spread of an English or British national identity, they have not been at all clear-cut. The spread of Scots in Lowland Scotland in the Middle Ages long predated English political control; whether Scots is a dialect of English or not is debatable, but it is certainly closely related to Anglo-English, particularly to northern dialects. It is not at all clear why it gradually replaced Gaelic, the language of the dominant ethnic group in medieval Scotland (see Mitchison 1982, 36). What is clear however is that its spread actually coincided, paradoxically, with the growth of a Scottish national identity (see Mitchison 1982, 43). In recent times Scots has itself been replaced to a considerable extent by Scottish English, that is by a variety which is very clearly the same language as Anglo-English. While there have been some attempts to reverse this shift, at least in the realm of poetry, there has been no clear general view of this variety as an alien imposition; indeed modern Scots strongly identify with it as a symbol of Scots identity, even though its differences from Anglo-English are largely restricted to the phonetic and phonological levels (see Price 1984, 186–93, Abrams and Hogg 1988). The original language of the Scots ethnic group, Gaelic, has been the object of strong disapproval, even persecution, on the part not only of the English but even more so on the part of (Scots-speaking and English-speaking) Scots (see Price 1984, 48–70). Among the indigenous population of Scotland today it is fully justified to distinguish between a Gaelic-speaking (though bilingual) and an English-speaking or Scots-speaking ethnic group (with Orcadians and Shetlanders arguably constituting a further ethnic group or groups).

In Ireland too, language has generally not been seen as an important element in national identity. The strong movement promoting the language did not get under way until the end of the last century, when the language had probably irretrievably declined; as late as the early nineteenth century the popular national hero Daniel O'Connell saw Irish as a barrier to modern progress (see Curtis 1961, 359–60, 401–2). The decline, even unpopularity, of the language seems unrelated to the strong persistence of a sense of Irish identity. Taking Ireland as a whole, both the Republic and Northern Ireland, the ethnic division which overrides all other potential ones (such as a potential one based on language) is, of course, that between Protestant Loyalists, who would describe their national identity as 'British', and Catholic Nationalists, who identify themselves as 'Irish'. The Ulster Protestant British identity goes back partly to an older British national identity, now changed beyond recognition in England, which contained an important religious dimension.

Only in Wales, which, of the 'subject nations', has been the most closely institutionally bound to England, is language a potent symbol of national identity, albeit a sometimes divisive one, alienating some people who are monoglot English speakers, but who nevertheless feel themselves to be Welsh (see Williams 1985, 290–5, 299–300). It is perhaps justified to postulate two indigenous ethnic groups in Wales: English-speakers and bilinguals.

In England language plays little part in national identity; since English is overwhelmingly dominant in Britain and is the foremost language of international communication, English people often regard it as simply 'natural' that they should speak English, not as an expression of ethnic or national identity. Given this view, and also given their mistaken equation of 'British' and 'English', many English people regard the desire of some of their fellow Britons to speak minority languages as simply perverse.

Language, then, functions in rather different ways in relation to nationalism in the English-speaking and in the German-speaking areas of Europe. In explaining the differences in the sociolinguistic configuration, work in political science and history is very helpful. Both British or English and German national identities, according to Anthony D. Smith, are, like most such identities in Europe, developments of the ethnic identity of the dominant ethnic group (*ethnie* in Smith's terms) in the nation (see Smith 1991, *passim*).[3] However, the development proceeded quite differently in the two cases.

We can see modern English ethnic identity developing in the Middle Ages. Smith describes medieval England as a 'lateral' ethnic community (Smith 1991, 52). This means that the dominant ethnic group, the Normans, formed an upper stratum in a stratified society. In time their ethnic identity was extended to the whole society, in the process changing beyond recognition to become first Anglo-Norman then English, changing its language from French to a heavily French-influenced English, and developing into a national rather than an ethnic identity. Alternatively we can see the Norman and English strata of society slowly merging, although the strongly stratified nature of English society persists to this day and still has a limited linguistic aspect with an RP-using upper stratum contrasting with the rest. In the English case the upper stratum, within England, has generally not felt so threatened in its position that it has tried to impose its language and culture in an obvious and aggressive fashion on the majority – there has simply been a long convergence of language and culture.

The process can be seen as successful in England, but as in many ways a failure in Wales, Scotland and Ireland, since the attempt to extend a British or English identity to these countries occurred significantly later, after competing ethnic identities, even embryo national identities, had already begun to crystallize there. Any history of Wales, Scotland or Ireland (for example Williams 1985, Mitchison 1982, Kee 1980) bears ample evidence of that failure. What has been successful (although of course not completely so by any means) has been the imposition of the English language. This has occurred because it has long been in the economic interests of Irish, Scots or Welsh to use English, and because it has often not been seen to conflict with their national interests. As Smith (1991, *passim*) explains, lateral ethnic communities cohere primarily around the power of the dominant ethnic group and its institutions (still seen in the importance of the monarchy in English national identity), and only secondarily around its language and culture (indeed the dominant ethnic group in England itself switched from French to English during the crucial medieval period). The attempt to extend an English national identity to the 'subject nations' has hence been institutional in thrust rather than cultural and linguistic. Where minority languages have been opposed it has been as obstacles to 'progress', or, in the Scottish Highlands and Ireland, as marks of Catholicism. Opposition to Catholicism is of course partly an attempt to eradicate a minority culture, but even here the institutional aspect has usually been dominant: Catholics were seen as disloyal, as potential allies of the Crown's Catholic enemies in

France or Spain (see for example Curtis 1961, 147–411, particularly 204). Scottish Presbyterianism did not represent such a threat and has hence been tolerated in recent centuries as a minority denomination in Britain as a whole, which even has established status in Scotland.

In Smith's terms Scotland, Wales and Ireland represent vertical ethnic communities (Smith 1991, *passim*), the entire majority community sharing a single ethnic identity, with Loyalists in Ireland not being part of the Irish majority community. The 'British', 'English' or 'Anglo-Irish' élite in the 'subject nations' has not succeeded, as it has in England, in unifying élite and majority ethnic identities. In modern Europe as a whole such vertical ethnic communities form the basis of very many nations, particularly east of the Rhine, and frequently have a strong linguistic element. The weaker linguistic element in the identity of the Irish nation and of the minority nations in Britain can be explained by the clearly defined national territories in Ireland or Scotland and by the lack of a strong linguistic element in the opposing British or English nationalism. In contrast vertical ethnic communities in most of Europe have chronic difficulty in defining and maintaining a clear national territory, witness the current conflict in the former Yugoslavia, and have been faced by powerful neighbouring nationalisms, German, Magyar or Russian, which also originate from lateral ethnic communities, and which are also strongly linguistic in character. In Wales the Welsh national territory is ill-defined by comparison with Scotland or Ireland, and Wales is much more thoroughly incorporated into the British state than either of the other two ever were. This partly explains the greater importance of the Welsh language as a mark of national identity; this is also partly explained by the fact that Welsh was and is a vehicle for a Protestant religious life, while Irish and (in part) Scottish Gaelic have long been associated with Catholicism (see Price 1984, 97–102).

We have seen above how political science and history can begin to explain complex sociolinguistic patterns. I now turn to a case where linguistics can illuminate historical and political phenomena. The persistence of linguistic identification over very long periods and against considerable odds is emphasized in the work of many linguists (I would cite for example Fishman 1989, and other works by the same author). The gradual changes in the structure of languages over long periods, while they are constantly viewed by their speakers as remaining 'the same languages', provide many well-documented cases of human cultural phenomena (in as far as language is a cultural phenomenon) retaining an identity despite profound changes in content. This backup from linguistics can help to dispel the notion that there is something anomalous in the persistence of an ethnic identity (partly a cultural phenomenon) in the face of ongoing changes in its nature.

Such changes are seen in both English-speaking and German-speaking areas. Irish national identity was, as we have seen, originally not closely linked to language, but it has gained a significant linguistic dimension in the twentieth century (see Curtis 1961, 400–2), partly inspired by the popular modern notion, which is to a considerable extent a German creation, that every self-respecting nation must have a national language (see Johnston 1990, 49–64).

In the German-speaking area many immigrant ethnic Germans recently arrived from eastern Europe, particularly from the former Soviet Union, do not share the otherwise more or less universal view of the importance of the language for national identity. Despite clearly seeing themselves as German, many have negligible command of the language and some have little motivation to learn it, as I discovered on a recent visit to a reception centre for such immigrants in Freiburg (see Hoffmann 1991).

Not only can ethnic and national identities change over time in their content; they can even change in type. In modern times German nationalism has suggested a vertical type of ethnic identity, since that sense of identity propelled the mass of the population, spurred on by intellectuals, to desire, not integration with an élite, but the sweeping away of an élite which was seen as anti-national, the petty particularist princes and their entourages (Johnston 1990, particularly 1–26). Yet the origins of German ethnic identity lie far back, in the early medieval Holy Roman Empire, where a group of speakers of West Germanic dialects were united by the Carolingian and Merovingian dynasties; almost the only factor uniting these peoples and distinguishing them from speakers of other West Germanic dialects was their subjection to these Frankish rulers, indeed their earliest name for their language, which is passed down to us in its Latin form *theodiscus*, seems also to have been applied to other West Germanic dialects (see Barbour 1991). Conversely the only factor uniting them, and separating them from other subjects of the Frankish dynasties, was their Germanic speech. It is in fact possible that they did not form an ethnic group at all at this period, but rather several groups; evidence for this comes from the extreme dialectal diversity of Continental West Germanic in this period, which persists into modern German; probably no other European language is so diverse, and groups of dialects elsewhere which show a similar diversity are considered to be several languages, for example Portuguese-Galician, Spanish and Catalan; Danish, Norwegian and Swedish; Slovene and Serbo-Croatian; Polish, Czech and Slovak (see Barbour and Stevenson 1990, 23–40). We can even speculate that a German ethnic identity scarcely predated the rise of national identity and that both of these identities have a strongly negative component and are hence rather weak in character; Germans are perhaps simply those Europeans who are not clearly anything else. We can further speculate that a clear German nationalism only arose as the various nation-shaping pressures of the modern world, so vividly described by Anderson (1991), began to take effect, but that while these forces found promising material elsewhere, in the German-speaking area they did not. There was almost nothing uniting German-speakers apart from a highly internally differentiated language; many of the existing principalities were simply not viable as modern states; and the area was divided by religion into Catholic and Protestant regions, with this divide, however, not producing two areas which were internally coherent on any basis other than a religious one. It is possible that the virulent, often racialist, nature of German nationalism can be at least partly explained by over-compensation for its inherently weak basis (Barbour 1991). To the discussion of this political phenomenon linguistics can contribute the insight that, from the point of view of structural distance and mutual intelligibility, leaving aside political factors, a linguist would be unlikely to conclude that German was a single language.

A cursory reading of the literature on ethnic and national identity could possibly leave one with the impression that linguistic differences are a given factor, which may or may not be exploited to shape identities. However, a study of developments in language can show how a national or ethnic identity can create or accentuate linguistic differences. In the early years of this century Swiss German, in the sense of Swiss dialects, was losing ground to Swiss standard German, that is the speech of German-speaking Swiss was gradually approaching something more like the speech of Germans. Since the Second World War the desire of German-speaking Swiss to distance themselves from an unfavourable German identity has contributed to a remarkable resurgence of Swiss German speech. In the 1950s Ferguson described the relationship between Swiss German and Swiss standard German as diglossic (Ferguson 1972, originally published 1959–60), with the two speech forms occupying secure but different spheres in national life. Such has been the resurgence of Swiss German that contemporary writers describe the situation as bilingual, since although Swiss standard German still predominates in certain spheres, there are now very few in which it does not compete with Swiss German dialects (see Barbour and Stevenson 1990, 212–17).

In *The Languages of Britain*, Glanville Price commends the example of the Swiss Germans to the Welsh (1984, 126). If, he suggests, proponents of Welsh had been content to espouse the goal of diglossia, with Welsh restricted to the spheres where its use seems more natural, the language might be faring better than it is in the current situation where bilingualism is the aim, with Welsh then not catching on in spheres where its use seems unnatural, producing a sense of failure in its supporters. I would add to this that the message of the resurgence of Swiss German is that in an area such as German-speaking Europe, where language is the prime symbol of national identity, if a declining minority language becomes a symbol of national identity, it can be reborn. Perhaps the view that the decline of minority languages is inevitable is at least in part a product of an English-speaking world view, less used to the idea of language as an all-important mark of ethnic and national identity. It is questionable whether the minority languages of Britain could revive in the same way, given that identities here are not so based on language, but the Swiss German case can nevertheless certainly give us hope.

Notes

[1] It will sometimes appear in this paper that ethnic identities and national identities are being equated; the reason for this is that for the purposes of the present discussion the distinction is not always crucial. In other contexts it is crucial (see Smith 1991, 19–70).

   I am grateful to Clare Mar-Molinero and Keith Moor for directing my attention to important literature on the topic of national identity.

[2] This statement actually begs many questions in the definition of what we mean by 'German', and hence has to be treated with great caution (see Barbour 1991). It is, however, not too misleading in the context of the present discussion.

[3] See Note 1 above. This statement requires considerable modification in the German case (see below).

References

Abrams, D. and Hogg, M. A. 1988. 'Language attitudes, frames of reference and social identity: a Scottish dimension', in Gudykunst, W. B. (ed.), *Language and Ethnic Identity*, Clevedon and Philadelphia: Multilingual Matters, 45–57.

Anderson, B. 1991. *Imagined Communities*, London and New York: Verso.

Barbour, S. 1991. 'Language and nationalism in the German-speaking countries', in Meara, P. and Ryan, A. (eds.), *Language and Nation (British Studies in Applied Linguistics, 6)*, London: CILT, 39–48.

Barbour, S. and Stevenson, P. 1990. *Variation in German*, Cambridge: Cambridge University Press.

Curtis, E. 1961. *A History of Ireland*, London: Methuen.

Ferguson, C. A. 1972. 'Diglossia', in Giglioli, P. P. (ed.), *Language and Social Context*, Harmondsworth: Penguin, 232–51.

Fishman, J. A. 1989. *Language and Ethnicity in Minority Sociolinguistic Perspective*, Clevedon and Philadelphia: Multilingual Matters.

Grundmann, H. 1973. *Wahlkönigtum, Territorialpolitik und Ostbewegung im 13. und 14. Jahrhundert (Handbuch der deutschen Geschichte, Band 5)*, Munich: DTV.

Gustavsson, S. 1990. 'Socialism and nationalism. Trends and tendencies in the language, nationality and minority policy of the socialist countries in post-war Europe', in Ammon, U., Mattheier, K. J. and Nelde, P. (eds.), *Minderheiten und Sprachkontakt/Minorities and Language Contact/Minorités et contact linguistique (Sociolinguistica 4)*, Tübingen: Niemeyer, 50–83.

Haugen, E. 1976. 'Dialect, language, nation', in Pride, J. B. and Holmes, J. (eds.), *Sociolinguistics*, Harmondsworth: Penguin, 97–111.

Hobsbawm, E. 1990. *Nations and Nationalism since 1780*, Cambridge: Cambridge University Press.

Hoffmann, C. 1991. 'Language and identity: the case of the German *Aussiedler*', in Meara, P. and Ryan, A. (eds.), *Language and Nation (British Studies in Applied Linguistics, 6)*, London: CILT, 49–60.

Johnston, O. W. 1990. *Der deutsche Nationalmythos*, Stuttgart: Metzler.

Kee, R. 1980. *Ireland. A History*, London: Weidenfeld and Nicolson.

Lockwood, W. B. 1976. *An Informal History of the German Language*, London: André Deutsch.

Mitchison, R. 1982. *A History of Scotland*, London: Routledge.

Price, G. 1984. *The Languages of Britain*, London: Arnold.

Russ, C. V. J. 1987. 'Language and society in German Switzerland. Multilingualism, diglossia and variation', in Russ, C. and Volkmar, C. (eds.), *Sprache und Gesellschaft in deutschsprachigen Ländern*, Munich: Goethe-Institut, 94–121.

Smith, A. D. 1991. *National Identity*, Harmondsworth: Penguin.

Williams, G. A. 1985. *When was Wales?* Harmondsworth: Penguin.